AFRICA

YEMEN

Assab

FRENCH
SOMALILAND

Gulf of Aden

Djibouti

Dire
Dawa

Jijiga   SOMALIA

Harar

Harar

ETHIOPIA

Bale

Indian
Ocean

200 km

KING OF KINGS

KING OF KINGS

The Triumph and Tragedy of
Emperor Haile Selassie I of Ethiopia

Asfa-Wossen Asserate

Translated by Peter Lewis
Foreword by Thomas Pakenham

First published in English in 2015 by

HAUS PUBLISHING LTD
70 Cadogan Place
London SW1X 9AH
www.hauspublishing.com

Originally published in German as
Der Letzte Kaiser von Afrika: Triumph und Tragödie des Haile Selassie
by Asfa-Wossen Asserte © by Ullstein Buchverlage GmbH, Berlin.
Published in 2014 by Propyläen Verlag

Translation Copyright © 2015 by Peter Lewis

A CIP catalogue record for this book is available from the British Library

ISBN: 978-1-910376-14-0
eISBN: 978-1-910376-19-5

Typeset in Sabon by MacGuru Ltd
info@macguru.org.uk

Printed in Spain

Contents

This book is dedicated to my maternal great-grandmother and the caring Mother of All Ethiopians, H.I.M. Empress Menen Asfaw, with great admiration and heartfelt devotion.

Asfa-Wossen Asserate

Foreword

By Thomas Pakenham

For many years there was a missing piece at the centre of the jigsaw of African history. There was no full-scale biography of the Emperor Haile Selassie. Yet no other African ruler had kept his grip on power for so many decades. Regent from 1916 to 1930, Emperor from 1930 to 1974, he excited the admiration of African leaders of later generations – even those who had come to power by democratic means. To many of his own subjects in Ethiopia he seemed almost like a god. To the Rastafarians of Jamaica he was the Messiah. Yet when he finally fell from power, and was secretly killed by the *Derg*, the revolutionary junta, he seemed already like a ghost from the past.

Now Asfa-Wossen Asserate has gallantly risen to the challenge. This is an insider's account, based on many personal sources not available to other historians. He has exploited a unique advantage: the history of his own family was, for three generations, interwoven with the history of the emperor. His paternal grandfather, *Ras* Kassa, was one of the five leading Ethiopian nobles who had chosen *Ras* Tafari (as the future emperor was then styled) to become regent after the overthrow of Emperor *Lij* Iyasu. In fact *Ras* Kassa was Tafari's cousin and had a better dynastic claim to the throne than Tafari, as his family was descended not only from the Shoan branch of the Solomonic line, which had ruled Ethiopia since 1889, but also from the Imperial Gondarine-Lasta line, which had ruled the country in previous centuries. But neither *Ras* Kassa nor Asfa-Wossen's father, *Ras* Asserate, had the appetite for imperial power. Both men remained stubbornly loyal to the emperor – by contrast with most of the other feudal nobles. Yet the loyalty of *Ras* Asserate, as his son poignantly describes, was tested almost to breaking point in the final years of the Haile Selassie's reign.

Asfa-Wossen begins his story in the declining years of the Emperor Menelik. *Ras* Tafari's father, *Ras* Makonnen, was one of Menelik's most loyal and most accomplished generals. After helping to defeat the Italians at the Battle of Adwa in 1896, Makonnen was given control of the south-eastern province of Harar, and it was here that the future emperor spent his boyhood and was educated by Europeans. However, the early death of his father catapulted Tafari forward into the dynastic struggle. At thirteen he was already the titular governor of Salale; at eighteen he assumed control of Harar, his father's old province; at twenty-four he was regent and effectively in control of the country. Already he had had to crush a revolt by *Lij* Iyasu, Menelik's wayward grandson, who had been the first heir apparent but was deposed on the pretext he had converted to Islam. (The charge was probably false, but *Lij* Iyasu was placed under house arrest, watched over by *Ras* Kassa, Asfa-Wossen's grandfather.) There was nothing wayward about Tafari. Although slightly built and a head shorter than most Ethiopian nobles, he seemed every inch the man of destiny. He preferred to out-manoeuvre his enemies rather than to crush them, and had a genius for playing off one faction against another. But when directly challenged he could be ruthless enough. After his rival *Lij* Iyasu escaped from *Ras* Kassa's care, *Lij* Iyasu was recaptured and chained to a post, then mysteriously killed in 1935 – perhaps on the emperor's orders.

By 1920 Haile Selassie had taken the first steps to modernise the country. He built schools and hospitals and invited Europeans to staff them. There was even a nod in the direction of democracy: promise of a parliament, a senate and a written constitution. In fact he had created an absolute monarchy for himself and his family. But there was one enemy it was not in his power to subdue: Mussolini's Italy. Smarting over their defeat at Adwa forty years earlier, the Fascist armies pushed south into

Ethiopia from their colonial base in Eritrea on the Red Sea. By 1936, their motorised columns had smashed the ill-equipped Ethiopian warriors, and the emperor (accompanied by Asfa-Wossen's father and grandfather) was a fugitive in England. For most Ethiopians the war was a catastrophe. (Three of *Ras* Kassa's sons, fighting with the partisans, had surrendered on the promise of safe conduct and were then shot by the Italians.) But for the emperor this was in a way his finest hour. Out of the humiliation of defeat he had created an astonishing moral victory. He was the first (and last) African ruler to address the League of Nations. He denounced the barbarism of the Italian invasion. And if the world could do little to help him, at least it had ears to listen – and in general to agree.

Five years later, in 1941, the Emperor was back in power, put back on his throne by British and South African forces. And for the next nineteen years, still playing off one opponent against another and depriving the aristocrats of their private armies, he ruled the country unchallenged. For two terms he chaired the Organisation for African Unity and earned much admiration from his fellow rulers. But back in Ethiopia the pace of reform seemed agonisingly slow, especially to the growing number of Ethiopians educated abroad. Of course this was the price of absolute monarchy: an absolute bottleneck. Press, Parliament and cabinet remained puppets in the hands of the emperor. And then, in 1960, the emperor's throne was shaken by a first political earthquake.

It is from this point that Asfa-Wossen, who was twelve years old in 1960, can speak as an eyewitness. His father, Asserate Kassa, was the leading loyalist who rallied the country against an attempted coup by two of the commanders of the emperor's bodyguard. The plan was to depose the emperor, while he was absent on a state visit to Brazil, and replace him with his son, the Crown Prince, appointed as a constitutional monarch. To many people's surprise, the Crown Prince played his part, and broadcast to the nation the news that he had replaced his father. (Asfa-Wossen cites evidence that the Crown Prince made this broadcast freely enough, although the official version, published later, claimed that he spoke with a gun in his back.) But the coup was botched. The main army, the students, the urban public, the landless peasants – they had no shortage of grievances. But who wanted to throw in their lot with the emperor's bodyguard? The coup ended in a massacre of senior ministers at the palace, which Asserate was lucky to escape. This was followed by the pursuit and suicide of two of the leading conspirators. Others were hunted down and publicly hanged.

What kind of lesson did the emperor draw from the attempted coup when he hurriedly flew back from Brazil? No lesson, perhaps, except that he had been betrayed by two of his most trusted commanders. It was different for Asserate Kassa and many of the others most loyal to the Emperor. Asfa-Wossen describes in graphic detail the torment that his father suffered in the final years of the emperor's reign, as the last chance for moderate reform was squandered. In 1972 the emperor celebrated his eightieth birthday. Asserate went to the palace to offer his congratulations – then suddenly fell at the emperor's feet. Lying there, he begged for one favour. 'Please say this to your subjects: "My beloved people of Ethiopia. I have served you for almost sixty years. Now the time has come for me to abdicate ... Here is my son, into whose care I commend you."

The emperor was visibly moved. Then he told Asserate to get up, and replied: 'Tell me, did King David abdicate ... We shall reign as long as the Almighty allows us'.

Two years later the killer wave of revolution, long feared by the loyalists, swept over the country. Sixty senior ministers, including Asserate, were tied up, two by two, and shot against the wall of the main prison. Tens of thousands died in the bloody purges ordered by the *Derg*, the Soviet-backed army junta. Tens of thousands more, including Asfa-Wossen himself, escaped and fled the country. Asfa-Wossen's mother and sisters were less fortunate. For fourteen years they, and other members of the royal family, were imprisoned in a room like a cage. Meanwhile the emperor, still in his own room in the palace, was quietly smothered with a pillow.

It was all so predictable – and avoidable. That was at the heart of the tragedy.

Asfa-Wossen concludes this masterly biography with a cool assessment of the emperor and his legacy. 'His many services to the country will carry more weight than the great mistakes he undoubtedly made.' And he might have added Haile Selassie's many services to the world at large. To Europeans he represented the pioneer in the struggle against fascism. To millions of Africans he came to symbolise their own struggle for independence. He gave them back the dignity robbed by centuries of European exploitation. This was the ultimate irony: a despot at home (even if a benevolent one), he was regarded abroad as the champion of liberty.

Who Was Haile Selassie?

There is a well-known story in Ethiopia concerning *Ras* Tafari Makonnen, who ascended the country's throne in November 1930 as Emperor Haile Selassie. In the early summer of 1892, it is said that a hermit came to see *Ras* Makonnen, the governor of the Ethiopian province of Harar – whose wife had suffered a series of miscarriages – and revealed the following prophesy to him: 'This time, the child your wife is pregnant with will come into the world in the best of health and survive. He will grow up to be a fine boy; and when he is still a young man, he will rise to become the ruler of Ethiopia and govern the whole country with a firm hand. He will bestow greatness and pride upon Ethiopia and make it renowned the world over. But ultimately he will destroy everything he has built with his own hands and leave the country in ruins.'[1]

Who was Haile Selassie, the little man with the proud face who ruled Ethiopia for almost sixty years? Some people demonise him as a ruthless dictator, while others revere him as a saint. In September 1974, a news picture was wired around the world, showing him – by now a visibly aged and frail old man – being escorted out of his palace by the ringleaders of a military coup and driven away in a light-blue Volkswagen Beetle. Forty-four years before, when he was crowned *Negusa Negast,* or 'King of Kings', the whole world had sent its envoys to attend the coronation celebrations in Addis Ababa. The reports of this occasion that were dispatched to Europe by the English novelist Evelyn Waugh and others read like fairytales from *A Thousand and One Nights*.

As emperor of Ethiopia, he took the name of Haile Selassie, which literally means 'the Power of the Trinity'. His dynasty descended from the Biblical King Solomon, and the world called him the 'Victorious Lion of Judah'. Just six years after ascending the throne, the King of Kings appeared in Geneva in front of the General Assembly of the League of Nations. The forces of Mussolini's Fascist Italy had invaded Ethiopia and the exiled monarch made a moving appeal to the world's conscience. The words he spoke that day have gone down in history: 'Catastrophe is inevitable if the great states stand by and watch the rape of a small country.' *Time* magazine chose him as its Man of the Year in 1935. In 1941, when the combined forces of Ethiopia and Great Britain had driven Mussolini's Blackshirts from the country, he returned in triumph to reclaim the Ethiopian throne.

In the 1950s, the 'Anti-Fascist on the Throne' positioned himself at the head of the African decolonisation movement. To this day, Haile Selassie continues to be revered as the 'Father of Africa' by many of the continent's leaders. Nelson Mandela called him the 'African Giant'. Bob Marley, meanwhile, set his speeches to reggae beats: '*Coming from the root of King David, through the line of Solomon, His Imperial Majesty is the Power of Authority: Spread out, spread out, spread out....*' run the lyrics of the song 'Blackman Redemption'. Like many others who called themselves Rastafarians, Bob Marley saw in Haile Selassie the reborn Messiah.

But there were – and still are – other less reverential voices: the Polish journalist Ryszard Kapuściński portrayed him in his book *The Emperor* as a despotic ruler besotted with pomp and surrounded by obsequious dignitaries and accomplices. On his accession, Haile Selassie had made it his goal to modernise Ethiopia along Western lines. Yet the Ethiopian students, who as part of his modernisation policies were sent abroad in the 1950s and 1960s to study in Western Europe and the United States, only ended up being struck by the economic and political backwardness of their native country in comparison with developed Western democracies. As a result, they came out onto the streets to protest. In the autumn of 1973, the years before Haile

Selassie was overthrown, television pictures of starving children who had fallen victim in their tens of thousands to a devastating famine in the Ethiopian provinces of Wollo and Tigray were broadcast around the world.

Who was Haile Selassie? Almost all those who got to know him in person found it hard to resist the sheer charisma he radiated. 'Every conversation gave me further reason to admire and acknowledge this Sovereign, who is so different from those who surround him and from his own people,' wrote the French physician Dr Sassard, who was the emperor's personal doctor for many years. 'In his motionless face, only his eyes seem alive – brilliant, elongated, extremely expressive eyes. They bespeak boredom as well as polite indifference, cold irony or even anger. The courtiers know these different expressions well and retire suddenly when the monarch's glance becomes indifferent, then hard. On the other hand, especially when he is dealing with Europeans, his eyes know how to be soft, caressing, affable – and even sincere.'[2]

My first memories of the Ethiopian emperor take me back to my childhood, in 1956. I was eight years old at the time and had come down with mumps, which stubbornly refused to clear up even after treatment with a course of drugs. The doctors in the Haile Selassie Hospital in Addis Ababa decided to operate on me, removing parts of my parotid gland that had become infected. To this day, I can clearly remember this procedure: being anaesthetised with ether and the intense nausea that subsequently overcame me. But above all I recall the moment when I woke up from the anaesthetic: as I slowly came to, the first person my gaze focussed upon was none other than the *Negusa Negast*, the King of Kings. He was wearing his field marshal's uniform, over which he had draped his *kabba*, the traditional cloak of the Ethiopian nobility. Next to him stood my grandfather *Ras* Kassa and my father *Ras* Asserate, both looking worried. The emperor laid his hand on my forehead and said: 'Now wait just a moment, my boy, and there will be ice cream as a treat!' Saying this, he took his leave in French of Professor Leutze, the hospital's German clinical director, and of the German surgeon who had performed the operation, thanking them for their splendid work. I later learned that the doctor who had operated on me was given a gold coin in gratitude by the emperor, while my parents sent him a set of gold cufflinks. I lived the next few days in a world of make-believe. For a whole week, as I lay in my sick bed, I received daily deliveries of a large Thermos flask, emblazoned with a golden imperial lion and filled with the most diverse and wonderful flavours of ice cream. These delicacies were specially prepared for me from fresh ingredients by the emperor's Swiss head chef in the nearby *Genete-Leul* Palace.

I will also cherish my memories of the emperor at the Red Cross Festival, which was held every year in January on 'His Majesty's Lawn' in Addis Ababa. As children, there was scarcely an event that we looked forward to with greater anticipation. On this day, the embassies of all the nations with diplomatic representation in Ethiopia put up tents on the lawn, where they sold the culinary specialities of their country in aid of the Red Cross. The emperor let my cousins and me accompany him as he did his round of the marquees. Everywhere the emperor stopped, he was given a present, which – provided it wasn't a bottle of wine or spirits – he immediately handed over to us before moving on to the next tent. So it was that at one Red Cross Festival, I became the proud owner of a doll in traditional Black Forest costume from the German tent, and on another such occasion a Black Forest cuckoo clock, which subsequently took pride of place in the drawing room of our house. I used to stand in front of it mesmerised, waiting for hours on end to see the cuckoo emerge from its little hut and hear its piercing cry echo down the corridors of our villa

Likewise, I vividly recall my drives through Addis Ababa with the emperor. Each afternoon, Haile Selassie would get into one of his cars and have himself driven around the capital to see how things stood with his empire. Every so often, he would let us children accompany him on these impromptu tours of inspection. The emperor would often take the Cadillac that President Franklin D. Roosevelt had given him, a stretched limousine with three rows of seats, which I was incredibly impressed by.

Between the chauffeur and the passengers, there was a glass partition, set in a surround made of rosewood. On the panel below the glass, fine inlay work spelt out the three initials 'H.I.M': 'His Imperial Majesty.' We were allowed to sit in the middle row of seats; up front, next to the driver, was the emperor's adjutant, while the emperor himself sat behind us. Like the consuls in Ancient Rome, on his tours through the city, the emperor took pleasure in distributing alms to beggars. Sometimes, he would pass a bundle of banknotes over to us to pass out through the window, which was only opened just a crack. That was all it took, for no sooner had one poked a bill through the window than it was snatched by one of the grasping hands that appeared from every direction.

As a child, I found it hard to understand: on the one hand the emperor was part of our extended family – my grandfather, *Ras* Kassa Hailu, was his cousin and one of his most loyal companions from childhood to old age – yet at the same time he was unapproachable; he was the King of Kings, *Abbaba Janhoy*, the Great Father of the Nation, and everyone around him would bow and prostrate themselves as a sign of their great reverence for him. I, too, always found him to be surrounded by this imperial aura except for one single occasion. This encounter took place in the 1960s in Eritrea. The emperor had come to Asmara and taken up residence during his visit at the Viceroy's palace, my father's official seat of administration as governor-general of the then-province of Eritrea. When Haile Selassie and his cousin *Ras* Imru came to call on us one afternoon at my father's private residence in the palace grounds, the emperor's interest was piqued by the pool room. Evidently he felt inclined to have a game of pool. He slapped *Ras* Imru – who was actually several years younger than his cousin but looked somewhat older – on the shoulder and said: 'Come on, old man! Can you still remember how we used to play in *Lij* Iyasu's house when we were boys? Let's see if you're still up to it!' *Ras* Imru laughed, and the emperor took off his suit jacket and handed it to my father. 'Come on, Asserate, you too!' *Ras* Imru challenged my father. His Majesty's jacket was duly passed to me, and the emperor broke off. Even after just a few shots, it was apparent that Haile Selassie was markedly superior to his cousin and his kinsman – though none of us or any of our acquaintances had ever seen the emperor with a pool cue in his hand. This was the first and only time I ever saw the emperor in shirt sleeves. All the gravitas of his office had fallen away from him, and at this moment he was just an ordinary person enjoying a game. I stood there rooted to the spot. Holding the emperor's jacket in my outstretched hand, I watched enthralled as the emperor potted ball after ball. After the final one, the black eight-ball, had also disappeared into one of the pockets, he laid his cue aside and I passed him his suit jacket. He slipped into it, and in a trice he was transformed back into the Emperor of Ethiopia.

At all these meetings with my great kinsman, we never talked politics. Only once did I ever get involved in a brief discussion with him about the political state of the country – during his final visit to the Federal Republic of Germany, on 12 September 1973, exactly a year to the day before he was seized by rebel army officers and led away from his palace into captivity. In the autumn of 1973, pictures of the terrible famine that hit the Ethiopian provinces of Wollo and Tigray began to be shown around the world. In Frankfurt, where I was studying at the time, I myself had organised a benefit concert for the 'flying doctors' who were working in Ethiopia and raised a decent sum. A large crowd had gathered on the Castle Square in Stuttgart, where the emperor was due to meet Hans Filbinger, the state president of Baden-Württemberg; most of them were there to cheer Haile Selassie and wave Ethiopian flags, but a handful of protesting students from the nearby University of Hohenheim had also mingled with the crowd. They were holding up placards with slogans proclaiming 'Haile Selassie – Go Home and Feed Your Starving People!' and 'Death to Imperialism!' and handing out leaflets to passers-by. The emperor and his entourage had been put up at the Monrepos Lake Palace in Ludwigsburg, just north of Stuttgart, and I was summoned to his suite there for an audience with Haile Selassie.

As I entered the room, he handed me a piece of paper and commanded: 'Translate this for me!' It was one of the leaflets the demonstrators had been handing out. I wondered how best to extricate myself from this tricky situation and replied: 'Your Majesty, wouldn't it be better to pass this over to the Foreign Ministry and get one of the official interpreters to translate it?' – His response was instant: 'So, We've sent you to Germany to study and you can't even perform this small service for Us?' I answered: 'If it may please Your Majesty, it was my father, and not you, who sent me to Germany.' – 'And are you saying he is not one of Us?' Haile Selassie responded, fixing me with a steely glare combined with a fatherly smile. 'Of course he is, Your Majesty!' I picked up the leaflet and started to translate it into Amharic. It was a confused diatribe by a self-proclaimed 'League Against Imperialism'. I kept my eyes fixed on the flyer as I translated, making a conscious effort to keep my voice as deadpan as possible. Now and then, I faltered as I groped around for the best way to render such terms as 'imperialist lackey' or 'the profit of monopoly capitalism' into Amharic. The emperor tried not to show any emotion, but I could sense that the words were hitting home. After I had finished translating, a painful silence filled the room. Then, out of the blue, the emperor asked me: 'By the way, who told you the Ethiopians were starving?' I knew he didn't approve of my fundraising initiative, but I was determined to fight my corner.

'Your Majesty,' I replied cautiously, 'I don't believe that I am doing anything wrong. The flying doctors perform an important role, they've already proved that in Kenya. I'm sure their aid will be good for our country as well.' Haile Selassie said nothing for a moment, then continued: 'Anyone can start something ... but the real art lies in carrying it through to the end.' His head was slightly bowed as he said this, and his dark eyes flashed. Then he looked up at me and said: 'We will talk again in Addis Ababa.' My audience was at an end. I bowed to him and left the room. Just a few months later, the Ethiopian Empire, which had existed for millennia, was consigned to history.

Who was Haile Selassie? Among those who would have been best placed to answer this question were two of my closest relatives. My grandfather, *Ras* Kassa Hailu, was a cousin of the emperor and his closest confidant over many decades. As an 'Imperial Duke' (the meaning of the Ethiopian title *Leul-Ras*) and a field marshal of the Ethiopian Army, *Ras* Kassa Hailu was one of the foremost politicians of the imperial family. In 1916, when Haile Selassie was installed as regent by the Crown Council, *Ras* Kassa renounced his own claim on the Ethiopian throne. My grandfather fought alongside the emperor against the Italian invaders, and went into exile with him. My father *Ras* Asserate Kassa also served the Imperial Ethiopian Government in several capacities. He grew up in the imperial palace and during the war attended Monkton Combe School in Bath; later, he trained as an army officer at the Soba Military Academy near Khartoum in the Sudan, a sister establishment of Sandhurst. In the spring of 1941, aged 18, he entered Ethiopia in a British uniform as part of the emperor's military contingent. After the war, *Ras* Asserate got to know the most far-flung and diverse provinces of his native country, being appointed successively as governor-general of Gondar, Wollegga, Arusi, Shoa (including the capital Addis Ababa), and finally Eritrea. In the final years of his life he served as President of the Imperial Crown Council, in terms of protocol the highest office in the Ethiopian Empire after that of King of Kings. My grandfather died in 1957, at the height of Haile Selassie's reign; my father was one of the sixty dignitaries who in the bloody night of 23 November 1974, a few weeks after the arrest of Haile Selassie, were executed by the *Derg*. He was 52 years old.

Neither my grandfather nor my father had the opportunity to give a written account of their time with the emperor – despite the fact that there was so much they could have recounted.[3] Yet at least some of the things they experienced while serving the emperor lived on in our family's fund of stories. For decades, I had entertained the idea of writing a book about my great kinsman Haile Selassie, but I did not simply want to produce a family memoir and a hagiography. I must confess that I am deeply indebted to my father for his readiness to share his thoughts and tribulations and his visions with me, as if I was his younger brother, at an early stage of my life – a relationship between father and son that was very unusual in those days. Hitherto, there has been a paucity of wide-ranging, serious historical biographies charting the life of Haile Selassie from his earliest childhood to his final hours. There are various reasons for this: in Ethiopia over the past forty years there has been little inclination to revisit the topic of the Ethiopian Empire and its last ruler. Indeed, the regime that immediately succeeded it was hell-bent on erasing every last trace of that period.

Nor did this determination to make a clean break with the past stop short of the archives of the Imperial Palace and the Imperial Ministry of the Pen, whose holdings were dispersed to the four winds. This makes it all the more difficult for any historian trying to research the empire. Although Haile Selassie wrote memoirs covering his reign up to 1945, these afford only a very limited insight into what really made the emperor tick. While 20th-century historiography in Europe took it for granted that it would have recourse to a multitude of archives and documents, the source material available to those writing about the history of Africa in general and Ethiopia in particular is extremely sparse. The overwhelming majority of written sources are of Western provenance – including memoranda and protocols from Western embassies, travel reports, personal memoirs and reportage. Several of these sources paint a picture of an alien, often impenetrable country – and yield to the only too understandable tendency to try and make the unfamiliar more familiar by adding embellishments. This is also the case for a number of books that English, American or German authors have written about Haile Selassie.

This present work does not lay claim to being a wholly scholarly biography; even so, I did consult academic sources and documents and made strenuous efforts to come to as objective a view as possible of my subject. In the course of my researches I had many conversations with others who knew Haile Selassie: members of the imperial family, former ministers and dignitaries of the imperial administration, but also with many people who took a critical attitude to the former emperor. This book has no pretensions to be the definitive biography of the last ruler of the Ethiopian Empire, merely a contribution to what I hope will become a growing body of work on this topic: it will take many mosaic tiles before we are finally able to compose a complete picture of the man.

The story of Haile Selassie is also the story of the 20th century – its upheavals, promises and terrors. In 1916, when *Ras* Tafari began his regency, Kaiser Wilhelm II was still sitting on the throne in Germany, while Franz Joseph I reigned supreme in Vienna and Tsar Nicolas II in Moscow – all crowned heads whose era in Europe was about to draw irrevocably to a close. Haile Selassie too was a child of his time, which was still very much characterized by the attitudes and mores of the late 19th and early 20th centuries. The year he was deposed, there was only one other reigning monarch left who had come to the throne before him: Japan's Emperor Hirohito. He had outlasted all the rest as the crowned head of state, most of them by several decades – until the autumn of 1974, when – with his demise and partly through his own agency – three thousand years of history in Ethiopia was brought to an abrupt close. In between his accession and his end lies the eventful and moving life of Haile Selassie.

Asfa-Wossen Asserate
Frankfurt-am-Main, May 2015

Notes on the text

Ethiopian naming conventions have no concept of the division into Christian name and surname that is usual in Europe; instead, people have a single given name. This is often followed by the father's name. Thus, Tafari Makonnen is 'Tafari, the son of Makonnen'. Whenever names are cited in abbreviated form in the text, they appear without the addition of the patronymic, though these should not be construed in any way as familiar forms.

Aristocratic titles (*Ras*, *Leul*, *Dejazmatch*, *Fitaurari*, etc.) are shown in italic in the text: an explanation of the most common imperial titles can be found on pages 348 and 349. Furthermore, the glossary on page 350 elucidates the more important Amharic terms that are used in the text. To facilitate reading, I refrained from giving Amharic names and concepts in their full academic transliterated form, with diacritical marks. The transcriptions I have used here follow the forms employed in non-academic English publications. The difficulties in transliterating Amharic are illustrated in my own family, where 'Asserate' is written in at least three different ways by various family members, including my late father.

The Ethiopian dating system follows the Alexandrian or Coptic calendar, which is around seven years behind the Gregorian calendar in universal use in the West. For ease of understanding, I have therefore followed the latter system for all dates given in this book.

CHAPTER ONE

A childhood in Harar

1892 to 1910

Even nowadays, only narrow tracks lead from the shining white city of Harar in eastern Ethiopia, close to the border with Somalia, up into the mountains to the small town of Egersa Goro. It was there, a good fifty kilometres from the provincial capital, that *Ras* Makonnen Wolde-Mikael Gudissa, governor of the province of Harar from the 1880s onwards, had a villa built. Its veranda afforded a marvellous view over the fertile valleys of the region. Every year in May, when it began to get oppressive and humid within the precincts of Harar and the likelihood of a typhoid outbreak increased, *Ras* Makonnen and his entourage would decamp to his villa in Egersa Goro to spend the rainy season there. And so it was in May 1892. On this occasion, as always, he was accompanied by his wife Princess Yeshimebet Ali Gonshor, to whom he was utterly devoted. She was the daughter of a nobleman from Wollo and was widely renowned for her beauty. Prior to this relationship, *Ras* Makonnen had been married once before, and this union resulted in the birth of a son named Yilma. But in 1876 he left his first wife for the beautiful young princess from Wollo; his marriage to Princess Yeshimebet was what may genuinely be termed a love match.

Even so, a shadow lay over the marriage. The princess had become pregnant no fewer than nine times, yet all the children were either stillborn, or died soon after being born. In the spring of 1892, the Princess was expecting another child. And when, on 23 July 1892, in Egersa Goro, she duly gave birth to a healthy boy, the household's joy was unconfined. He was baptized in the name of Haile Selassie.[1] No one could have suspected then that the radiant new mother Yeshimebet would die two years later giving birth to a second child.

At that time, the province of Harar, with the eponymous white city at its centre, one of the oldest centres of Islam in East Africa, had shortly before become part of the Ethiopian Empire once more. At the beginning of the 16th century, the notorious Imam Ahmed Gran 'the Left-handed', who had proclaimed a jihad against the Christian Empire of Ethiopia, then proceeded, step by step, to bring the Abyssinian heartland under his sway, including Harar.[2] For three hundred years thereafter, Harar was a Muslim city-state. Its city ramparts, over three kilometres in length, protected the city from foreign invaders. One of the first Europeans to penetrate its defensive walls, in 1854, was the British explorer Sir Richard Francis Burton. Then, from 1875 onwards, Harar was under Egyptian rule for a decade until, in January 1887, *Negus* Menelik of Shoa – the later Emperor Menelik II – and his forces took control of the city. His commander-in-chief was *Ras* Makonnen, who was also his cousin, and in gratitude for his military achievements, Menelik named him governor of Harar province. The region is particularly fertile and to the present day remains one of the principal places where coffee is grown. Within an Ethiopian state that boasted a diversity of different peoples, the population of Harar was particularly heterogeneous, with the capital alive with a multitude of ethnicities and languages. But above all, Harar – together with the national capital Addis Ababa – was Ethiopia's gateway to the world. The city became an important marketplace for caravans, attracting large numbers of merchants. In addition, there were delegations from the colonial powers of France, Great Britain and Italy, whose territories bordered directly on Harar province. And finally, in the very heart of this predominantly Muslim region with its many prominent mosques, the Roman Catholic Capuchin mission also decided to base itself in Harar after the monks had been expelled from Addis Ababa during the reign of Emperor Yohannes.

Lij Tafari Makonnen, the future Emperor Haile Selassie, as a child.

Before long, the governor of Harar had earned himself an enviable reputation among those under his rule: *Ras* Makonnen respected the rights of the Muslim majority, and he succeeded in bringing both the Muslim Harari and the dominant ethnic group of the Oromo under his jurisdiction. The mosques that formed the characteristic skyline of Harar were soon joined by a Coptic church, and the two institutions entered a peaceful co-existence.[3] From the troops of the Oromo, who were renowned as outstanding horsemen, *Ras* Makonnen formed a powerful cavalry army, which gave him loyal support. Its great efficacy was soon to be demonstrated when it was deployed in the war against Italy in 1895–96 – notably at the legendary Battle of Adwa on 1 March 1896, when a combined contingent of Ethiopian troops comprehensively routed an invasion force of Italian units attacking from the north, so preventing their country from being absorbed as an Italian colony. In this decisive engagement, the governor of Harar, riding in the vanguard of his army, gave ample proof of his courage, fighting on until victory was assured despite having sustained a wound.

But above all – and this was anything but customary for an Ethiopian prince of that period – *Ras* Makonnen was an inquisitive, open-minded individual. He sought out contact with the merchants and foreigners who flocked to Harar to trade in the wake of the city's opening up to the outside world. Among these was the writer Arthur Rimbaud, who in the 1880s had fled from his French home town of Charleville to Ethiopia and settled in Harar. He also conducted business with the court there; for example, he supplied *Ras* Makonnen with a consignment of 500 flagons, who promptly sent them back, with the tart observation that in Italy he would get these kinds of vessels for nothing.[4] All the same, after the poet's untimely death, Rimbaud's business partner Armand Savouré maintained that Rimbaud had been highly regarded at the Harar court, 'especially by *Ras* Makonnen'.[5]

Ras Makonnen also campaigned for the construction of a railway line from Djibouti to Addis Ababa. In 1902, work began on laying the section between the coast and the station at Dire Dawa, not far from Harar. The governor imported the first printing press to be seen in Harar. He also had a hospital built and was responsible for endowing a number of schools in the province he controlled. Whenever he consulted with Emperor Menelik in Addis Ababa, his preferred modes of communication were the telephone and the telegraph. His natural curiosity and openness predestined *Ras* Makonnen for diplomatic missions, which took him to Europe. As early as 1889, he travelled to Rome to attend ratification of the Treaty of Wuchale, an Italo-Abyssinian friendship and trade agreement. In 1902, as the representative of Emperor Menelik, he attended the coronation of Edward VII in London, after which he visited Paris and Zurich. He was fascinated by the innovations he encountered in European countries.

Following its victory over Italy, overnight Ethiopia was accorded an important role in the community of international powers. The European nations – from Great Britain to France to Russia – sent delegations to pay their respects to Emperor Menelik II, the victor over the Italian forces. The British delegation, with five officers in attendance, was headed by Lord Rennell Rodd. One of those accompanying him was Lord Edward Gleichen, who subsequently published a comprehensive account of the mission. On their way from Somalia to Addis Ababa, the legation had also stopped off in Harar, where it was met by a guard of honour firing a 21-gun salute. The governor of Harar invited the British delegation to visit him at his palace, whose splendour Lord Gleichen describes in his account:

'Here, there was once more a guard of honour drawn up for us, dark warriors with rifle and silver shield, and dressed in cloaks and silks of all colours of the rainbow. Up the wooden stairs and on the landing above were more of them, mostly coiffed with a strip of lion's mane to denote their valour, and then – we found ourselves in a little room, so dark after the sunlight without, that at first we hardly distinguished Ras Makunnen sitting by the window and pointing graciously to eight cane chairs arranged along the walls.'[6]

On meeting the prince himself, Lord Gleichen's report continues:

'During this short interview Ras Makunnen had produced on us a pleasing impression. He is a small dark man with delicate hands, large expressive eyes, a small black beard and moustache, and a most intelligent cast of countenance. His voice is very gentle, and his manners extremely dignified and quiet. What he said was little, but to the point, and he gave us then, and thereafter, the impression of a man who wielded a good deal of power in a quiet way. His dress was also quiet, consisting of a black silk shirt with narrow orange stripes, a white robe of fine linen, and a black silk cloak with a gold throat-fastening, whilst a broad-brimmed grey felt hat rather detracted than otherwise from his appearance.'[7]

Lord Gleichen's book contains no specific mention of the governor's son Tafari Makonnen, who by this stage was five years old; there is, however, an account of the delegation's meeting with the head of the Roman Catholic Capuchin mission, Monsignor Taurin,[8] 'a charming old gentleman in a brown cowl and long white beard,' who along with his monks was responsible for educating the children of the Ethiopian aristocracy.[9] Among his pupils were the son of the governor and his cousin Imru, who was almost the same age and who – as Haile Selassie later wrote in his autobiography – was like a twin brother to him.[10] After his mother's death, the two-year old Tafari Makonnen had been placed in the care of the family of his uncle, *Fitaurari* Haile Selassie Abayneh and his wife Mezlekiya. His aunt assumed the role of his late mother, while his uncle became like a second father to Tafari. This was doubtless also due to the fact that his actual father found himself obliged by his many duties and responsibilities to spend much of his time away from home, usually on military or diplomatic missions. Even though, as yet, there was no such official post in the Ethiopian empire, General *Ras* Makonnen fulfilled the role of foreign minister for Emperor Menelik II. Furthermore, the routes that had to be travelled within Ethiopia were circuitous and onerous – the journey from Harar to Addis Ababa alone took almost an entire month.

Yet *Ras* Makonnen set great store by his son's education, insisting that it be as broad as possible. In his autobiography, Haile Selassie writes that he and his cousin Imru's education was no different from that of the sons of ordinary Ethiopians[11] – an understatement if ever there was one. Ethiopian priests were engaged to teach Tafari both Amharic and *Ge'ez*, the traditional liturgical language of the Ethiopian Church. Another of Tafari's teachers in these early years was Dr. Joseph Vitalien, a physician from Martinique who was director of the hospital in Harar and was appointed to teach the boy French. But the busy doctor was unable to devote more than an hour a day to his language tuition. As a result, the young governor's son and his cousin ended up being sent to the French Capuchin school run by Monsignor Taurin and Monsignor Jarosseau, known as *Abba* Andreas, who became Taurin's successor after his death.[12] When, in early 1896, *Ras* Makonnen was appointed as commander-in-chief in the Italian-Abyssinian War, he entrusted his son to *Abba* Andreas' care: 'If I die,' he told the French priest, 'be his father. I give him to you and God will do the rest.'[13] *Abba* Andreas was deeply moved. He hung his pectoral cross over the boy's shoulder, as a visible sign of his adoption, and had him photographed in this pose. The picture still survives today.

Among the teaching staff at the Capuchin school, one in particular exerted a decisive influence upon the young Tafari Makonnen: the Ethiopian monk *Abba* Samuel Wolde Kahen. '*Abba* Samuel,' Haile Selassie later wrote, 'was a good man with a wide range of knowledge, who dedicated himself to the vocation of learning and teaching, who like a bee gathered knowledge with goodness and modesty, who had devoted himself to the love of God and of his fellow man and who never lusted after the pleasures of the flesh, but exclusively pursued the spiritual joys. I am in a position to say this, because I knew him well. We spent some ten years together.' This emphatic endorsement by Haile Selassie of his former teacher is also remarkable in as much as the emperor treats his own childhood only very cursorily in his memoirs, devoting just a few pages to this phase of his life. And in truth *Abba* Samuel really did fill the roles of mentor, advisor and secretary for Haile Selassie, right up to the priest's death in June 1915. Even so, Haile Selassie did not divulge the whole truth about his relationship with *Abba* Samuel.

On 7 July 1915, Tafari Makonnen and a retinue of nine followers took a boating excursion on Lake Haramaya, some

20 kilometres northwest of Harar. In the middle of the lake, however, their boat began taking on water. The men tried bailing the water out using their hats, but all to no avail. 'Once we had become convinced of the fact that the boat was leaking, that it was impossible to cross with us inside it, and that we were all of us sinking with the boat,' writes Haile Selassie, 'we began to swim with great difficulty. But as the lake was wide and it was impossible to cross it by swimming, seven men became exhausted and drowned.' Haile Selassie then goes on to list them all by name, including *Abba* Samuel. He himself, the emperor claims, was helped first by one of his servants until more assistance arrived in the form of some men on the shore who had seen what had happened and dived in. But in actual fact it was *Abba* Samuel who saved the life of his emperor – who clearly couldn't swim – and in the process sacrificed his own that day.[14] We can only speculate why Haile Selassie chose not to mention this fact in his autobiography. Did it perhaps strike him as unseemly to admit openly to the world that he might be beholden to another person?

By the age of ten, Tafari Makonnen could read and write both Amharic and *Ge'ez* and converse in French.[15] Haile Selassie's Catholic education and his closeness to the Catholic monks of the Capuchin mission would later give rise to the accusation that he had secretly converted to the Roman faith. Groundless suspicions like these bespoke a deep-seated mistrust in Ethiopia of anything foreign. Many conservative Ethiopians took an extremely sceptical view of foreign expatriates in their midst, especially Europeans. But the cosmopolitan atmosphere in Harar and the broad-minded attitude of his father left a profound impression on the young Tafari Makonnen, as would become apparent later in his regency.

It was evident that his father had great expectations of his son and intended to prepare him for greater things – and just as clear that Tafari had the requisite talent to fulfil his father's wishes. For many people, *Ras* Makonnen was the natural heir to the throne, and so it came as no surprise when, in 1898, Emperor Menelik II formally named his cousin as his successor.[16] On 1

November 1905, after Tafari Makonnen had turned thirteen, his father bestowed upon him the title of *Dejazmatch* (Count) and made him his heir. He also appointed him as the regional governor of Garamuleta, a district within Harar province.[17] Since this was merely a ceremonial enfeoffment, a trusted official, *Fitaurari* (Baron) Qolatsch, was put in place to govern the region in his name. Nevertheless, the young Tafari was deeply gratified at receiving this solemn mark of respect. He later reported that he had been especially proud to be admitted, as an officially nominated *Dejazmatch*, into his father's circle of advisors alongside his most senior officers.[18]

There is a record of a meeting between the young Tafari and a delegation sent to the Ethiopian court by the German emperor Wilhelm II in December 1904. The Extraordinary Imperial Mission to Abyssinia, under the leadership of Friedrich Rosen, special advisor on the Middle East to the German Foreign Ministry, was tasked with concluding a trade and friendship treaty with Emperor Menelik II. In January 1905, the delegation reached the province of Harar, where it was formally received at the governor's palace by his son and deputy Tafari Makonnen. In his account of the visit, Felix Rosen, a university professor and the brother of the head of the delegation, gives a vivid thumbnail sketch of the twelve-year-old prince:

'Lidj Tafari is delicate and slight for his age. His features are pure Semitic, while his skin is fair; in Abyssinia, both of these traits are a sign of noble blood. He was dressed in a flowing cloak of black silk with small gold buttons, attire customarily worn by the upper echelons of Abyssinian society. His bearing was measured and dignified and yet at the same time charmingly childlike. The conversation was confined to civilities and compliments and at the request of the prince was conducted in Amharic, although it is rumoured that he speaks French tolerably well. Here, lively discussion is not considered polite. People of good breeding tend rather to listen attentively to what is being said and only to give a response, in the form of some courteous remark, after a brief pause for thought.'[19]

After they had been served *Tedj*, the traditional honeyed wine of Ethiopia, and cognac, the envoy gave the governor's son a gold watch as a present: 'At this juncture, too, *Lidj* Tafari showed his noble upbringing; he received the gift with gracious thanks, but did not once look at it nor gave any sign that he was pleased, since only common people display their pleasure.' Rosen continues:

'The only thing that excited his interest was our bodyguard. The young prince gazed up in awe at our tall cavalrymen, and being the son of a renowned general himself, the questions he asked about their weapons and equipment were keen and well-informed. I wanted to photograph him with the soldiers, but the prince asked me not to, as his father had not expressly authorized it.'[20]

Even at this early stage in his life, it is clear that Tafari Makonnen was preparing to take on great responsibilities – and as son of the heir-apparent a glittering future lay in store for him. But then something occurred that, at least for the time being, was to dash all plans and hopes. On 12 January 1906, *Ras* Makonnen set out for the capital Addis Ababa. En route, he began to feel unwell and fell ill, finally seeking medical help at the town of Kollubi. He called for his son, who set off immediately to see his father. 'When I entered his bedroom,' Haile Selassie reported, 'to see his condition and he saw me standing by his side, he motioned me with his eyes to sit down, since it was difficult for him to speak with his tongue on account of the severity of his illness. As I was convinced that it was his wish that I was not to part from him, I spent the whole day sitting by his side.'[21] *Ras* Makonnen died in his hospital room in Kollubi on 21 March 1906. Haile Selassie does not reveal what illness his father was suffering from, but in all likelihood it was typhoid.[22] Soon after, the once-powerful governor of Harar and designated heir to the throne was interred in the Church of St Michael in Harar, which he had built, and a forty-day period of mourning began.

In Addis Ababa, the Imperial German delegation were witness to the obsequies which Emperor Menelik II organized for his late cousin *Ras* Makonnen after the mourning period was over. Felix Rosen quotes from the last letter that the gravely ill governor of Harar sent to the emperor shortly before his death: 'Now that I feel my end is nigh, I commend into your care the welfare of my beloved son Tafari. Protect him well, and be assured that I will hold you to account for this in the Afterlife before a Higher Judge.'[23]

Evidently, *Ras* Makonnen anticipated that the emperor would appoint Tafari to be his successor as governor of Harar, as indeed did Tafari himself: a few days after his father's funeral, he sent *Abba* Andreas his draft design for a governor's seal of office and asked the monk to have it cast for him in France.[24] The young nobleman's hopes were anything but unfounded. After all, on many previous occasions the emperor had, on the death of a great prince, bestowed control of the father's province upon the son of the deceased and formally named him as the rightful successor. But Menelik II did not appoint the thirteen-year-old *Dejazmatch* Tafari as governor of Harar, opting instead for his half-brother *Dejazmatch* Yilma, ten years his senior and the offspring of *Ras* Makonnen's first marriage. The suspicion that Empress Taitu had a major hand in this decision cannot be entirely discounted. The empress was related to Yilma's mother, *Ras* Makonnen's spouse before he married Yeshimebet. Furthermore, Yilma's wife was her niece.

All the same, both Tafari Makonnen's closest advisors and the general populace of Harar were profoundly shocked at the emperor's decision. Everyone knew that Tafari was his father's favourite son and that he had made him his heir; and to help him in his role as governor the plan was to appoint an experienced administrator alongside the young prince – and this is also what happened in the case of *Dejazmatch* Yilma. It was more than even a 23-year-old could manage to rule such a large province on his own.

Yet Emperor Menelik was fully aware of the responsibility he bore for the young *Dejazmatch*, as imparted to him by the latter's father on his deathbed. And so he decided to bring Tafari Makonnen to court and take personal charge of his continuing education. In addition, Tafari was installed as district governor of Selale – a region around one hundred kilometres north of Addis Ababa. No one expected Tafari to take up residence in Selale; the region was governed in his name. Instead, the prince from Harar and his cousin Imru were enrolled at the palace school in the capital. His advisor and mentor, *Abba* Samuel, also accompanied him to the court. To scotch once and for all the rumours that he had secretly converted to Roman Catholicism, Tafari had himself baptized for a second time by the priests at the palace, in accordance with the rituals of the Ethiopian Orthodox Church.[25]

Addis Ababa was the capital at the heart of the Ethiopian Empire. From here, the *Negusa Negast* ('King of Kings') Menelik II ruled over his extensive realm. After centuries of anarchy, he finally succeeded in unifying the provinces that were threatening to secede as well as regaining the country's southern provinces, which had been lost previously. He also secured Ethiopia's independence against the European colonial powers. His strong personal leadership ensured that the Ethiopian people's national consciousness and will to remain independent were immeasurably strengthened. Menelik II did not speak any European languages, and had never ventured beyond the borders of his own country. But he was open to modernity and to the benefits of Western civilization. Under his rule, all the advances that made Europe so outstanding were introduced into Ethiopia: the telephone and the telegraph, paved roads, bridges and railways; modern buildings, hospitals and schools; technical innovations and modern weapons technology. Menelik surrounded himself with a staff of foreign advisors, among them the Swiss engineer Alfred Ing, who was primarily responsible for building the railway line which was to link Addis Ababa with the sea. He also implemented a far-reaching process of modernization in the country's administration, beginning by centralizing the provinces, appointing a council of ministers, and officially prohibiting slavery (even though in practice this ban was flouted in many parts of the country). And yet, even though his position as absolute ruler was unchallenged, it still took a great deal of finesse in the exercise of power to rule this multi-ethic state with its powerful regional princes. For the *Rases*, the country's dukes, governed their provinces as personal fiefdoms and maintained powerful private armies which they could mobilize against the emperor if they so wished.

The extent to which Ethiopia was transformed under Menelik II was apparent not least in the capital Addis Ababa. The city had changed beyond all recognition since being founded in 1881, the date when Menelik, then still King of Shoa, set up camp here amid the Entoto Hills and his wife Queen Taitu gave the pleasant region in the valley, with its warm springs, the name Addis Ababa, or 'New Flower'. Twenty-five years later, the small settlement had become a pulsating metropolis with more than 50,000 inhabitants – a vast expanse of round huts spread across the foothills of the Entoto. A few stone structures rose up above this sea of huts, including the imposing post office building and several hotels. All the roads leading into the capital were still rough mule tracks, but the main central street was tarmaced. Telephone and telegraph networks were already in place. The villas of the foreign ambassadors were equipped with all the amenities of modern civilization, like mains electricity, baths and flushing toilets. This was also the case in the imperial *Gebbi* palace complex in the centre of the city. Admittedly, when measured against the standards that European potentates were accustomed to, this complex more resembled a collection of modest stone buildings. The emperor's residence, where Menelik II lived with his retinue, was a two-storey, whitewashed building with a red tiled roof, several balconies and a series of external staircases brightly painted in blue, red and green. On the fringes of the compound were barracks and administrative blocks; the complex also housed a private chapel and an enclosure for the palace lions, a special attraction for foreign guests.

We may judge how seriously Emperor Menelik II took his affairs of state from the account written by Lord Gleichen, who during his sojourn in Addis Ababa had the opportunity to observe the daily routine of the *Negusa Negast*:

'The emperor rises every morning at 3 a.m., goes to early morning chapel, and at 6, or sooner, receives the reports of his secretaries. For the next three hours he is busily engaged in answering letters, and deciding on matters in which his judgment is appealed to. During the rest of the day he is extremely active, and supervises every detail of government, no matter being too small for his attention. He also aims at being a popular sovereign, accessible to his people at all hours, and ready to listen to their complaints. In this he appears to be quite successful, for one and all of his subjects seem to bear for him a real affection.'[26]

If Lord Gleichen had visited the court at Addis Ababa some decades later, he would have been able to write the same about Haile Selassie.

The young *Dejazmatch* Tafari was schooled in the company of other aristocratic children of in Addis Ababa. Alongside *Lij* Imru and the future defence minister *Ras* Birru, this group also included *Lij* Iyasu, grandson of the Emperor Menelik and son of the powerful Prince of Wollo, *Ras* Mikael. In the palace school, they were prepared for higher responsibilities. They were instructed in statecraft and taught about the country's two basic statute books: the *Kebra Negast*, the 'Glory of the Kings', which records the history of Ethiopian imperial rule; and the *Fetha Negast*, the 'Kings' Law Book', a sort of penal code for Christian Ethiopia, which had been in use since the 16th century. They were familiarized with all the commonly used forms of address and other aspects of court protocol, had lessons in strategy and the art of war, and learned how to ride and fence. Last but not least, they were also introduced to the country's leading lights, who frequented the imperial court.

The contrast between Tafari Makonnen and his cousin *Lij* Iyasu, who was two and a half years younger, could not have been greater. Tafari, who was naturally slight, was a quiet and reserved boy with a studious and disciplined character. *Lij* Iyasu was the precise opposite:[27] tall and athletic, he was mad about sport and had an aggressive disposition. He shunned reading, preferring to spend his time in bars and brothels. The two cousins did not get along well, possibly because they were conscious of the dynastic rivalry between them, but even so they tried to reach some kind of accommodation with one another.

In 1907 Tafari Makonnen had cause to feel himself passed over once more by Emperor Menelik II. On 10 October, after just seven months in office as the governor of Harar, his half-brother *Dejazmatch* Yilma died suddenly and unexpectedly of pneumonia. But instead of Tafari Makonnen, the emperor again chose someone else as his successor: *Dejazmatch* Balcha Safo, a decorated military commander, who had fought bravely at the Battle of Adwa. On this occasion, too, the emperor compensated Tafari Makonnen for his disappointment by bestowing on him the office that the new governor of Harar had previously held: stewardship of the district of Darassa in Sidamo province. This time, the emperor did not want it to be a merely symbolic appointment, either. The young prince would be given a chance to prove his mettle by performing the role in person. Accordingly, that year Tafari Makonnen and his retinue, including three thousand soldiers from his father's army, made their way to Darassa.

Looking back in his memoirs, Haile Selassie describes the period he spent in Sidamo as 'a time of perfect joy'.[28] In his administrative duties, he was able to call on the support of *Dejazmatch* Abba Tabor, a thoroughly able civil servant. Meanwhile, his maternal grandmother Wolete Giorgis took care of court affairs and his personal well-being. As governor, Tafari Makonnen was also the supreme legal authority in his district, a new experience for the young prince. Now, week-in, week-out, he was expected to hold court sessions every Wednesday and Friday and pass judgment on the various disputes that were brought before him. Increasingly, he came to enjoy this role, once he realized that he could quickly command the respect of the head men in his district despite his tender age of fifteen.

In the event, though, Tafari Makonnen's tenure of the district governorship of Darassa would last for barely eighteen months. At the beginning of 1909 news reached him that the emperor's health was failing. And so in April Tafari returned to the court in Addis Ababa. Menelik II had already suffered a minor stroke back in 1906, and by the time another year had elapsed, there was no disguising the fact that he was seriously ill and no longer in full command of his faculties.[29] A council of ministers was put in place to take over the day-to-day running of government. Menelik's union with Empress Taitu had been without issue, a fact that caused much consternation at court and among the princes. Speculation about who might succeed the emperor became increasingly rife. The ensuing power vacuum played into the hands of Empress Taitu above all, who from the moment of her marriage on had claimed a political role and served as an advisor to her husband.[30] She also accompanied Menelik II on his military campaigns. During the war against the Italian invaders in 1896, she had led a group of noblewomen who went to the front with a mule train to care for the wounded. My grandfather *Ras* Kassa, who took part in the war as a junior officer and page in the personal tent of Emperor Menelik II, would often regale me as a child with the story of the rousing speech that the empress delivered to the assembled generals and princes of Tigray, Harar, Gojjam, Wollo and all the other provinces on the eve of the Battle of Adwa, to stiffen their resolve. 'Don't give an inch!' she urged them, 'Any ground you give today will become a ladder that will then be propped against your citadel, and tomorrow you'll wake to find that the enemies of Ethiopia are already within your walls!'

Now, as Menelik's condition worsened, the empress' political influence grew ever stronger – until ultimately she was the only person to have unrestricted access to the *Negusa Negast* at all times. She found an important ally in Princess Zauditu, a daughter of Menelik from a previous marriage. The empress brought Zauditu to the court at Addis Ababa and arranged her marriage to the son of her brother, *Ras* Gugsa Wale. Although as empress, she could not wield absolute power, she calculated that with her protégée Zauditu on the throne, her influence would still be felt at the highest level. For here it was a fortunate coincidence that a prophesy by Ethiopian monks was doing the rounds at that time, claiming that an empress would rule the country after Menelik.

Yet beside the empress there were others who were eager to stake a claim to the throne. The most influential of these was *Ras* Mikael, prince of Wollo province, who commanded a large, well-equipped army. Lord Gleichen described him as 'a man of pleasing address, of strong character and many rifles'.[31] He was connected to Emperor Menelik II in many ways – a connection that bore fruit principally in Menelik giving Mikael his daughter Shoaragad's hand in marriage. *Lij* Iyasu was the offspring of this union. And the powerful prince of Wollo made no bones about the fact that he considered his son the sole legitimate successor to Menelik.

In January 1909, Menelik suffered another, far more serious stroke which left him partially paralyzed. On 13 May, he summoned the country's dignitaries to his bedside and announced to them that his grandson *Lij* Iyasu was to be the heir apparent. *Ras* Tesemma Nadow, an experienced general and statesman who enjoyed the emperor's full confidence, was assigned to be his guardian and regent. The capital was by now abuzz with rumours that the empress would refuse to accept this decision on the succession and that she, Princess Zauditu and her husband *Ras* Gugsa Wale were organizing resistance. Yet one thing was patently clear: a situation in which the emperor was no longer capable of conducting the affairs of state and where two influential rival camps vying for supremacy were locked in a permanent state of hostility was threatening to cripple the country. A year later, in March 1910, the group around the regent *Ras* Tesemma finally prevailed and Empress Taitu was banished from the court. Henceforth, she was to play no further part in political developments in Ethiopia.

In this power struggle, Tafari Makonnen had behaved both tactically and shrewdly, refusing to throw his lot in with either side and keeping his eyes firmly fixed on the goal that he had been striving after for years: namely, to be appointed governor of his father's former province of Harar. And he duly achieved this aim. The incumbent governor *Dejazmatch* Balcha was recalled to Addis Ababa and dismissed, and Tafari Makonnen installed as the new governor of Harar.

The increased power that control over this economically and militarily important province brought was plain for all to see – as was the continuing tension between Tafari and the heir apparent *Lij* Iyasu. The fact that Tafari, as the son of *Ras* Makonnen, could also claim descent from the Solomonic line – the most important prequisite for eligibility to succeed to the Ethiopian throne – unsettled the regent. Could it be that, even at this early stage, *Ras* Tesemma intuited that Tafari harboured his own ambitions for the throne and that he might eventually pose a threat to *Lij* Iyasu? In any event, the regent decided upon a remarkable step: when Tafari Makonnen informed him of his imminent departure for Harar, *Ras* Tesemma summoned Princes Tafari and Iyasu to him and took them to the house of the archbishop *Abuna* Matewos. In the Ethiopian primate's presence, the regent demanded that the two warring cousins take a solemn vow.[32] *Lij* Iyasu was to swear that he would in no way hinder Tafari's work as governor of Harar and that he would always guarantee him the central government's full support and cooperation. For his part, Tafari Makonnen was required to swear that he would make no move to wrest the throne from *Lij* Iyasu and forswear from making common cause with *Lij* Iyasu's opponents. Directed by the regent, the two cousins concluded a kind of friendship treaty, or perhaps more accurately a non-aggression pact, with the new governor of Harar pledging always to remain loyal to the Crown Prince, and Iyasu promising to treat his cousin like a brother.

Almost exactly a year later, *Ras* Tesemma died after suffering a series of strokes. The seriously ill emperor Menelik II was still alive at this point, but had withdrawn entirely from public life. It was at this moment that *Lij* Iyasu seized his opportunity. He refused to share power any longer or to accept a new guardian as regent. In so doing he became, at the age of fourteen, the *de facto* ruler of Ethiopia. And when Menelik II finally passed away in December 1913, Iyasu also became ruler *de jure,* though he was never to be crowned. The pact between the two cousins lasted until September 1916, when Iyasu ordered Tafari to be dismissed as governor of Harar. This act marked the beginning of the end of the uncrowned emperor Iyasu's rule – and the start of the reign of the regent *Ras* Tafari and the future emperor Haile Selassie.

CHAPTER TWO

Two cousins vie for power

1911 to 1916

Tafari Makonnen was still not quite eighteen when he took up his new post as governor of Harar province in May 1910. 'He hides his youthfulness behind his brown beard,' remarked Monseigneur Jarosseau in his diary. But even then, as the Capuchin monk also noted at the time, his thin face displayed that mixture of pride, maturity and melancholy which was later to captivate so many of those who encountered him.[1] His previous role as provincial governor of Salale had endowed Tafari Makonnen with a growing maturity, and taught him how to take responsibility. In Harar, as the son of the legendary *Ras* Makonnen, he was given an ecstatic welcome by the populace. The governors who had succeeded *Ras* Makonnen had not left the province of Harar in a good state. Farmers were up in arms about the excessive tributes they were expected to pay, while soldiers were aggrieved about outstanding salaries and their officers about inadequate accommodation. The oppressively high tax burden had choked off the country's economy. The new governor was concerned to redress this situation: he did so by placing an upper threshold on the tributes payable to the feudal lords and curtailing their powers. He also divided Harar into twelve districts and appointed fitting people to administer their affairs, as well as establishing courts of law.[2] The reforms that he instigated in Harar were later to serve as a blueprint for him when, as Emperor Haile Selassie, he set about reorganizing Ethiopia as a whole.

His Imperial Highness Abeto *Lij* Iyasu Menelik.

In the meantime, the pact between Tafari Makonnen and *Lij* Iyasu was destined to be strengthened through familial ties. In 1911, Tafari married Princess Menen Asfaw, a granddaughter of King Mikael of Wollo and a niece of *Lij* Iyasu. Iyasu had personally engineered this liaison. To enable Menen to marry Tafari Makonnen, he arranged for her divorce from her then husband, *Ras* Leul Seged. Yet despite the fact that this was an arranged marriage, the 22-year-old Menen was by common assent one of the most beautiful women at the Addis Ababa court, and the couple were evidently devoted to one another. The wedding was duly celebrated in a church ceremony in Harar on 31 July 1911. In his autobiography, Haile Selassie later wrote of the Empress Menen: 'Her character is such that, apart from goodness, there is no evil or malice in her. Ever since we were married we lived together, by virtue of her being fertile, in one family sharing joy as well as sadness.'[3]

Yet this arrangement could not prevent the impending confrontation between the two cousins. Looking back today on this period, which culminated in the deposition of the uncrowned emperor Iyasu, one finds oneself confronted with a host of accusations and reproaches, the veracity of which is hard to determine. How much of this was propaganda, or to what extent did it represent verifiable misconduct or at least well-founded concerns? If we stick purely to the facts, there is no denying that Iyasu did not acquit himself well in his role as regent of Ethiopia. He was erratic, anything but diplomatic, and lacked any sense of proportion. After taking charge of the affairs of state following the death of *Ras* Tessema in April 1912, he summarily dismissed most of the ruling Ethiopian hierarchy and replaced them with his own appointees. This act earned him the enmity of the large majority of the country's princes and governors. And more than a few Ethiopian aristocrats may well have had a quite different cause for resentment against Iyasu, having found themselves cuckolded by the young ruler.

Lij Iyasu struggled ceaselessly to assert his authority. The long shadow of Menelik II weighed heavily upon him. No one knew whether the old emperor was still alive or not. And as long as his death was not proclaimed, *Lij* Iyasu was not emperor but merely the heir apparent. The death of the emperor was only officially announced in 1916 – he is thought to have died during the night of 12–13 December 1913.[4] And yet the powerful regional princes managed to prevent him from ever being crowned. For his part, *Lij* Iyasu scarcely missed an opportunity to snub these parvenu Ethiopian dignitaries; a whole series of reports testify to this. For instance, when *Lij* Iyasu and the powerful minister of war *Fitaurari* Habte Giorgis once encountered one another while out riding in Addis Ababa, *Lij* Iyasu ordered the minister to dismount in his presence. 'How dare you address me while you are still on horseback?' he barked at Giorgis. No sooner had the minister leapt down from his horse than the emperor told him: 'Now you may get back in the saddle again.'[5]

Lij Iyasu once paid an unscheduled visit to the reformer and later author of Ethiopia's first written constitution, *Begirond* Tekle Hawariat, in Harar. Tekle Hawariat had been educated in Europe and lived for a long spell in Russia. Without more ado, on entering the house, which was furnished in the European style, *Lij* Iyasu began looking at the pictures hanging in the parlour and asked his host to explain what they were about. But rather than indulge him, Tekle Hawariat took Iyasu to task: 'Your Majesty, it simply isn't done for an emperor to enter the house of one of his subjects unannounced. And even if he does, he's duty bound to behave like a guest and accept his host's hospitality humbly and quietly.'[6] Whereupon, as Tekle Hawariat recounts in his autobiography, the emperor picked up an inkwell from the desk and tipped its contents over his host's head. 'Up to that point I had been a loyal servant of the emperor,' Tekle Hawariat wrote, 'but in this instant I thought: this man cannot remain emperor of Ethiopia. He had put frivolity at the centre of his rule and completely sidelined sensible government.'[7]

By contrast, *Ras* Tafari displayed a far defter touch in his dealings with the Ethiopian nobility. An anecdote from Tekle Hawariat's autobiography makes this clear:

> 'On the day when *Ras* Tafari was introduced to us as the emperor's successor, I was standing behind the minister of war's chair. *Ras* Tafari entered the room, dressed in his official robes and with a prince's crown on his head. He walked up to the war minister and kissed his feet. To try and provoke *Ras* Tafari, I asked: "Do you really think those narrow shoulders of yours will be strong enough to support such a great land as Ethiopia?" *Ras* Tafari just smiled benignly and replied; "I'll find everything easy with masters like you to guide me."'[8]

However, what proved to be *Lij* Iyasu's undoing was not his dissolute lifestyle, nor even his volatility or his violent temper. Rather it was the grand vision that lay at the heart of his political agenda: namely, reconciliation between the Christian and Muslim sectors of Ethiopia's population. For although Muslims, who made up around 35–40 percent of the country's population, were officially on an equal footing with Christians, they were far from enjoying equal living standards. Ethiopian Muslims, *Lij* Iyasu announced, had been abandoned and persecuted, and issued the following unequivocal policy statement: 'Though we differ in religion and tribe, I would wish all of us to be united through a nationalist sentiment [...] cooperation with the rest of your Ethiopian brothers will keep your country united and her frontiers secure.'[9] Admittedly, his opponents were quick to exploit those character flaws of Iyasu's which made him an easy target for criticism. They recalled that his father had been born a Muslim and that, before he was christened in the name of Mikael and elevated to the aristocracy, his name had been Mohammed Ali. Before long rumours began to circulate that *Lij* Iyasu had converted to Islam and was intending to transform Ethiopia into a Muslim state.

Lij Iyasu saw the province of Harar, with its majority Muslim population, as being of key strategic importance to his policies. Accordingly, and much to the displeasure of the governor Tafari Makonnen, he began to interfere in regional affairs in Harar, appointing one of his placemen, a Syrian Muslim called Ydlibi, to the post of *Nagadras*, the province's director of customs and markets. The *Nagadras* was invested with extensive revenue-raising and tax-collecting powers – income that was henceforth channelled directly to central government. Tafari Makonnen's administration found itself effectively with the financial rug pulled from under its feet.

Another factor in *Lij* Iyasu's downfall that should not be underestimated – indeed, it may even have played a decisive role in it – was the influence of the European powers on Ethiopian politics. With the outbreak of the First World War, the country found itself once more a subject of interest to the Allies led by Britain and France on the one hand and the Central Powers of Germany and the Ottoman Empire on the other. Ethiopia's official stance during the war was one of neutrality. However, the Allies viewed the new direction Ethiopian policies were taking under Iyasu with great suspicion. In August 1915, the emperor travelled incognito to French Somaliland without informing French diplomats beforehand of his plans. Even though the visit was more in the nature of a holiday excursion, the Allies were deeply alarmed.[10] It was also well known at the time that *Lij* Iyasu was supplying rebellious forces in Somalia who were then staging an uprising against the colonial powers of Britain and Italy with arms and ammunition. The rebel leader Sheikh Mohammed Abdullah Hassan was referred to disparagingly by the British as the 'Mad Mullah'. Furthermore, *Lij* Iyasu was suspected of organizing a campaign against the Italian colonial authorities in neighbouring Eritrea. As far as the Allies were concerned, it was therefore only a matter of time before *Lij* Iyasu formally joined the conflict on the side of Germany and Turkey. Quite how out-landish these fears were may be gauged from the intense diplo-matic alarm triggered in Great Britain in 1915 by the news that the German ethnologist Leo Frobenius, founder of the Africa Institute that was later to bear his name, was leading an expedi-tion to Abyssinia. The British government suspected the explorer of going to Ethiopia on behalf of the Emperor Wilhelm II to arrange a clandestine pact with *Lij* Iyasu. As the flurry of frantic telegrams sent between London and Britain's representatives in Addis Ababa indicates, the British were so concerned that they watched the German delegation round the clock. Furthermore, Whitehall also ultimately ensured that Frobenius and his com-panions were refused entry by the Italian colonial authorities in Eritrea and forced to turn back before they even managed to set foot on Ethiopian soil.[11] It is therefore hardly surprising that the British also used every means at their disposal to fan the flames of the rumour that *Lij* Iyasu had converted to Islam, even going so far as to circulate faked photographs showing the Ethiopian ruler clad just in a loincloth in the manner of a Muslim nomad. These images, which were passed around from hand to hand in rural regions, achieved their desired effect.

According to his own account, Haile Selassie had not the slightest involvement in *Lij* Iyasu's downfall, though this is hard to believe, given that Tafari Makonnen had a clear vested inter-est in the toppling of his cousin and rival. In 1916, *Lij* Iyasu sum-moned Tafari Makonnen to a meeting in Addis Ababa. But at the same time, unbeknownst to his cousin, Iyasu left the capital and travelled to Harar. Once there, on 14 August 1916, *Lij* Iyasu issued a proclamation relieving Tafari Makonnen of his duties as governor of Harar and giving him charge instead of the remote province of Kaffa. In one fell swoop, Iyasu's action both publicly demoted the former governor of Harar and ostentatiously revoked the 1910 pact between the two men.

What might have impelled *Lij* Iyasu to take this drastic step? It was evident that the administrative reforms which Tafari Makonnen had begun to institute in Harar were not to his liking. Moreover, Iyasu cannot fail to have construed Makonnen's public antagonism toward his favourite *Nagadras* Ydlibi, whom he had foisted on the governor, as an open act of insubordination. Yet clearly the main thing that bothered Iyasu was the great popularity that his cousin Tafari Makonnen had attained during his time as governor of Harar.

It was this summary act, the deposition of Tafari by proclamation, which proved to be the straw that broke the camel's back and led directly to the coup against the uncrowned emperor. On 27 September 1916 – when Ethiopians were celebrating the *Masqal* holiday, the traditional 'Feast of the Exaltation of the Holy Cross' – a group of Ethiopian princes gathered in Addis Ababa under the chairmanship of the defence minister Habte Giorgis, the same person whom *Lij* Iyasu had once so publicly humiliated by making him climb down from his horse in the centre of the capital. At this meeting *Lij* Iyasu, who was absent in Harar at the time, was accused of treason and apostasy. The princes called upon the Coptic bishop *Abuna* Matewos to excommunicate the emperor. However, he was reluctant to do so and demanded incontrovertible proof of Iyasu's guilt. First and foremost he insisted that *Lij* Iyasu be given an opportunity to answer the allegations made against him. In his memoirs, Haile Selassie listed the specific charges which the minister of war Habte Giorgis, the strongman at the Addis Ababa court read out against *Lij* Iyasu:[12]

'*Lij* Iyasu had followed Islamic practice in taking four wives, all of whom came from Muslim homes.'

He had used government funds to build a mosque for the Muslim community in the town of Djijiga.

To mark the beginning of the feast of Ramadan in 1916, he had presented the Turkish consul Mahazar Bey with an Ethiopian flag showing the Lion of Judah and the legend 'The Lion of the Tribe of Judah has prevailed' on the front, and on the reverse an embroidered inscription of the first *surah* (chapter) of the Qur'an – 'There is no God but Allah, and Muhammad is his Prophet'.

1. He had been seen wearing Somalian clothing and a turban and carrying Muslim prayer beads. Furthermore, he was said to have prostrated himself towards Mecca in a mosque.
2. He had read the Qur'an and prayed from it, and had also had it transliterated into Amharic.
3. He had ordered the first *surah* of the Qur'an to be inscribed on the headgear of members of his palace bodyguard.
4. In Harar, he had expelled Catholic priests from a church that had formerly been dedicated by *Ras* Makonnen to the Ethiopian Orthodox Church and handed the building over to the Muslim community.
5. When one of his wives bore him a daughter, he commanded that she be brought up in the Islamic faith.
6. Rather than trace his ancestry back to the genealogy of Emperor Menelik I, he claimed instead to be a descendant in the fortieth generation of the Prophet Muhammad.
7. On the day that the death of Menelik II was announced, rather than attending the funeral service and interment, he played polo instead.

After this formal indictment was read out, the grand marshal of the court *Ligaba* Beyene drew his sword and declaimed: 'Now let anyone who is still a Muslim make himself known!' Then, on the basis of the 'charge sheet,' sentence was passed: The emperor was found to have converted to the Muslim faith and was excommunicated as a result. Finally *Etshege* Wolde Giorgis, the head of the Ethiopian Orthodox Church and subordinate only to the Coptic Pope, formally proclaimed the emperor's banishment, stating that he had clearly been part of the conspiracy himself.[13] In the same verdict, the emperor was declared deposed. The daughter of Menelik II and the aunt of *Lij* Iyasu, Princess Zauditu, was named empress, and at the same time Tafari Makonnen was invested as regent and heir apparent. Hand-in-hand with this, Tafari was also elevated to the rank of *Ras*.

There was no disputing that Zauditu should succeed *Lij* Iyasu on the throne. But because she was a woman, she required a regent and since she was also childless – and evidently unable to bear any children – the person who was installed as her regent would also be Zauditu's successor to the throne. There are several different versions of the story as to how *Ras* Tafari came to be appointed to this position. One account, which was told to me by my grandfather's secretary, claimed that *Ras* Kassa, the highly influential governor of Salale and *Lij* Iyasu's close relative, was actually the first person to be nominated crown prince and regent.[14] *Ras* Kassa was in a strong position to lay claim to the throne, seeing that he was a descendant not only of the Royal House of Shoa, but also of the Imperial House of Gondar and the Royal House of Lasta-Lalibela.[15] He was certain of the support of the Ethiopian Orthodox Church and also had an unimpeachable character. The representatives of Great Britain knew and admired him, after he attended the coronation of George V in London in 1911 as head of the Ethiopian royal delegation. But *Ras* Kassa did not have any driving ambition where secular power was concerned. Accordingly, he is said to have waived his claims and declared that his cousin Tafari Makonnen was far better suited to the role than he was.

Another version was recounted to me in a personal conversation by the *Dejazmatch* Zawde Gebre-Selassie, the long-serving foreign minister and deputy prime minister under Haile Selassie.[16] The strong man behind the throne, war minister Habte Giorgis, supposedly told a close circle of friends that no one was better suited to this post than *Ras* Kassa, and that the only black mark against him was that he was too powerful, since he had inherited the large forces of his grandfather *Ras* Darge. On the other hand, this young man Tafari Makonnen, the defence minister continued, who had no father and no mother, who was at everyone's beck and call and who kissed everyone's feet, would make an ideal regent.[17] If we accept this version as true, then it would appear that the princes were after a weak regent without strong dynastic ties, whose strings they could pull. And Tafari Makonnen appeared to fit this bill admirably. With Tafari Makonnen at the helm, the lords thought, they would once more have a free rein on power, which they exercised as quasi-sovereign rulers of their respective provinces and enforced with the private armies they maintained. However, it would not be long before the Ethiopian dignitaries' assumption was proved incorrect. War minister Habte Giorgis later expressed his great regret at having opted for *Ras* Tafari: 'We sat down and chose him as emperor, but when we stood up and tried to be rid of him we found it couldn't be done.'[18]

We do not know if Tafari Makonnen attended this historic meeting of the Ethiopian dignitaries, thought he certainly was present in Addis Ababa during this fateful period. In his autobiography, he writes that the circle of Ethiopian aristocrats around the defence minister came to him at this time and confided in him their plan to depose *Lij* Iyasu. When he learned that *Lij* Iyasu had turned his back on the Ethiopian Orthodox Church, he claims, he signalled his willingness to collude in the plot. There is no way of verifying the truth of this account. It seems, however, scarcely credible that Haile Selassie was actually the prime mover in toppling his cousin from the imperial throne. His position at that time was not so strong that he could have organized a conspiracy of this kind. It is also highly improbable that the empress-in-waiting Princess Zauditu played any significant role. Other figures were the real king-makers in this enterprise, notably the minister of war Habte Giorgis.

The decision to topple *Lij* Iyasu plunged Ethiopia into civil war: the deposed emperor, who may well have anticipated what was about to befall him, was not about to accept his fall from power without a fight. He assembled his forces in Harar and marched at their head towards Addis Ababa. Half-way to his destination he found his way barred by an army deployed by the aristocratic rulers of Shoa; he promptly withdrew back to Harar before swinging south, into the Afar region. On 9 October, an army under the command of *Dejazmatch* Balcha entered Harar. A massacre of the Muslim population of the city ensued, in which hundreds of people were killed. *Lij* Iyasu's hopes now rested entirely on the powerful army led by his father King Mikael, the *Negus* of Wollo. It was his prevarication that decided the outcome of the civil war. If he had marched on Addis Ababa with his army, which numbered almost 100,000 men, without delay he would have encountered little resistance there. Yet the *Negus* had good reasons for his caution. For one thing, he trusted in the assurances given to him by the defence minister Habte Giorgis, who wrote him a letter advising him not to do anything rash. His son *Lij* Iyasu had behaved in an ill-mannered way, Habte Giorgis told him, and steps were merely being undertaken to re-educate him and remind of of his responsibilities; but no one was thinking of breaking their oath of loyalty to the emperor. It took a while for *Negus* Mikael to realize that this was precisely what Habte Georgis and his co-conspirators had already done. This ploy helped the Ethiopian nobility win valuable time in which to assemble its forces and put them into the field against King Mikael.

The decisive engagement took place on the morning of 27 October 1916 at Sagale, barely 100 kilometres from Addis Ababa, where the forces of *Ras* Mikael confronted a government army of 120,000 troops under the command of Habte Giorgis. *Ras* Mikael had thirteen machine guns at his disposal, but these proved to be of little use as his artillery quickly ran out of shells. The government forces managed to capture the King of Wollo alive as his army dissolved into disarray. Around 10,000 Ethiopians lost their lives that day on both sides.

Ras Tafari did not remain idle during this period. Prior to this, he had never personally commanded an army in a campaign, but he was adamant that his place was at the front, in order, as he put it, 'to ensure discipline'.[19] Haile Selassie later described the Battle of Sagale in his autobiography: 'When we had fought from early morning for about five hours and when the Shoan army, leaping like a leopard seeing a goat, like a lion seeing a cow, entered in battle formation – swords drawn and fighting hand to hand – *Negus* Mikael was defeated and captured.'[20] Yet there is much evidence to suggest that *Ras* Tafari remained behind the front lines and only intervened in the fighting when the outcome of the battle was already decided.[21]

Side by side with the defence minister, *Ras* Tafari then took part in the victory parade staged by government forces in the Ethiopian capital on 3 November 1916. The Hon. Wilfred Gilbert Thesiger, British Consul-General in Ethiopia, painted a vivid picture of the occasion in a letter to the Foreign Secretary Sir Edward Grey. When *Ras* Tafari marched past at the head of his troops, he was greeted with 'a great ovation'. Thesiger elaborated: 'Then *Negus* Mikael was brought in. He came on foot and in chains, an old, fine-looking man dressed in the usual black silk cloak with a white cloth bound round his head, stern and very dignified, to bow before the empress before being led away [...] only a month before Mikael had been the proudest chief in Abyssinia and it must have been a bitter moment for him to be led in triumph before the hated Shoans.'[22]

Yet the deposed emperor *Lij* Iyasu was still at large. He saw himself as the victim of an intrigue, but he had no significant supporters left among the princes or governors. He remained in hiding for several years in the northeast of the country, in the remote Danakil Desert region. He was finally apprehended on 11 January 1921 and brought to the court at Addis Ababa. *Ras* Tafari Makonnen shied away from any triumphalism towards his rival, and the same was true of the other Ethiopian princes. In common with the other conspirators who had plotted against *Lij* Iyasu, he was troubled by a guilty conscience: after all, in taking the action they did, the Ethiopian aristocracy had knowingly flouted the express wishes of Emperor Menelik II. For in their presence, Menelik had once named *Lij* Iyasu his rightful heir apparent, and had required from the princes that they swear an oath of allegiance to his grandson. They remembered only too well the curse that the *Negusa Negast* had pronounced against anyone who refused to do obeisance to his chosen successor: 'May those who break this oath of loyalty give birth to black dogs.'

The princes' council decided to place the deposed emperor in safe custody. They chose my grandfather, the governor of Salale, as the ideal person for this job, possibly because he was related to both the regent *Ras* Tafari and *Lij* Iyasu. Haile Selassie wrote of Iyasu's detention: 'We despatched *Lij* Iyasu to Salale, to Fiche and arranged that he should reside there guarded by our faithful *Ras* Kassa.'[23] The princes got *Ras* Kassa to swear an oath pledging that *Lij* Iyasu would come to no harm while he was in his charge. They knew that they could rely upon *Ras* Kassa not to turn his prisoner over to any third party, not even to *Ras* Tafari if he should demand it.

Ras Kassa took *Lij* Iyasu to Fiche, the capital of his province. There, in a house specially constructed for him, the royal internee had several rooms and even a balcony at his disposal. My father *Ras* Asserate Kassa told me that my grandfather was punctilious about treating *Lij* Iyasu in a manner befitting a former emperor. Whenever he entered the room where Iyasu happened to be, *Ras* Kassa would remove his shoes, take off his cloak (*kabba*) and bow three times before addressing his prisoner. He implored the Empress that a 'golden' (in actual fact, brass) bedstead should be brought from the royal palace so that *Lij* Iyasu could sleep in the style to which he was accustomed. The empress duly sent it, along with various Persian rugs and silk curtains. For fear that the resident cook might be bribed to put poison in the former emperor's food, *Lij* Iyasu's meals were all personally prepared by *Ras* Kassa's wife, Princess Tsige Mariam Beshah. The precautions taken to guard against any potential assassination attempt were so stringent that, before *Lij* Iyasu's meals were taken to him, they were placed inside a wooden box with a padlock, to which only the princess herself and *Lij* Iyasu had a key.[24] All in all, then, *Lij* Iyasu's stay in Fiche was more like being under house arrest than a gaol sentence.

But although it was a golden cage that had been set up to house *Lij* Iyasu, it was still a cage. So it is perfectly understandable that

Empress Zauditu on the day of her coronation, 11 February 1917.

the deposed emperor should have hankered after his freedom. In May 1932 – with the aid of his former father-in-law *Ras* Hailu, who was at that time governor of Gojjam province – he managed to escape. News of this reached Haile Selassie when he was in Addis Ababa attending the marriage of his son, Crown Prince Asfa-Wossen, to Princess Wolete-Israel Seyoum. *Ras* Kassa, who had also been invited to the wedding, approached the emperor and told him: '*Lij* Iyasu was my responsibility alone – do with me what you will.' The emperor simply gave a brief nod and replied: 'You couldn't help what happened; others will be called to account for that.'[25] *Ras* Hailu's plot was duly uncovered, and the prince of Gojjam placed under arrest and later expropriated. And when *Lij* Iyasu was recaptured soon after, Haile Selassie took a far less indulgent attitude than before to his cousin; this time, *Lij* Iyasu found himself incarcerated in a prison cell in the town of Gara Muleta in Harar province. The conditions in which he was held there could scarcely be described as humane, involving as they did a very meagre diet of bread and water and the prisoner shackled both with a neck brace and leg irons.

The final occasion on which *Lij* Iyasu appeared in public was in the autumn of 1935, soon after the outbreak of war with Italy, at Dire Dawa railway station, where he was seen boarding a train to Addis Ababa in the company of *Abba* Hanna, the emperor's confessor.[26] By chance, two prominent dignitaries were on the platform at the same time, having just arrived on the down train from the capital. The men in question were the later Ethiopian foreign minister Lorenzo Taezaz and the governor of Harar, *Nagadras* Nasibu Zamanuel. *Lij* Iyasu turned to them and said: 'We shan't see one another again' before bidding them farewell with tears in his eyes. Nothing more is known about what became of him hereafter. There has been much speculation about the precise fate that befell the former emperor. But a few days later, just before Haile Selassie left for the front, the empress was officially notified of the death of *Lij* Iyasu, and a session of lamentation was held in the royal palace. In the summer of 1966 *Dejazmatch* Belai Ali, a close relative of *Lij* Iyasu who was visiting my parents in Asmara, described to me how he and two other prominent dignitaries from Wollo were summoned to the palace one morning. As they entered the Great Throne Room, Haile Selassie came towards them wailing and crying, with his burnous worn inside-out – a traditional sign of mourning – and informed them that *Lij* Iyasu was dead.

There is no denying the fact that the death of his disagreeable cousin and rival was an extremely convenient development for the emperor at this point in time. Haile Selassie was afraid that Mussolini might use *Lij* Iyasu to further his own political ends, by installing him as the figurehead of a puppet government in Abyssinia. As it turned out, such fears were largely groundless. Following his escape from Fiche in May 1932, Iyasu's aides had urged him to make contact with the Italian consul in Debre Markos and seek his help. *Lij* Iyasu was furious at this suggestion and lost no time in putting his advisors in their place: 'If I were to turn to one of the *Ferenji* (foreigners) for help and sign a pact with him, that would be high treason. I would effectively be disowning the Ethiopian Empire, a state that has been revered and feared by all since time immemorial. The people who are challenging my right to rule it are my own sister and my own brother; but at least they're not some foreigner who has no claim whatsoever on my country and simply wants to colonize it.'[27]

However, Haile Selassie could never rid himself of his guilty conscience that, in deposing *Lij* Iyasu, he had actually toppled the legitimate ruler of Ethiopia. The conspiracy against his cousin that marked the start of his rise to power was a stain which would tarnish his regency for decades to come. Repeatedly, *Ras* Tafari sought to have his claim to the title and office of *Negusa Negast* – 'King of Kings' – officially recognized and legitimized. Right up to the very end of his regency, his relations with the province of Wollo, homeland of *Negus* Mikael, remained strained.

The picture that Haile Selassie painted of *Lij* Iyasu in public and in his autobiography coloured the official verdict on the former ruler for many decades. *Lij* Iyasu was declared a nonperson and most European authors, who were likewise driven by personal interest, fell in line with this assessment. He was branded as the Ethiopian emperor who lapsed from the Christian faith and called for jihad – though to date there is no incontrovertible proof that *Lij* Iyasu ever became a Muslim. He is shown on several photographs in the uniform of an Ottoman pasha. He may well have given the Turkish consul in Harar an Ethiopian flag with the first *surah* of the Qur'an embroidered on the back, but this was a symbolic gesture on his part to the Muslim community in his realm, to indicate that they too were an integral part of the Ethiopian people. In the 1920s, for instance, the young Edward Prince of Wales (the future Edward VIII) went on a state visit to India, where he was photographed dressed in a turban and wearing the uniform of a Sikh regiment in the Indian Army. Yet no one in Britain at the time thought to accuse the heir apparent of having converted to Sikhism.

In the 1990s, the grandson of *Lij* Iyasu, Professor Girma Yohannes, succeeded in getting the primate of the Ethiopian Orthodox Tewahedo Church, *Abune* Paulos, to issue a written declaration stating that *Lij* Iyasu had never renounced his Orthodox Christian faith. Even so, to the present day he has not been rehabilitated or his excommunication rescinded. If one asks Ethiopian Muslims about *Lij* Iyasu, a particular refrain crops up time and again, namely: he was the only one of Ethiopia's leaders who really understood us Muslims. It is only in recent years that a more nuanced picture has started to emerge,[28] which recognizes the progressive nature of many of his policies, notably his insistence that Christians and Muslims should enjoy equal rights and his vision of making Ethiopia a haven of religious tolerance. Another point of prescience was his instinctive mistrust of Great Britain, France and Italy – all countries whose primary aim turned out to be the dismantling of Ethiopia as a sovereign state. And one final forward-looking policy was *Lij* Iyasu's pan-African perspective, as manifested in his support for the Somali rebels in their struggle against the colonial powers; in this, he anticipated the postcolonial period in African politics.

Though Ethiopian historians and the bulk of European and American studies of the country were loath to admit it, *Lij* Iyasu was a man of conviction and a great Ethiopian patriot, whose tragedy lay in the fact that he was too liberal-minded for his time. The same was undoubtedly true of his successor Haile Selassie, but he far outstripped his unfortunate cousin in both political

The Prince Regent Ras Tafari holding court with Fitawrari Habte
Giorgis on his right and Ras Hailu on his left. Addis Ababa 1918.

acumen and ambition. And as would soon become abundantly
clear, in contrast to *Lij* Iyasu, Haile Selassie possessed one price-
less quality: he proved to be a master of diplomacy and tactics,
which he quickly employed to free himself from the grip of the
powerful Ethiopian princes and attain the position of absolute
ruler of the country.

CHAPTER THREE

The Ethiopian Machiavelli

1917 to 1929

Princess Zauditu ascended the throne on 11 February 1917. This was the first time that a woman had been crowned empress in Ethiopia since the legendary Queen of Sheba. 'Zauditu's sole qualification for the throne was her birth, as the daughter of Menelik,' wrote the Ethiopian historian Bahru Zewde. 'Her attraction to the nobility was her political innocuousness.'[1] The powerful princes and lords to whom she owed her elevation to rulership flocked to her coronation in St George's Cathedral in Addis Ababa. Standing directly behind her during the ceremony was the heir apparent *Ras* Tafari, whom the assembled aristocracy regarded as something of a political lightweight. At his instigation, for the first time in Ethiopia's history European dignitaries – the governors of Anglo-Egyptian Sudan, of British Somaliland and of French Somaliland – had also been invited to attend the coronation festivities. They were all present to witness the moment when *Abuna* Matewos anointed Zauditu's head with holy oil before placing the crown of Menelik II upon it.

A surviving photograph of the occasion (see illustration on page 33) shows the empress seated on her throne, which is draped with swags of silk, clad in her gold-emboidered *lanka* ceremonial robe, and clutching the imperial sceptre. From beneath the massive crown, a tiny face peers out. She almost seems to disappear amidst the magnificent trappings of imperial office. Zauditu was the empress, and *Ras* Tafari her regent. But who really held the reins of power in the Ethiopian Empire, which had been in existence for millennia but which had recently been shaken to the core and weakened by the armed clashes that broke out after *Lij* Iyasu was deposed? In her coronation address, the empress left her audience in no doubt that she had not the slightest intention of restricting herself to ceremonial duties, envisaging instead a thoroughly active role for herself. She solemnly swore to protect her people. She would look upon the nobility as her fathers and upon the common people as her brothers, she declared. And above all, the rule of law would prevail in the country. Anyone who suffered an injustice should tell her representative, the prince regent, 'and I shall set them to right'.[2] The empress lost no time in giving a clear sign of her hunger for power when, just a week after her coronation and without the prior agreement of the privy council or the heir apparent, she promoted her uncle *Ras* Wolde Giorgis, the conqueror of the kingdom of Kaffa, to the position of *Negus* of Gondar.

Yet Zauditu had little experience in dealing with people, and was even less well versed in political intrigue. Her education, Bahru Zewde wrote, did not go beyond a reading of the holy books, to which she was especially attached.[3] Even before she ascended the throne, she had been obliged to seek a divorce from her husband, *Ras* Gugsa Wale, the Prince of Begemder. Both *Lij* Iyasu and *Ras* Tafari mistrusted this powerful prince, and he had even spent several years under house arrest. Now, at least, he regained the governorship of his province. It was far enough away from the Ethiopian capital, the powers-that-be calculated, for him not to pose any threat to the country's new rulers.

Ras Tafari also made clear his desire, in his capacity as regent and the designated successor to the throne, to control the affairs of state – and if possible without any tiresome interference on the part of the empress. But it was difficult for him to make any headway against the sheer splendour and aura of the imperial crown. The final decision in all matters of any substance lay with the empress, and any attempt to rule against her settled will was impossible. Consequently, a blend of skilful diplomacy, tact and sensitivity and subtle persuasion were called for in order to convince the empress that those decisions which the regent was minded to reach were in fact of her own making. However, as soon became apparent, she was not the one from whom *Ras* Tafari encountered the most resistance. The young regent found himself surrounded by forces which threatened to stifle any attempt of his to govern. These comprised the powerful minister of war Habte Giorgis and a coterie of ministers under his control, most of whom had been appointed by Emperor Menelik II. Then there was the privy council, an assembly of the ministers and the leading princes, and the princes of the provinces, who insisted upon their respective privileges and exclusive rights. Furthermore, the Ethiopian Orthodox Church with its primate, the Coptic archbishop *Abuna* Matewos, was one of the forces within the country that set great store by tradition and adherence to the status quo.

The new regent wanted to institute reforms, while his opponents were determined that everything should remain just as it was. *Ras* Tafari knew that it would be a long struggle for him to reshape the country according to his own ideas. And he also knew that he would have to proceed with the utmost caution – if only so as not to give his far more powerful adversaries any excuse for getting rid of him. But *Ras* Tafari had read his Machiavelli: over the following twelve years he would gradually manage to eliminate all his opponents. 'In fact,' writes Harold G. Marcus, 'so wily was Tafari that no one remarked on his wiliness.'[4]

The regent's first pressing concern was to bolster the firepower of his own personal armed forces and equip them with modern weapons, in order to create a counterweight to the armies of the provincial princes. Wherever he could, he installed trusted confederates in key positions, above all in the administration of the capital Addis Ababa, which he established and developed as his power base. Here, at one remove from the traditional aristocratic ruling elite, he found ambitious young men who shared his desire to change the country and whose loyalty he could count upon. He appointed the prince whom he trusted the most, *Ras* Kassa Hailu, as governor of the province of Shoa, which surrounded the capital. Over the ensuing years, he came to play a key role: whenever *Ras* Tafari found himself at loggerheads with the empress or the privy council, *Ras* Kassa would attempt to arbitrate and mediate between the parties, and not infrequently his efforts in this regard were crowned with success.

Initially, *Ras* Tafari focussed his main attention on foreign policy, as the realm where he was least likely to come into conflict with the regional princes. The man who had been given the position of foreign minister, *Ras* Mulugeta, later minister of war, had little ambition, which left the prince regent a largely free hand. In 1917, the European powers were still at war with one another – a conflagration that assumed the proportions of a world war with the entry of the United States into the conflict that same year. *Ras* Tafari worked to ensure that Ethiopia entered the fray on the Allied side – the triple entente between Great Britain, France and Italy. He offered the Allies his country's support in their campaign against the Turks in Arabia. In return he asked them to supply him with modern weapons and grant Ethiopia a seat at the forthcoming peace negotiations. However, the Allies declined. A country that was itself on the verge of a civil war, whose government seemed profoundly unstable, which was beset by internal strife fomented by a deposed emperor who remained implacably opposed to his successor the empress – such a country did not strike them as the kind of partner from whom any serious assistance could be expected in the war.

In addition, the European powers and their envoys in Ethiopia underestimated the willpower and resilience of the new regent. In March 1917, the Italian ambassador in Addis Ababa reported to his government that *Ras* Tafari lacked 'the skill and energy to lead the country out of the state of anarchy into which it has fallen'.[5] The British high commissioner for the protectorate of British Somaliland and the French envoy in Ethiopia took a similar view: in their estimation, the break-up of the Ethiopian Empire was imminent.

This may well have simply been wishful thinking on the part of the Europeans, especially in the case of Italy, which sought to benefit directly from the collapse of central power in Ethiopia.

In 1906 Rome had signed a pact with Great Britain and France, in which London recognized the existence of an Italian sphere of interest which spanned the territory between Addis Ababa and Eritrea. Italy had entered the war on the side of the Allies in 1915 on the understanding that, in the event of the Allies annexing German colonies at the cessation of hostilities, corresponding colonial concessions should be made to Italy. At least, this was the principle that was enshrined in Article 13 of the secret Treaty of London that was concluded on 26 April 1915. The dream of Imperial Italy was of an East Africa under her sway – with Ethiopia at its centre, flanked by the colonies of Eritrea and Somalia. Anything that weakened Ethiopia could therefore only be a welcome development where Italy was concerned. As a result, Rome fought tooth and nail to maintain the arms embargo that had been placed upon the country in 1916. It also tried to entice the fugitive *Lij* Iyasu onto its side by offering him support in his struggle against his cousin *Ras* Tafari. Yet the deposed emperor was shrewd enough not to be lured by this poisoned chalice: his dispute with *Ras* Tafari, he informed the Italian ambassador, was a matter between brothers which did not concern any foreign government. According to the French envoy in Addis Ababa, Italy did everything within its power to try and drive the Ethiopian Empire into 'a state of anarchy', to 'strip it of all its defences' and to 'seize the first opportunity that arose to turn Abyssinia into a kind of African Poland, from which it would secure the lion's share for itself when the country was carved up'.[6]

For the time being, though, the First World War absorbed all the energies of the European colonial powers, as *Ras* Tafari set about devising his initial plans for reforming his country. On 30 April 1917, the prince regent presented an historic memorandum, which had been drafted under the guidance of two European advisors – the German-born Adolf Jakob Mayer and a Cypriot by the name of Baldassare.[7] The Ethiopian Foreign Ministry '… a little hovel composed entirely of one small room, furnished with a table and a few chairs and a cupboard', appeared to them to be wholly unworthy of a country with pretensions to be considered on a par with the European nations and which wanted to proclaim to the rest of the world that it was 'capable and worthy of being independent.'[8] The urgent reforms that were listed in the memorandum included: the introduction of model farms to boost the agricultural economy, the establishing of independent bureaucracies in Addis Ababa, Harar and Dire Dawa, a single nationwide currency, the creation of a telephone network, the standardization of army equipment and reform of the education system.[9]

But to realize projects such as this, two things were necessary: access to a central authority which extended beyond the city boundaries of Addis Ababa and the corresponding financial wherewithal. For every proposal that the advisors put forward had a price tag. Yet when *Ras* Tafari embarked upon his term of office as regent, the central government lacked any regular income stream. Its main sources of income were excise duties and tribute payments by the provincial princes; tax revenues to the central administration were only at a very rudimentary stage. The key positions in matters of finance in the provinces and regions were held by the *Nagadras*, the senior directors of customs and markets. *Ras* Tafari succeeded in appointing people whom he trusted as the *Nagadras* in Addis Ababa, Harar and several other towns. Tafari's home province of Harar was of particular strategic importance in this regard; most goods arriving in the country came through the railway station at Dire Dawa, which lay close to the provincial capital, and it was there that import duties were levied. The man whom *Ras* Tafari put in place as the *Nagadras* of Harar, Gebre-Igziabher François, made sure that not only the newly-levied special tax for supporting the central goverment's budget was dispatched to Addis Ababa but also that monies which were earmarked for funding the personal regiment of the prince regent were collected on a regular basis.

New regulations were imposed upon the administrations of the towns and regions. Bureaucrats were banned forthwith from creaming off a certain percentage for themselves from every financial transaction that took place within their jurisdiction. Instead, they were granted a fixed salary. In this way, the foundations were laid for a whole new echelon of government in Ethiopia:

a professional civil service of the kind long since familiar in the developed nations of Europe. *Lij* Wassanie, one of those young Ethiopians who had completed their education abroad, became the mayor of Addis Ababa. In this capacity, he found himself under the direct command of the heir apparent. Over the following years and decades, many others were to follow the example set by *Lij* Wassanie; these were Ethiopia's *homines novi*, ambitious, well-educated young men from the middle classes, often with experience of living abroad, who were systematically promoted by Haile Selassie and who had a personal sense of loyalty to him – unlike the old aristocratic elite. Schools, hospitals, modernization on all fronts: *Ras* Tafari's vision of a modern Ethiopia was calculated to rally the 'young Ethiopians' to his cause. In turn, the provincial princes, who became alarmed at the prospect of their influence waning, looked down on these Young Turks as upstarts and 'men who came from nothing'.

In particular, the provinces that lay on the fringes of the Ethiopian Empire seemed far beyond the reach of central government. Arms dealers, bands of local brigands and warlords made these areas extremely unsafe. Various descendants of the former king of Tigray and emperor Yohannes IV were vying with one another for control of Tigray in the north of the empire, and the province stood on the brink of anarchy. Furthermore, the enduring economic crisis affecting the whole country – during the First World War, trade with European countries had dried up on several occasions – was another destabilizing factor. In March 1918, the central government decided to deploy a military task force to the troublesome northern province. Thousands of troops assembled in the capital. There was considerable unrest and discontent in their ranks, as many of them had been waiting months to be paid. Presently, their numbers were swelled by an army of day-labourers and unemployed men from Addis Ababa, who also held the country's ministers responsible for their desperate situation.

Ras Tafari skilfully exploited the highly-charged situation in the capital for his own ends, in order to strengthen his own position. He seized this opportunity to undermine the authority of the unpopular ministerial council by clandestinely making common cause with disgruntled army officers. The demands that this group issued on 20 March 1918 were entirely consistent with his ideals. The officers' ultimatum demanded the dissolution of the ministerial council and the transfer of governmental authority to a triumvirate comprising Empress Zauditu, the war minister Habte Girorgis and *Ras* Tafari. The administration turned a deaf ear, but found itself unable to sit out this crisis: six days later, 8,000 soldiers and officers staged a mass show of strength outside the gates of the palace complex, and refused to disperse until their demands were met. After a while, the principal seneschal of the palace appeared before the crowd and handed the protesters a letter from the empress confirming the dismissal of her ministers. In addition, he proposed that a meeting should take place between the empress and a delegation from the demonstrators. The name that this delegation chose for itself – *Derg* ('coordinating committee') – represented the first usage of this term in Ethiopian history. Fifty-four years later, the cadre of officers that overthrew Haile Selassie and toppled the Ethiopian Empire deliberately harked back to this earlier occasion by adopting the same name. The demonstrators outside the gates remained distrustful and refused to enter the palace grounds. It was only when *Abuna* Matewos, *Etshege* Wolde Giorgis and *Ras* Tafari's private secretary appeared in person to confirm that the ministers had indeed been dismissed that the crowd believed the news. Satisfied with what they had achieved, the protesters dispersed.

In his autobiography, Haile Selassie maintains that he was against the dismissal of the ministers at this time – since it wasn't in the gift of the people to decide upon the appointment and sacking of ministers. To this he added, by way of complaint, the remark: 'Until new ministers could be selected and appointed, the entire work had to be carried out on Our responsibility alone, and this caused great fatigue to Us.'[10] This account seems barely credible, for there can be no question that this development rid *Ras* Tafari of a whole series of hostile ministers. But even though the position of the prince regent was clearly consolidated, he was not empowered to merely select a new cabinet to his own liking. And above all the power of his principal adversary, the war minister, remained intact.

In the same year, the Spanish flu pandemic that had already ravaged other parts of the world hit Ethiopia. It swept the country in two waves, the first in August and September and the second in November and December 1918. Ten thousand people fell victim to the flu in Addis Ababa alone, while across the country as a whole it claimed at least 40,000 lives. In many regions, public life came to a complete standstill, as also happened in the capital. *Ras* Tafari was among those struck down. He collapsed on 2 September; European doctors were summoned and for several days his life hung in the balance. He was even given the last rites. Rumours began to spread through Addis Ababa that *Ras* Tafari was dead and *Fitaurari* Habte Giorgis announced that he was 'taking over the reins of government until further notice'. 'The government is in complete turmoil,' noted the British envoy Thesiger at this time, concluding that Tafari's 'threatened demise has brought home forcibly how much influence he has quietly acquired during the past one and a half years.'[11] To scotch these rumours, the seriously ill prince regent was led out onto the balcony of Menelik's Palace during the Ethiopian New Year celebrations on 11 September. The sight of the jubilant crowd waiting on the square may well have stiffened his resolve not to succumb to the illness. Yet it was still several months before *Ras* Tafari was able to resume work. The only mention by Haile Selassie of his illness in his autobiography, however, is the terse observation: 'But I, after I had fallen gravely ill, was spared from death by God's goodness.'[12]

In the meantime, the Great War, which had kept the world on tenterhooks for the past four years, finally drew to a close. The map of Europe had changed radically: the German and Austro-Hungarian empires had been swept away, and with them their rulers Wilhelm II and Franz Joseph I. The victorious Allies were demanding reparations. In this context, Africa in general and Ethiopia in particular once more came under the scrutiny of the European nations. Now Italy began prosecuting its claims for recompense for having participated in the war, as laid down in the secret Treaty of London. Rome's stated aim was to take control of British and French Somalia and of the railway line from Addis Ababa to the port of Djibouti. In doing so, it would establish a de facto protectorate over Ethiopia. Great Britain would have been willing to quit the Horn of Africa and leave it to Italy, but France demurred, since it saw Djibouti as vital for safeguarding its own trade with Madagascar and Indo-China. Paris did not have the slightest intention of giving up the lucrative railway line, either, as it ensured the prosperity of French Somaliland. In a skilful piece of diplomatic chicanery, in which England and France did not annexe Germany's former colonies *de jure* but merely took them over as mandated territories, Italy's claims arising from the London treaty had been effectively annulled.

The arms embargo imposed on Ethiopia and *Lij* Iyasu in 1916 had outlasted the war. France was well aware that Ethiopia was in need of modern weapons if it was going to successfully establish central authority across the whole country. But Great Britain and Italy opposed this move with every means at their disposal. Every import of weapons to Ethiopia required the joint agreement of the British, Italians and French. *Ras* Tafari realized that there was only one way to free the empire from the stranglehold of the colonial powers surrounding it, namely by embedding Ethiopia in an international system of collective security. In January 1918, US President Woodrow Wilson had unveiled his striking 'Fourteen Points' policy. The last of the fourteen points enshrined an important vision for future international cooperation: 'A general association of nations must be formed under specific covenants for the purpose of affording mutual guarantees of political independence and territorial integrity to great and small states alike.' This was a reiteration of the notion of a 'peaceful … continuous community of all peoples on Earth,' which Immanuel Kant had first formulated in the late 18th century. The 'League of Nations' was ultimately brought into existence by the ratification of the Versailles Peace Treaties in 1919.

Ras Tafari was in no doubt that Ethiopia should become part of this community of nations in order to secure its long-term sovereignty. For their part, Italy and Great Britain did everything they could to try and sabotage Ethiopia's entry to the League. The prince regent not only had to contend with their resistance, but also with opposition from within the Ethiopian ruling elite, which vehemently rejected the incorporation of the country into international frameworks. For certain members of this class, any contact with the representatives of a European power was tantamount to a betrayal of national interests.

One of the chief impediments which needed to be resolved before Ethiopia could join the League of Nations was the country's slave trade. The British and Italians never tired of picking at this particular sore as a way of thwarting *Ras* Tafari's plans. Up to the late 19th century and beyond, slavery was widespread in Ethiopia – as it was in many other countries at this time, not only on the African continent.[13] Especially in the border region between Ethiopia and the Sudan, organized gangs of slavers went about their nefarious business, conducting mass raiding expeditions to seize people and sell them into slavery. Even so, the great majority in slaves in Ethiopia had originally been prisoners of war. They were either traded within the country or shipped via the ports on the Red Sea or the Gulf of Aden to Arabia, Egypt, the Middle East, India or Europe.

Most of the people-traffickers were Muslims, and in many cases the captives were forced to convert to Islam. In the heavily Christian Ethiopian Highlands, adherents of this faith were traditionally forbidden to trade in slaves, but were not prohibited from buying or owning them. Slaves were also to be found at the courts of princes, kings and emperors. Admittedly, there were all manner of gradations and nuances in this regard: it wasn't always easy to determine where a normal relationship of servitude ended and a state of slavery began.[14] Indeed it was not uncommon for slaves to occupy quite exalted positions in the civil service or the army. Many commentators have pointed to the fact that domestic slavery in Ethiopia was relatively benign in comparison to the brutality that had been meted out to slaves in the European colonies or in the United States.[15] Many of those who were nominally slaves were paid and as a rule it was taken for granted that their entire families, which were often very large, would also be cared for. Not infrequently, bondsmen employed at royal courts were actually proud of their positions, and even among ministers it was even common practice and a badge of honour for ministers to refer to themselves as the *baria* ('slaves') of their emperor or empress.

Charles Fernand Rey, a British colonial official who regularly visited Ethiopia during the 1920s, described the following incident:

> 'A distinguished Abyssinian of advanced ideals, a cultured and broad-minded man, recently freed his own slaves: they seemed mildly interested, but refused to depart from the precincts where they had lived quite happily for many years. They were consequently told they could remain, and were fed as usual, receiving also a small monthly wage. But they declined firmly to do any work except at such times as the spirit moved them, for, as they pointed out, what was the point of being free if they had to work?'[16]

Rey's account may be somewhat embellished, but the experience of serfs in Ethiopia reacting with incomprehension when they were told that they were now free men is well attested.

Every Ethiopian ruler who set about combatting slavery was under no illusion that this was an extremely arduous undertaking whose progress could be counted not in years but rather in generations. The institution of slavery was simply too deeply ingrained in the country's social psyche and was intimately bound up with tradition and economic interests. Attempts to curtail slavery went back to the reign of Emperor Menelik II. When this ruler came to the throne in 1889, he issued a decree banning slavery, but exempted from this the enslavement of prisoners of war. Empress Zauditu renewed the ban in 1918, and *Ras* Tafari followed suit. In September 1923, he proclaimed an expressly-worded ban on slave trading, followed six months later by an official statute which set out severe penalties for convicted traffickers. This law was far from being merely an empty gesture, as the following years were to prove. Charges were brought against many slave traders, and numerous trials were staged. Anyone who was convicted faced the prospect of a heavy fine or a gaol sentence, or in some cases even capital punishment. 'All the foreign envoys know that We have punished them even with the death penalty,' Haile Selassie later recalled in his autobiography.[17]

Opposition to the abolition of slavery also came from the ranks of the Ethiopian aristocracy, dignitaries and landowners, right up to the highest ministers: ' Where will this all end?' complained *Fitaurari* Habte Giorgis, for instance: 'I can see my wife being forced to go down to the river to fetch water, and me having to go off and chop firewood.'[18] And one aristocratic landowner declared: 'We could just as soon do without slaves as Europeans could run around barefoot.'[19] *Ras* Tafari was fully aware that in tackling this question he was taking on his country's ruling class and that there would be no quick solutions. But he also knew that solving the problem of slavery depended upon economic development: at that time, some 90 percent of Ethiopia's economy was comprised of agriculture. As long as the country was in the grip of a feudal agrarian society, corresponding dependencies would continue to exist between landowners and feudal masters on the one hand and their vassals on the other. Slavery would only diminish in importance in proportion to the growth of cash crop cultivation and the development of labour markets.

In July 1923 the council of the League of Nations called upon its member states to prepare reports on the state of slavery in regions under their jurisdiction: France announced that although slavery existed in Ethiopia and that slaves were transhipped from there through the port of Djibouti to Arabia, the slave trade had nevertheless declined markedly since 1916 – a signal achievement of the government led by *Ras* Tafari. It also pointed out that the Ethiopian central government needed arms and ammunition in order to effectively stem the slave trade. Italy flatly rejected this request, and attempted to block every move aimed at strengthening Ethiopian sovereignty. The total embargo that Italy continued to place upon all trade with the country would finally lead to a collapse of the accord between Rome and London over their foreign policy towards Ethiopia. For all that Great Britain was also driven by the imperial dream of British hegemony in Africa from the Cape of Good Hope to Cairo, it had no desire to take an openly hostile stance towards Ethiopia. Above all, London was mindful of one of its own pet projects: the construction of a dam on Lake Tana in the Ethiopian Highlands, at the source of the Blue Nile. The planned dam was designed to ensure a regular supply of water to the Sudan and enable the development of a cotton-growing industry there. In order to secure the agreement of the Ethiopian government to this scheme, Great Britain was therefore also prepared to make concessions to *Ras* Tafari in the matter of arms supplies.

When the discord between Rome and London became public, this seemed to *Ras* Tafari an opportune moment – once again with the tacit support of France – to lodge an official application for Ethiopia to be accepted as a member of the League of Nations. But first the empress and the leading nobility had to be convinced of the necessity for this step. The discussions in the palace lasted several days and nights. The reformers around *Ras* Tafari hoped that Ethiopia's entry into the League would act as a catalyst for the modernization of the country. Yet the conservative forces, who would have preferred to see Ethiopia isolated from the rest of the world, nevertheless found the argument thought-provoking that no one would be able to enact the kind of arms embargo that had by now hamstrung Ethiopia for the past seven years on a sovereign country that belonged to the League of Nations. As for the empress, she was only minded to give her assent after scrutinizing the precise wording of the application to join.

On 1 August 1923, *Ras* Tafari despatched an official communiqué to the League of Nations, asking that the matter of his country's accession to the League be tabled at the forthcoming meeting of the General Assembly in September of that year. The British and the Italians maintained their opposition for a while, until *Ras* Tafari cabled the governments in London and Rome directly and challenged them to make their position publicly known.[20] This was a shrewd move on the part of the Ethiopian prince regent. Neither London nor Rome wanted to risk an open rift with Ethiopia, especially since the Ethiopian delegation in Geneva, under the leadership of *Ras* Nadaw, had already secured the support of a wide range of states – from Belgium to India, Persia and China. A few days before the vote, *Ras* Tafari finally managed to win over the final doubters within his own country: the empress and the Imperial Privy Council, who finally threw their weight behind the application.

Ethiopia signed a declaration that it would bend all its efforts towards eradicating slavery in the country. Accordingly, on 28 September 1923, the General Assembly of the League of Nations voted unanimously to accept Ethiopia into the community of nations. 'There was great joy at Addis Ababa,' recalled Haile Selassie, 'the rejoicing was for no other reason than We thought that the Covenant of the League would protect us from the sort of attack which Italy has now launched against us!'[21] As the emperor realized when he wrote those words, the initial euphoria at Ethiopia's accession was sadly misplaced.

Ras Tafari saw Ethiopia's acceptance into the League as a kind of stage victory – against the European powers and their colonial ambitions, but also against the opponents of reform within his own country. He had realized that international connections and recognition by the world community could only be to his benefit. Now it was his aim to make his proud nation known to the outside world. It was under these conditions that *Ras* Tafari embarked on his first major tour of Europe in April 1924. But the trip also had a very practical purpose. The prince regent wanted to convince the European powers that access to the sea was vital if Ethiopia was to flourish economically.

This was the first ever occasion on which an Ethiopian emperor had set foot outside the African continent. 'This decision truly is an event of quite extraordinary significance for the heir apparent and for the small world of political intrigue,' the German ambassador to Abyssinia wrote to his foreign ministry in Berlin. 'Another thing to be borne in mind is that, since the mythical journey of the Queen of Sheba to the court of Solomon almost three millennia ago, no ruler of Abyssinia has ever dared to leave the country for months on end or even shown any interest in such a venture; in fact, quite the contrary – until very recently, leaving the country was put on a par with high treason.'[22]

To guard against any potential revolt breaking out during his absence, the regent had taken precautions as best he could, by taking those princes whom he most deeply mistrusted with him on his state visit, foremost among them *Ras* Hailu, the prince of Gojjam, and *Ras* Seyoum, the prince of Tigray. On 16 April 1924, the regent and his entourage left Addis Ababa on a trip that would take five months. Their journey took them first to Jerusalem and Egypt. In Alexandria they boarded a steamer bound for Europe, crossing the Mediterranean to Marseilles in six days. *Ras* Tafari was clearly impressed by the squadron of aircraft and the flotilla of mighty French warships with their long-range guns that were assembled to greet him. On 15 May, the royal party arrived in Paris. Under the headline 'A Picturesque Scene', *The Times* reported that the visit of the '*Roi Noir*' to the French capital attracted great public attention. The newspaper's correspondent lighted upon the regent's dignified and elegant appearance: '*Ras* Tafari [...] was seen to be a man rather under middle height, slightly built, and with a gentleness of manner which did not detract from his dignity of bearing. His face was of the colour of bronze. His small, refined features, framed in a heavy black beard, gave an impression of vivacity. The Regent was wearing a beautiful long cloak of white silk, embroidered in gold, and tight white trousers. Across his breast was the Green Ribbon of an Abyssinian Order, and on his right side a White Star.'[23] The members of his retinue were no less imposing: 'Among the *Rases* and their suite were a number of tall men. They brought other colours to the scheme – blue and green and gold. They also brought the most striking combination of coloured cloaks in the Abyssinian fashion, and hats closely resembling the ordinary soft grey felt hat of Western civilization.'[24]

The Ethiopian delegation visited Versailles and Les Invalides, to view the tomb of Napoleon, before ascending the Eiffel Tower. Their itinerary also included trips to the Paris Opera and

Le Bourget Airport. Ever since the prince regent had climbed aboard an aeroplane two years before during an air show in Aden – the first Ethiopian ever to do so – he had been enthralled by this revolutionary new mode of transport. And though many people in Ethiopia – where there were only a few dozen automobiles and hardly any tarmaced roads at that time – poked fun at his enthusiasm for new technologies, he cherished an ambition that before long aircraft would be taking off and landing in his country as well. Yet the discussions over Ethiopian access to the sea were to end in disappointment for the prince regent. The French Prime Minister Poincaré and his foreign minister clearly gave their distinguished guest to understand that he could not count on France's support in this matter. As things stood, almost all trade with Ethiopia was conducted through the French port of Djibouti, and France had no interest in sacrificing this commercial advantage.

Ras Tafari utilized the breakdown in the Paris talks to take an excursion to Belgium – where he visited the stock exchange in Brussels, the cities of Antwerp and Ghent and the battlefield at Waterloo – Luxembourg and Sweden. On the way to Stockholm he stopped off, incognito, in Hamburg. He stayed in the Atlantic Hotel, where he was greeted with a glass of champagne and then treated to an 'automobile ride through the city' before resuming his train journey to the Swedish capital the following morning.[25]

An official state visit to Germany was never envisaged on this trip, although the German government, which viewed Ethiopia's close ties to France with suspicion, had high hopes such a visit would take place. A report by the German ambassador to Ethiopia at this time waxed lyrical on the subject:

'For the development of our relations with Abyssinia, the last independent nation-state in Africa, the significance of the planned visit should not be underestimated. A sojourn in Germany, however brief, and even the train journey through the German countryside in all its summer glory, the sight of workshops in full swing and of a hard-working population industriously going about their business will achieve more than mere verbal propaganda ever could, and clearly demonstrate to our Abyssinian visitors the sheer untenability of the French fantasy of excluding Germany from the rivalry between the industrialized powers of Europe. Furthermore, its repercussions will also help Germany secure its rightful place in efforts to reform Abyssinia, an enterprise which is bound to come sooner or later.'[26]

This passage displays the typically condescending attitude taken by European states of this period towards Africa and Ethiopia. *Ras* Tafari had declined Germany's offer of a state visit out of consideration for his French hosts. As regarded Ethiopia's desire for an outlet to the sea, the prince regent now pinned his hopes on Italy, the next stop on his tour. When his train pulled into Rome on 16 June, he was received with full military honours at the station by King Victor Emmanuel III and his prime minister Mussolini. An entire wing of the royal Quirinal Palace was set aside for the distinguished guest's use. When he appeared on the balcony of the palace with the Italian king, he was greeted by a cheering crowd shouting 'Long live Italy! Long live Ethiopia! Long live His Highness Crown Prince Tafari!' Looking back later on these events, Haile Selassie wrote: 'When they think of this today, how extraordinary must this appear to them?!'[27]

Sightseeing visits to all the usual tourist attractions were the order of the day in Rome as well. These were followed by a state banquet and an address by the king, while in the Vatican the Ethiopian heir apparent was granted an audience with Pope Pius XI. Italian diplomacy now shifted its stance from a policy of outright obstruction to an attempt to co-opt Ethiopia into its own colonial plans for the region. Mussolini offered *Ras* Tafari a 99-year lease to establish its own Red Sea port at Assab, but demanded far-reaching concessions in return: not only the harbour itself, but also the roads linking it to Adwa, Gondar and Mekele as well as a railway connection were to be built under Italian supervision. In addition, Italian firms were as a point of principle to be given preferential treatment in the country's economic development.[28] *Ras* Tafari was loath to acquiesce in

The Ethiopian regent *Ras* Tafari with the Duke of
York (the later King George VI), on the occasion
of his first state visit to London in 1924.

such a comprehensive interference on Italy's part in the domestic economy of Ethiopia, and so these talks also ended without agreement.

But besides French Djibouti and Italian Assab, in their attempt to gain access to the sea the Ethiopians had one more card up their sleeve: a port in British Somaliland, which might be secured in return for their agreeing to Britain's dam project on Lake Tana. And yet, compared to the euphoria in Rome, the Ethiopian heir's reception in London was a decidedly chilly affair. The king and the British government were unashamedly condescending towards their official guest. George V regarded *Ras* Tafari as an envoy from a wild, uncivilized country. He acceded only reluctantly to the government's request to hold a reception for him at Buckingham Palace. But he was adamant that he would not allow the prince regent to stay there, on the pretext that the palace was 'not suitable for such accommodation as would be required'.[29] And Labour Prime Minister Ramsay MacDonald agreed to issue an official invitation to *Ras* Tafari to visit Britain only under intense pressure from the Foreign Office. 'I am inclined to think that a refusal to issue an invitation, when similar invitations have already been issued by the French and Italian governments, could only be regarded as a display of ill temper, and would scarcely be calculated to further British interests in Abyssinia [...] You should extend an invitation to Ras Taffari [*sic*] accordingly,' the head of the American and African Department urged his prime minister.[30]

In a memorandum to Ramsay MacDonald by the British envoy to Ethiopia, Claud Russell, the members of the Ethiopian delegation are described in decidedly unflattering terms:[31] *Ras* Hailu, the prince of Gojjam – the province where Britain was planning to dam Lake Tana – is characterized as 'energetic, intelligent and enterprising, but quite uneducated', while *Ras* Seyoum, the prince of Tigray, is described as 'not intelligent or educated.' *Ras* Nadaw, who the year before in Geneva had negotiated Ethiopia's entry to the League of Nations, was 'one of the old school, rough and uneducated and generally opposed to European innovations, with the exception of Scotch whiskey, for which he has a liking.' Finally, the governor of Adwa, Gebre Selassie, 'is reputed cunning and shifty, and is anti-English.' The British ambassador also gave his assessment of *Ras* Tafari: although he was 'amiable, humane and invariably couteous' and moreover 'honest in money matters', in the long term, the envoy invested little hope in the prince regent:

'He is, I think, genuinely anxious to improve the state of his country, but, so far, his powers have not been equal to moving the rooted conservatism of the Abyssinian people, and it may be doubted whether, even if he succeeds to the throne, he would have the strength of character to effect much in the way of progress and reform. He is a politician and a diplomatist rather than a warrior and a man of action, and it is this latter type that carries weight in Abyssinia.'[32]

When *Ras* Tafari finally got to broach the question of a Red Sea port with the prime minister, he was brusquely snubbed. The only topics Ramsay MacDonald wanted to discuss with the prince regent were arms smuggling and the Tana dam project. The following memorable exchange is said to have taken place between George V and *Ras* Hailu, the man the British dossiers deemed 'uneducated': through his interpreter, the British monarch asked the prince of Gojjam: 'Can you speak English?' When *Ras* Hailu replied that he did not, the king asked: 'French? Arabic?' – only to get the same response. In a somewhat indignant tone, the king then enquired of his guest: 'Well, what *do* you speak?' *Ras* Hailu countered: 'Can you speak Amharic? Gallinga? Gurage?' And when George V was forced to admit that he knew nothing of these languages, *Ras* Hailu responded: 'I am glad to see that we are both equally ignorant!'[33]

In contrast to the official agencies, though, the ordinary people and the overwhelming majority of the British press received the Ethiopian delegation with a mixture of curiosity and undisguised sympathy. The London newspapers were full of articles and pictures depicting he exotic life at the court of 'medieval Abyssinia … where an empress reigns and a regent

Leul-Ras Kassa and the Ethiopian delegation at the
coronation of King George V in London, 1911.

governs.'[34] With his 'extraordinarily attractive face not exactly
black, with his high curly hair, his trim black beard, his think
hawk-like nose and his large shining eyes', Ras Tafari was a
truly captivating presence.[35] Occasionally, however, this fasci-
nation blossomed forth in strange ways. The *New York Times*,
for example, served up the following headline and subhead on 5
May 1924: 'Ethiopian Royalties Don Shoes In Cairo: Prince and
Eight Field Marshals Submit to Tortures in Tribute to Western
Civilization.' Evidently, the reporter was labouring under the
misapprehension that this was the first time the Ethiopian dignitaries had ever had shoes on their feet: 'They are retaining their
rich, picturesque court dress, but they have struggled into shoes.
These shoes apparently pinch everywhere, and not only make
walking a torture, but are always liable to precipitate a dignified
Field Marshal across the floor or down the steps.'[36]

The sight of *Ras* Tafari inspired the English artist Rex Whistler to sketch a caricature, showing the regent in an unflattering

pose, wearing the traditional *kabba* and with a yellow puddle at his feet (see illustration on page 64).[37] Thirteen years before, the official Ethiopian delegation to George V's coronation had electrified the London public: these envoys from far-flung Africa, led by *Ras* Kassa, attended the coronation ceremony in Westminster Abbey dressed in their traditional warriors' garb, complete with lion's mane head-dresses, scimitars, spears and gilded rhinoceros-hide shields. Vita Sackville-West immortalized the scene in her famous novel *The Edwardians*: 'The Ethiopian [*Dejazmatch* Kassa] wore a bristling lion's mane swathed about his head-dress, which tickled the face of his neighbour in the next choir-stall every time he turned his head to observe the movements of some fresh dignitary taking up his position.'[38]

Many people in Britain may also have recalled the notorious 'Dreadnought' hoax of February 1910. On that occasion, a small band of young British artists, dressed in blackface and sporting turbans and oriental robes, had inveigled themselves aboard the pride of the British fleet, the battleship HMS *Dreadnought*. They presented themselves to the ship's captain as a group of Ethiopian princes. This supposed royal delegation – which included the writer Virginia Woolf (then Virginia Stephen), wearing a false beard glued onto her chin and the painter Duncan Grant – was greeted with full military honours and invited to inspect the vessel and the rest of the Home Fleet lying at anchor in Weymouth Bay. This prank by members of the Bloomsbury Group only came to light when the perpetrators themselves took the story to the newspapers. For several weeks thereafter, the Royal Navy was a public laughing-stock.[39]

The genuine warmth he encountered among the wider public in London made up in some measure for the frosty reception that *Ras* Tafari had received from the British government. He was especially proud at being granted an honorary doctorate by Cambridge University on 18 July. In his acceptance speech, he stressed the importance of education to his programme of national renewal: 'Since Ethiopia entered the League of Nations last year, it is appropriate for her to draw closer to the nations of Europe. As we have sent Ethiopian youths to study in Europe and in other countries and as they are very diligent in their studies, I hope that in a few years' time they will come to Cambridge for their university education and then serve their country when they return after graduation.'[40]

On 4 September 1924, after having visited Geneva and Athens, the crown prince and his entourage embarked on their homeward journey back to Addis Ababa. While *Ras* Tafari had made absolutely no progress in his quest to secure an Ethiopian seaport, the European trip was nevertheless hailed as a great success. Ethiopia was now a household name throughout Europe and beyond. And everywhere that *Ras* Tafari had set foot, the populace had welcomed him with open arms. In the USA, Marcus Garvey, one of the most influential American Black activists, read the reports of the prince regent's triumphant European tour with rapt interest. For many years, he had been promoting a new sense of self-awareness among African-Americans and calling for them to revert to their own traditions and values. In 1914 he had founded the *Universal Negro Improvement Association and African Communities League* (UNIA), a Pan-African movement whose principal objective was the emigration of all Black peoples to Africa. The aspiration was for them to live in a continent liberated from all colonial masters, under the leadership of a Black king. Hundreds of thousands flocked to hear Garvey speak in huge assembly halls and sports stadiums. He prophesied to his followers: 'Look to Africa. When a Black king shall be crowned there, the Day of Deliverance is at hand.'[41] Before long, Garvey and his followers would identify the 'Black king' whom they hoped would bring them salvation as *Ras* Tafari.

At the station in Addis Ababa, *Ras* Tafari and his companions were met by *Abuna* Matewos and a delegation of ministers and other state officials, surrounded by a crowd of cheering onlookers. Even the empress seemed fit to burst with pride at the prince regent's achievements, notwithstanding the fact, as her welcoming address revealed, that she only had a rudimentary grasp of certain details, such as the climatic conditions in Europe and the forms of government that existed there. In the royal palace, the 'Minister of the Pen' read out her words of thanks: 'And you, my trusted son went, like your father, to countries you did not know and patiently endured the turbulence of the sea and the heat of the sun, carrying out the plan which we had devised for the prosperity of our country and the good fortune of our people; you extended the friendship and affection of kings which had existed of old, and now I am very pleased about your return after carrying out my wishes!'[42]

The things that *Ras* Tafari had seen in Europe – the schools and universities, the hospitals and businesses, the impressive technological and military achievements – had confirmed him in his reforming zeal. Now, however, back in Addis Ababa, *Ras* Tafari found himself faced with all the tribulations arising from the humdrum aspects of rule. In his autobiography, Haile Selassie lists thirty-two planned reforms that he managed to enact between the start of his term as regent and 1935: the reorganization of the Ethiopian ministries, civil service and judicial system; the creation of electricity and telegraph networks, the promotion of automobiles and road-building; the acquisition of a printing press; the construction of schools and hospitals; the creation of a central bank independent of Egypt; training and modernizing the country's armed forces; and last but not least the introduction of a national anthem.[43]

With the aid of the recently-imported printing press, the first copies of the newly-founded government weekly *Berhanena Selam* ('Light and Freedom') were produced, in which *Ras* Tafari's reform programme was announced.[44] The Ethiopian state had a great deal of catching-up to do, especially in education and healthcare. For instance, prior to 1922 the country was served by a single hospital, the Menelik II Hospital in Addis Ababa, and before 1924 there was only one school where foreign languages were taught. Illiteracy stood at well over 95 percent. A major school and hospital construction programme now began, with doctors, teachers and other professionals recruited from Europe.

Among the many foreign advisors whom the prince regent gathered around him were the Sandfords, a married couple from Britain. Daniel Arthur Sandford, a discharged British Army officer, was appointed as a personal advisor to *Ras* Tafari, while his wife Christine established, and later became headmistress of, the first private high school in Addis Ababa. Writing about Haile Selassie in her memoirs, she recounts a conversation she had in the 1920s with a young Ethiopian who had originally been in her service before joining the regent's palace guard. When she enquired how he liked his new job, he replied: 'I like it very much, and his Highness treats us very kindly, but there is one thing that is a terrible trial. One of us has, of course, to stay up until his Highness goes to bed – and he never goes to bed until the early morning' – 'Why, what is he doing?' Sandford asked – 'Oh nothing,' the man replied, 'he sits alone in his study just thinking and thinking and thinking.'[45]

And indeed, not just the situation in his own country and internal opposition to his plans but also the further development of international relations gave *Ras* Tafari plenty to think about. A resolution passed by the League of Nations in May 1925 – with the strong support of France – had seen the arms embargo against Ethiopia finally lifted. But in December of that same year, a memorable exchange of diplomatic notes took place between London and Rome: in the resulting declaration, ratified by Mussolini and the British ambassador to Italy, Sir Ronald Graham, Britain reasserted her right to build a dam on Lake Tana, while Italy staked her claim to build a railway line from Somalia to Eritrea, cutting right across Ethiopian territory. Western Ethiopia was assigned to Italy as an exclusive zone of economic influence. Quite clearly, the colonial powers were acting as if Ethiopia did not exist as a sovereign state. *Ras* Tafari was profoundly alarmed when he learned of this accord. He formally advised the governments in Rome and London that their agreement represented a violation of his nation's sovereignty and that he intended to raise the matter at the League of Nations. This open threat, combined with a press campaign in the pages of the government newspaper *Berhanena Selam*, were apparently enough to force Italy and Great Britain to row back on their plans. *Ras* Tafari took this as a vindication of his foreign policy: Ethiopia's membership of the League of Nations

A scurrilous caricature of *Ras* Tafari (1924)
by the British artist Rex Whistler.

had paid off, and the colonial powers had been put firmly in
their place. But in this instance, too – as in the lifting of the
arms embargo – the support of France, which had been tirelessly
working behind the diplomatic scenes on Ethiopia's behalf, was
of crucial importance.

In December 1926, *Ras* Tafari's opponents lost two of their
most prominent leaders and figureheads, when *Abuna* Matewos
and the war minister *Fitaurari* Habte Giorgis both passed away.
At one fell swoop, the balance of power swung decisively in
favour of the prince regent. *Ras* Tafari grasped this opportunity
to consolidate his authority. Never again under his rule would a
single minister be allowed to amass such power and influence as
Habte Giorgis had. Accordingly, the regent devolved the responsibilities of the War Ministry to two office holders. Now, alongside the war minister, there was to be a Chief of Staff of the
Armed Forces as well. Their areas of competence and responsibility overlapped to some extent; but this competitive relationship would, in turn, only serve to strengthen the position of the

regent. The new war minister was named as *Ras* Mulugeta, who had formerly held the finance and foreign affairs portfolios, while the post of Chief of Staff of the Armed Forces went to the empress' grand marshal *Ligaba* Wodajo. The regent also appointed a loyal ally to the vacant position of finance minister. In another deft political move, *Ras* Tafari summarily absorbed the 15,000 soldiers who made up the personal army of the deceased war minister into his own regiment.

The Coptic *Abuna* Matewos, who for decades had controlled the destiny of the Ethiopian Orthodox Church, had also been a sworn enemy of *Ras* Tafari's reform policies. After the *Abuna*'s death, the prince regent made it his aim to limit the political influence of the Church. Above all, he strove to make it completely independent from the Coptic Pope in Alexandria.

According to tradition, the Ethiopian Orthodox Church did not have the right to appoint its own Patriarch. This dependence of the Ethiopian Orthodox upon the Coptic Church had been codified in the *Fetha Negast*. It was stipulated there that no bishop of the Ethiopian Church should come from Ethiopia. As a result, right up to the 20th century every Metropolitan (archbishop) and all other bishops of the Ethiopian Church had been delegated by Alexandria. This practice became the source of increasing resentment among the circle of reformers around the prince regent, as well as among ordinary priests in Ethiopia. The talk was of 'Coptic imperialism'. *Ras* Tafari did not shrink from seeking a confrontation with the Coptic Pope.[46] He demanded from Pope Cyril V of Alexandria the right for the Ethiopian Orthodox Church to elect its own Ethiopian archbishop. Cyril V rejected this request outright. And when *Ras* Tafari announced that he was transferring all the fundamental ecclesiastical powers of the *Abuna* to the Ethiopian *Etshege,* Cyril responded by refusing to appoint a new Metropolitan to Ethiopia. The Alexndrian Pope died in August 1927 without the matter having been resolved. Only with the appointment of his successor Yohannes XIX did it become possible to reach a compromise. Finally, in May 1929, the New Pope of Alexandria granted the Ethiopian Orthodox Church the right to consecrate four Ethiopian bishops: *Abuna* Petros, *Abuna* Yesahak, *Abuna* Mikael, and *Abuna* Abraham. The supreme head of the Ethiopian Church, however, would continue to be Coptic. Yet the newly-appointed Coptic Metropolitan *Abuna* Cyril, unlike his predecessor *Abuna* Matewos, was now surrounded by four powerful and influential Ethiopian bishops. For *Ras* Tafari, this represented an interim victory on the way to an autocephalous Ethiopian Orthodox Church. It took until 1959 for the Coptic Church in Alexandria to finally agree to the installation of the first Ethiopian Patriarch.

Two of the Ethiopian bishops – *Abuna* Petros and *Abuna* Mikael – were subsequently murdered by the Italians during their invasion of Abyssinia. *Abuna* Petros was shot in Addis Ababa, while *Abuna* Mikael was beaten to death at Gore in the province of Illubabor. Those who confess the Ethiopian Orthodox faith continue to commemorate them as martyrs to this day.

Ras Tafari used the greater freedom of action afforded him by the death of the war minister and the Metropolitan to launch a new foreign policy initiative. In May 1927, he received a high-ranking Italian delegation headed by Luigi Amadeo of Savoy, Duke of the Abruzzi, in Addis Ababa. Hitherto, all his diplomatic efforts to secure Ethiopian access to the sea had come to nothing and since no cooperation in this matter would be forthcoming from France, he turned once more to the Italians for support. In a series of negotiations involving the Duke of the Abruzzi, the Italian ambassador in Addis Ababa and the Italian governor of Eritrea, the basic points of a friendship treaty were set out: these included the creation of a free-trade zone within the Eritrean port of Assab, as well as the construction of a road under Italian control from Assab to the Ethiopian town of Dessie. But *Ras* Tafari also made a point of demonstrating Ethiopia's independence and strength to the Italian colonial power. Even before the talks began, the Italian delegation was obliged to endure a parade of the Ethiopian armed forces lasting three and a half hours. As a special gift to his host, the Duke of the Abruzzi presented the prince regent with a tank that had been retired from frontline duty with the Italian colonial army.[47]

It would take more than a year for the negotiations between Ethiopia and Italy to reach their full conclusion. On 2 August 1928, Empress Zauditu and King Victor Emanuel III signed the treaty of friendship between the two nations. One issue that was the subject of intense wrangling was the Ethiopian demand that any border disputes or other conflicts between the countries should henceforth be referred to the League of Nations for arbitration. Conversely, the Ethiopians feared that an Italian-administered highway might be used as an invasion route. Ultimately, Ethiopia secured its free-trade zone in Assab, while Italy was granted the concession to build a road from Eritrea to Dessie. The key clause where Ethiopia was concerned, however, was Article 5 of the agreement, in which Rome and Addis Ababa jointly undertook 'to submit to conciliation or to arbitration-judges any matter arising between them on which they cannot agree and which is incapable of being resolved by the customary diplomatic means – without recourse to the force of arms.'[48] Yet although the friendship treaty was designed to remain in force for a period of twenty years, it was clearly ill-suited to ensure a successful coexistence. Before long, quarrels broke out over who should supervise construction of the planned road; another bone of contention was the line of the frontier between the Italian colonies and Ethiopia.

Following protracted negotiations, the same year also saw the conclusion of an accord with Great Britain: Addis Ababa at last gave Britain the go-ahead for a dam on Lake Tana, with the proviso that it should be built under US supervision. *Ras* Tafari's mistrust of the European colonial powers, especially Great Britain and Italy, was as strong as ever, and so the regent set his sights on extending Ethiopia's political and economic links to the wider world. Both the USA and Japan opened embassies in Addis Ababa in 1928, and trade agreements were signed with India and several other countries. The inevitable consequence of this energetic pursuit of internationalization was a cooling of relations with France, Ethiopia's most important ally in Europe. Consequently, the French began gradually to disengage from Ethiopia.

The first fruits of *Ras* Tafari's reform programme became apparent in the second half of the 1920s – both economically and politically. The Ethiopian economy was experiencing an unprecedented boom. But the regent still had some determined opponents within the country. One of these was *Dejazmatch* Balcha Safo, the long-serving governor of Sidamo province in southern Ethiopia. He had served as one of Emperor Menelik II's commanders at the legendary Battle of Adwa in 1896. As one of the principal coffee-growing regions, Sidamo had profited enormously from the economic upturn. But right from the outset, Balcha Safo found himself at odds with the regent's reformist course. Increased contributions to the government in Addis Ababa, which were part and parcel of the policy of centralization, were a particular source of irritation to the governor. The paltry sums that he sent to the capital bore no relation to the size of the income that his province generated. It was an open secret that he was defying the central government's directives within his own fiefdom. Eventually, *Ras* Tafari summoned him to Addis Ababa. At first, the governor ignored the summons for several months before complying.

But when he did finally deign to come to the capital, it was not alone. On 11 February 1928, *Dejazmatch* Balcha Safo appeared before the city gates at the head of an army of 10,000 men. And to leave no one in any doubt that he saw himself as a sovereign ruler, he announced his arrival with an imposing drum roll. After a while, he followed the regent's orders that he could only enter the capital with his personal bodyguard, and left his main body of troops to set up camp in the suburb of Akaki. However, at the ensuing talks with the empress and the regent he took an uncooperative stance, shunning all the concessions they offered. Accordingly, *Ras* Tafari had no qualms about persuading the privy council to strip Balcha of his governorship and take control of his domain. When the provincial prince returned to his army, he found the camp deserted.[49] While Balcha had been negotiating in the palace, the regent had dispatched one of his commanders, *Ligaba* Beyene, to Akaki with a number of sacks full of Maria Theresa thalers. No lengthy perorations or shows of force were required to convince the governor of Sidamo's troops to come over to the regent's side. The deposed governor, now deprived of his army, was taken prisoner and later placed under house arrest.

This would not be the only coup attempt against the increasingly powerful regent. In September of the same year, the commander of the palace guard, *Dejazmatch* Abba Weqaw Berru, tried to topple *Ras* Tafari. Christine Sandford, who witnessed this coup attempt, described the events in her memoirs:

'The Regent had gone down, as was his almost daily custom, from his own house – the little *gebbi* – to the palace in which state affairs were conducted – the big *gebbi*. Hardly had he set foot within the hall when the gates of the palace were closed behind him, and held shut by troops within. Machine-guns, posted on the Menelik mausoleum, which stands within the wall of the palace enclosure, were trained on the entrances. Within, the Empress was questioning the Regent on rumours reported to her that he was aiming at supreme power. Disposing scornfully of such allegations of disloyalty, *Ras* Tafari maintained complete self-possession in the face of the threatening soldiers of the palace guard. Ordering the great doors of the *gebbi* to be thrown open, he passed out and down the steps of the assembly hall. The force of his personality held the crowd. Outside the main gates there had already arrived retainers from his own palace, who had been hastily armed with any weapons which his wife, *Woizen* Menen, who had been apprised of the situation, could lay hands on. The gates were opened at his orders, his own servants poured in; in the silence of surprise *Ras* Tafari mounted his mule and rode slowly towards his own house; his calm confidence had won the day.'[50]

Soon after, *Ras* Tafari ordered his own soldiers to surround the palace, and the rebels surrendered. By all accounts, one of the pieces of military hardware deployed that day was the tank that the regent had received from his Italian visitors the year before.

The four Ethiopian Princes of the Blood. From left to right: *Leul-Ras* Seyoum, *Leul-Ras* Kassa, *Leul-Ras* Hailu and *Leul-Ras* Gugsa.

Had the empress really lent her support to the revolt, as Sandford's account appears to suggest? This seems unlikely, despite the fact that the ringleader of the uprising was a close confederate of Zauditu. On the other hand, there can be little doubt that the commander of the palace guard sincerely believed that he was acting in the empress' name. In the days and weeks leading up to the coup attempt, she had repeatedly made known to the regent her displeasure at the terms of the friendship agreement with Italy, to which she had only reluctantly assented. And so *Ras* Tafari could not help but suspect her of being involved in the attempt to overthrow him.

In any event, the failed revolt acted as a catalyst on *Ras* Tafari's path to absolute power. He now turned his gaze towards the title of king. In this matter as well, if we are to believe Haile Selassie's own account in his autobiography, he was not the prime mover. Rather, a group of 'ministers, noblemen and commanders of the armed forces' supposedly went to the empress and demanded that he should be elevated to the rank of *Negus*. Furthermore, he himself, Haile Selassie claimed, took a sceptical view his elevation to the kingship and had even tried to persuade those who were promoting his cause to desist – admittedly to no avail.[51] Finally, Empress Zauditu was presented with an ultimatum giving her three days to accept *Ras* Tafari's appointment as *Negus*.[52]

Another – more plausible – version of events was confided to me in the summer of 1968 by a close relative of the Empress Taitu and a favourite of *Ras* Tafari, *Dejazmatch* Haile Marian Gessesse. He assured me that *Ras* Tafari really had been the driving force behind what happened at that time. The prince regent, he maintained, had sent his closest allies to the empress with their ultimatum that he be named king. The last prince to hold the title of *Negus*, the King of Gondar Wolde Giorgis, had died a few months previously. *Ras* Tafari's supporters argued that the Empress Zauditu would only be entitled to style herself 'Queen of Queens' if she had at least one king beneath her. To this, the empress is said to have replied: 'What is his hurry? I cannot bear any more children and I am ailing – so he will become my successor sooner or later anyhow.'[53] But the empress had no choice but to recognize where real power now resided and fall in line. On 7 October 1928, *Ras* Tafari was crowned King of Gondar.

Christine Sandford has given us a vivid account of the coronation ceremony:

'A silken tent had been pitched in the palace grounds over against the old Church of the Trinity. Here at an early hour assembled the participants: the Empress Zauditu and her officers of state, Tafari with his own personal officers, the *Etshege* or chief of the monks, who was acting Head of the Church in the absence of an *Abuna*. There were present the *corps diplomatique* and one or two privileged spectators – the author's husband being one. After some intoning by the priests Tafari rose and, descending from the throne erected for him, advanced slowly towards the Empress and knelt at her feet. Silk hangings were draped over the pair as the crown was placed upon his head. Then the hangings fell apart and as Tafari – the king – rose to his feet there was a startling zip as swords whizzed from their sheaths and were waved on high. His officers thronging round him seemed almost to carry him back to his throne. Ensued a dramatic pause, and then again as though on a sudden impulse the whole concourse surged round him and bore him off in triumph to the church hard by, where he was to receive the acclamation of the people – leaving the Empress alone, a forlorn figure in the almost deserted tent.'[54]

When *Ras* Tafari duly became King of Kings two years later, the argument that there could be *Negusa Negast* without a *Negus* no longer pertained. Before Haile Selassie appointed a *Negus* and thereby brought a potential rival onto the scene, he preferred to create the entirely new title of *Leul-Ras*. In a private conversation, *Fitaurari* Nebeye-Leul, former secretary to my grandfather *Ras* Kassa, told me that in the 1920s *Ras* Tafari had promised the latter that if he, *Ras* Tafari, ever became emperor, he would make the Premier Prince of the Empire king.[55] Had he done so, he would have been obliged to also elevate the other three Princes of the Blood – the two governors of Tigray *Ras* Seyoum and *Ras* Gugsa Araya, and the governor of Gojjam, *Ras* Hailu – to the kingship. Instead, he chose to name these four *Leul-Ras*, a title that had never existed before.[56]

Ras Tafari's coronation as *Negus* called forth another adversary: *Ras* Gugsa Wale, the former husband of the empress, who had been sent to govern the far-flung province of Begemdir in the north of the country. Frustrated by political developments in the capital, the de facto disempowerment of his ex-wife and the unstoppable rise of Tafari, he decided to stage an open rebellion. In 1928–29, northern Ethiopia suffered a severe drought and a plague of locusts, leading to widespread unrest. Fears grew in the capital that Italy would exploit this situation of instability for its own ends and use *Ras* Gugsa as its proxy. King Tafari duly summoned *Ras* Gugsa to a meeting in the town of Dessie, but the governor of Begemdir refused. Instead, he threw his weight behind the local uprising. *Ras* Gugsa hoped that the two governors of Tigray would join forces with him, but in this he was fatally wrong.

King Tafari responded to the revolt in his customary manner. In February 1930 a government army under the command of war minister *Ras* Mulugeta marched north to bring *Ras* Gugsa to heel. The renegade *Ras* had no chance against a government force equipped with modern weapons. On 31 March 1930, his army suffered a crushing defeat at the Battle of Anchem. *Ras* Gugsa himself was killed in this engagement. This battle saw the very first deployment of the Ethiopian Air Force, which at that time consisted of a single aircraft. King Tafari had acquired it the year before, together with a French pilot, whom he appointed to his staff. In his study of Haile Selassie's rise to power, the historian Harold G. Marcus remarks: 'Tafari had won a crown by using a modern tank; the airplane would confirm his kingship.'[57]

Two days later, on 2 April 1930, sometime between two and three o'clock in the afternoon, Empress Zauditu died. She had been ill and suffering from diabetes for some while, but just prior to her death she lapsed into a typhoid-like fever. She was offered treatment at the hospital in Addis Ababa by its Swedish head clinician Hanner but declined, preferring instead to rely on the succour of the Church. The assembled priests immersed her body in ice-cold holy water, which in all likelihood only hastened her demise. There is no evidence whatsoever to suggest that she died of unnatural causes. Even so, rumours to this effect began to circulate in the capital – among them a scurrilous rhyme based on a pun deriving from the identical sounds of the Amharic word for lynx ('*Aner*') and the name of the Swedish doctor, Hanner: '*Wotrom labetachew demat ayhonatchew, Negesta Zawditun Aner gadaletchew*' ('Cats were never welcome in her house, and now Empress Zauditu has been killed by a lynx!').

That same night, the empress was laid to rest in Menelik II's mausoleum in the palace grounds, and barely 24 hours later the following communiqué was read to the Ethiopian people:

'Proclamation in the name of the Crown Prince and appointed regent of the Ethiopian Empire, His Majesty King Tafari Makonnen, on his ascent to the imperial throne under the name of His Majesty Haile Selassie the First, King of Kings [*Negusa Negast*] of Ethiopia: True to the Word of our Creator, who resides within us humans and has made us his chosen ones, We have lived like mother and son without breaking our bond. Because, according to God's law and commandment, there is nothing that is human which can avoid returning to dust, Her Majesty the Empress has departed this life after a short illness. Her Majesty's passing is painful for me and for the whole empire. Ancient tradition dictates that whenever a king, the shepherd of his flock, dies, another shall succeed him. And so from the Throne of David, to which I am now called, I will watch over you with the help of God's grace. Merchants, trade! Farmers, plough! I will rule over you in keeping with the law and with the authority that has been vested in me by my forefathers.'[58]

Tafari Makonnen had achieved his goal. Now, at the age of thirty-seven, he was Emperor of Ethiopia.

CHAPTER FOUR

The Elect of God

1930 to 1936

On 2 November 1930, under the title of Haile Selassie I, the Conquering Lion of the Tribe of Judah, Elect of God, Tafari Makonnen was crowned as the *Negusa Negast*, the King of the Kings of Ethiopia. Other Ethiopian emperors before him had chosen a special regnal name in order to proclaim a particular programme for their rule. Zera Yakob, for example, whose reign during the 15th century as Emperor Constantine I saw the dawning of a Golden Age for the Ethiopian empire, selected this name as a way of indicating that he saw himself as a religious reformer. Likewise, on his accession to the throne in 1889, the *Negus* of Shoa Sahle Mariam harked back to the legendary King Menelik, the supposed son of King Solomon and the first emperor of Ethiopia, in his choice of imperial name. In his turn, Tafari Makonnen opted for his baptismal name: Haile Selassie, whose literal meaning is 'the Power of the Trinity'.

Hitherto, following the death of an emperor, it had been customary for his successor to be crowned immediately, generally speaking even before the former's death had been announced. But this time, almost seven months were to elapse between the announcement of Zauditu's death and the new emperor's coronation. Haile Selassie later explained the reasoning behind this departure from convention: 'Now that Ethiopia had concluded treaties of commerce and friendship with twelve foreign governments, had entered the League of Nations and had established firm friendly relations, We were convinced that it was proper – in accordance with the practice of the most civilized governments in the case of their coronations – to invite to Our coronation the countries which had set up legations and consulates in Ethiopia.'[1] These countries included Great Britain, Italy, Japan, Belgium, Sweden, The Netherlands, Egypt, France, the USA, Germany, Turkey and Greece. Yet it was not only the representatives of these twelve nations who were to witness the celebrations. Rather, the intention was that the imperial coronation would showcase the pomp and might of the sovereign Ethiopian Empire to the rest of the world and also demonstrate that it was just as civilized a country as those from which the invited guests hailed. In addition, Haile Selassie was keen to impress upon the regional princes and the common people of Ethiopia that the authority of an emperor elected by God was absolute.

The coronation festivities were planned for the beginning of November, once the rainy season had come to an end, and were scheduled to last for ten days. The preparations required for such an undertaking were extensive. Above all, it was essential that the capital of the Ethiopian Empire should appear spick and span: '... arrangements were made for the principal streets of Addis Ababa and the houses along each street to be repaired as well as for electric light to be installed along the main street and in all the houses by which the guests would pass.'[2] In as much as these streets existed in the first place, that is: in many cases, they first had to be built from scratch and surfaced with tarmac.

Presently, the area around the palace complex and St George's Cathedral became a hive of activity, as mules and donkeys carted stones and other construction materials to building sites and the main city streets and arterial roads resounded to the noise of steamrollers. Telephone cables and electrical power lines were laid, and guest houses put up to accommodate the visitors who were expected from all four corners of the globe. Temporary triumphal arches made of wood and muslin were erected along the route of the planned parades. The city police and the imperial bodyguard were issued with modern khaki uniforms specially imported from Belgium. Lepers and beggars were banned from setting foot in the city centre. Indeed, anything that it was thought should be concealed from the gaze of foreigners vanished behind high whitewashed fence panels.

Haile Selassie kept himself informed on a running basis about all the coronation preparations; in the process, scarcely a single detail escaped his attention. In his diary, the British consul recounts a memorable encounter on the day before the coronation celebrations were due to commence. The consul had called on the office of an Ethiopian minister to convey a message from the British ambassador in Addis Ababa: 'I found him out, but he was said to be in a certain street. Here I saw a little group of men in the twilight in the middle of the road. I got out of the car and walked towards them and someone said in a subdued tone: "*Janhoy!*" (Majesty!). There he was with a handful of men, within a few hours of his Coronation, inspecting a patch in the road which was being mended with a steamroller.'³

Various accoutrements for the ceremony – the imperial robes, the crown, the orb, the imperial sceptre and sword (both fashioned from gold and encrusted with diamonds) – were commissioned personally by *Negus* Tafari. Emissaries were sent to Paris, London and Moscow to acquire historically valuable artefacts for the ceremony. The coronation coach, for instance, was found in Berlin: a former state carriage from the Prussian royal court, previously used by Kaiser Wilhelm I. This conveyance was specially restored for the occasion before being handed over to the Ethiopian ambassador in Berlin. The *Berliner Lokal-Anzeiger* newspaper reported proudly and at some length on this little piece of Prussia that was being shipped off to Abyssinia, while at the same time reassuring its readers: 'The administration of the state palaces has given us to understand that, despite its great age – it was built in 1880 – the carriage has no historical significance. All the coaches that have real historic value are, we are informed, housed in the Hohenzollern Museum at Monbijou Palace.'⁴ The team to pull the coach, meanwhile, was ordered from Vienna: four magnificent white horses, together with a coachman who used to drive the former Habsburg Emperor Franz Joseph, were dispatched to the Ethiopian capital.

A triumphal arch made of wood and muslin, erected in Addis Ababa
for the coronation of Emperor Haile Selassie I in November 1930.

None of the invited nations wanted to forego the spectacle
in far-off Addis Ababa, and all duly sent their envoys. Haile
Selassie proudly lists all the visiting dignitaries in his memoirs:
the Duke of Gloucester and a delegation represented the British
crown, while the Prince of Udine came on behalf of the King
of Italy; the plenipotentiary ambassador Gérard was there
for the King of Belgium, as was Baron Bildt for the King of
Sweden, while the Queen of the Netherlands was represented by
Jonkheer Hendrik Maurits van Haersma de With, the Emperor
of Japan by his special envoy Isaburo Yoshida and the King of
Egypt by Muhammed Tawfiq Nasim Pasha. Marshal Franchet
d'Ésperey attended on behalf of the French Republic, alongside US special envoy Herman Murray Jacoby, privy councillor
Baron Waldthausen, representing the German Weimar Republic,
Count Metaxas (the Greek Republic), Muttihin Pasha (Turkey)
and Count Dzieduszycki (Polish Republic).[5] Also included on the
list of invitees were the governors of the neighbouring colonies
of British and French Somaliland and Eritrea, along with envoys
and attachés from a number of other countries. And when word
began to spread about the major social event that was about to
take place in far-off Ethiopia, the world's press began whipping
up public interest in the proceedings.

The envoys and diplomats from the invited nations now racked their brains about what gifts might be appropriate for the coronation of an African emperor. The delegation from Belgium brought along a vast crystal vase, while the Egyptians came bearing furniture to fill two salons and the Greeks a classical bronze figure depicting a discus thrower. Baron von Waldthausen, the German envoy, presented a portrait of President Paul von Hindenburg in a gold frame and 800 bottles of German wine. In one of his despatches to the Foreign Ministry in Berlin, he noted that the Ethiopian ambassadors from London and Paris, whom he had met on the voyage from Port Said to Djibouti, had 'professed themselves very happy with our presents, including the wine, for which they were particularly grateful; they said this was a friendly and personal gift, which was meeting with widespread approval.'[6]

The gifts brought by the European powers with colonies on the Horn of Africa were far more lavish by comparison: Britain gave two gilded sceptres for the royal couple, and Italy presented Haile Selassie with an aeroplane and his empress with a valuable Venetian veil. Alongside a field gun, the French Republic also gave the emperor an aeroplane; however, as the German envoy reported back to Berlin shortly after the coronation, during the festivities this machine 'crashed as the result of a collision, killing both the pilot and the flight engineer.'[7]

During the second half of October, the delegations and other guests began arriving in dribs and drabs in the Ethiopian capital. For the great majority of them, it had been a long and arduous journey. Like the German envoy Baron Waldthausen, they had travelled by ship to Djibouti, and from there by train to the capital. The railway journey alone took two days. According to their rank, they were met at Addis Ababa station, which was decked out with the flags of all the guest nations, either by Haile Selassie himself or by the crown prince, the 14-year-old Asfa Wossen. The emissaries of the great powers were given their own princely attendant: *Ras* Kassa, for example, accompanied the Duke of Gloucester, *Ras* Gugsa Araya the special envoy of the United States, *Ras*

Hailu the Prince of Udine and *Ras* Seyoum Mengesha Marshal Franchet d'Ésperey.

The sights that the foreign guests and delegations found themselves confronted with over the following days were described by some as being like scenes from *Alice in Wonderland*, while others felt they had been transported to the world of *A Thousand and One Nights*. In a succession of ceremonies, processions, parades and banquets – and for the last time in its two-thousand year history – the ancient empire of Ethiopia celebrated a coronation with a lavish, kaleidoscopic extravaganza lasting the best part of fourteen days.

Several Western guests and observers captured their impressions of the events in Addis Ababa in writing. The most famous of these is the account written by the English novelist Evelyn Waugh, who reported on the coronation in his role as special correspondent for *The Times* and the *Daily Express*. He published his sketches a year later as a book, entitled *Remote People*.[8] Unfortunately, Waugh's attention was mainly drawn to what he saw as the comic aspects of the coronation ceremony and to the foibles and *faux-pas* of his colleagues and of the diplomats in attendance. Yet Waugh cut a decidedly odd figure himself: a typical English snob under the blazing African sun, as his compatriot and fellow author Wilfred Thesiger – the Ethiopian-born son of the former British ambassador to Addis Ababa, who had also invited to the coronation – recalled with distaste: 'I disapproved of his grey suede shoes, his floppy bow tie and the excessive width of his trousers: he struck me as flaccid and petulant and I disliked him on sight. Later he asked, at second-hand, if he could accompany me into the Danakil country, where I planned to travel. I refused. Had he come, I suspect only one of us would have returned.'[9] So it is that Waugh's sketches of the event, which are a thoroughly entertaining read, actually reveal more about himself, the journalists who attended and the European envoys than they do about the ceremony itself. It is tantalizing to imagine the kind of book that an author of his stature might have produced if he had taken a genuine interest in Ethiopia. In the 1980s, I once asked Princess Alice of Gloucester, whose

Emperor Haile Selassie I and Empress Menen on
the day of the coronation, 2 November 1930.

husband represented Great Britain at the coronation, how
the Duke had got on with Evelyn Waugh. She replied, rather
indignantly: 'I am afraid the two did not get on very well – my
husband felt he was not grand enough for him.' Waugh later saw
fit to describe the Italian occupation of Ethiopia as a 'civilizing

mission' and heaped praise of the achievements of Mussolini's fascist regime.

The coronation ceremony began on the morning of 1 November 1930 with the consecration of the newly erected monument to King Menelik II in front of St George's Cathedral, in the presence of the foreign delegations. Haile Selassie wanted to demonstrate in front of the whole world and his own people that he saw himself as being firmly rooted in the tradition of his great imperial forebear, who had restored Ethiopian unity and stoutly defended the country against European colonial intervention. *Ras* Tafari gave the head of the French mission, Marshal Franchet d'Ésperey, the honour of unveiling the colossal equestrian statue in bronze.

The coronation itself took place the next day, after the emperor and his wife and the assembled priesthood had spent the whole night at a prayer vigil in the cathedral.[10] Because the building was too small to hold all the guests, a cavernous tent extension had been put up specially for the occasion. Baron Waldthausen gave the following account of coronation day:

'On entering the huge hall [...] a magnificently colourful, indescribably beautiful sight unfolded before our eyes. Along the side facing the cathedral hung a very striking red silk curtain of gigantic proportions, in front of which stood the high priesthood dressed in the most picturesque vestments imaginable, and at their head the Archbishop or *Abuna*, the primate of the Abyssinian Church. Opposite the curtain in the middle of the hall, which was decorated with the most exquisite carpets, two baldachins with thrones had been set up, a red one for the Emperor and on it right a blue one for the Empress. To the left and right of the baldachins, on grand chairs, sat the country's high dignitaries – resplendent in uniforms that had been tailored for them in the capital and which were fashioned on European lines, with an abundance of tasteful gold braid – along with the members of the foreign delegations and missions, organized in such a way that alternate chairs on the front row on either side were occupied by an Abyssinian dignitary and a foreign ambassador or other delegate. The four most prominent princes – *Ras* Kassa, *Ras* Hailu, *Ras* Seyoum and *Ras* Gugsa Araya – wore crowns while the rest, such as the governor of Sidamo, who had been detailed to escort me, sported tall helmets decorated with lion's manes.'

Everyone awaited the arrival of the royal couple with bated breath:

'Sometime after 7.30 a.m. they entered the hall from the church, and the priests led them singing to the baldachins, first the Emperor and then the Empress, where they sat down on the thrones. The 14-year-old heir apparent took a seat to the left of the Emperor's baldachin, while the second, highly intelligent son of the Emperor, the 7-year-old Prince Makonnen [...] stood for the entire duration of the ceremony between his father and brother. It was a charming scene. Over the course of the ensuing ceremony, which lasted for several hours, the Emperor swore to uphold the Alexandrian Coptic Orthodox faith, to observe its laws, to protect the Ethiopian people to the best of his ability, to respect the laws of Abyssinia and the inviolability of the empire, and wherever possible to promote the founding of schools engaged in both religious and secular education and in the teaching of the Gospels. He corroborated his oath with a signature. Then the imperial regalia – daggers, sceptres, orb, ring, two spears, robe, crown and Bible – were all consecrated and presented one by one to the Emperor. Finally, after his head had been anointed by the Archbishop, the crown was set upon his brow.'[11]

The sequence of the coronation was conducted according to the liturgy of a church ceremony hallowed by centuries of tradition: on the eve of the coronation, the imperial regalia were carried into the innermost sanctuary (*qedusa qedusan*) of St George's Cathedral, and each item was individually blessed by Archbishop Kerillios. Now they were ceremonially presented to the emperor:

'1. The bishop of northern Ethiopia, *Abuna* Yeshak, and the abbot of Lalibela brought the gold-embroidered imperial cloak and draped it around Haile Selassie's shoulders.

2. The great sword, encrusted with precious jewels, was carried up by the bishop of southern Ethiopia, *Abuna* Sawiros, and the abbot of Tedbara Maryam, who girded their emperor with it.

3. The imperial sceptre was brought by the bishop of central Ethiopia, *Abuna* Mikael, and the abbot of Haiq, who placed it in the monarch's right hand.

4. The diamond-studded imperial ring was brought by the bishop of western Ethiopia, *Abuna* Abraham, and the abbot of Martula Maryam, who placed it on the emperor's ring hand.

5. The two golden spears were carried by the bishop of eastern Ethiopia, *Abuna* Petros, and the abbot of Debre-Wagag (Asebot), who handed them over to the Defender of the Empire.'[12]

Then the coronation ceremony proper could commence:

'Now it fell to the archbishop of Ethiopia, *Abuna* Kerilios, as the envoy of His Holiness the Pope of Alexandria, Yohannes XIX, to perform the coronation and anointing of the Orthodox emperor. He was assisted in his duties by the bishop of Debre Libanos, who held the golden urn containing the anointing oil, and the abbot of Axum, who carried in the three-tiered imperial crown on a velvet cushion. After a short prayer, in which he called upon the Holy Ghost for help, he announced: "Just as Zadok the priest anointed King David and Nathan anointed King Solomon, so I anoint you with sacred myrrh." Whereupon he anointed the head, shoulders and heart of Haile Selassie while reciting the words: "O Thou, our devoted Lord, we beseech you to bless this crown. Just as Thou crownest Thy servant, Our Emperor Haile Selassie, with the crown of pure gold, so crown him also with the quality of mercy." He then placed the crown upon the head of the "Elect of God".

Presently, they were joined by the former confessor of the Empress Zauditu and bishop of Ethiopia, who handed the emperor the golden sword with the words: "With this sword may Thou always deliver just verdicts. May Thou wield it in defence of the Orthodox Church, and in setting all crooked matters to right. To those who bear Thee goodwill, may Thou use it to elevate them to glory. To those who harbour ill will against Thee, may Thou use it to condemn and punish them!" The Emperor responded: "May God my Creator help me to accomplish all the tasks that Thou, My Father, have set out for me." '[13]

The crown prince's swearing of the oath of allegiance followed the coronation of Haile Selassie: 'Crown Prince Asfa-Wossen knelt down before his imperial sovereign and swore his oath of fealty. The emperor held out the sceptre to him and said: "May God Almighty make you the heir to my power and authority, my throne and my crown." Whereupon the crown prince kissed his father's right hand and replied: "May the Lord hear your words." Then he received the prince's crown from the hand of the archbishop.'[14]

The final act of the coronation ceremony saw the crowning of the Empress:

'Bishop Sawiros now took a gold ring set with diamonds and placed it upon the ring finger of Empress Menen with the words: "With this ring, the symbol of our religion, may God raise Thee up and inspire Thee to do deeds that shall please Him." The Emperor rose from his throne and addressed the following words to Archbishop Kyrillos: "As I have received the crown granted to me by God from your hand, so it is my wish that my wife the Empress Menen shall receive the crown which is due to her and share my renown with me. And so I beseech Your Blessedness to set this crown upon her head." The archbishop stepped forward, took hold of the crown and prayed: "Lord Our God, may Thou crown Wolete-Giorgis [the baptismal name of Empress Menen] with the crown of honour and joy! May it also be the crown of grace and mercy, of wisdom and learning." Saying this, the archbishop read out the felicitations sent to the royal couple by His Holiness *Abuna* Yohannes XIX of Alexandria and pronounced the *Ite, missa est*. This concluded the ecclesiastical part of the centuries-old coronation ceremony.'[15]

Yet not every element of the ceremony was dictated by long-standing conventions. The emperor's placing of the princely crown on his son's head in the course of the coronation ceremony was a new departure in Ethiopian history. Dynastic succession was not a traditional feature of the Ethiopian Empire; rather, every prince from the House of Solomon had always been free to lay claim to the throne. By contrast, Haile Selassie was determined, from the moment he ascended the throne, to found a dynasty. It was the new emperor's fervent wish that the princes of Ethiopia should never again be allowed to conspire in back rooms and play at being king-makers. Instead, he resolved that princes of royal blood should stake their claim to the throne with the full authority at their disposal.

At the conclusion of the ceremony the assembled dignitaries bowed down before the newly-crowned emperor. There was loud applause, followed by the national anthem and a 101-gun salute.[16] Then the royal couple returned to the cathedral to receive Holy Communion. The duration of the ceremony – from 7.30 in the morning to 12.30 – proved something of an ordeal for a number of the foreign guests. Evelyn Waugh, for example, took a typically wry view of proceedings:

'The ceremony was immensely long, even according to the original schedule, and the clergy succeeded in prolonging it by at least an hour and a half beyond the allotted time [...] Psalms, canticles, and prayers succeeded each other, long passages of Scripture were read, all in the extinct ecclesiastical tongue, *Ghiz*. Candles were lit one by one; the coronation oaths were proposed and sworn; the diplomats shifted uncomfortably in their gilt chairs, noisy squabble broke out round the entrance between the imperial guard and the retainers of the local chiefs [...] Presently the bishops began to fumble among the bandboxes, and investiture began. At long intervals the emperor was presented with robe, orb, spurs, spear, and finally with the crown. A salute of guns was fired, and the crowds outside, scattered all over the surrounding waste spaces, began to cheer; the imperial horses reared up, plunged on top of each other, kicked the gilding off the front of the coach, and broke their traces. The coachman sprang from the box and whipped them from a safe distance. Inside the pavilion there was a general sense of relief; it had all been very fine and impressive, now for a cigarette, a drink, and a change into less formal couture. Not a bit of it. The next thing was to crown the empress and the heir apparent; another salvo of guns followed, during which an Abyssinian groom had two ribs broken in an attempt to unharness a pair of the imperial horses. Again we felt for our hats and gloves. But the Coptic choir still sang; the bishops then proceeded to take back the regalia with proper prayers, lections, and canticles [...]

For the first time throughout the morning the emperor and empress left their thrones; they disappeared behind the curtains and into the improvised sanctuary; most the clergy went too. The stage was empty save for the diplomats; their faces were set and strained, their attitudes inelegant. I have seen that look in crowded second-class railway carriages, at dawn, between Avignon and Marseille. Their clothes made them funnier still. Marshal d'Esperez [sic] alone preserved his dignity, his chest thrown out, his baton poised on his knee, rigid as a war memorial, and, as far as one could judge, wide awake.'[17]

When the ceremony was finally over and the imperial couple emerged from the church, where the carriage from Berlin awaited them, scuffles broke out among the press contingent:

'There was a slightly ill-tempered scramble among the photographers and cinema-men – I received a heavy blow in the middle of the back from a large camera, and a hoarse rebuke: "Come along there now – let the eyes of the world see." Dancing broke out once more among the clergy and there is no knowing how long things might not have gone on, had not the photographers so embarrassed and jostled them, and outraged their sense of reverence, that they withdrew to finish their devotions alone in the cathedral.'[18]

Evelyn Waugh's reportage provides a comprehensive inventory of all the mishaps that occurred during the coronation, at least all those that the English writer noticed: from the aeroplanes that were meant to salute the royal couple during the ceremony, but which took off ahead of time, to the celebratory fireworks that were let off too early. Even so, he did find himself having to concede: 'If in the foregoing pages I have seemed to give undue emphasis to the irregularity of the proceedings, to their unpunctuality, and their occasional failure, it is because this was an essential part of their character and charm.'[19]

Yet the impressive military parades and manoeuvres that took place in the days following the coronation commanded respect even from the notorious sneerer Evelyn Waugh. Baron Waldthausen wrote of one of these manoeuvres: 'The street scenes with the masses of warriors and onlookers, an endless sea of humanity that seemed to stretch as far as the surrounding mountains, and the magnificent colours and peculiarity of the costumes worn by the chiefs from every province of the empire simply defy description ... as the head of the foreign ministry told me, around 120,000 warriors had assembled for this occasion – a figure which I am sure is no exaggeration.[20]And he appended the following note to his report to the German Foreign Ministry: 'I can only reiterate here what I said to the emperor and empress at the gala dinner which was held that same night in the imperial palace, namely that I have spent time in almost all the countries of the world, but that I have never witnessed such a magnificent spectacle as took place here, not even in India.'[21]

However, neither Evelyn Waugh nor Baron Waldthausen were invited to the great ceremonial coronation banquets, the

Geber, which were reserved exclusively for Ethiopians. No fewer than 24,000 Ethiopian dignitaries and soldiers gathered for the *Geber*; they were fed in four groups of 6,000, one after the other. The German envoy had it on good authority that, for this banquet alone, 700 oxen and 2,000 sheep had been slaughtered. *The New York Times,* by contrast, put the figure at 5,000 oxen, and the costs for the entire coronation ceremony at a staggering US $3 million – albeit without explaining how it had arrived at this sum.[22]

The official celebrations ended on 9 November. The delegations and journalists began trickling homewards. Without a doubt, the coronation had been an impressive demonstration both of the Ethiopian Empire's self-confidence and of the new *Negusa Negast* Haile Selassie's appetite for power. Internally, the newly-crowned emperor had certainly put on a powerful display of his authority to his people and the provincial princes, but had he achieved the desired effect beyond the country's borders? International reporting of the event – especially in England and Germany – did not turn out to be as universally positive as Haile Selassie would have wished. An independent press which revelled in finding the fly in the ointment was a totally alien concept to the emperor.

Even while the festivities were still going on, a report that appeared in one British newspaper, to the effect that the Duke of Gloucester's quarters, the old *Gebbi* palace in Addis Ababa, was swarming with flies, caused a diplomatic stir. *The Times* gave a more sober, though by no means wholly uncritical, assessment of the coronation:

'There were two main objects behind the pageantry and hospitality of the coronation. First, the Emperor wished to impress his countrymen, and particularly the *Rases*, that he was accepted by the Royal Families of Europe. In this he succeeded. Secondly, the Emperor wished to impress his European visitors with the fact that Ethiopia was an up-to-date, civilized nation. In this he was only partially successful, for the Abyssinians are still so radically backward in culture and progress that evidence of the true state of things inevitably appeared from time to time. Enormous efforts had been made to prepare Addis Ababa for the European visitors, and if some of the improvements excited amusement, there was more to admire in the degree of success with which the authorities were able temporarily to disguise the nature of the people. Many of the visitors, however, availed themselves of the opportunity to see a little more of the country than was officially prepared for them, and these realized that the gold braid, brass bands and fine motor-cars of Addis Ababa, the caviare and sweet champagne, were a very superficial introduction to the national life.'[23]

This introduction was followed by a long litany of Ethiopia's continued shortcomings:

'It is absurd to pretend that Ethiopia is a civilized nation in any Western sense of the word. Communications are still hopelessly bad. Except for a few miles outside Addis Ababa there is not a single motor road in the country. The railway from Jibouti to the capital does not pass through a single town except Dire Dawa, which sprang up on the line at the time of its construction. Harar, an important commercial centre, 35 miles from Dire Dawa, can only be reached by a two-days' mule ride up the circuitous mountain caravan route. The cities of the north can only be reached by organizing a caravan and trekking to them. [...] The finances of the country are still rudimentary. [...] Intertribal raids and crimes of atrocious violence are common in the countryside. Public mutilations have been abolished from the penal system, but the conditions of the prisoners are grossly unhealthy, and deaths from typhus frequently follow imprisonment for trifling debts. Slavery is still universal, although many modifications are being made in the trade.'[24]

Haile Selassie himself was only too well aware of his country's situation in comparison to, say, England or other European states.

But he was aggrieved at being given no credit for the goodwill he had shown and the great efforts he had already made as prince regent. He made personal representations to the government in London, and also in Berlin, where articles of a similar nature appeared. The German Foreign Ministry responded to his complaint by writing to the Imperial Ethiopian Consulate-General 'concerning the unwarranted attacks by various German writers on the person of His Majesty the Emperor Haile Selassie'. In this letter, Berlin was at pains to reassure the Ethiopians that it 'had already done everything within its power to prevent, wherever possible, any such regrettable lapses on the part of German writers in future.' And indeed, the Foreign Ministry had already taken several German newspaper proprietors and editors to task over the matter.[25]

Not just among certain European correspondents, in some government departments too the coronation occasionally provoked a different reaction to the one the emperor had hoped for. The very self-confidence of Ethiopia that had been so ostentatiously on show at the coronation ceremonies antagonized some foreign governments. For example, on March 1931 the German embassy in Addis Ababa wrote to Berlin:

'The negative consequences of the excessive European participation in the coronation ceremonies in November, which seasoned observers of the Abyssinian character predicted would happen, have surpassed all our most gloomy prognoses. Members of the diplomatic corps here are also in no doubt that this participation, in the manner in which it unfolded, was a serious mistake from a European point of view, an error which not only the nations represented here will end up paying for, but which will also cost Abyssinia dear.'[26]

The concrete cause behind such grievances was a complaint against local authorities, who had banned a German farmer from driving his car. Yet the harsh terms in which it is couched reveal that a more fundamental issue was at stake; at that time, no European nation – irrespective of whether it (still) had its own colonies – would countenance the idea of a self-assured African state decisively pursuing its own political, economic and security interests, actions which might begin to instil the populations of neighbouring European colonies with thoughts of independence.

The conception of the state cherished by Haile Selassie, who invoked a right to rule that stretched back a thousand years and more, must also have struck European governments as odd. According to tradition, the Ethiopian imperial dynasty descended from King David, a lineage which made the emperor a relative of Jesus Christ. Plus, he carried the title of 'Elect of God'. For his coronation as the King of Kings, Haile Selassie made a highly symbolic gesture that was intended to underline his descent from the House of David: the throne in the tented extension to St George's Cathedral, where Haile Selassie was anointed king on the morning of 2 November 1930, stood on a slab which had been hewn from the bedrock beneath Solomon's Temple in Jerusalem.

It was *Ras* Kassa who had transported this piece of rock, on which the Temple of Solomon had once stood, from Jerusalem to Addis Ababa. In June 1911, at the coronation of King George V in London, he had heard the story of the 'Stone of Scone', which in the late 13th century was taken from its original location in Scotland (where it was used in the crowning of Scottish monarchs) and installed beneath St Edward's Chair in Westminster as the English coronation stone, and which to this day still forms part of the coronation ceremony. On his return, *Ras* Kassa stopped over in Jerusalem and asked the representative of the caliph there if he might have the piece of rock from the sacred temple. At his coronation, Haile Selassie adopted this ceremony as his own; in the same way that English kings used the Stone of Scone in their coronation ritual to stress the unity of the realms of England and Scotland, so the Ethiopian emperor now demonstrated his descent from the dynasty of King Solomon by means of the stone from the holy site in Jerusalem. When I returned to Addis Ababa in 1991 – for the first time since my enforced exile in 1974 – I asked the priests at St George's Cathedral what had become of the coronation stone. It was no longer there. They told me that even in 1955, when Haile Selassie had celebrated twenty-five years on the throne, the stone was missing and so played no part in the church service marking the jubilee. In all likelihood, it disappeared without trace during the period of Italian occupation.

In the Solomonic Dynasty, Haile Selassie was the 225th successor of Menelik I to ascend the Ethiopian throne. Through the act of anointing, the central element of the coronation ritual, Tafari Makonnen was transformed into the *Negusa Negast*, elected by God. The title 'Elect of God' carried by the Ethiopian emperor was much more than simply an expression of godliness. In any event, right up to the very end, Haile Selassie was steadfast in his belief that he really had been chosen by God to be king. Accordingly, this title was affirmed in the two Ethiopian constitutions that Haile Selassie enacted in 1931 and 1955.[27] The consultations on the renewed constitution of 1955 saw lively debate on this passage among members of the constitutional commission. In particular, the American advisor John H. Spencer, who had been called in to help draft the new constitution, saw it as an anachronism. He spoke to the secretary of the constituent assembly, *Lij* Imru Zelleke, and asked him to prevail upon the emperor to have this clause dropped. But when *Lij* Imru approached the emperor with this request, Haile Selassie reacted furiously: 'How can you presume to doubt it?' he shouted at Imru Zelleke, 'Where would We be if We weren't elected by God?'[28] And not just the emperor himself, also his retainers and the majority of Ethiopians believed he was the Chosen One; this fact also went a long way towards explaining the unconditional loyalty that many people showed him right up to the end – while a new generation of Ethiopian intellectuals bridled at the very idea.

With the promulgation of a constitution in 1931, six months after his coronation, the emperor surprised both his own people and the world at large. There are very few instances in history of a ruler enacting a constitution without any external pressure and voluntarily curtailing his power in the process. In the 19th century, European nations had had to force their rulers

to introduce constitutions and cede control to elected parlia-
ments, not infrequently as a result of unrest and revolution. But
things were quite different in the case of Haile Selassie; there
was no pressure whatsoever and no public call for a constitution, either within the country or among the European powers
or world opinion. Haile Selassie later explained that, as regent,
he had already tried to persuade Empress Zauditu to create a
constitution. But the empress, in collusion with the princes, had
blocked all attempts to do so. According to the account in his
autobiography, the constitution that the emperor now enacted
was designed to lend to his administration 'a form of rule that
is based on law and to bring Our people into partnership in the
work of government.'[29]

Previously, those engaged in the affairs of government in Ethiopia referred to the two great traditional texts: the *Fetah Negast*
('Law Book of the Kings'), which was translated from the Arabic
in the 15th century and which was thought to have been drafted
by the 318 Church Fathers present at the First Council of Nicaea
in AD 325. The *Fetah Negast* combined matters of civil law with
religious observances; parts of it were transcribed from the Old
and New Testaments. However, its use as a statute book was, as
Cardinal Paulos Tzadua (1921–2003) of the Ethiopian Catholic
Church pointed out, extremely limited: many people knew of
it by hearsay, but only a few – educated priests and religious
scholars – could understand it.[30] The *Kebra Negast* ('The Glory
of the Kings'), the second sacred book of Ethiopia, was even
less use as a practical constitutional guide. The *Kebra Negast*
embraces the history and apotheosis of the Solomonic Dynasty
– from the Jewish kings David and Solomon to the Christianiza-
tion of Ethiopia. The centrepiece of the book concerns the legendary meeting between the Queen of Sheba and King Solomon,
a liaison that resulted in the birth of the child who would later
become Emperor Menelik I of Ethiopia.[31]

Despite the fact that Haile Selassie only mentions him fleet-
ingly in his autobiography, the true architect of Ethiopia's first
constitution was the finance minister Tekle Hawariat. After
being charged by the emperor with the task of producing a

working document, he studied various written constitutions, supplied to him by foreign embassies in Addis Ababa. The resulting draft, which was produced in conjunction with the emperor, was shown to the most important princes and ministers for their approval. But what the great *Rases* read there could not fail to provoke their opposition: the constitution represented a de facto transformation of the Ethiopian state into a hereditary monarchy. The royal succession was stipulated in article 3, according to which the crown prince now had to be not merely a descendant of Solomon from the lineage of David, but also come from the branch of the dynasty to which Haile Selassie belonged The emperor had already laid the foundations of his succession by installing his eldest son Asfa-Wossen as crown prince. Now the succession was to be codified in the constitution. In agreeing to it, the princes would be relinquishing their power as king-makers. Among the princes, it was Ras Kassa who was most vociferous in his objection to this arrangement: 'All of us here present,' he told Haile Selassie, 'have accepted Your Majesty as supreme ruler and sworn absolute loyalty to Your Majesty. But we cannot possibly sign away our sons' birthrights in this way.'[32]

The Coptic archbishop, *Abuna* Kyrillos, brokered a meeting between the emperor and the princes who opposed him. Eventually, albeit through gritted teeth, the four leading princes – *Ras* Kassa Hailu, *Ras* Hailu Tekle-Haymanot, *Ras* Seyoum Mengesha and *Ras* Gugsa Araya – went along with the ruling on succession to the throne. For his part, Haile Selassie assured the princes of royal blood that in future royal princely titles would be the sole preserve of their families. Henceforth the princes were forbidden to conclude any treaties independently with foreign countries or to import weapons without the express permission of the emperor. They were to be permitted to continue to command their own forces within their territories and to endow aristocratic titles on others up to the rank of *Dejazmatch* (count). *Dejazmatch* Zawde Gebre-Selassie, the emperor's last foreign minister and the son of the governor of Adwa, *Dejazmatch* Gebre-Selassie Baria-Gabre, once told me that when his father learned of this arrangement, he exclaimed: 'Did God agree to this as well, then?'[33]

Alongside the clause on the royal succession, one of the central provisions of the constitution,[34] which contained a total of fifty-five articles, was the introduction of a parliament in Ethiopia. It was to comprise two chambers – a senate and a house of representatives. As laid down in article 31, the senators were to be elected from the upper echelons of the nobility, such as princes, ministers, judges and long-serving military officers and be appointed by the emperor. Yet also the members of the house of representatives, who were to be drawn from the ranks of lesser dignitaries and civil servants, were to be chosen personally by the emperor – at least (as article 32 stipulated) 'until such time as the populace is in a position to elect them for themselves.'[35] All resolutions passed by both chambers could only acquire legal force through an imperial decree. The remaining articles of the constitution also underpinned the emperor's sovereign authority. It was in his gift to appoint and dismiss ministers, he was the supreme legal authority and had the power to decide whether to go to war or to remain at peace. Moreover, as commander-in-chief of the armed forces, all soldiers swore loyalty and obedience to the emperor. The emperor's aforementioned state of being divinely elected was enshrined in article 5.

What to the outside world must have seemed like a restraint upon the power of the emperor actually served to secure his position of absolute sovereignty. It was Haile Selassie's wish that the Ethiopian constitution should transform 'a completely feudal system of rule into an absolute monarchy.'[36] The princes had fought to the bitter end to maintain their hold on power in the provinces they controlled. For the time being at least, Haile Selassie found it impossible to divest them of all their authority: they were only to lose their age-old privilege of raising their own armies after the Italian invasion and the emperor's eventual return from exile. The general anti-feudal tenor of the constitution also found expression in the fact that the president and the vice-president of the senate did not come – as might have been expected – from the ranks of the great princes but rather from among the new aristocracy, the *homines novi*. This was a tangible sign that the decisive power of the *Rases* was finally broken.

One final factor should be borne in mind, however: if *Ras* Kassa, the premier Prince of the Empire, had refused point-blank to accept the constitution and organized a boycott by the princes, then it would never have been promulgated. It was only the great friendship and loyalty that the *Ras* Kassa had always felt towards Haile Selassie that prevented him from open revolt against the proposal.[37]

The *homines novi*, who were later referred to as 'progressists', emerged the clear winners from this struggle. But were they really in a position to influence the country's destiny, or merely being cleverly manipulated by Haile Selassie to undermine the traditional princely class? *Fitaurari* Tekle Hawariat, the architect of the constitution, and other progressists saw it as just a first stage on the road to a democratic future. For Haile Selassie, on the other hand, it was a stepping-stone towards autocratic rule, which he had had sanctioned by the reformers. And yet it would be wrong – as many European commentators continue to do even now – to simply dismiss the constitution as a meaningless piece of window-dressing. In actual fact the constitution and the parliament helped smooth the path to centralization and the unification of the country. As the historian Bahru Zewde put it: 'Parliament acted as a school of national unity.'[38] The fact that Ethiopia even had a constitution at all represented a major step forward. And those who decry the constitution as 'backward' forget that the route to parliamentary democracy in most European countries was a long and arduous one.

Professor Menno Aden, a constitutional lawyer in Germany, offers the following succinct appraisal of the 1931 constitution:

'The introduction of the "theocratic" constitution of 1931 in Ethiopia provided a crash-course in a development which Europe had taken centuries to achieve, namely the proclamation of the state as the only legitimate authority entitled to wield open force. In this constitution, Emperor Haile Selassie precisely did not maintain l'état c'est moi! Rather he proclaimed, in the Prussian sense, that l'état: c'est le roi! In other words, the state was coterminous with the office of emperor and, as in all Western states, the absolute (sovereign) plenitude of supreme power was invested in this state. The state was the absolute ruler, not the personage of Haile Selassie, who, he firmly believed, had been entrusted with this office by God. The sum of state power was thus concentrated in the office of emperor and not in the person of the office holder.'[39]

Wherever a parliament had been established, however limited its rights may have been, sooner or later there had always arisen among its members the demand for genuine representative participation and control. And so it was in Ethiopia, too. If Haile Selassie had taken the reformers' demands seriously, the history of the country would no doubt have taken a different course. It is tempting to speculate that Ethiopia might have been spared the revolution that swept the country in 1974 and the ensuing reign of terror.

The promulgation of the constitution by the emperor in Addis Ababa in early November 1931, exactly a year after his coronation, was accompanied by several days of celebration in he capital. Despite his successful rapprochement with the princes, Haile Selassie still preferred to take no chances, and so, in order to forestall any potential revolt, had summoned all the princes and provincial governors to Addis Ababa and detained them there for the duration. The extensive celebrations surrounding the constitution were followed in January 1932 by the opening of the senate. Even as the princes were solemnly setting the seal on the curtailment of their own powers, the emperor dispatched his envoys to the provinces to lay the foundations of local bureaucracies and tax authorities.

The four great *Rases* had acquiesced in this *fait accompli* – all, that is, except Hailu Tekle-Haymanot, the *Ras* of Gojjam. He defied the summons to come to Addis Ababa to witness the promulgation of the constitution, preferring to remain in his capital Debre Markos. *Ras* Hailu was the son of the last *Negus*

of Gojjam, Tekle-Haymanot, who had once been one of Menelik
II's rivals to succeed to the throne. By the time Menelik II
became emperor, Tekle-Haymanot had already been appointed
as *Negus*. His son, who had ruled the province of Gojjam since
1908, was convinced that he too had more than earned the title
of king. But even in the absence of such a title, *Ras* Hailu's rule
over Gojjam was tantamount to that of a king. He was among
the wealthiest and most flamboyant princes of Ethiopia. The
memoirs of European travellers and envoys abound with reports
of the legendary parades, banquets and receptions that were
held at the court in Debre Markos, and of the prince's imperial
demeanour. The sums in taxation and tribute that he sent to
the central government were entirely at his own discretion. *Ras*
Hailu saw the reform policies of Haile Selassie and his efforts
to introduce centralization for what they undoubtedly were: a
direct assault on his own position as the absolute ruler of his
province. This deep mistrust was evidently mutual: in 1924, *Ras*
Hailu had been one of the princes whom the regent *Ras* Tafari
had taken with him on his European tour as a precaution.

In 1931, when *Ras* Hailu refused the imperial invitation to
attend the promulgation of the constitution, the emperor first
tried mollifying the stubborn prince in a manner that had a long
tradition in the Ethiopian Empire. He proposed that *Ras* Hailu's
second daughter should marry Crown Prince Asfa-Wossen. This
offer ultimately moved the prince of Gojjam to come to the celebrations in Addis Ababa after all. But his reception in the capital
was anything but friendly. Haile Selassie accused *Ras* Hailu of
maladministration and placed large parts of his province under
imperial supervision.[40] There was now no longer any talk of
forging a family bond between the emperor and *Ras* Hailu.
Instead, *Ras* Hailu recalled another such familial tie: in 1910,
his own daughter Sable Wongel had been married to *Lij* Iyasu.
Although the union was annulled soon after, *Lij* Iyasu had for
a short while been his son-in-law. In 1931, after Haile Selassie's
coronation and his bid for absolute power, the deposed emperor
Iyasu was still languishing in Fiche under house arrest as the
prisoner of *Ras* Kassa. So it was that *Ras* Hailu began to hatch

a plot to free *Lij* Iyasu. On 15 May 1932, with *Ras* Hailu's help, *Lij* Iyasu made good his escape.

It took no time for the conspiracy to be uncovered. *Ras* Hailu was arrested, while *Lij* Iyasu was recaptured a few days after his escape. The prince of Gojjam was put on trial before the privy council, the great dignitaries and the leading churchmen and sentenced to death. The clergy interceded on his behalf and the sentence was commuted to life imprisonment. The prince of Gojjam's property was impounded, and as the new governor of the province, Haile Selassie appointed his cousin and loyal confederate since childhood, Imru, whom he elevated at the same time to the status of *Ras*.

In 1932, alongside *Ras* Hailu Haile Selassie also managed to rid himself of another political adversary, the Sultan of Jimma in the southwest of Ethiopia. Menelik II had granted the Sultan of Jimma, *Abba* Jifar, autonomy in 1884. However, the special status of the sultanate increasingly became a thorn in the side of the new Ethiopian emperor, whose whole programme was based on centralization. The grandson of the ageing sultan, *Abba* Jobir, embarked on a campaign of open resistance to the new course set by Haile Selassie. His response was to send a regiment of troops to Jimma and to declare the sultan deposed.

This effectively seemed to bring an end to the revolt of the princes against the emperor's policy of centralization. The emperor was convinced that *Ras* Kassa was a loyal ally, while he concluded family alliances with the two princes of Tigray, *Ras* Seyoum and *Ras* Gugsa Araya. The crown prince, who not long before had found himself betrothed to *Ras* Hailu's daughter, now received one of *Ras* Seyoum's daughters as his bride: Princess Wolete-Israel. *Ras* Gugsa, meanwhile, was married to one of the emperor's nieces, Princess Yeshashi Work Yilma, and his son, Haile Selassie Gugsa, to the emperor's daughter Zenebe Work.

Now that he was furnished to a large extent with absolute power, the way seemed clear for Haile Selassie to pursue his course of modernizing the country. In the meantime, the emperor had assembled a whole staff of foreign advisors around him in

the capital: the Swiss jurist Jacques Auberson advised the government on legal affairs, while matters of domestic policy were
handled by the British diplomat Frank de Halpert. The latter was
tasked in particular with coordinating efforts to abolish slavery.
The American Everett A. Colson was sent to Ethiopia on the rec-
ommendation of the US State Department to assist in the realm
of foreign affairs and relations with the League of Nations. A
compatriot of Colson's, the Afro-American F. E. Work, was
responsible for education. David Hall, a descendant of a business family of Russian-German extraction who had long been
active in Ethiopia, was appointed as Imperial Privy Councillor,
reporting directly to Haile Selassie. In 1922, he had founded the
St George Brewery in Addis Ababa, where beer is still brewed
to the present day in accordance with the 500-year-old German
Purity Law. As privy councillor, Hall organized the postal and
telephone services, while as press liaison officer for the coronation festivities in 1930, he was responsible for looking after the
foreign journalists and other guests.[41]

In addition, there were around a hundred Russian engineers
and technicians working for the Ethiopian government. Haile
Selassie also entrusted the training and education of his armed
forces to European military advisors. Swiss officers trained the
Ethiopian Army on the border with Somalia and the newly formed
Imperial Bodyguard, which comprised 1,300 handpicked troops,
was under the command of Belgian officers. Over the following
years, this unit expanded to a strength of 2,200 men. The Imperial Ethiopian Air Force at this time boasted a total of just eight
pilots and officers, all of whom were French. A military academy
was established at Genet, forty kilometres south of Addis Ababa.

By now, the country also had its own state bank. This institution pressed ahead with the issuing of banknotes, which increasingly supplanted Maria Theresa thalers, the most widespread
form of currency throughout the country. These silver coins
made Ethiopian public finances dependent upon the wildly fluc-
tuating price for this metal on international markets. The creation of a national currency was designed to remedy this situation
and make monetary transactions far more straightforward

The early 1930s saw the capital and many regions of Ethiopia enjoy an economic boom, stimulated among other things by a succession of good harvests and an absence of any natural disasters. The Great Depression that had held the world in its grip for some years was over by this time. Haile Selassie had succeeded in creating a central governmental and administrative apparatus, presided over by loyal civil servants. An ever-growing number of foreign firms arrived in Ethiopia and opened branch offices in Addis Ababa. Many Europeans were engaged in trading coffee, herbs and oilseeds. In the space of fifteen years, the population of the capital had more than doubled, from 50,000 to well over 100,000. Construction work was going on everywhere: among the new buildings that arose to grace the Addis Ababa skyline were the city's new railway station, completed in 1929, the parliament building with its clock tower, which was dedicated in 1934, and the imperial palace or *Genete-Leul* (literally 'Princes' Paradise'), which was finished soon after.

Haile Selassie's modernization programme went into overdrive in the three years between 1931 and 1934: new schools and hospitals sprang up, numerous road-building projects were set in motion and a programme for the electrification of the country was begun.

Even before Haile Selassie was crowned emperor, though, Ethiopian foreign policy scored a major success. On 21 August 1930, Ethiopia, France, Great Britain and Italy signed a 'Treaty Regulating the Importation into Ethiopia of Arms, Ammunition, and Implements of War'. In it, the three European powers guaranteed Ethiopia the right to 'obtain the arms and ammunition necessary for the defence of its territory against all outside aggression and for the maintenance of internal public order.'[42]

The seeds that Haile Selassie had sown in the few short years of his reign were about to bear fruit – in domestic politics as well as foreign affairs. Ethiopia now had diplomatic representations in France, Great Britain and at the League of Nations, and in January 1935 hosted its first official state visit when the Swedish Crown Prince Gustav Adolf, accompanied by his wife Princess Luise, son Bertil and daughter Ingrid (the future Queen of Denmark) arrived in the country. However, this visit was overshadowed by a serious incident that had occurred the previous month. On 5 December 1934, at the Wal-Wal oasis on the Ogaden plateau in the south of the country near the frontier with Somalia, Italian colonial troops clashed with a detachment of Ethiopian troops escorting a British border commission, resulting in a number of deaths on both sides. This incident made headlines in the European press, and supplied Mussolini with a welcome pretext to put into action a plan that he had been harbouring for some time: to attack Ethiopia and annex it as an Italian colony.

CHAPTER FIVE

The darkest hour

1935 to 1940

The Italian invasion of Abyssinia was a long-standing ambition of Mussolini's. The first intimations of such a plan appear just a few years after he seized power in Italy with his 'March on Rome' in October 1922. In July 1925 he instructed his minister for the colonies to 'take all military and diplomatic steps necessary in order that we might profit from a possible collapse of the Ethiopian Empire.'[1]

Il Duce dreamt of reviving the *Imperium Romanum* with himself at its head. After the First World War, France and Britain reneged upon the promise they had made to expand Italy's colonial possessions. This made Mussolini all the more determined to establish Italy as a colonial power and keep pace with London and Paris. He was no longer prepared to make do with a handful of barren desert regions in Africa. Ethiopia occupied a special place in the dictator's plans for global power. Italian public opinion still smarted at the memory of their defeat at the hands of the Ethiopians in 1896. Time and again there were calls for the 'Disgrace of Adwa' to be avenged. It therefore seemed only a matter of time before Fascist Italy trained its sights on Ethiopia.

It took some time, however, before Mussolini had consolidated his hold on power sufficiently to risk the adventure of a foreign war. In the interim, he relied upon diplomatic means to try and achieve his goal. In the aforementioned exchange of diplomatic

notes with Great Britain in December 1926, the two countries
staked out their respective spheres of interest within Ethiopia.
But when this agreement became public knowledge, and *Ras*
Tafari filed a complaint with the League of Nations, Italy was
forced to back down. The following years saw Mussolini adopt
a dual strategy in Ethiopia:[2] In the northern provinces and the
regions bordering the Italian colonies in the Horn of Africa, he
instituted a covert policy of subversion. Thus, in Tigray, Begemder, Gojjam and Wollo, where the ties to the central government of Ethiopia were weak, he threw his support behind local
rebels and warlords who opposed the imperial administration.
On the other hand, he pursued a strategy of friendly rapprochement towards the regent *Ras* Tafari. The Treaty of Friendship
of 1928 and the establishment of Italian consulates in Ethiopia
were designed to serve this latter purpose. By 1932, there were
six such diplomatic missions – in Adwa, Gondar, Dessie, Debre
Markos, Makale and Harar. With the help of Italian traders and
advisors, these consulates were intended as bases from which
Ethiopia could be gradually infiltrated and made compliant.

Yet this Italian 'Trojan Horse' strategy soon proved fruit-
less. Haile Selassie greatly mistrusted all the European colonial
powers, but Italy most of all. None of the many foreign advisors
with whom he surrounded himself were Italian. The emperor
also made no efforts to press ahead with the infrastructure projects agreed in the friendship treaty, namely the construction of
a road from Assab to Dessie. And while Mussolini outwardly
continued to give the impression that he was committed to
a policy of compromise, behind the scenes he began preparations for a military invasion. The final decision to invade Ethiopia was taken in 1932 at the latest. In January of that year,
the colonial minister Emilio de Bono presented the *Duce* with
a draft invasion plan, which was fleshed out and modified over
the coming months.[3] The Italian colonies of Eritrea and Somalia
were steadily built up as military assembly points, while back in
Italy munitions production was stepped up significantly. These
measures were supported by a sustained campaign in the Italian
press. Countless articles accused Ethiopia of fomenting unrest in

Italian soldiers boarding a troopship bound for Ethiopia, 1935. Fixed to the mast is a large banner portraying the *Duce*, Benito Mussolini.

neighbouring Eritrea and spread unfounded rumours of alleged border incidents. The Ethiopian Empire was denounced as a 'barbarian state', which had wilfully overridden the terms of the 1928 friendship treaty.[4] Even so, a specific pretext was still needed to justify a war of aggression. The clash on the border at Wal-Wal on 5 December 1934 came at just the right moment.

The Wal-Wal oasis in the Ogaden Desert of Ethiopia, close to the border with Somalia, was a favoured meeting point for nomadic Somalis from Ethiopia, Somalia and British Somaliland to converge upon and water their cattle. The precise line of the Ethiopian–Somali border was an enduring bone of contention between Addis Ababa and Rome, but the fact that the oasis itself belonged to Ethiopia was beyond dispute. In November 1934, a British frontier commission began a tour of inspection in the region. To protect its members against attack, the delegation was provided with an escort of 600 Ethiopian troops. When they reached Wal-Wal on 23 November, they found that Italian troops had set up a fortified military base there. The Italian commanding officer, a Captain Roberto Cimmaruta, denied the delegation access to the oasis. The following afternoon, the British and Ethiopian encampment was harassed by two Italian aircraft buzzing their tents. The British C.O. accompanying the commission, Lieutenant-Colonel E. H. M. Clifford of the Royal Engineers described the incident in a note to the colonial office: 'It was observed that one of the occupants of So.4 [the serial number of one of the Italian planes] was aiming a light automatic weapon at the members of the Commission and at personnel in the two camps, in each of which the national flag was flying.'[5] Concerned to avoid an escalation, Clifford decided to withdraw the British delegation, while leaving the Ethiopian detachment in place.

For twelve days, the Ethiopian and Italian troops faced off against one another until finally, on 5 December, the Italians opened fire. The outcome of the ensuing battle was never in doubt: the Ethiopian infantrymen had no chance against the aircraft, tanks and machine guns that the Italian commander could bring to bear. This brief but bloody skirmish left 107 Ethiopians dead and 45 wounded, while on the Italian side 30 Somali irregular colonial troops (*Dubats*) were killed.[6] Mussolini lost no time in exploiting this incident, which the Italians had deliberately provoked, to escalate the conflict still further. The Italian ambassador in Addis Ababa demanded compensation to the tune of £20,000 and an official statement recognizing Wal-Wal as an Italian possession. Furthermore, he insisted that an Ethiopian delegation should come to Wal-Wal and salute the Italian flag.

Haile Selassie did not rise to this provocation, falling back instead on a strategy that had served him well in the past: he lodged a protest against Italy's actions with the League of

Nations. In doing so, he was counting on the support of Great Britain, whose representatives had, after all, been present in Wal-Wal and personally witnessed the stand-off. Yet the political landscape of Europe had changed fundamentally in the space of just a few short years. The Nazi Party (NSDAP) had come to power in Germany in 1933, and the new Reich Chancellor Adolf Hitler made plain his ambition that Germany should become the dominant power in Europe. By announcing its exit from the League of Nations in October 1933, the new regime in Berlin sent out a clear message that it no longer considered itself bound by any international agreements. During the early years of Hitler's dictatorship, National Socialist Germany and Fascist Italy found themselves at loggerheads with one another, despite their ideological kinship. Above all, it was the question of the annexation (*Anschluß*) of Austria into the Third Reich that was the source of major tension between Mussolini and Hitler. For their part, Britain and France hoped to lure Rome into joining an alliance against the German dictator. In any event, these two nations were eager to avoid doing anything that might drive Mussolini into Hitler's arms.

This trial of strength between Mussolini and Hitler did, however, provide Ethiopia with an unexpected, if temporary, ally. In December 1934, the arms dealer Major Hans Steffen, the Ethiopian honorary consul-general in Berlin, travelled to Addis Ababa at the request of the foreign affairs department of the NSDAP.[7] Steffen was regarded as a close friend of Haile Selassie. Before working in Ethiopia, he had acted as an advisor on military procurement to both King Faisal I of Iraq and the king of Saudi Arabia, Ibn Saud. Now this German middleman was tasked with using 'all available means' to ensure that war broke out between Ethiopia and Italy as quickly as possible. Steffen, it was hoped, would persuade Haile Selasssie to launch a pre-emptive strike against Italian interests in the Horn, and in return Germany would guarantee him plentiful arms shipments.[8] A few months later, the Ethiopian Privy Councillor David Hall travelled incognito to Germany. On his return to Addis Ababa, he visited the German ambassador, Dr Prüfer, on 17 July 1935 and asked him to transfer of a sum of 3 million Reichsmarks for the purchase of arms.

This matter was too sensitive for the German envoy to simply act on his own authority and sanction the payment, because officially Germany was taking a neutral stance in the Abyssinian conflict. So he forwarded Hall's request to the German foreign minister at the time, Konstantin von Neurath, who in turn secured Hitler's approval. Ultimately, the Ethiopian privy councillor was paid the money he requested from a special fund of the German Foreign Ministry.[9] For this sum, Major Steffen procured 10,000 Mauser rifles, plus quantities of machine guns and hand grenades. These weapons, together with 36 field guns bought from Switzerland, were loaded aboard an English freighter in Lübeck and shipped to Ethiopia. In addition, Privy-Councillor Hall also acquired 30 German anti-tank guns produced by the renowned arms manufacturer Rheinmetall-Borsig. Before these weapons were shipped, however, all the company's identification plates were removed from them. In an interview with *Le Figaro* in 1959, Haile Selassie maintained that Germany had been the only country 'which gave us any real help, supplying us with arms and ammunition through secret shipments and parachute drops. Even after the cessation of formal hostilities, Germany still continued to provide some assistance to our guerrilla fighters. [...] While Germany overtly smiled upon Mussolini's invasion, covertly it did its utmost to harm him.'[10]

'My enemy's enemy is my friend' – Haile Selassie appropriated this well-known adage and made it his own. Even though he continued to have faith in a settlement brokered by the League of Nations, he set about preparing for every eventuality. His hope that the League would intervene came to nothing, though: in Geneva, the matter was referred to the appropriate standing committees and kicked into the long grass. The French government played a large part in this, having been pressurized by Mussolini into withdrawing their protective support for Ethiopia. In a memoir dedicated to Hitler, Foreign Minister von Neurath wrote:

'As long as France continues to play the role of Abyssinia's protector, it is scarcely conceivable that an armed conflict will come about between Italy and Ethiopia. [...] But if Mussolini should succeed in effecting a *désinteressement* on France's part for Abyssinia, the path would be cleared for Italian action. England would in all likelihood adopt a sympathetically neutral position, in order that it might ultimately be rewarded for its stance with territorial gains, as provided for in the secret 1906 treaty between Italy and Great Britain.'[11]

The accord between Rome and Paris that Mussolini had been seeking was duly signed in January 1935. The way was now clear for the *Duce*. Hundreds of thousands of men and heavy armaments, tanks and munitions were dispatched to Eritrea and Somalia to prepare for the assault. While this was happening, France and Great Britain imposed an arms embargo on the two potential adversaries. But while this action barely affected Mussolini, it hit Ethiopia hard. *Fitaurari* Tekle Hawariat, Ethiopia's representative at the League of Nations, protested in Geneva that the arms embargo highlighted the 'unequal combat [...] between two Members of the League of Nations, one of which, all powerful, is in a position to employ, and declares that it is employing, all its resources in preparing for aggression, while the other, weak and pacific, and mindful of its international undertakings, is deprived of the means of organising the defence of its territory and of its very existence, both of which are threatened.'[12]

A few weeks later, on 11 September 1935, the British Foreign Secretary Sir Samuel Hoare delivered a rousing speech to the League of Nations general assembly in Geneva: 'The League stands, and my country stands with it, for the collective maintenance of the Covenant in its entirety, and particularly for steady and collective resistance to all acts of unprovoked aggression. The attitude of the British nation in the last few weeks has clearly demonstrated the fact that this is no variable and unreliable sentiment, but a principle of international conduct to which they and their Government hold with firm, enduring, and universal persistance.' This was a specific reference to article 11 of the League's covenant, which stated that: 'Any war or threat of war, whether immediately affecting any of the Members of the League or not, is hereby declared a matter of concern to the whole League, and the League shall take any action that may be deemed wise and effectual to safeguard the peace of nations.'[13]

Anyone listening to Hoare's address could only have construed it as meaning that Britain would come to Ethiopia's defence in the event of an attack. Indeed, this was the understanding of the overwhelming majority of the British people, who firmly rejected Mussolini's policies. But the actions of the British government over the following weeks and months were to give the lie to its high-minded declarations. At the beginning of December – by which time the Italian invasion was well underway – Hoare, in concert with the French prime minister Pierre Laval, put forward a plan to end the conflict. In it, a substantial part of the Ethiopian provinces of Ogaden and Tigray – totalling around one-fifth of Ethiopia's national territory – was ceded to Italy, along with exclusive commercial rights in the south of Ethiopia. In return, Ethiopia would be given access to the port of Assab. This virtually amounted to a de facto renunciation of the sovereignty of the Ethiopian state.[14] Publication of the Hoare–Laval Pact prompted a public outcry in both Britain and France. The then British Secretary of State for War, Duff Cooper, later described the popular mood at the time in his autobiography *Old Men Forget*:

'But before the *Duce* had time to declare himself there was a howl of indignation from the people of Great Britain. During my experience of politics I have never witnessed so devastating a wave of public opinion [...] My post-bag was full and the letters I received were not written by ignorant or emotional people but by responsible citizens who had given sober thought to the matter. That outburst swept Sir Samuel Hoare from office.'[15]

The general sense of outrage in Britain and France was more than matched by public opinion within Ethiopia. Haile Selassie rejected the plan out of hand, pointing to his country's 3,000-year history of independence.[16] Even Mussolini ultimately turned it down, banking instead on a swift victory by his armed forces and seizure of the entire country.

On the morning of 3 October 1935, an Italian army of 100,000 men under the command of General Emilio de Bono crossed the River Mareb, which marked the border between Ethiopia and Eritrea. At the same time, Italian troops led by General Rodolfo Graziani invaded the south of the country from Somalia. There was no official declaration of war. Mussolini's strategy was to subdue Ethiopia in a lightning pincer movement. On the day of the invasion, Haile Selasssie issued an order for general mobilization in Ethiopia. As commander-in-chief and coordinator of the Ethiopia's entire northern army, *Ras* Kassa was dispatched to Tigray; at the same time, *Dejazmatch* Nasibu was named as supreme commander of the southern army. In the lightly defended border region in the north, the invading Italian troops advanced rapidly without encountering any significant resistance. After three days, they took Adwa, and by 15 October they had pushed forward as far as Axum, the ancient capital of the Ethiopian Empire. General de Bono's campaign was assisted in no small measure by the defection of *Dejazmatch* Haile Selassie Gugsa, the emperor's son-in-law and husband of Princess Zenebe-Work, together with his army of 10,000 men, to the Italian side.

Two days later, on 17 October, the emperor's own army, under the command of the minister of war *Ras* Mulugeta, was assembled and made ready to march north from Addis Ababa. There, it would join forces with the armies of *Ras* Kassa, *Ras* Seyoum and *Ras* Imru to launch a combined offensive against the Italians in Tigray. The imperial troops were sent off with a grand march-past before the emperor. Below the Menelik Palace, a huge tent with velvet furnishings was erected and in front of it a dais with gilded chairs. George Steer, the correspondent of *The Times*, was there to report on the military parade:

'The Emperor, in khaki field uniform, took his seat upon the highest chair next morning at ten. His ministers, all except

Blattengetta Herrouy, the Foreign Minister, carrying service rifles, squatted on the ground before him. Fearsome yells, reminiscent of *Maskal*, announced the head of the procession. The Emperor's guards loosened their swords and rhino-whips as the leaders of the *Yamahal-Sarawit* [the army of the war minister *Ras* Mulugeta] approached the tent entrance. The ramshackle buildings on the edge of the plain were filled with spectators who bellowed encouragement to the vanguard of Ethiopia. Dust rose into the pale air and confused the wheeling hawks. It took four hours, from ten-thirty to two-thirty, for the army to pass the Emperor's dais. It proceeded in jerks, some running by, others marching in order, others stopping to shriek a précis of their warlike achievements or to demand new arms of the King of the Kings of Ethiopia. The troops ranged from the Imperial Guard, followed by Vickers guns on well-trained mules, to fierce fighting men from the provinces armed with nothing better than sticks and empty cartridge belts.'[17]

The parade of Ethiopian warriors, accompanied by the incessant beating of war-drums, was a spectacle the like of which the European journalists present had never seen before. The aged war minister *Ras* Mulugeta, who as a young man had fought under Emperor Menelik II at the Battle of Adwa thirty-nine years before, 'passed the throne about noon, preceded by hornblowers dressed in European uniform, their gigantic antlers lifted high. Drawing his sword of modern temper, the towering grizzled figure with the face of an eagle approached the dais and the Emperor slowly rose and saluted.'[18]

As a sign of his loyalty and allegiance the geriatric war minister laid his sword at the emperor's feet and dispensed the following advice:

'Do not interest yourself overmuch in politics. Your weakness is that you trust the foreigner too much: kick him out. What are all the fools of the Press doing here? I am ready to die for my country, and you are too, we know. War is now the thing and to conduct it you had better remain in the city of Addis

Ababa. Send all the foreigners packing. I swear you perfect loyalty.'[19]

Eventually the parade came to an end. 'Mulugeta's army marched off,' wrote George Steer, before continuing:

'We watched the curious procession pass the British Legation gates by twos and threes. What could they do? They thought that they could do everything. Barefooted, in their ragged dirty jodhpurs, their swords sticking far away behind them, they moved along with a steady stride [...] The men themselves went ahead carrying the tent-poles, from the ends of which dangled sandals and a few pouches and calabashes; more pouches, holding food, hung about their persons. The woman leaning forward in her long broad skirts to haul the mule brought up the tent and sacks of *mashila* or dried peas.'[20]

The Ethiopian soldiers were steadfast in their determination to confront the enemy: they had triumphed over the Italians in 1896, so why should they not do so again? Yet the war that Fascist Italy visited upon Ethiopia was quite different to that waged by their colonial forces forty years previously. Concerned to avoid another Adwa at all costs, Mussolini had thrown everything that Italy could muster in the way of men and materiel into the invasion. In May 1936, the Italian generals on the Ethiopian front had over 476.000 men under their command, including 87,000 so-called 'Askaris', African mercenaries fighting for their colonial masters. In addition, the Italians also had 100,000 horses, mules and donkeys, 19,000 lorries and other forms of motorized transport, 500 tanks, 1,500 artillery pieces, 350 aircraft, over half a million rifles and muskets and 15,000 machine guns. It was the largest fighting force ever assembled on the African continent.[21] Even the bravest and most motivated Ethiopian warriors could not hold the line against such overwhelming odds in the long run. The Ethiopian army comprised some 250,000 men all told, and was equipped with just a couple of dozen tanks. Of its fifteen aircraft, only eight were airworthy,

Accompanied by his imperial bodyguard, Emperor
Haile Selassie rides to war on a mule, 1935.

and even these were just transport machines for the most part.
The majority of its troops were ill-equipped to fight a modern
war. Only the 20,000 men of the Imperial Guard were a real
match for their Italian opponents.

Here is not the place to enter into a detailed account of the
course of the Second Italo-Abyssinian War. Nor indeed is there
any need to do so; a host of books have already been written on
the subject, and the period of the Italian invasion and occupation has over time become by far the most well-researched era
in Ethiopian history.[22] A few brief remarks should suffice at this
point. In the event, Italy's hopes of delivering a swift knockout
blow to the Ethiopian army did not come to pass. As it made
its way through the mountains, the Italian advance slowed to a
crawl. After just forty-five days in charge of the operation, the
Italian supreme commander General de Bono was dismissed and
replaced by Field Marshal Pietro Badoglio, who would hereafter
prosecute the war with unprecedented brutality.

On 28 November 1935, the emperor travelled in person to the front: 'It was Our duty to defend Our country's independence in the midst of Our troops,' he wrote in his autobiography.[23] In Dessie, the capital of Wollo province, Haile Selassie took up residence in his headquarters, the former residence of the Italian consul, which had been converted into a makeshift palace. In the period before his departure from Addis Ababa, the death of his former adversary *Lij* Iyasu had been officially announced. This at least had served to allay any concerns that the former emperor, who had been deposed in 1916, might fall into enemy hands and be installed as a puppet leader by the Italians.

In accordance with tradition, the emperor made his last will and testament before going to war. If he should die in battle, Haile Selassie instructed that the empress and his children should be taken to the British embassy, where they would seek asylum. The senior commanders and officers were to regroup in an unoccupied part of Ethiopia and choose a leader from among their number, who would assume overall command. The intention was that they should then continue their brave struggle. If Ethiopia should lose her independence, patriotic forces in the country should start a guerrilla war against the occupiers and do everything they could to ensure that the nation regained its sovereignty as quickly as possible. The whole world should be informed about the country's fate and the crime of the Italian war of aggression. Haile Selassie's will was entrusted to *Etshege* Basileos, the senior abbot of the monastery at Debre Libanos, for safe keeping.[24]

As commander-in-chief of the Ethiopian army, the emperor bore full responsibility for the strategic conduct of the war. Because he was well aware of the difficulty of this task, he imposed a particularly strict discipline on himself at his head-quarters in Dessie. His working day began at 5 a.m., and before reading the day's urgent dispatches and holding a briefing with the officers and heads of the armed forces, he would withdraw to the chapel for half an hour of morning prayers. 'It was a marvel to me how this frail little man – the complete physical oppo-site of the brawny Italian dictator – could cram so much work into the twenty-four hours,' wrote the British journalist Stuart Emeny, who was reporting from the Abyssinian front for the *News Chronicle*.[25]

His colleague from *The Times*, George Steer, noted:

'In the house he worked day and night, organizing the last detail in the construction of the two northward roads, that to Korem and the branch road to Lalibela. Seeing that the food caravans went through Dessye regularly. Negotiating with troublesome chiefs. Writing to his wife and his Council in Addis Ababa about his League policy ... air-raid precautions ... the decent treatment of Europeans. Codifying and improving his regulations for the Ethiopian tactic against Western arms – all except the spraying of mustard gas, which he did not foresee.'

Even in these surroundings, as George Steer remarked, Haile Selassie maintained his air of imperial dignity: 'The Emperor of Ethiopia had the gift of appearing at all times, even in the middle of war, completely detached and poised above the mêlée. Pursuing his quiet, rather delicate and well-dressed life without noticing overmuch the noise which surrounded him.'[26]

The correspondent of *The Times* wrote that the emperor:

'... went into the war in every point a European gentleman. At his table four courses of well-cooked European food were served, with Ethiopian *Wot*, chicken spiced with sauce of chillies, to crown the banquet. A cellar was laid in. In the front hall lay a selection of solar topees and, in a corner, stood a series of walking-sticks for going to church, which the Emperor attended daily, for visiting the town, for walking on the mountain, for inspecting the troops and the Red Cross hospitals. His best Arabs were brought up to Dessye.'[27]

Almost nothing at the Dessie residence betrayed the fact that it was the headquarters for military operations: 'The only evidences of war, besides his khaki uniform, were hidden away behind the house. Here, under branches of mimosa and bluegum, was the anti-aircraft machine-gun which he had learned to handle.'[28]

In December, the emperor ordered a thrust against the Italian troops in Tigray, an action since commemorated as the 'Christmas Offensive'. The combined forces of the four Ethiopian armies of the north – commanded by *Ras* Seyoum, *Ras* Kassa, *Ras* Imru and *Ras* Mulugeta – would, he hoped, drive a wedge between the Italian forces, splitting them in two. The offensive succeeded in recapturing a number of the towns the invaders had seized and in the battle that took place at the Dambagwina Pass in mid-December, the Ethiopian forces scored a signal victory. Field Marshal Badoglio reacted by employing a gruesome mode of warfare – an aerial bombardment of the Ethiopian positions with poison gas.

The gas attack took the Ethiopian troops completely by surprise. *Ras* Imru described one of the bombardments:

'The sight was terrible to behold. It was only by chance that I survived. On the morning of 23 December [1935] – I had just crossed the Tacazze River – a group of planes appeared on the horizon. I wasn't particularly alarmed, because in the meantime we had got used to bombing raids. On this morning, however, the aircraft did not drop bombs, but instead curious-looking canisters, which burst open the moment they hit the ground or the water. Before I could grasp what was happening, hundreds of my men had been sprinkled with a strange liquid and were screaming in pain. Their bare feet, hands and faces were covered with blisters, Those who had drunk from the river writhed around on the ground for hours in their death throes. A number of farmers who had come to water their cattle at the river were also affected, along with the inhabitants of the surrounding villages. In the interim my officers had gathered round, seeking instructions from me. But I was in a daze; I had no idea what to say to them or how to combat this burning, deadly rain.'[29]

This was not the first time poison gas was deployed by the Italian army. General Graziani had already used it on the southern front. In total during this conflict, over a thousand tons of poison gas were dropped on Ethiopian troops and civilians alike, in the form of Yperite, or mustard-gas, bombs, as well as some 60,000 arsine-gas (Lewisite) shells fired by the Italian artillery.[30] Marcel Junod, a member of the International Committee of the Red Cross, likened the situation in one of his reports to a 'veritable Hell': 'Men were stretched out everywhere beneath the trees. There must have been thousands of them. As I came closer, my heart in my mouth, I could see horrible suppurating burns on their feet and on their emaciated limbs. Life was already leaving bodies burned with mustard gas.'[31]

Over the coming weeks and months, Italy waged a brutal war of extermination against Ethiopia. The bomber squadrons of the Black Brigades drew no distinction between combatants and civilians. Red Cross field hospitals and dressing stations were repeatedly and deliberately targeted, too. In his HQ at Dessie, it must have become clear to Haile Selassie during these days that he could not possibly prevail against the hugely superior Italian force, and that he could rely on no help from the international community. Although the League of Nations had passed sanctions against Italy after the war began, these were half-hearted at best, and had no bearing on the outcome of the conflict. All the Ethiopian government's protests at the League of Nations against Italy's use of chemical weapons were ignored. Following the signing of the Geneva Protocol of 1925, to which Italy was also party, the use of poison gas was universally outlawed, but Mussolini simply denied that any such attacks had taken place.

The situation was growing increasingly perilous at the emperor's headquarters at Dessie, as well. The US historian John Spencer, who was present during the Italian invasion and from 1941 on became one of Haile Selassie's principal foreign policy advisors, gave an account in his memoirs of this tense period at the front:

'On January 19, 1936, consultations were suddenly interrupted by another air raid warning when we were all assembled at headquarters. Three tri-motor Capronis were not long in

appearing. They flew so high that it was difficult to make out
their silvery silhouettes in the flashing sunlight. The Emperor
immediately went out in front of headquarters and let himself
down into a trench, put on a steel helmet and swung into position an Oerlikon gun, swiveling on a heavy tripod set into
the trench. As I stood nearby fascinated by the operation, His
Majesty frantically motioned to me to run for cover. Reluctantly, I moved aside a few feet under a eucalyptus tree so that
I could continue to see what the Emperor might do. When the
planes came overhead the Emperor started firing.'[32]

February 1936 saw the beginning of the end: on the 19th, *Ras*
Mulugeta's army was routed at the Battle of Amba Aradam. The
war minister himself was killed in this engagement, when he was
hit by shrapnel from a bomb dropped from a plane. His bodyguard carried him from the field of battle. George Steer commented on his death: 'So died the last of Menelik's high officers,
the man who had stopped more lead in his rhino-skin shield
and killed more men with the sword than any in Ethiopia.'[33] At
the end of that same month, the armies of *Ras* Kassa and *Ras*
Seyoum were defeated at the Battle of Tembien – followed just
a few days later by *Ras* Imru's troops at Shire. Nevertheless, the
emperor decided to launch one last offensive. Under his personal
command, he planned to lead his Imperial Guard, combined
with what remained of *Ras* Kassa's and *Ras* Seyoum's armies,
into a final decisive engagement. On 27 March he radioed the
empress with this message: 'Since our trust is in our Creator and
in the hope of his help, and as we have decided to advance and
enter the [Italian] fortifications, and since God is our only help,
confide this decision of ours in secret to the *Abuna*, to the ministers and dignitaries, and offer up to God your fervent prayers.'[34]

The day of the attack was 31 March 1936. Haile Selassie
described the course of events during the Battle of Maychew,
which began around dawn at 5.45 a.m., in his autobiography:

'As Our army moved forward with enthusiasm and reached
the enemy's fortifications, the enemy troops abandoned the

Haile Selassie manning a 20-mm Oerlikon anti-aircraft gun before the Battle of Maychew in late March 1936.

forward positions and were seen to defend a second, more heavily fortified line towards the rear. Within four or five hours, enemy aircraft arrived, dropped bombs and cut off Our army at the rear, preventing it from coming to the aid of the advance troops at the front [...] Our forces spent the whole day fighting with an ardent spirit and with daring. The battle did not cease until five o'clock at night [= 11 p.m.]. In this day's fighting many nobles and army officers died, sacrificing their lives for their country.'[35]

The battle of Maychew ended with around 11,000 Ethiopian troops dead, while on the opposing side 400 Italians and 873 Eritreans were either killed or wounded.[36] The war was now irretrievably lost for Ethiopia.

On 2 April, the emperor ordered a general retreat. Steady rain hampered this operation. To make matters worse, as it withdrew the Ethiopian army came under attack from some of its compatriots. During the battle, warriors from the Oromo tribes of the Raya and Azebo, who had been won over by the Italians, had remained neutral, but now fell upon the fleeing imperial troops from the rear. Ultimately, these attacks were to claim more lives than the actual battle.[37] Furthermore, elements of the army from Wollo province, where word had got around about the death of the former emperor *Lij* Iyasu, the son of the *Negus* of Wollo, also now rose up against Haile Selassie. Finding their planned path of retreat through Wollo blocked, the imperial troops could not take the most direct route through Dessie back to Addis Ababa. As sections of his own people denied him their support, this was a bitter moment for the Ethiopian emperor. His disillusion clearly did not exempt the empress either, as the granddaughter of *Negus* Mikael of Wollo. He sent a telegram to her in the capital, complaining: 'Since Your relatives have barred Our way, we cannot return to the capital through Dessie and so find Ourselves forced to join *Ras* Kassa in making the long detour through Lasta and Lalibela.'[38]

On reaching the holy city of Lalibela, with its ancient rock-cut churches, the emperor withdrew into the monastery and spent three days in retreat there, praying with the monks. During this time, he made a solemn vow: if he should ever regain the Ethiopian throne, he would henceforth hear all cases brought before the *Chilot* – the imperial court of justice, which was convened twice weekly – from a standing position, in honour of the Justice of Christ. When Haile Selassie duly returned to Addis Ababa from exile in 1941, he honoured this pledge and to the end of his reign always insisted on standing during the *Chilot*.[39]

Meanwhile, the Italians overran Dessie and the imperial field headquarters. On the southern front, matters were now decided too: On 14 April 1936, Graziani's troops had defeated the southern army under *Dejazmatch* Nasibu. And as the emperor was making his arduous journey back to the capital, the international press concocted the rumour that Haile Selassie had taken flight from the Italians on a mule and had shaved his beard off so he would not be recognized.[40] When the emperor and his retinue finally arrived in Addis Ababa – on 30 April, exactly a month after the disaster at Maychew – news of the defeat had already spread throughout the city. The capital itself was to all intents and purposes completely unfortified, and there were no troops worthy of the name left to defend it anyhow. The governor of Addis Ababa, the young, energetic patriot *Blatta* Takele Wolde-Hawariat, had assembled 800 volunteers in St George's Cathedral, who banded together to form a Patriotic Front. In the presence of the *Abuna*, they swore a solemn oath that they would never betray their fatherland.

The day the emperor returned, the members of the Privy and Ministerial Councils had been summoned to the Menelik Palace to discuss the grave situation. It was clear to all those present that the war was lost. And it was now surely only a matter of days before Italian troops reached the capital. What was to be done? As long as the emperor remained free, the Italian occupation would have no legitimacy, therefore the safety and security of the *Negusa Negast* was the top priority. The ministers all agreed that the emperor should leave Addis Ababa as soon as possible. *Blatta* Takele proposed making Gore in the far western province of Illubabor the provisional capital. This inaccessible region beyond the Blue Nile could easily be defended against the Italian invaders, and in addition a good supply route ran from there to the Sudan. From this remote stronghold the emperor could direct guerrilla operations against the Italians.[41] But the more cautious of the princes, chief among them *Ras* Kassa, did not consider this a viable option. What would happen if Haile Selassie were to fall into Mussolini's hands, sooner or later? Under the prevailing circumstances the emperor's safety could not be guaranteed. After some further discussion on this matter, *Ras* Kassa requested a private audience with the emperor. Once they were alone, he impressed upon his cousin that he should leave Ethiopia and present the country's grievances in person to the League of Nations in Geneva. And because the Italians might be liable at any moment to cut the railway line, there was no time to lose: the emperor should depart at the earliest opportunity.

A King of Kings abandoning his country in the hour of defeat – such a thing had never happened in the 3,000-year history of the Ethiopian Empire. When the plan was put before the assembled princes and other dignitaries, it sparked a heated and emotional debate. *Blatta* Takele reached for his pistol and put the muzzle in his mouth. '*Janhoy*,' he shouted, 'are you not a son of Téwodros!' The allusion was not lost on Haile Selassie; when his citadel at Maqdala was stormed by British troops in 1868, Emperor Téwodros II had shot himself to avoid falling into enemy hands.

Finally, a vote was taken: twenty-one of those present were in favour of the emperor going into exile, while just three were against – among them the governor of Addis Ababa, *Blatta* Takele, and the foreign minister *Blattengetta* Heruy.[42] *Times* correspondent George Steer, who was waiting in the palace grounds with fellow journalists, saw the emperor as he emerged from the meeting: 'He was dressed in khaki as a general. His aspect froze my blood. Vigour had left his face, and as he walked forward he did not seem to know where he was putting his feet. His body was crumpled up, his shoulders drooped: the orders on his tunic concealed a hollow, not a chest.'[43]

Haile Selassie havered over whether to follow the resolution of the Privy Council and go into exile. Only after a long conversation with the empress and another with *Ras* Kassa did he finally decide to comply with the will of the Ethiopian princes and ministers.[44] That same night, a special train was made ready for his departure. The emperor's confessor, *Abba* Hanna, was instructed to gather together the most important documents and equipment from the royal household. It took some while for the coaches to be loaded – the imperial paraphernalia included a Buick and a Chrysler. On 2 May 1936, at four in the morning, the imperial family and their entourage boarded the train. Along with Empress Menen, the royal couple's five children were also preparing to bid farewell to their native land: Crown Prince Asfa-Wossen and his two brothers the 17-year-old Prince Makonnen and the 5-year-old Prince Sahle Selassie, along with the emperor's two daughters, the 23-year-old Princess Tenagne-Work and the 16-year-old Princess Tsahai-Work.[45] The dignitaries accompanying the royal party into exile included *Ras* Kassa and Foreign Minister Heruy. Haile Selassie joined the train in the suburb of Akaki; he had a prominent prince with him when he stepped aboard – the prisoner *Ras* Hailu. The emperor had him fetched from prison to accompany them, as he feared Hailu might defect to the Italians.

On the evening before their departure, Haile Selassie had dispatched telegrams in which he issued three more important orders: *Ras* Imru, who at that time was in Debre Markos with the remnants of his scattered force, was named as regent. Secondly, a provisional government was to be established at Gore in the far west. And finally, he ordered the remaining forces of the Imperial Guard to place themselves under the command of *Dejazmatch* Aberra Kassa, one of *Ras* Kassa's sons, in Fiche. As the emperor made his appeal to the world in Geneva, the fight against the occupying army in Ethiopia was to continue.

The train stopped at Meeso, half-way between Addis Ababa and Dire Dawa. It was not enemy troops who forced the locomotive to come to a halt there, but a long-standing confidant of the emperor, *Fitaurari* Tekle Hawariat, the author of the constitution. He had not been present at the crucial meeting of the Privy Council in the capital, and when he learned that the emperor was about to leave Ethiopia he was determined to persuade him to turn back. Accompanied by a military escort, he boarded the train, strode into the emperor's compartment and told Haile Selassie: 'Your Majesty, an Ethiopian emperor does not leave his country in the lurch!' But his attempt to get Haile Selassie to reconsider at the eleventh hour was to no avail. The train proceeded on its way to the border.[46]

Quite by chance, a few days later, John H. Spencer came face to face with Tekle Hawariat and recounted: 'Although I must have been for him almost a complete stranger, he lost no time in unburdening himself to me of his thoughts about Haile Selassie, whom he denounced as a traitor to Ethiopia, a coward, and one unworthy to bear the name of Emperor after his flight into exile. It was no surprise to me later that, following the Liberation, Tekle Hawariat himself chose exile.'[47]

The train came to a halt once more in the station at Dire Dawa. The emperor waited there for the British Consul from Harar, to seek Britain's assistance in his onward journey to Europe.

Haile Selassie took this opportunity to release *Ras* Hailu from his custody. It is unclear what prompted him to take this step. Perhaps he hoped that the Prince of Gojjam would join the patriotic resistance. In the event, *Ras* Hailu lost no time in returning to Addis Ababa to offer his services to the Italians. During the occupation, he became one of the principal Ethiopian collaborators with the Italian regime.

Eventually, Haile Selassie's train reached French Somaliland. Adamant that no armed Ethiopian soldiers should set foot on their territory, the French authorities ordered the fifteen officers of the Imperial Guard escorting the emperor to surrender their weapons. In response, the emperor dismissed his guard and instructed them to go and join the partisan resistance movement. On 4 May 1936, in Djibouti, the imperial party boarded the Royal Navy cruiser HMS *Enterprise*, which was to take them to the port of Haifa in Palestine.

The ship's captain later sent a report to the Foreign Office: 'My first impression on being presented to His Majesty [...] was how very tired he looked. It felt somehow that he was almost at his last gasp and from his first few remarks I knew he was a very frightened man. He had a hunted look in his eye ... .' The emperor asked the captain whether his personal safety could be guaranteed. 'I assured him at once that as soon as he stepped over my gangway he would be as safe as the Bank of England,' the captain replied.[48] This bought a smile to the emperor's face, the first for a long time. And so it was that Haile Selassie I, Conquering Lion of the Tribe of Judah, Elect of God, King of the Kings of Ethiopia, went into exile. He had undertaken to endure this test that God had set him with his customary imperial dignity. At the end of the passage to Haifa, the captain of the *Enterprise* was moved to remark: 'I have seldom been so impressed with any man, black or white, and his consideration, courtesy and above all his dignity, has left a very deep impression on every officer and man in my ship.'[49]

The day after the emperor departed Djibouti, Marshal Badoglio marched into the Ethiopian capital. Four days later, on 9 May, Mussolini stepped onto the balcony of the Palazzo

Venezia in Rome and announced to the enraptured crowd below that Ethiopia had been annexed. By the time the seven-month war came to an end, there were around 150,000 dead on the Ethiopian side. Yet this was merely the prelude to a five-year regime of occupation that was characterized by unparalleled brutality towards the country's civilian population. So-called 'mopping-up actions', reprisals, rapes, executions and massacres were everyday accompaniments to Italian rule in the Horn of Africa. Conquered Ethiopia was united with the Italian colonies of Eritrea and Somalia to form an empire that was christened *Africa Orientale Italiana* (AOI), Italian East Africa. The Italian king Victor Emmanuel III was proclaimed as the new emperor of Ethiopia and the commander of the southern army, Rodolfo Graziani, as its viceroy. During the five years of occupation, many more Ethiopians fell victim to the invaders than in the war itself. A total of almost 400,000 Ethiopians met a violent end during this period. Set against this were some 25,000 killed on the Italian side.

The Italian war against Ethiopia had all the hallmarks of a Fascist war of extermination, while the occupation regime associated with it revealed itself to be a racist system of apartheid.[50] The Italian colonial minister Alessandro Lessona decreed that separate residential areas were to be set up for the indigenous population and Italians. A series of racial laws were enacted to prevent the 'commingling' of the 'Italian race' with the 'Ethiopian race'. These laws made little impact on the Italian soldiers and their officers, many of whom took Ethiopian women as lovers or wives. Yet there is still much truth in Swiss historian Aram Mattioli's comment: 'Seen from a global perspective, the Abyssinian war represents a "bridge" between the colonial wars of the imperial age and Hitler's war to secure *Lebensraum*.'[51]

But for all the reprisals and brutality they meted out, at no time did the Italians succeed even remotely in bringing Ethiopia fully under their control. The radius of their authority barely extended beyond the urban centres. Right from the start of their occupation, the dogged resistance of the Ethiopian people was brought home forcefully to the Italians, from virtually all sectors of the population and most parts of the country. Among those princes who spearheaded the resistance were the regent *Ras* Imru, the emperor's son-in-law *Ras* Desta Damraw, and Ras Kassa's sons – *Dejazmatch* Wond-Wossen Kassa in Lasta, and *Dejazmatch* Aberra Kassa and *Dejazmatch* Asfa-Wossen Kassa in Selale. A resistance cell of officers and civilians calling themselves the 'Black Lions' formed around *Ras* Imru; this group came to play a leading role in the struggle against the occupiers. One of the foremost Ethiopian patriots, organizing resistance from his base in Shoa province, was *Ras* Abebe Aregay; after the war, he was to serve the country in a number of important roles, as war minister, minister of the interior and chairman of the Council of Ministers, before being murdered in the attempted coup of 1960.

The darkest chapter in the Italian occupation came on 19 February 1937, after two Ethiopian resistance fighters had attempted to assassinate Marshal Graziani. On that day, the Italian viceroy was hosting a reception for Italian and Ethiopian dignitaries at the royal palace to mark the Prince of Naples' birthday.

A Hungarian doctor, Ladislas Sava, witnessed events as they unfolded:

> 'Then suddenly bombs were thrown towards the table at which Graziani was sitting with his lieutenants. At the moment of the explosion he was hiding under the table, while the other Italian officers had flung themselves to the ground [...] A moment of silence followed, which lasted until the Italians realized that no more bombs were to be feared. Then the shooting was started by Cortese [secretary-general of the Fascist Party in Addis Ababa], who fired with his revolver into the group of Ethiopian dignitaries. The Italian Carabinieri followed this example. In a few moments there were more than 300 dead in the courtyard and around the Palace alone. Hardly a single Ethiopian escaped alive from the courtyard.'

Graziani himself sustained only relatively minor shrapnel wounds in the grenade attack. The reprisals against the Ethiopian populace that he immediately ordered were dreadful, and have gone down in history as the 'Graziani Massacre'. Blackshirts, Carabinieri and soldiers combed the capital, indiscriminately shooting Ethiopians on sight:

'... blood was literally streaming down the streets. The corpses of men, women and children, over which vultures hovered, were lying in all directions. Great flames from the burning houses illuminated the African night. [...] Whole streets were burned down, and if any of the occupants of the houses ran out from the flames, they were machine-gunned or stabbed with cries of *"Duce! Duce!"*. From the lorries in which groups of prisoners were brought up to be murdered near the Palace, the blood flowed on to the streets, and again from the lorries we heard the cry of *"Duce! Duce! Duce!"*'[52]

This systematic pogrom in Addis Ababa claimed the lives of more than 4,000 Ethiopians. But the Italians' thirst for bloody revenge did not stop there. Over the following few days, the country's intelligentsia – well-educated Ethiopians, including those who had studied abroad – were deliberately targeted for execution. The campaign of revenge did not even spare clerics, with between 1,500 and 2,000 monks, priests and deacons murdered at the monastery in Debre-Libanos and other holy sites.[53]

All this, however, was still some way in the future when Haile Selassie went into exile in May 1936. One cannot say for certain whether he counted on ever being able to return to his homeland. Throughout his life, the emperor never gave any inkling of his innermost hopes and fears, and this was also true of this momentous period. But if he hadn't harboured any hope of returning, he would surely never have exiled himself in the first place. From Port Said, Haile Selassie travelled on to Jerusalem, where he learned of Mussolini's speech proclaiming the annexation of Ethiopia. He immediately sent a telegram to the secretariat of the League of Nations. Whatever may have happened, the Lion of Judah was in the mood to fight: 'We now demand,' the text of the telegram ran, 'that the League of Nations should continue its efforts in order to secure respect for the Covenant, and that it should decide not to recognize territorial extensions, or the exercise of an assumed sovereignty resulting from an illegal recourse to armed force and from numerous other violations of international agreements.'[54]

The British government under Prime Minister Stanley Baldwin was ready to grant Haile Selassie asylum; public pressure on this matter was simply too great to ignore. At the same time, though, it was still the case that Great Britain did not want to do anything that might bring Fascist Italy and National Socialist Germany closer together and create a Rome–Berlin Axis. At the port of Haifa in Mandatory Palestine, the Royal Navy cruiser HMS *Capetown* took the imperial party on board for the voyage to London. But as the warship approached the Atlantic, the prime minister began to have doubts about the wisdom of allowing the Ethiopian emperor to sail all the way to Great Britain on a vessel flying the White Ensign. And so, on the pretext that she needed repairs, the *Capetown* was promptly ordered to put into Gibraltar. A naval officer, Commander (later Vice Admiral) Brian B. Schofield, recalled an incident during the emperor's brief sojourn there that points up his ambivalent attitude towards the British:

> 'One day the exiled King of Abyssinia, Haile Selassie, arrived at Gibraltar in one of our cruisers and was invited to lunch by the Commander-in-Chief in HMS *Nelson*. As he spoke French but no English, I was invited to act as interpreter. During the lunch the conversation was confined to generalities but afterwards when I was showing him around the ship and pointed out to him the *Nelson*'s big 16-inch guns, he remarked rather ruefully that it was a pity they had not been used in the cause of liberty and justice.'[55]

Haile Selassie and his entourage were duly transferred to the SS *Orford*, a passenger liner bound for Britain. Baldwin was determined that, when the Ethiopian emperor set foot on British soil, he would do so 'strictly incognito' rather than enjoying the status of an official state guest. The emperor and his family disembarked at Southampton on 3 June 1936. When their train arrived in London, they were greeted at Waterloo Station by a large and enthusiastic crowd. One of the thousands who came to cheer the emperor was the famous suffragette and socialist Sylvia Pankhurst. Before the First World War, she had demonstrated in favour of votes for women, and during the war was a prominent pacifist. Now, she threw all her campaigning weight behind the cause of a free Ethiopia. During Haile Selassie's years in exile, she would become one of his most important supporters in the spheres of politics and public relations. To draw attention to the plight of Ethiopia, she even started a new weekly magazine with the title *New Times and Ethiopia News*.

The pugnacious suffragette formally bade the emperor welcome at Waterloo. But when she met him a few days later to interview him, she lost no time in telling him frankly: 'I am a republican. I support you not because you are an emperor, but because I believe your cause, the cause of Ethiopia, is a just one.' The emperor replied evenly: 'I know.'[56] He couldn't afford to be choosy where his supporters were concerned.

The Jewish philanthropist Sir Elie Kadoorie had offered to put the emperor and his family up at his home in Princes Gate, Kensington, almost next door to the Ethiopian Legation. This house soon became a hub of feverish diplomatic activity in preparation for Haile Selassie's upcoming address to the General Assembly of the League of Nations, which was scheduled for 30 June. In the meantime, the British government scarcely missed an opportunity to make it clear that Haile Selassie was anything but a welcome guest in London. The Foreign Office informed the Ethiopian ambassador to Great Britain that the emperor should avoid public appearances which might 'cause any unpleasantness' for His Majesty or the Ethiopian people. A civil servant in the Egyptian-Ethiopian section of the Foreign Office also minuted: 'I feel sure that if we don't try to exercise some moderation, our guest will be both a nuisance and a danger.'[57]

At a meeting with Foreign Secretary Anthony Eden, which the British government designated 'private', Haile Selassie expressed a wish to meet King Edward VIII. However, the British monarch stubbornly refused to receive the emperor at Buckingham Palace. The prime minister, Stanley Baldwin, also went to great lengths to avoid meeting him. In his memoirs, John H. Spencer recounted a memorable near-encounter in the early days of June between Baldwin and the emperor, or 'The Lion Incognito' as the English-speaking press had latterly taken to calling him:[58]

'One day in June, Stanley Baldwin was taking tea with one of his colleagues on the terrace at Westminster when he saw a small group of persons, in the midst of whom was a diminutive figure in a long cape and strange hat, slowly approaching his table. The prime minister swiftly turned to one of the waiters to inquire who the visitors were. "Haile Selassie, the Emperor of Ethiopia, and some Ethiopians, sir." Since the prime minister's path was cut off by the approaching group, he faced the choice of jumping over the parapet into the river or ducking around the tables until he could find a door or passageway behind which he could disappear. An alert attendant found the alternative to a bath in the Thames.'[59]

The British prime minister had his reasons for wishing to give the emperor a wide berth. Shortly before, Anthony Eden had announced to the Commons that His Majesty's government saw no further grounds, now that Ethiopia had been overrun, for upholding the sanctions against Italy. Accordingly, Britain would be seeking to have them lifted at the forthcoming meeting of the General Assembly of the League of Nations. The parliamentary debate which followed this statement was extremely heated. Ministers were heckled from the opposition benches with shouts of 'cowards!' 'poltroons!' and 'jellyfish!' David Lloyd George, the Liberal elder statesman who had been prime minister for much of the First World War, was outraged: 'The Foreign Secretary is going to Geneva to smash the League of Nations. There is nothing but international anarchy as an alternative. For nearly half a century I have sat in Parliament and never before have had I heard a British Foreign Secretary confess that Britain had been

Emperor Haile Selassie delivering his renowned address to the
General Council of the League of Nations in Geneva, 30 June 1936.

defeated. This is British surrender to Italy without the firing of a
shot! Surrender in fear of the Italian air force.'[60] In his memoirs,
Eden drily remarked, 'The debate was vehement and accusing,
with Mr. Lloyd George at the height of his debating powers.'

The British government exerted all the diplomatic means at
its disposal to try and prevent Haile Selassie from travelling in
person to Geneva to plead Ethiopia's case at the League. 'Tell
your Emperor,' Anthony Eden imperiously informed the Ethiopian ambassador, 'that no head of a state has ever addressed the
League – it would be unprecedented! The emperor really must
not appear. It would compromise his imperial dignity.'[61]

Haile Selassie was undeterred by such threats. On the afternoon of 30 June 1936, the Emperor of Ethiopia rose to address
the General Assembly of the League of Nations in Geneva. In
the run-up to the session, the Ethiopian delegation's main fear
had been that the newly-elected president of the Assembly, Paul
van Zeeland of Belgium, might veto the emperor's speech. It was

no secret that as a colonial power in Africa Belgium pursued its own national interests and, where the war was concerned, were on the side of the Italians. Once the session had been declared open, the president allowed a letter from the Italian foreign minister Count Galeazzo Ciano to be read out, which began with the words: 'Italy considers it an honour to be able to inform the League of Nations about her efforts to civilize Ethiopia [...] Italy sees this as her sacred duty.'[62] Then Haile Selassie came to the podium. John H. Spencer, who was accompanying the Ethiopian delegation, related what happened next: 'At that instant, a chorus of cat-calls and shouts arose from the Fascist journalists in the gallery behind us. I recall no moment in the many years spent with Haile Selassie when, despite his small stature, he so instantly summoned up such majesty of presence. The tumult was quelled – not by van Zeeland, president of the Assembly – but by Titulescu of Rumania who shouted, "À la porte les sauvages! (Throw out the barbarians!)"'.[63]

It was ten minutes before the Swiss police managed to clear the building of the fascist agitators. Originally, Haile Selassie had intended to deliver his speech in French, since he hoped that this would have a more immediate impact on the assembled ministers and envoys. But standing at the lectern now, he reached for the Amharic version of his address. The emperor was determined to convey the message he wished to impart to the world in his native tongue. Even mediated through the simultaneous translators present, its effect was not lost on the Assembly:

'I assert that the problem submitted to the Assembly today is a much wider one [than merely the lifting of sanctions]. It is not merely a question of the settlement of Italian aggression. It is collective security: it is the very existence of the League of Nations. It is the confidence that each State is to place in international treaties. It is the value of promises made to small States that their integrity and their independence shall be respected and ensured. It is the principle of the equality of States on the one hand, or otherwise the obligation laid upon small Powers to accept the bonds of vassalship. In a word, it is international morality that is at stake [...] . Apart from the Kingdom of the Lord there is not on this earth any nation that is superior to any other.'

An embarrassed hush fell over the Assembly as the delegates listened to the following words:

'It is my painful duty to note that the initiative has today been taken with a view to raising sanctions. Does this initiative not mean in practice the abandonment of Ethiopia to the aggressor? [...] Placed by the aggressor face to face with the accomplished fact, are States going to set up the terrible precedent of bowing before force? [...] I ask the fifty-two nations, who have given the Ethiopian people a promise to help them in their resistance to the aggressor, what are they willing to do for Ethiopia? And the great Powers who have promised the guarantee of collective security to small States on whom weighs the threat that they may one day suffer the fate of Ethiopia, I ask what measures do you intend to take? Representatives of the World, I have come to Geneva to discharge in your midst the most painful of the duties of the head of a State. What reply shall I have to take back to my people?'[64]

The end of the emperor's speech was greeted with a tumult of applause. 'Everyone agreed,' reported *Time* magazine, 'that it was a great speech – one of the noblest, most factual, irrefutable and moving ever made before the League of Nations. Yet it was totally without effect on Geneva's sleek, hard, slippery statesmen.'[65] In the course of the ensuing proceedings, an overwhelming majority of member states decided to lift the sanctions that had been imposed on Fascist Italy. Haile Selassie's appeal to the world's conscience had fallen on deaf ears. His hopes for international support lay in tatters. Depressed and disillusioned, the Ethiopian delegation made its way back to London. A sententious leader article which appeared in *The Times* on 2 July must have given him scant comfort:

'For the little good it can now do him – his legend may not be without a growing force hereafter – Haile Selassie has taken and will hold a high place in history. The authority and reasoned strength of his final appeal to the Council must have moved many to regret, however impotently, that "not Heaven itself upon the past has power". Is there another in history who has deserved more of fortune and his fellows and received less?'

Quite how right Haile Selassie's prophetic words to the League of Nations were would become apparent over the following years. Beginning with Austria and Czechoslovakia, as Hitler's Germany set about bringing one country after another under the Nazi yoke, there presently ceased to be any League of Nations at all and no system of collective security on which these countries might have been able to rely for help. A premonition of what was to come was provided by an incident on the fringes of the Assembly in Geneva, which the British foreign secretary Anthony Eden took note of: 'These were wretched days at Geneva. One morning during an Assembly session about Abyssinia, I suddenly heard a report and saw a figure fall on the benches at my right hand. Until the police ran up to him, I did not understand what had happened. A Czech spectator had shot himself dead after a cry of warning, apparently about the fate of small countries. His death was a message to his countrymen sealed with his life.'[66]

On 15 July 1936 the League of Nations sanctions against Italy were officially lifted. Great Britain would become the first country to recognize Victor Emmanuel III as the emperor of Ethiopia and hence to acknowledge the country's annexation by the Italians as lawful. Most other countries followed Britain's lead, with only the United States, Mexico, New Zealand and the Soviet Union demurring. It now gradually dawned on Haile Selassie that he would have to steel himself for a lengthy exile. The plight not only of his country, but also of the hordes of Ethiopian refugees in Sudan, Kenya and Jerusalem must have weighed heavily upon him. Not to mention the thought of how his wife the empress and their children would cope with a life in exile.

The imperial family spent August 1936 in the West Country town of Bath, where a wing of the Spa Hotel had been rented for them. The town's inhabitants welcomed their exalted visitors with friendly curiosity. People flocked from far and near to catch a glimpse of the emperor. One of the hotel's employees recalled the mood of popular excitement:

> 'The best place to see him [i.e. the Emperor] was in the Pump Room. Apparently he had some colonic trouble and daily he went to the baths for treatment, Saturdays and Sundays excluded. He would arrive in the afternoon and then we had to do something about the crowds [...] He arrived by car, always dressed in his sombre clothes – a bowler hat and a dark suit with black cape. With him he used to bring his two sons, who were learning to swim.'[67]

Why did Haile Selassie come to Bath, of all places? A short but fascinating paper on the emperor's years of exile in Britain, written in 1992 for the Anglo-Ethiopian Society, provides a plausible explanation for the emperor's choice:

> 'It is very likely that the city may have suited his mood: it was elegant, but not fashionable as Monte Carlo or Cannes. Shabby in places, but dignified in a provincial way, cheaper than London, yet sufficiently near for consultations with supporters in the capital. There was, in fact, more to the visit than holidaying, making friends and influencing people. He needed a home and to plan his future as an exile.'[68]

After several weeks at the hotel, the family took possession of Fairfield House, a large Victorian villa with an extensive garden on the outskirts of Bath. This was to be their home for the next few years. Alongside the royal couple and their children, the Ethiopian foreign minister *Blattengetta* Heruy, a secretary and two Coptic monks also lived there. *Ras* Kassa, whose son Prince Asserate Kassa was at school in nearby Monkton Combe, also stayed at Fairfield House for a spell. The emperor's sons, Prince

At one of the many fundraising functions he attended during his five-year exile in Britain, Haile Selassie is pictured here in 1938 in the company of Princess Tsahai-Work (second from left), Crown Prince Asfa-Wossen (third from left), and *Leul-Ras* Kassa (fourth from left).

Asfa-Wossen and Prince Makonnen, were sent off to study respectively at Liverpool University and at Wellington College boarding school in Berkshire, and only spent their holidays at the house in Bath. This was the case for Princess Tsahai-Work, too, who lived in London at Great Ormond Street Hospital, where she was training to be a nurse. The imperial household at Fairfield House also comprised a number of Ethiopian servants, including a butler and a cook. Compared with the court life that the emperor had led in Addis Ababa, these were relatively straitened circumstances.

'Our life in Bath was very hard,' Haile Selassie wrote in his autobiography. 'We also encountered great financial difficulties. Some [....] had spread the rumour that we had taken a great deal of money with us when leaving the country, but it is a complete lie. The fact that we had serious financial problems was plain for all to see. In the hope that, with the help of the League of Nations, We would soon be returning to Our homeland, We took what We thought was sufficient for a certain time, but even that was soon finished as We used it to help the exiles.'[69] The funds that Haile Selassie had brought from Ethiopia to England did indeed dwindle alarmingly fast. Thanks to the reports written by the Foreign Office, which kept a meticulous account of the emperor's finances during this period, we now know a great deal about this aspect of his life. When Haile Selassie arrived in Britain, he was carrying cash, silver and jewellery to the value of £25,000 (around £650,000 in today's prices).[70] With this, he had to meet not only his family's living costs but also all the official expenses, such as his servants' and advisors' wages, his trip to Geneva, the purchase of Fairfield House and sundry other outgoings. Within a year all the cash had been spent. The emperor could count on no financial support from the British government. Private individuals and bodies like the Abyssinia Association organized fundraising parties and donation drives, but the sums these raised were only very modest. A British film company offered Haile Selassie US $100,000 to take part in a movie about his life entitled 'Escape Under Cover of Darkness'. The emperor politely declined.[71] Eventually, he was forced to sell his wife's jewellery and the imperial silver tableware. Later, individual pieces from this set kept appearing at auction. The latest item to come up for sale was in June 2013, when a Copenhagen auction house advertised a silver dining service for 24 persons from the imperial household, engraved with a monogram of the initials 'TM' – for 'Tafari Makonnen' – surmounted by a crown.[72]

The winter of 1937 marked the low point of Haile Selassie's time in exile. The empress found the clammy English climate intolerable and was plagued by severe rheumatism. It was decided that they should spend the rest of the winter in warmer climes, and so in January 1938 the empress decamped, along with their youngest son Sahle Selassie, to Jerusalem. That winter the financial situation became so strained that there wasn't even enough money for coal – in Fairfield House, a fire was lit in only a single grate. And in December 1937, while on the way to a

The Emperor and Crown Prince Asfa-Wossen at Dunham
Massey, Greater Manchester in 1938, with their hosts Roger
Grey, 10th Earl of Stamford and the Countess of Stamford.

radio interview at the BBC, the emperor's car was involved in an
accident in which Haile Selassie broke his collarbone. Betraying
no hint of the pain he was in, he went ahead with the broadcast
and afterwards found time to attend a Christmas party at Great
Ormond Street Hospital. It was only when he got back to Bath
that he finally went to see a doctor about the fracture.[73]

The dire financial straits the imperial family found themselves
in alarmed the British government, which was keen to avoid anything that put Haile Selassie in the headlines. The Foreign Office
speculated whether the Italians might be prepared 'to give the

Negus and his family either a pension or a lump sum in exchange for an act of abdication in favour of the King of Italy.'[74] But Haile Selassie would not agree to such a step under any circumstances. Following a meeting in February 1938 with Lord Halifax, Anthony Eden's successor as Foreign Secretary, the emperor issued a statement on 2 March, expressing the hope that Britain was 'not seeking to do a deal over the dead body of Ethiopia.'[75] However, the Chamberlain/Halifax administration, like its predecessor, opted for a policy of appeasement: In April, it concluded a treaty with Mussolini which, without mentioning Ethiopia by name, nevertheless tacitly recognized its annexation by Italy.[76] The emperor's financial worries were eventually allayed in June 1938 by an anonymous donor who put up the sum of £10,000, from which £500 was paid quarterly to Haile Selassie.[77]

The longer the emperor remained in exile, the quieter things grew around him. During the first months of his stay in Bath, the local paper, the *Bath Chronicle*, had dogged his every footstep, but by now public interest in him was only sporadic. The emperor led a reclusive life. He went for a walk every day and set about writing his memoirs. Occasionally, he received invitations from English aristocrats to come and stay in their country houses – for example the Duke of Gloucester at Barnwell Manor, the Earl of Glasgow at Kelburn and the Earl of Wemyss in East Lothian. Foremost amongst the English aristocrats who were sympathetic to the Emperor's cause was Roger Grey, 10th (and last) Earl of Stamford (1896–1976). A left-leaning peer and member (though not very active) of the House of Lords, Roger Grey was a great supporter of the League of Nations and a friend of Sylvia Pankhurst. In 1938 he entertained the Emperor and Crown Prince Asfa-Wossen in his ancestral home, Dunham Massey, a large estate on the edge of Greater Manchester now belonging to the National Trust. The Imperial party stayed there for four days and a lifelong relationship was formed. The Ethiopian connections with Dunham Massey are marked every year on 23 July (the birthday of Haile Selassie) with the flying of the Ethiopian flag from the hall building itself and from the Stamford Estate building, a tradition introduced in 2011.

Fairfield House in Bath.

Hilda Seligman, an English artist and anti-fascist campaigner, was also staunch in her support of Haile Selassie, holding several receptions for the emperor at Lincoln House, her residence in London, where she introduced him to various politicians of all parties. The bust that she sculpted of Haile Selassie, recently restored, can now be seen in Cannizaro Park in Wimbledon.

Haile Selassie never gave up hope that his hour would eventually come. But as the years passed he became ever more isolated. On health grounds, the empress had relocated permanently to Jerusalem, where a large expatriate community of Ethiopians had grown up in the meantime. *Ras* Kassa had also turned his back on England and moved there. In September 1938, Foreign Minister Heruy, one of Haile Selassie's closest advisors, had died at Fairfield House after a long illness. He was buried in Bath. But the family, his children and grandchildren continued to be a great source of strength to Haile Selassie. Few others paid the emperor of Ethiopia and the fate of his country much heed any more. The whole world was now transfixed by Adolf Hitler, who in September 1939 invaded Poland. The desperate policy of concessions and appeasement, which France and Britain had pursued for so long, had ultimately failed to fend off war. In May 1940, Neville Chamberlain stepped down as prime minister. His successor, Winston Churchill, was determined to stand firm against the threat posed by National Socialist Germany. The new British premier certainly met with the emperor's approval: on 16 May, just six days after Churchill's appointment, Haile Selassie wrote to him from Bath: 'Peace be unto you. It was with great pleasure and renewed hope that I learned of your appointment as Prime Minister, not only because your gifts and energy will secure victory for the Allies, but also because you have always been a loyal supporter and advocate of the League of Nations.'[78]

A month later, on 10 June 1940, Italy entered the Second World War as an ally of Nazi Germany. Overnight, Haile Selassie was transformed from a forgotten exile languishing in a sleepy spa town in the West Country into a key figure on the stage of world history. Soon after, he found himself a passenger on an aircraft flying to the Sudan. The years of inactivity and exile were finally at an end.

CHAPTER SIX

The Lion of Judah returns

1941 to 1954

On 24 June 1940, a fortnight after Italy entered the Second World War as an ally of Hitler's Germany, under conditions of great secrecy Haile Selassie boarded an RAF Sunderland flying boat in Plymouth, along with his second son, the Duke of Harar, and his two private secretaries Lorenzo Taezaz and Wolde-Giorgis Wolde-Yohannes. To preserve his anonymity, the Ethiopian emperor had been given the alias of 'Mr Smith'. A night flight across Nazi-occupied France took the royal party to the island of Malta. There, they transferred to another flying boat bound for the Egyptian port of Alexandria. After spending a night at the Italian Yacht Club, recently commandeered by the British, the following day Haile Selassie was taken to Cairo to meet Edwin Chapman-Andrews, the first secretary of the British Embassy, who was to act as his political advisor over the coming months. Chapman-Andrews was an old acquaintance of the emperor, having been British vice-consul in Harar in the years immediately before the Italian invasion. From Cairo, 'Mr Smith' flew on to Wadi Halfa in the Sudan.

It was Winston Churchill's express wish and order that the emperor be sent to this region, as he was convinced that Haile Selassie would act as a magnet for the revolt of the Ethiopian patriots against the Italian occupation force. The British generals and colonial officers were far from happy with this decision. They did not believe that the emperor would be of any use

Edwin Chapman-Andrews, British political advisor to Haile
Selassie during the 1941 campaign to liberate Ethiopia from
Italian occupation, formally greets the Emperor as he sets foot
back on his native soil for the first time after five years in exile.
Standing immediately to the right of the Emperor are Major
Orde Wingate, *Leul-Ras* Kassa and the Crown Prince.

to them in the liberation of Ethiopia, or indeed that he ought
to play any significant role in a future Ethiopia. Ethiopia was
just one of several territories in the wider region under enemy
occupation – along with Libya, Eritrea, and Italian Somaliland
– which needed to be captured from the Italians. And the British
made no secret of their intention, at the end of this campaign,
to create a large integrated territory in East Africa in the form
of a British Protectorate. Their belief in Great Britain as wield-
ing unrestricted colonial power in Africa was undimmed – and
if faced with the choice of accepting either an Ethiopian colony
under Italian control and an independent Ethiopia under the
leadership of Haile Selassie, the British colonial officers would

have chosen the former in the blink of an eye. Their colonial mindset made this kind of thinking inevitable.

In the Sudan Haile Selassie was treated as a decidedly unwelcome guest. It was only after sustained pressure from London that the governor-general of the Sudan, Sir Stewart Symes, and the British commander-in-chief for the area, Major-General William Platt, allowed him to remain in the country.[1] Eventually, the emperor installed himself in the so-called 'Pink Palace', a country house on the outskirts of Khartoum. The dismissive attitude of the British Sudan Service and the disagreement among Britain's war leaders about his role were an open secret to him. He had come to the Sudan full of great hopes and the expectation that he would soon be leading a military offensive, but now found himself condemned once more to inactivity.

For months, virtually nothing happened. Although Great Britain had begun to assemble a joint Commonwealth force comprising troops from the Sudan, Kenya, South Africa, India and Australia, there was as yet no sign of definite preparations for an invasion of *Africa Orientale Italiana*. In August 1940, Italy advanced into British Somaliland and took possession of it. In the same month, a British unit under the command of Brigadier Daniel Arthur Sandford – the former English advisor and confidant of Haile Selassie who had already been in his service before the war – set out from the Sudanese town of Gallabat to enter the Gojjam region of Ethiopia, which was under partisan control. Sandford's detachment established its headquarters in the mountainous region around Sakale, not far from the source of the Blue Nile. The purpose of this military action, designated as 'Mission 101', was to whip up support among the patriots there for a revolt against the Italians. Sandford supplied the local Ethiopian guerrillas with weapons and ammunition, as well as holding out the prospect of imminent British assistance in their struggle. Yet still no detailed plan existed for an all-out invasion.

The British commander in the Sudan saw no reason for swift action. He made no bones about the role he envisaged for Haile Selassie in the drama that was about to unfold in Ethiopia under British direction, as he once frankly admitted to a visitor: 'Haile

Selassie will enter Abyssinia by the grace of William Platt, and with his baggage.'[2] However, the emperor was already making preparations to regain control of the script, drafting an Imperial Proclamation announcing his imminent return to his people. In it, he urged those of his compatriots and subjects who had already thrown in their lot with the Italians to desert. The proclamation, emblazoned with the seal of the Lion of Judah, was duplicated; presently, tens of thousands of leaflets with this call to arms were dropped over Ethiopia by British planes. The emperor also set up a newspaper to report on the Ethiopian liberation campaign. It was entitled *Banderachin*, a portmanteau word formed from the Ahmaric term for 'our' (*achin*) and the Italian *bandera*, 'flag'. The former *Times* correspondent in Ethiopia, George L. Steer, was appointed as its publisher, and at the same time made chief of the Imperial Propaganda Unit.

'While We were preparing Our patriots and Our people in these ways, the British authorities were holding back from Us information about what was really going on. Thus We heard everything belatedly.' Haile Selassie was later to write in his autobiography, 'While We did not openly protest the Sudanese administration's indifference to Our cause, Our dissatisfaction with it was made known to the British government.'[3] Haile Selassie sent Churchill a letter in which he called for the immediate mobilization of troops and the arming of Ethiopian refugees in Somaliland and Kenya.

It took some weeks for the emperor's direct approach to bear fruit. At the end of October Churchill sent Anthony Eden – whom the prime minister had first appointed as war minister; soon after, Eden resumed his former post as foreign secretary – to the Sudan with instructions to expedite matters. Churchill and Eden had identified the ideal man to lead the Ethiopian operation, a young major by the name of Orde Wingate, a truly idiosyncratic character. There was no doubting the enormous military experience of this 37-year-old graduate of the Royal Military Academy at Woolwich: in the late 1920s he had commanded a company of the Sudan Defence Force. In 1936, he was transferred to Palestine, where he led a paramilitary commando unit made up of

British soldiers and members of the Jewish settlers' police force. There, he found himself drawn to the Kibbutz movement and Zionism. It was Wingate's great dream to ride triumphantly on a white horse into a liberated Jerusalem. Consequently, it came as no surprise that he named the guerrilla unit that would undertake the mission to free Ethiopia 'Gideon Force' – a reference to the Old Testament judge Gideon, who was chosen by an angel to deliver the Israelites from oppression by the Midianites.[4]

'He was an idealist and a fanatic,' recalled Wilfred Thesiger, who served under Orde Wingate in Gideon Force. 'He needed a cause with which he could identify himself but his intolerance and arrogance required him to be in command. He should have lived in the time of the Crusades. I can picture him in that brutal age, fighting with a mad gleam in his eye to liberate the Holy City, but equally determined, when it fell, to be crowned King of Jerusalem.'[5]

Shortly after his arrival in Khartoum, Wingate met Haile Selassie for the first time. The major bowed to the emperor and read out a prepared statement: 'I bring you most respectful greetings, Sire. In 1935 fifty-two nations let you and your country down. That act of aggression led to this war. It shall be the first to be avenged. I come as adviser to you and the forces that will take you back to your country and your throne. We offer you freedom and an equal place among the nations. But it will be no sort of place if you have no share in your own liberation. You will take the leading part in what is to come.'[6]

Wingate's tone was an unfamiliar one to the emperor, who was becoming increasingly frustrated at the continuing lack of action and his dismissive treatment at the hands of British officialdom in the Sudan. He may well have harboured quite justified doubts as to whether Wingate really was speaking for his superiors. But the gung-ho, Zionist British major and the Ethiopian emperor hit it off right from the start. In Haile Selassie – the Lion of Judah, who could cite King Solomon and the Queen of Sheba in his lineage – Wingate had found his true lodestar, and from this moment on, he was determined to do everything in his power to restore the emperor to his throne.

Thesiger described his first encounter with Orde Wingate in Khartoum in November 1940:

'As I came into his office, he was studying a map on the wall. He swung round, said, "I've been expecting you," and immediately launched into his plans to invade Gojjam, destroy the Italian forces stationed there, reach Addis Ababa before the South African Army from Kenya could do so, and restore Haile Selassie to his throne. While expanding his seemingly impossible plans, he strode about his office, his disproportionately large head thrust forward above his ungainly body, in his pale blue eyes, set close together in a bony, angular face, as more than a hint of fanaticism [...] Wingate took me round various offices at Headquarters. As he shambled from one to another, in his creased, ill-fitting uniform and out-of-date Wolseley helmet, carrying an alarm clock instead of wearing a watch and a fly-whisk instead of a cane, I could sense the irritation and resentment he left in his wake.'[7]

Major Wingate eagerly set to work on his mission. In a typically bold move, on 28 November 1940 he took a flight to Gojjam, to the base of Mission 101, to confer with Sandford. They agreed that Haile Selassie should set foot on Ethiopian soil as quickly as possible in order to rally behind him the disparate guerrilla movements in Ethiopia, some of which were bitterly opposed to one another, and to send out a powerful message to his people to rise up against the Italian occupation. In December, Wingate cabled the British supreme commander in the Middle East, Sir Archibald Wavell, in Cairo: 'Give me a small fighting force of first-class men, and from the core of Ethiopia I will eat into the Italian apple and turn it so rotten that it will drop into our hands.'[8] In return for his initiative, he received the full backing of the British government. On 30 December Churchill sent the following directive to his foreign minister Eden: 'I am strongly in favour of Haile Selassie entering Ethiopia. Whatever differences there may be between the various Ethiopian tribes, there can be no doubt that the return of the Emperor will be taken as a proof

Haile Selassie conferring with two leading commanders of Gideon
Force, the guerrilla unit tasked with the liberation of Ethiopia:
Brigadier Daniel Sandford (left) and Major Orde Wingate (right).

that the revolt has greatly increased, and will be linked up with
our victories in Libya.'⁹

A special department of Britain's War Office furnished Wingate
with the sum of a million pounds in Maria Theresa thalers (the
Ethiopian currency at that time), to pay for troops and military
hardware. He used these funds to buy 18,000 camels to transport
the equipment up into the Ethiopian Highlands and to hire 5,000
camel drivers. The original invasion plan devised by Colonel
Sandford – 'Plan X' – envisaged Haile Selassie re-entering Ethiopia at the head of a massed Ethiopian army. Wingate rejected
this idea. A large force under the emperor's command struck him
as too unwieldy and unfit for purpose – especially since it would
have made Haile Selassie a prominent and easy target for the

enemy. To the contrary, Gideon Force was expressly forbidden from engaging in any set-piece battles with the Italian occupiers. Instead, Wingate created a number of guerrilla units, each consisting of 200 Ethiopian fighters, a British officer and five NCOs. Wingate believed that these highly mobile detachments afforded the emperor the best chance of protection.[10] Conversely, Gideon Force's main unit would comprise two battalions; one recruited from British-Sudanese troops commanded by British officers, with the other, smaller battalion made up of Ethiopian volunteers and officers who had for the most part been prominent commanders in Haile Selassie's army before the war. In addition, the ranks of the patriots were swelled by Ethiopian refugees who had returned to the Sudan from Kenya and Somaliland, plus sundry other volunteers: British, French, Kenyans, South Africans and Australians. Many of these men lacked any military training: as one commentator unflatteringly described them, 'They were a heterogeneous band of scholars, writers, adventurers, white hunters, scamps and drunks.'[11] But Wingate managed to inspire them with the goal of liberating Ethiopia and to forge them into an effective fighting force.

News of the British incursion into Gojjam and of Haile Selassie's arrival in the Sudan soon reached the Italians. To try and weaken the Ethiopian resistance, they restored Haile Selassie's old adversary *Ras* Hailu as governor of Gojjam. Despite his collaboration with the Italians, many local leaders and a large proportion of Gojjam's inhabitants continued to regard *Ras* Hailu as the legitimate ruler of the province. A number of rebellious tribal elders promptly laid down their arms and rallied to *Ras* Hailu; nevertheless, this could do little to halt the impending Allied offensive.

The campaign began in the third week of January 1941. British troops converged on *Africa Orientale Italiana* from all sides: as a British Commonwealth army under the command of Sir Alan G. Cunningham attacked Italian Somaliland from Kenya, Major-General Sir William Platt invaded Eritrea from the Sudan with several divisions. Meanwhile, Gideon Force under Orde Wingate had already set out from Khartoum in December to advance into

Gojjam through the mountainous Belaia region. Three weeks after their departure, the imperial newspaper *Banderachin* was able to report its first piece of good news:

> 'On January 20, His Majesty the Emperor Haile Selassie I accompanied by the Crown Prince and the Duke of Harar, by the *Etshege, Ras* Kassa, *Dejazmatch* Makonnen Endalk-atchew, *Dejazmatch* Adafrisau, by his delegate to the League of Nations *Ato* Lorenzo Taezaz and by his principal secretary *Ato* Wolde-Giorgis, by the Chief of His Imperial Guard *Kengazmatch* Mokria, by the two powerful Ethiopian and English armies equipped with war material and men superior to the Italian, crossed the frontier of the Sudan and Ethiopia and entered into his own [...] Therefore we rejoice in the tender mercies of our God and of Jesus Christ and we give thanks before the Divine Throne.'[12]

The report was undoubtedly somewhat exaggerated – in fact, the two 'powerful armies' of Gideon Force consisted of no more than 1,700 soldiers[13] – but even so this was an historic moment. The crossing of the Sudanese–Ethiopian border occurred near the town of Omedla. The place had been specially chosen by Wingate, since its location in the shelter of a dried-out river bed (*wadi*) rendered it 'practically incapable of detection or interception by the enemy.'[14] Haile Selassie did not march at the head of his troops, but was transported by air to the border on 20 January, escorted by two Hawker Hurricanes of the South African Air Force. His royal personage was deemed too valuable to expose him to any unnecessary risks. The ceremony that took place in this remote, uninhabited spot was staged primarily for the press photographers and the history books. 'As he [the Emperor] crossed an imaginary line representing the border,' reported a British captain who was present, 'up went the Imperial Standard on the flagstaff and we gave the Royal Salute and Present Arms. The bugler really surpassed himself and blew the General Salute without a single mistake.'[15] *Ras* Kassa had arrived from Jerusalem, accompanied by his son Asserate Kassa, to join the invasion force. His other three sons had all been murdered on Graziani's orders during the occupation.

The route into the interior through scrubland and dense undergrowth was arduous. The lorry carrying the emperor and his British advisor Chapman-Andrews struggled to cross this harsh terrain. It was abandoned eighty miles from Belaia, and Haile Selassie continued his journey on horseback. Like some religious procession, the royal convoy made its stately way past the officers: 'First Wingate, then the Emperor (on horseback) then if you please the High Priest with his venerable beard, gallantly padding along on foot through the African bush with his black robes flapping and his prayer book in his hand.'[16] The camels, laden down with baggage and weapons, soon proved entirely unsuited to this gruelling trek through the mountains. They died in their hundreds along the way, and the animals' decomposing corpses gave off a pestilential stench. Pointing at one of these unfortunate beasts lying by the roadside, Haile Selassie is reputed to have remarked: 'He too has died for Ethiopia.'[17]

To his officers and others accompanying him, the commanding officer of Gideon Force, Major Wingate, also cut a decidedly odd figure. He didn't wash, and sported an unkempt beard that he never shaved off: 'He apparently carried no change of clothes except for a dressing gown,' reported Wilfred Thesiger. On the march to Belaia, the Reuters' war correspondent attached to the unit, Kenneth Anderson, noticed Wingate's rudimentary ablutions: All the commander did was 'to lower his trousers and cool his bottom in the occasional waterholes, from which, incidentally, others would have to drink.'[18] Had the emperor ever witnessed this ritual of Wingate's, he would no doubt have taken a stoical view. When they halted at one waterhole, Haile Selassie showed one of the British officers how to fish using a mosquito net.[19]

On 6 February 1941, the convoy reached Belaia, where the emperor met with Ethiopian patriot fighters and local tribal leaders. It immediately became apparent that he had lost none of his magnetic charisma during his five years of enforced exile from the country. People flocked from all around, shouting

'*Janhoy!*' and prostrating themselves at his feet. Notwithstanding the prophesies of doom issued by the British Sudan Service,
the authority that the returning King of Kings exerted over his
people was clearly as strong as ever.

From Belaia, Gideon Force made its way through Gojjam. On
3 April, it reached the regional capital Debre Markos, which was
under the control of *Ras* Hailu. There, the emperor received the
news that the British force in the north under General Platt had
defeated the Italians. For almost two months, Italian troops had
managed to stall the British offensive at the Eritrean town of
Keren, but finally, on 27 March, the British made the decisive
breakthrough. The first day of April saw the capture of the Eritrean capital Asmara, where the governor of Tigray, *Ras* Seyoum,
and his force of 7,000 men surrendered to British troops. *Ras*
Seyoum had also recently been reinstated as governor by the
Italians. Following their victory in the Italo-Abyssinian War, he
had been deported to Italy and interned there for a spell. Later
he lived in Addis Ababa under Italian supervision, but in an
attempt to stop the population from going over to the Allies, in
February 1941 the prince was made a *Negus* by the Italians and
recalled to Tigray. Yet his loyalty to the occupiers was always
highly questionable and clandestinely he supported the Ethiopian patriots.

Now the emperor and Major Wingate pondered what *Ras*
Hailu might do in Debre Markos. The Italian commander of the
region, Colonel Saverio Maraventano, had abandoned the city
and withdrawn his two brigades, leaving *Ras* Hailu in command
of a force of irregular troops, plus a huge stockpile of weapons
and ammunition. As well as having 6,000 heavily-armed men at
his command, he also occupied well-defended high ground just
outside the city. Haile Selassie, together with *Ras* Kassa and the
rest of Gideon Force, took up position a suitable distance away.
As the sun went down, the Ethiopian flag was hoisted over *Ras*
Hailu's encampment. Yet still he made no move to capitulate.
He was clearly enjoying keeping his old rival Tafari Makonnen
on tenterhooks. But he was also aware that he could ultimately
do little against the alliance of the emperor and the British. *Ras*

Hailu held out for two days before finally surrendering without a fight.

Haile Selassie marched into Debre Markos on 6 April, and in so doing effectively liberated the whole of Gojjam from Italian occupation. In a solemn ceremony, the crown prince was promoted to lieutenant-general, his brother Prince Makonnen to major-general and Prince Asserate Kassa – my father – to colonel. It was still far too early to celebrate outright victory, but even so Orde Wingate raised a glass to toast the emperor's health, and delivered a memorable speech:

'Myself and the British officers under my command have borne their part with the patriot Ethiopian forces in this campaign, in the knowledge that, in so doing, they were supporting that same cause for which England is fighting throughout the world. The right of the individual to liberty of conscience, the right of the small nation to a just decision at the tribunal of nations, these are the causes for which we fight. Until Ethiopia was liberated the major wrong, which brought in its train the present war, had not been righted and success for our arms could not be expected.'[20]

And indeed, the liberation of the whole of Ethiopia was close at hand. A British army under General Cunningham had taken Harar on 27 March 1941. By now, very little serious Italian opposition remained. On 6 April, the same day the emperor and Gideon Force entered Debre Markos, Cunningham and his army marched into the Ethiopian capital. When Wingate received news of this, he asked General Platt to send him an aircraft to fly Haile Selassie down to Addis Ababa. His request was turned down, with the following explanation: 'We need to restrain him a bit because there are 100,000 Ethiopians there and 40,000 Italians and we don't want a massacre or incidents as the Ethiopians will all go mad at the triumphal entry.'[21]

In actual fact, this was a specious argument; the British military evidently wanted to buy time in order to effect certain *faits accomplis* in Ethiopia. Anticipating the impending collapse

of *Africa Orientale Italiana*, the British formed an organization known as the Occupied Enemy Territory Administration
(OETA), which encompassed not only the former Italian colonies of Eritrea and Somaliland but also Ethiopia. In addition, the
Ethiopian province of Tigray was summarily declared to be part
of Eritrea. These high-handed decisions by the British leadership
must have profoundly alarmed the emperor. The classification of
his country as 'enemy territory' suggested that Great Britain was
unwilling to recognize the sovereignty of the Ethiopian Empire.
Furthermore, the incorporation of Tigray into Eritrea indicated
that the British were also questioning the territorial integrity of
Ethiopia.[22]

The British generals detained Haile Selassie in Debre Markos
for almost two weeks. On 22 April, Wingate received a telegram from General Cunningham, ordering him to prevent the
emperor from leaving for Addis Ababa 'by all means short of
force.' But Haile Selassie refused to wait any longer, and neither
Wingate nor Sandford were minded to stop him.[23] And so, on the
morning of 27 April 1941, the emperor and his escorts, including *Ras* Kassa and the prisoner *Ras* Hailu, set off from Debre
Markos in two lorries. The Imperial Bodyguard and the two
battalions of Gideon Force had already begun their march to
the capital. The column stopped off at Fiche, *Ras* Kassa's home,
and the emperor and *Ras* Kassa took the opportunity to pray
for the souls of the three murdered sons of the governor of Shoa,
who had been killed in cold blood by the Italians in 1937. In the
nearby half-destroyed monastery of Debre Libanos, a requiem
mass was held for the monks and deacons who had been slaughtered there during the Graziani Massacre.

On 4 May the emperor reached the Entoto Heights overlook-
ing the Ethiopian capital. He was received by the leader of the
Patriot resistance fighters in Shoa, *Ras* Abebe Aregay, who had
pitched camp there with 15,000 of his followers. Haile Selassie took a pair of field glasses and surveyed Addis Ababa. The
unmistakable scent of eucalyptus, which covered the hill surrounding the city, hung in the air. The odyssey of exile was at an
end. A total of eighteen men from Gideon Force had been killed

Ras Abebe Aregay, commander of patriot
forces in Shoa during the liberation.

in the course of the campaign. And of the 18,000 camels that had set out from Khartoum in January, just 53 reached their final destination. These doughty survivors met an undeserved fate, shot by British officers outside the gates of the city because no fodder could be found for them. 'We were simply horrified to watch this incredible cruelty,' wrote Haile Selassie in his autobiography.[24]

Five years to the day after the Italian commander Marshal Badoglio had seized the city, on the morning of 5 May 1941, Haile Selassie returned to Addis Ababa. All the way down from the Heights of Entoto to the city centre, to mark his triumphal return, the streets had been strewn with flowers and decked out with flags and bunting in the Ethiopian national colours. *Ras* Abebe's patriots, in full warriors' regalia, formed a guard of honour along the route and were joined by tens of thousands of men, women and children, cheering and waving the imperial standard. 'When We saw the abject condition of Our people and witnessed their affection for Us, We could not control Our tears and deep emotion,' admitted Haile Selassie.[25] The parade was led by the tanks of the South African division. After them, riding on a white horse, came Major Wingate, while behind him marched the Imperial Bodyguard and Gideon Force's two battalions. Then came the emperor in an open-topped car, escorted by a phalanx of cavalry officers. Bringing up the rear were the Ethiopian and Somalian troops. At the Menelik Palace, the homecoming Lion of Judah was met by General Cunningham and an honour guard of Nigerian soldiers. Haile Selassie hoisted the Ethiopian flag, and a 21-gun salute reverberated around the capital. Then he mounted the podium to address the nation. In his speech, the emperor proclaimed a 'new era in the history of Ethiopia' and called for calm: 'Do not return evil for evil. Do not indulge in the atrocities which the enemy has been practicing in his usual way, even to the last. Take care not to spoil the good name of Ethiopia by acts which are worthy of the enemy. We shall see that our enemies are disarmed and sent out the same way they came.'[26]

The emperor's words struck a chord with his subjects. The revenge attacks on Italian nationals that the British generals had so feared never happened – not on that triumphal day nor in the weeks that followed. On 23 May a combined army of *Ras* Kassa's troops and Gideon Force accepted the surrender of an 8,000-strong army under Colonel Maraventano.[27] Those taken prisoner in this engagement were taken to Fiche, where the emperor planned to stage a parade of captured troops. Wilfred Thesiger was sent to Maraventano to inform him of this. 'But that is uncivilized,' the Colonel protested, 'It is barbarous to humiliate prisoners in this way.' Thesiger could barely contain his fury:

'Don't dare to speak to me about barbarous treatment of prisoners. You Italians shot *Ras* Desta, the Emperor's son-in-law, who commanded the armies in the south, after he had surrendered to Marshal Graziani. You Italians shot *Ras* Kassa's sons after they had surrendered to you. You shot four hundred priests near here in the monastery of Debre Libanos. Your blackshirts massacred ten thousand men, women and children in Addis Ababa after you took the town. Now you have the effrontery to stand there and talk about barbarous treatment of prisoners [...] Tomorrow at ten o'clock you will march past the Emperor or be driven past him by *Ras* Kassa's men. I don't care which.'[28]

In his memoir, Thesiger goes on to describe the march-past the following day:

'The Emperor sat in an open-sided tent with his son Asfa Wossen, Chapman-Andrews and a few retainers. The presence of this small, indomitable man endowed the proceedings with a strange dignity and significance. For him, as ruler of a warrior race, the parade may well have been a necessary manifestation of victory, but no hint of triumph showed on his face; he watched in silence, his expression sombre and rather sad. *Ras* Kassa, old and heavy, sat his mule between Johnson and myself, and watched with an impassive face the parade of the men who had murdered his sons. Nor did the assembled crowds, women as well as men, give vent to their feelings, though the relatives of many had died at Italian hands.'[29]

The parade of the victorious Ethiopian forces was led by *Ras* Kassa's only surviving son, Colonel Asserate Kassa.[30] What must have been going through the Premier Prince's mind on that momentous day?

On the day the emperor returned to his capital, by way of salutation the BBC in London broadcast the Ethiopian National Anthem. However, the victory celebrations could only hope to paper over for a few hours the serious rifts that existed between the emperor and the British military administration in Ethiopia. That same evening, Haile Selassie moved back into the *Genete-Leul* Palace and set up his court there. General Cunningham, meanwhile, had established his office in the nearby Menelik Palace. He invited the emperor over to meet him in his new HQ, but Haile Selassie had no intention of paying court to the British general in such a manner, which would have amounted to a de facto acknowledgment of Cunningham's superior rank. Eventually, the emperor managed to persuade the general to come to the *Genete-Leul* Palace by the adroit stratagem of promising to honour his military services with a decoration.[31] Back in London, official opinions on how to proceed with Ethiopia continued to differ. On 4 February 1941, in the House of Commons, Foreign Secretary Anthony Eden had affirmed Ethiopia's independence: 'His Majesty's Government would welcome the reappearance of an independent Ethiopian State and recognize the claim of the Emperor Haile Selassie to the throne.'[32] Eden was also at pains to stress that Great Britain had no territorial ambitions of its own in Ethiopia. This stance also clearly reflected Churchill's attitude. 'The Emperor,' Eden continued, 'has intimated to His Majesty's Government that he will need outside assistance and guidance. His Majesty's Government agree with this view and consider that any such assistance and guidance in economic and political matters should be the subject of international agreement at the conclusion of the peace. [...] In the meanwhile the conduct of military operations by Imperial forces in parts of Abyssinia will require temporary measures of military guidance and control. These will be carried out in consultation with the Emperor and will be brought to an end as soon as the situation permits.'[33]

For all their ostensible clarity, though, these explanations left plenty of room for interpretation. Just a few weeks before Eden's speech in the House, a memorandum had been circulated in the Foreign Office, in which it was stated: 'It is difficult to believe that the restoration of the former Ethiopian Empire as an independent state is a practicable political aim. That Empire survived as long as it did, only because the three Great Powers bordering on it – Great Britain, France and Italy – were unable to agree on its control. A solution might be to aim at the restoration of the ex-Emperor as the ruler of a native African state under European protection.'[34] The War Office took a very similar view of matters. This stance, as opposed to the Foreign Secretary's line, was evidently also the approach favoured by the British generals and officials in Addis Ababa.

It is worth speculating at this point about the relationship between Haile Selassie and Anthony Eden, Earl of Avon. One curious fact to emerge from my research is the lack of any Ethiopian decoration given to this former British foreign secretary (and later prime minister), who championed the cause of Ethiopia when it came under mortal threat from Italian fascism. I met Eden on two occasions. The first was in 1971.[35] While still a student at Cambridge University, I was asked by the Anglo-Ethiopian Society to propose the toast of its President at the annual dinner on 7 May.[36] At this meeting, I spoke about the great gratitude Ethiopia owed Lord Avon for his stand as foreign secretary during the Italian–Ethiopian crisis in 1936. After dinner, while we were having coffee, he thanked me for the kind words I had expressed and added: 'I wonder whether your great kinsman would agree with all you said?' His remark hinted strongly at some unresolved tension between the two men. Was it perhaps the case that the emperor blamed Eden for not asserting his more liberal stance against British colonialist 'hawks' in the postwar settlement for Ethiopia? Two pieces of circumstantial evidence seem to bear out this surmise. In 1965, the country's highest order, the Grand Cross of the Order of the Seal of Solomon, was conferred upon the Queen's cousin Lord Louis Mountbatten, a man with a highly distinguished service record but who had had nothing to do with the liberation of Ethiopia in 1941. No such honour was forthcoming for Eden. In an even more pointed snub, in the following year Eden was not invited to attend the 25th anniversary of the liberation of Ethiopia by British and Ethiopian forces.

The man appointed to head the OETA, the authority charged with administering 'occupied enemy territory' in East Africa, was Sir Philip Mitchell, a veteran British general, who had fulfilled a similar remit in the former German East Africa (Tanganyika Territory) after the First World War. From 1935 to 1940, he had been governor of the British colony of Uganda. It was hardly to be expected that Mitchell, an ardent champion of the British Empire, would suddenly throw his weight behind the cause of Ethiopian independence. Mitchell's second-in-command, or 'Deputy Chief Political Officer,' was Brigadier Maurice Stanley

Lush, a former provincial governor in British Somaliland. Haile Selassie gives an uncharacteristically frank assessment of this colonial officer in his autobiography: 'Among the British military officers in Ethiopia, there was a person called Brigadier Lush, who led a political group which had sinister intentions toward Our country. They spoke publicly that the purpose of their coming was to rule Ethiopia.'[37]

Brigadier Lush discharged his duties in Addis Ababa no differently to his counterparts in the British-occupied former Italian colonies of Eritrea and Italian Somaliland. Not infrequently, the stress he laid on his own superiority had unashamedly racist undertones. One particularly telling anecdote did the rounds at this time in Eritrea and beyond: During the advance by Ethiopian troops from Keren to Asmara, a British commander is said to have come across an old Eritrean woman, shrouded in the characteristic white robes of the Highlands. On seeing him, she launched into a traditional ululation in greeting, to signal her joy at her country's liberation from Italian Fascism. The British officer allegedly stopped her in mid-flow with the deeply offensive remark: 'I didn't do it for you, nigger,' before proceeding on his way to Asmara. News of this thoroughly unpleasant episode spread like wildfire and is still recalled even today – as a typical example of the colonialist attitude of the British 'liberators' of the Horn of Africa.[38]

The first clash between the emperor and Brigadier Lush came just a week after the former's triumphal return. Without consulting the British authorities, the emperor appointed a cabinet of seven ministers. The reaction was not long in coming. Brigadier Lush informed the emperor that he had no authorization to do such a thing, and added: 'His Majesty Haile Selassie cannot fully reassume his status and powers until a peace treaty with Eritrea has been signed by Italy. Until that happens, the King of Italy must remain the legal ruler of Ethiopia.'[39] If he had not been so before, from that point on, the brigadier was definitely *persona non grata* in the emperor's eyes.[40]

Haile Selassie had not the slightest intention of recalling his cabinet, yet he was still obliged to face facts. The emperor and the Ethiopian authorities were directed by Sir Philip '... to agree to abide in all important matters, internal and external, touching the government of the country, by the advice tendered to them by His Majesty's Government in the United Kingdom.'[41] Every step the emperor took and every decision made by his cabinet was carefully monitored. All official communiqués were under British control, as were all channels of communication and the police. The British military administration reserved the right to enact martial law across the whole of Ethiopia should the need arise. In addition, the emperor was forbidden from engaging in any military operations without British approval. In return, the imperial government was granted financial assistance and consultation by Great Britain.

The Anglo-Ethiopian Agreement, which was ratified on 31 January 1942 in Addis Ababa, along with the military convention signed at the same time, clearly reflect this imbalance of power. In many respects, the Agreement bore all the hallmarks of a protectorate arrangement over Ethiopia. For although Great Britain formally recognized Ethiopia as a 'free and independent state', the treaty still enshrined comprehensive control by Britain of all aspects of public life. The emperor was only permitted to consult external policy advisors if they were British, while the appointment of advisors of other nationalities was only possible with the express approval of the British government. The British ambassador in Addis Ababa enjoyed special status, and British approval was likewise required for the opening of any other countries' legations. British representatives occupied the key positions in the Ethiopian civil service and judiciary. The radio and telegraph stations, the telephone exchanges and the railways remained firmly under British control, and Britain was granted a monopoly over commercial air transport in the country. The British military authorities had the right to commandeer any facilities or sites formerly belonging to the Italian state – and this had in fact become common practice since General Cunningham's arrival in Addis Ababa. Any declaration of war required the consent of the commander-in-chief of British forces in East Africa. All Ethiopian imports and exports were strictly controlled. The currency used in British colonies in East Africa, the East African shilling, was introduced as the official currency of Ethiopia. And finally, following the British model, driving on the left was introduced on Ethiopia's roads.[42] In recompense for all this, the emperor received financial support from Britain to the tune of £1.5 million in the first year after the agreement came into force, followed by £1 million in the second year.

The agreement was due to run for a term of at least two years, but from the very moment of signing Haile Selassie started paving the way to eventually free himself from Great Britain's grip. For the present, though, he was dependent upon financial subvention from London and upon military support. In the autumn of 1943, the so-called 'Woyane Rebellion' in Tigray was put down with the aid of British troops. Over the course of the preceding summer, rebellious peasants had seized control of almost all of Tigray province. Only after a series of RAF bombing raids was the Ethiopian army finally able to crush the uprising in October.[43] But in the medium term, Haile Selassie's primary aim was to restore the full and absolute sovereignty of Ethiopia. As so often in his life, the Ethiopian emperor displayed extraordinary single-mindedness, perseverance and diplomatic skill in this matter. In the years that followed, this policy was to result in Ethiopia gradually turning away from Great Britain and toward the United States of America. This development saw the 'British Decade' of the 1940s in Ethiopia superseded by the 'American Era' of the 1950s and 1960s.[44]

As early as the 1920s, Haile Selassie had attempted, albeit without resounding success, to prompt the USA into a more active engagement in Ethiopia, as a counterweight to the European colonial powers. Now, with America's re-entry into global politics and the impending conclusion of the war, the time seemed ripe to rekindle this interest. Just a few weeks after the British took Ethiopia from the Italians, the United States had reached the conclusion that Great Britain was about to 'establish a protectorate over Ethiopia'.[45] Washington viewed London's colonial ambitions in East Africa with growing unease. Ethiopia was the first country in the Second World War to be freed from the clutches of the Axis powers; its fate should serve as an example to all the other countries that were still occupied by Nazi Germany and its allies.

One particularly painful aspect of the Anglo-Ethiopian Agreement for Ethiopia was the fact that Great Britain claimed control over both the former Italian colony of Eritrea and the Ogaden in the southeast of Ethiopia. The Ogaden had been an integral part of the Ethiopian Empire right up to the Italian invasion in 1936. But Eritrea, too, had for a long time belonged to Ethiopia. Prior to 1890, when it became an Italian colony, it had been the northernmost province of the empire. Twice, in 1896 and 1935, Italian-controlled Eritrea had acted as a jumping-off point for wars of aggression against Ethiopia. Therefore, not merely historic reasons, but also concrete security and political considerations argued in favour of supporting the Ethiopian claim on Eritrea. Economic factors also played a part: under Italian colonial rule, Eritrea's infrastructure and industrial base had also grown considerably. And last but not least, Eritrea offered Ethiopia the access to the sea that it had long sought.

An incident which illustrates both the decline in relations with Great Britain and the shrewdness of Haile Selassie's diplomacy was revealed to me in a conversation I had in March 2015 with a friend, Stephen Bell, whose father Ian had served for several years from the late 1940s onwards at the British embassy in Addis Ababa. In the early 1950s resentment began to grow in Ethiopia not only at Britain's continuing direct administration of the Ogaden but also its control over the country's military and police forces and, in the economic sphere, over the management of currency and banking. On one occasion, matters came to a head over the British military mission, based at the former cadet school at Holleta a few miles outside the capital. Developing from its principal training role, in the eyes of Ethiopia's senior military ranks and most likely of the emperor himself it had come to be seen as exercising an undue and overweening control over Ethiopia's own army, another instance of British high-handedness. Through a spy who was a frequent visitor to Haile Selassie's court, the British came to learn that the emperor was seriously considering – unilaterally and without forewarning

– expelling the military mission from the country altogether. The Foreign Office was determined to preempt this humiliation, instructing the Chargé d'Affaires in Addis to tell the emperor that the British government had recently been reviewing the scope and scale of its commitments in Ethiopia and that, with the country's own army now appearing to have organisationally developed into a position of sufficient self-reliance, it would seem that the British military mission had outlived its usefulness and that, unless the emperor felt strongly otherwise, it should be withdrawn. At the audience with the emperor at the Little *Gebbi* palace, conducted as was customary through an interpreter in Amharic and French, Haile Selassie professed great sadness at the news of the British government's proposal. The military mission had been of enormous value to his country and to the development of its own armed forces, and it would surely continue to do so were it to remain. This however was a decision for the British government and, notwithstanding his own regrets, the British must of course decide how to allocate their own resources. He wished further to record his warmest thanks for their help in the past and up to the present. The military mission was withdrawn soon after. Henceforth, Haile Selassie was to look elsewhere than Britain, and principally to the United States, for the development and progress of Ethiopia's military forces. As it turned out, the emperor had been aware all along that his supposed confidant was a British spy and that he had engineered the situation to achieve the end he desired without having to embark upon unilateral action himself.

Haile Selassie had reasonable grounds for hoping that, in the United States, he would also find an ally to support his territorial claims. In February 1941 Congress had passed the 'Lend-Lease Act', an arrangement by which the United States placed arms and other war supplies at the disposal of Allied countries fighting the Axis powers. Ethiopia and Eritrea were also to be included. By August 1942, following America's entry in the war in December 1941, 3,000 US soldiers and civilian personnel were already stationed in Ethiopia, and an American consulate had been opened in Asmara. The geostrategic importance of the

Horn of Africa for the Middle East made the region of interest to the USA as well. In the Eritrean capital, America was involved in the takeover of the former Italian radio station 'Radio Marina', and in 1943 acquired this news broadcast outlet from the British. Washington pressed for the reopening of the US Embassy in Addis Ababa, which duly came to pass in 1942. The USA also increasingly found reasons to take an economic interest in the region. The monopoly that the British claimed over all commercial air traffic in Ethiopia was a thorn in the side of the United States, which had plans to expand Pan American Airways flights in the Middle East.[46] In 1943 the Red Sea was opened to American merchant shipping and before long US trade in the Middle East had outstripped British exports by some margin.

In a letter to US President Franklin Roosevelt at the end of 1942, Haile Selassie assured the USA of Ethiopia's full support in the Allied war effort against the Axis. Roosevelt's reply was unequivocally cordial: 'It is a source of much satisfaction to me and to the people of the United States that your country, which fought so courageously against a ruthless enemy, has regained its independence and self-government. The steadfast friendship of the American people and their sympathy with you in your period of trial will continue to be manifested during the days of reconstruction now facing your country.'[47]

The American citizen John H. Spencer, who had already worked as an advisor to Haile Selassie in 1935–36, seemed to the emperor the ideal person to help foster closer ties with the United States. Ethiopia sent a delegation under the chairmanship of acting finance minister Yilma Deressa to the United Nations Conference on Food and Agriculture held at Hot Springs, Virginia in May 1943. This event provided a welcome basis for the beginning of discussions with representatives of the State Department. The negotiation of a new bilateral accord touched both upon the question of military and political assistance and on financial support for the creation of a new currency. Ever since the introduction of the East African shilling into Ethiopia, this new currency had been in free-fall, as it had gained little acceptance in the country. The Ethiopian people continued to place their trust in the Maria Theresa thaler, which as a result kept on being revalued. And so, behind the scenes, the imperial government made preparations for the introduction of a proper national currency. To this end, Yilma Deressa asked the United States for a loan in the form of one and a half million ounces of silver for the minting of new coinage: the new Ethiopian dollar, or *Birr*, was intended as a replacement for both the Maria Theresa thaler and the East African shilling.[48]

Yilma's mission was an unqualified success. In August 1943, the USA and Ethiopia signed a 'Mutual Aid Agreement', which, in the words of Roosevelt, provided Ethiopia with 'goods, services and information, so that we might be in a position to contribute to the defense of Ethiopia and, with the aid of other potential measures, be able to offer practical help to rebuild your country.'[49] Washinton granted Ethiopia the desired loan of silver bullion. But above and beyond that, the United States signalled its readiness to support Ethiopia in its attempts to regain Eritrea. A US State Department memorandum at the time states: 'We take the view that there might well be a particularly strong case for supporting the Ethiopian conviction that Eritrea, or at least a part of it, should be incorporated into Ethiopia.'[50]

The Mutual Aid Agreement represented 'a watershed in Ethiopian diplomatic, social, and economic history.'[51] An American government delegation visited Ethiopia in May 1944 to discuss further economic assistance. Before the Fellows Mission, named after its leader Perry Fellows, left the country, the emperor sent London a note terminating the Anglo-Ethiopian Agreement, combined with a wish to enter into negotiations over a new treaty with Britain. The notice period for termination was three months, but no response was forthcoming from the British government until just before the existing agreement was due to expire on 25 August 1944. On 18 August, the emperor forwarded a communication to the British embassy with an indication of the expectations that Ethiopia attached to the termination of the agreement. These included the immediate return of the Ogaden and Ethiopian control of the railway network. An instant reply was now received from London, and after a certain amount of

After liberation, the Emperor hoisted the Ethiopian flag once
more at the Menelik Palace in Addis Ababa, 5 May 1941.

to-ing and fro-ing over the conditions for a temporary suspen-
sion of the notice of termination, negotiations on a successor
agreement commenced on 26 September in Addis Ababa. The
Ethiopian delegation at these talks was led by the Ethiopian
prime minister *Ras-Bitwadad* Makonnen Endalkatchew; his
opposite number on the British side was Lord de la Warr. On
several occasions, the talks threatened to break down; secretly,
the Ethiopians kept both the American and the Soviet ambassadors informed on the proceedings.[52]

At the conclusion of the negotiations, an accord emerged, in
which most of the restrictions on Ethiopian sovereignty present

in the earlier agreement had been lifted; henceforth, the British ambassador in Addis Ababa was not granted special status. The Ethiopian minister of war would now assume leadership of the British Military Mission in Ethiopia (BMME). And although the Ogaden and other areas included in the umbrella term 'Reserved Area' were still to remain under British control – in order, it was claimed, to allow the war to be prosecuted more effectively – the end of the global conflict was now in sight. The new treaty between Ethiopia and Great Britain was ratified on 19 December 1944 in Addis Ababa. Anyone versed in diplomatic protocol could see that this signalled a downgrading of Ethiopia's relations with Great Britain.

On 13 February 1945 Haile Selassie met with Franklin D. Roosevelt for the first time. The American president invited the emperor to join him on a flying visit to Egypt aboard the heavy cruiser USS *Quincy*, which was patrolling the Great Bitter Lake section of the Suez Canal. The emperor and his entourage – which included *Ras* Kassa, his confessor *Abba* Hanna, the 'Minister of the Pen' Wolde-Giorgis, Foreign Minister Aklilu Habte-Wold, Finance Minister Yilma and John Spencer as foreign policy advisor – were picked up at five o'clock in the morning in Addis Ababa by a Douglas DC-3 Dakota of the US Air Force. The imperial government had not seen fit to inform the British embassy of the upcoming summit, nor had anything about it been leaked by Washington to the British government. According to Spencer's memoirs, the first thing British ambassador Robert Howe knew about it was when he was rudely roused from his sleep by the noise of the American aircraft as it took off: 'He heard the sound of a take-off at this unusual hour, jumped out of bed, and upon learning what had happened, frantically sought a plane to rush him to Cairo. He had, in the end, to settle for a tiny biplane out of Aden which could make only short hops over the 1,400 miles of desert to Cairo.'[53]

In preparation for the summit, the emperor had drawn up a memorandum comprising six points: first and foremost Haile Selassie continued to urge the USA to support him in his demand for the return of Eritrea. But the Ogaden question, the railway line to Djibouti and requests for further financial and military aid were also on the agenda. In addition, the emperor expressed a wish to take part in the drafting of the charter of the United Nations, which was to replace the League of Nations, and also to participate in the great peace conference that would take place at the end of the war. All these points were only briefly touched upon during the 90-minute discussion between the leaders. But the atmosphere between these two heads of state was exceedingly cordial, not least thanks to the presents that they exchanged. The emperor surprised the president with a special gift manu-factured by the palace jeweller, a four-inch diameter globe made of a shimmering, reddish 24-carat gold. Alongside the outlines of the continents, the site of their summit on the Suez Canal was also engraved upon it. 'I was quite surprised at the seem-ingly genuine enthusiastic response which Roosevelt reserved for this token of friendship,' reported Spencer, 'If it was not what he might have expected, or was what he did not particularly desire, he masterfully concealed his true feelings.'[54] In return, Roosevelt gave the emperor four military jeeps.

When Haile Selassie arrived in Cairo after the meeting, he was informed that Churchill wanted to meet him. When the British premier had learned from his ambassador about the emperor's summit with Roosevelt, he had immediately flown over to Egypt from Africa to pay his respects to Haile Selassie. A meeting in the British Embassy in Cairo was quickly arranged – this was in fact the first ever occasion on which the two leaders had come face-to-face. But in the event, the encounter was brief and chilly. When a member of Churchill's staff asked the emperor what points he wished to discuss with the prime minister, he replied: 'None.' And during the meeting, when the emperor broached the ques-tion of the return of the Ogaden, Churchill is said to have beck-oned over one of his advisors and asked him: 'What and where is the Ogaden?'[55] To conclude, after learning about the four jeeps, the British PM presented the emperor with a Rolls-Royce. But Roosevelt proceeded to nonchalantly overtrump even this gift; shortly after the emperor returned to Addis Ababa, there arrived from America a Cadillac stretched limousine with three rows of bench seats and a magnificently appointed interior: between the second and third rows was a glass partition, framed in rosewood. In the panel beneath were the initials H.I.M. ('His Imperial Majesty'), inlaid in fine marquetry. This was the very car in which, as a boy, I was often taken on drives around Addis Ababa with the emperor in the 1950s.

Barely two months after Haile Selassie's meeting with Roosevelt, the American president, who had been ailing for some time, died; yet the foundations of cooperation had been successfully laid, which Roosevelt's successor Harry S. Truman could build upon. There was a sea-change in British politics at this time, too. At the General Election in July 1945, Churchill suffered a surprise defeat, and for the new Labour administration under Clement Attlee, plans for a 'Greater Somalia' under British control were not high on the agenda. The vacuum that was left by Great Britain's gradual retreat from empire in the postwar world was readily filled by the United States. Many of Ethiopia's economic development plans, which had proved so arduous and tough to implement in collaboration with British colonial officers, were now realized with US help.[56] As early as 1945, the Ethiopian government signed an agreement with the American airline Transcontinental and Western Air (TWA) to develop a national carrier, Ethiopian Air Lines. Intensive cooperation also ensued in the realm of transport infrastructure. A host of new roads had been built during the Italian occupation, but many of them were destroyed in the liberation struggle. The Imperial Highway Authority (IHA), founded in 1951 under American leadership, made improvement of the transport network its chief priority. The necessary loans for this work were provided by the American International Bank of Reconstruction and Development. A deal was struck with the US firm International Telephone and Telegraph (ITT) to restore the country's wrecked telecommunications infrastructure. The United States also provided crucial support in creating the Ethiopian National Bank and in developing education. But it was in the realm of military aid that the USA soon proved an indispensable partner. From 1950 onwards, as part of an extensive programme of military assistance, a large number of US Army instructors arrived in Ethiopia to train the country's army. The various aid programmes finally culminated in 1952 in the so-called 'Point-Four Agreement,' which on the basis of the Point Four Program instigated by President Truman provided for large-scale aid in the areas of agriculture, healthcare, administration and education.

Immediately after he returned from Cairo, Haile Selassie also pressed ahead with the creation of a well-functioning governmental and bureaucratic apparatus. In this, the loss of the upper echelon of the Ethiopian population, who had gone abroad to complete their education in the 1920s and 1930s and who had been systematically eradicated by the Italian occupying power, was keenly felt.[57] As a result, in his reconstruction efforts, the emperor found it virtually impossible to avoid having recourse to those who had served the Italians during the occupation and who were seen as collaborators by the patriots of the resistance movement. Even so, the majority of those in the emperor's innermost circle after the liberation were part of the group that had gone into exile with him in 1936. These included, for example, *Ras-Bitwadad* Makonnen Endalkatchew, one of the seven ministers appointed by Haile Selassie in May 1941; after serving as interior minister, Endalkatchew occupied the post of prime minister from 1943 to 1957. This nobleman from Shoa was a steadfast and long-standing confidant of the emperor. When the Italo-Abyssinian war broke out, he commanded the forces in the Ogaden before going into exile in Jerusalem. In 1941, he was involved alongside the emperor and Gideon Force in the hard-fought campaign that began in the Sudan and ended in the liberation of Addis Ababa. Yet despite his elevated position as prime minister, Endalkatchew was never a decisive man of action or a person who made the political weather – in any event, the final word always lay with the emperor.

Post-liberation, for a period of fifteen years, the leading figure in Ethiopian politics was Wolde-Giorgis Wolde-Yohannes, who as Minister of the Pen was endowed with the traditional title *Tsehafe-Tezaz* (Chancellor). He occupied this influential post until 1955 in addition to serving terms as foreign minister and minister of justice. The son of a saddler, he had worked his way up in the Ethiopian capital despite having a somewhat basic education. Before joining the royal household, he had worked as a translator and clerk at the Menelik Hospital. As Haile Selassie's long-serving private secretary, he had shared the emperor's dark days of exile in Bath, and had also been with him on Gideon Force's campaign to retake Ethiopia. *Tsehafe-Tezaz* Wolde-Giorgis was one of the antifeudally-minded *homines novi*, whom the country's old aristocracy looked upon with suspicion.[58]

Other members of this 'progressist' group were the brothers Aklilu Habte-Wold and Makonnen Habte-Wold, who after the war rose to become key confidants of the emperor. They came from a poor family with a clerical background; their father had been a priest at the Church of Saint Raguel (*Qedus Rague'el*) in Addis Ababa. The whole family had spent the period of exile together in Paris, where Makonnen kept his head above water by running a restaurant, which became a favourite haunt of expatriate Ethiopians and other East Africans in the French capital. Aklilu was even more of a Francophile than his brother. He had studied at the Sorbonne and married a French woman in 1941. When the Germans overran Paris, he fled to Lisbon with the help of a forged passport. Back in Addis Ababa after the liberation, he could often be found sitting reading French magazines like *Paris Match*. 'Aklilu was the product of Western civilization with the French touch. He was married to a French lady and lived like a Frenchman rather than an Ethiopian,' Seyoum Haregot, later to become a minister, wrote of him. 'He was suave, debonair, affable, and urbane, and immediately put people at ease. He was a man of extreme patience, who never lost his temper [...] His patience was so extreme that it could make his colleagues impatient, but completely disarmed opponents.'[59]

Aklilu's main field of engagement in the new Ethiopia was foreign policy, and from 1943 on he occupied the post of foreign minister for fifteen years. In 1945, he headed the Ethiopian delegation to the United Nations Conference in San Francisco, at which the UN Charter was drawn up; the following year, he represented his country's interests at the Paris Peace Conference, where peace terms were also determined for the defeated Fascist Italy. In 1961, Aklilu finally took up the post of prime minister and was also granted the title of *Tsehafe-Tezaz*. He was to occupy this position until 1 March 1974, and so can be seen as one of the most important and influential political figures to serve in the postwar Empire, right up to its demise. His brother Makonnen also served Ethiopia in a number of prominent ministerial roles – including industry and agriculture, finance and trade – before being murdered by putschists in the notorious Palace Revolt of 1960. 'A man of frugal tastes and ascetic disposition,' the historian Bahru Zewde wrote about Makonnen, 'also known for his hard work and his generosity to those in need.'[60]

While the exiles gained influence in top positions after the war, Haile Selassie used the opportunity to curtail the preeminence of the nobility within Ethiopia. A boundary reform saw the country's provinces concentrated into thirteen administrative units. This deliberate act of centralization failed to provoke any significant resistance on the part of the regional princes. However, the decisive step toward consolidating the emperor's power came with the formation of the country's first national army, supplanting the patchwork of princely armies. The private forces that still existed were disbanded, and the princes were henceforth strictly forbidden from raising their own armies. This moment can be said to mark the beginning of Haile Selassie's absolute power: from then on, there were no more *Rases* for the emperor to take into consideration. Nor did he need to fear any longer that a powerful prince might march on the palace in Addis Ababa with tens of thousands of his warriors – a not uncommon occurrence in the past.

Yet the emperor did not want to forego the political contribution of *Ras* Kassa, who continued to be the most influential among the Ethiopian princes. After the campaign against Colonel Maraventano, *Ras* Kassa had told Haile Selassie that he was planning to spend the rest of his days in retirement on his estate in Fiche and would henceforth avoid the capital as far as possible. The emperor told his cousin that he couldn't do without his constant advice and urged him to reconsider his decision. When it became apparent that the *Ras* really meant it, the emperor sent the Ethiopian archbishop, *Abuna* Basileos, together with a bishop and a prominent nobleman, *Dejazmatch* Amde, to Fiche with the following message for *Ras* Kassa: 'If you do not wish to assume an active role in the government, then I must accept your decision, albeit with great reluctance. But you simply cannot leave me in the lurch, now that I need your advice at court more than ever.' After several days, the Premier Prince finally bowed to the emperor's will. He returned to Addis Ababa, and was appointed as the first president of the Imperial Crown Council.[61] And over the following fifteen years, until *Ras* Kassa's death, there wasn't a single important decision of the emperor's in which the prince was not involved, though this generally occurred behind the scenes. The weekly audience with *Ras* Kassa was a fixed point in the monarch's schedule. Every week without fail – unless the emperor was abroad on state visits – *Ras* Kassa would come to the palace at 4 o'clock on Friday afternoon to discuss the political situation with his cousin.

Alongside the traditional aristocratic class, during the years of struggle against the Italian occupying force, a new influential political grouping had also arisen; the 'Patriots'. Many of them had been bitterly opposed to the emperor's decision to go into exile while they were risking their lives fighting the Italians in their homeland. Many of the Patriot leaders had commanded their own detachments and grown accustomed to taking independent decisions. The fact that the emperor was now preparing to make common cause with collaborators made most of them profoundly distrustful. They felt themselves unfairly treated and insufficiently rewarded for their sacrifices for their country. The most prominent of the Patriot leaders was *Ras* Abebe Aregay, the head of the resistance in Shoa province, who had received the emperor on his return to Addis Ababa. He was one of the few whom Haile Selassie entrusted with a leadership position after the war: *Ras* Abebe was made mayor of Addis Ababa, and soon after appointed to the post of war minister. It was he who led the Ethiopian army in their suppression of the Woyane Rebellion in Tigray in September–October 1943. Later, he became governor of Tigray and also held the portfolios of internal affairs and defence. He was another of those who were murdered during the 1960 palace coup.

Not all the Patriots proved as loyal to the emperor as *Ras* Abebe. The first of them to organize an uprising was *Fitaurari* Belay Zeleke, one of the most charismatic of the freedom fighters. He had made a successful stand against the Italians in Gojjam and Wollo and attracted a growing number of supporters. Magnanimously, and quite without authority, he bestowed titles on them, such as *Dejazmatch*, *Fitaurari* and *Ras*. When his brother, *Dejazmatch* Eggugu, asked him 'What title will be left for you after you have handed them all out to your followers?' he replied, 'My mother called me Belay, so I don't need any title': in Amharic, this name literally means 'he who stands above all others.'[62]

In view of his service for his country, Belay also expected to be given a high position in the new Ethiopia. The emperor named him *Dejazmatch* and appointed him as governor of Bichena district in Gojjam, a post which seemed to Belay to be far beneath his rightful station. He soon found himself at odds with the regional governor and the central government over appointments to public offices and other positions. Belay called for an uprising, forcing the emperor to dispatch an army to Bichena in February 1943. The renegade governor took refuge in the mountains with his band of armed supporters; it took three months of fighting before he was finally taken captive. He was sent to Addis Ababa, where he was sentenced to life imprisonment. Incarcerated in a gaol in the palace grounds, Belay joined forces with a fellow inmate called Mamo Haile-Mikael, who had been gaoled for collaborating with the Italians. Together, they managed to murder their guards and stage a breakout; before long, however, the security forces tracked them down the north of the capital and recaptured them. This time, Belay was condemned to death, and on 12 January 1945 he, his brother, his co-conspirator Mamo and a number of other rebels were publicly hanged in Addis Ababa. It was not without a certain irony that the officer commanding the execution squad that day was none other than the later insurrectionist General Mengistu Neway. In 1961, he was hanged on the very same spot where he had placed the noose around Belay's neck fifteen years previously.

Despite the fact that Belay had thrown his lot in with a known collaborator, many Patriots still regarded him as some kind of martyr, and some of those who later rose up against the emperor did so in his name. These included *Bitwadad* Negash Bezabeh, a grandson of *Negus* Tekle-Haymanot of Gojjam. The plot that he hatched in 1951 had as its objective the assassination of Haile Selassie and the proclamation of a republic. The conspirators managed to win the support of various local officials, but were eventually betrayed by one of their number, *Dejazmatch* Gerassu Duki, before they could carry out their plan. *Bitwadad* Negash Bezabeh and several other ringleaders were handed long prison sentences.

Another Patriot who took up arms in the name of Belay was *Fitaurari* Hailu Kibret. He had battled the Italians in the mountainous region of Tembien in Tigray, gaining himself a reputation as a particularly determined fighter. In the field, he always carried a picture of Haile Selassie, wrapped in the Ethiopian tricolor, and made his men kneel before it.[63] After the emperor returned from exile, Kibret hoped to be given the title of *Dejazmatch*, a rank his father had held before him, but in the event he was only made a district governor in Lasta. In retaliation for this perceived slight, he murdered the brother of the governor of Lasta, a prominent dignitary from Sokota, and became a rebel. He landed in gaol and after a time was pardoned by imperial decree and recalled to Addis Ababa. But eighteen months after the attempted coup of 1960, he took up arms once more and proclaimed the crown prince as the new emperor. He and his men seized control of the Ras-Makonnen Bridge in the city centre for some days, but he was ultimately captured and put on trial for murder and high treason. Having been sentenced to hang for his crimes, he did not plead for mercy but defiantly announced; 'I have done what I have done.' The emperor left the final decision in the hands of the crown prince, who upheld the court's verdict.[64]

However determined Haile Selassie was to nip any resistance on the part of the Patriots in the bud, their resentment toward the emperor and his association with collaborators remained as strong as ever, and transferred to the next generation. The student leaders of the 1960s and 1970s were in many instance the children of Patriots, who had from an early age imbibed their parents' disaffection with the emperor – for example the militant student leader Tilahun Gizaw, who was shot dead in 1969.

Conversely, the *homines novi* and parts of the populace lumped together the Patriots and the aristocrats, referring to them disparagingly as the 'Party of *Kabba*-Wearers' (the *kabba* is the traditional black Ethiopian cloak. For both were deeply conservative and feudal in their outlook. Just as, before the war, the emperor had played off the *homines novi* against the aristocratic faction, now he exploited the mutual rivalries between the various groups – the aristocracy against bourgeois *arrivistes*, exiles against the Patriots, and the Patriots against collaborators – to reinforce his hold on power. In doing so, the dictum of 'divide and rule' became the hallmark of his reign. The power and influence wielded by the ministers he put in place and the prime minister were strictly limited, with the emperor reserving the right to take all important decisions. The parliament that was restored in 1943 was largely toothless – its members were, as stipulated by the 1931 Constitution, still appointed by the emperor. The ministerial council only met very infrequently, all the key decisions being taken in personal audiences with those who had direct access to the emperor. The absolute power of the *Negusa Negast* reigned supreme over all the rival groups of ministers, parliamentarians and dignitaries.

At the same time, the emperor continued to try and foster a new leadership elite that was beholden to him. The ministry of education, which he saw as key to Ethiopia's future, was headed by him personally. A host of new schools were founded in the 1940s and 1950s, above all in the capital. Haile Selassie paid regular visits to the country's high schools. Decades later, many

Ethiopians recalled the time when, as schoolchildren, they were given an orange by the emperor himself on the Ethiopian Orthodox Christmas Day, 7 January, every year without fail. And every student who went abroad to university was invited to meet the emperor beforehand. They were given the emperor's blessing for their journey to foreign parts – and were also asked to pledge that they would return home after their course of study to apply the skills they had learned in the service of Ethiopia. And whenever a student returned from abroad, he was given another audience with the emperor. Haile Selassie did everything he could to try and keep students in the country once they had graduated. The imperial government even paid for hotel rooms in the capital for returning scholars to stay in, so that they might resist the temptation to forsake their family *Tukul* (the traditional straw-roofed roundhouse of the Ethiopian countryside) for a New York apartment. All foreign graduates were guaranteed a job in the civil service. This paternalistic arrangement ensured that those who might otherwise have become the first wave of opposition to the emperor's rule were successfully integrated into the system for many decades.

Yet even though the emperor's paternalistic policy was able to hold the most important groups in the country in check, and the odd attempts at rebellion staged by the Patriots were scarcely any danger to him, Haile Selassie still felt the need for tight security. The deep sense of mistrust of his surroundings that he had developed during his rise to become regent, when his power base was still insecure, remained with him throughout his life. The Imperial Bodyguard, an elite unit of the Ethiopian Army, was there to ensure his personal safety. They were newly reorganized and expanded under the leadership of Swedish army instructors. For over 14 years, the commander of this unit was Brigadier Mulugeta Bulli. He had spent his time in exile in Djibouti and had come back to Ethiopia as part of Gideon Force. Under his command, from 1951 to 1953, Ethiopian troops took part in the military operation undertaken by the United Nations in Korea, a deployment that saw him promoted to Major General. He was also responsible for developing the Ethiopian secret service, the Department for Public Security, which reported to the interior minister. But this was not the only intelligence service established by the emperor. Every morning, Haile Selassie had himself personally briefed by his closest confidant Habte Wold Makonnen about the latest information gathered by the secret services. In 1959 Mulugeta created the so-called Imperial Private Cabinet, a new department of national security, which had a special remit to monitor the activities of the emperor's ministers. By this stage, Mulugeta was no longer in command of the Imperial Bodyguard; Brigadier Mengistu Neway, one of those who would later lead the Palace Revolt of 1960, had taken over this position in 1955. Fate decreed that Mulugeta Bulli was murdered by his successor as commander of the bodyguard in this failed coup attempt.

The country's involvement in the UN mission in Korea was a clear symbol to the rest of the world that Ethiopia had regained its national sovereignty. It was a matter of vital concern to the emperor that his country should be integrated into supranational structures. Ethiopia had been one of the founder-members of the United Nations, and Haile Selassie wanted to ensure that the frameworks within which the new organization operated were more robust than those of its predecessor, the League of Nations, which had failed so abjectly to counter the threat of Fascism and National Socialism. It was with the UN's help that some decisive progress was made in the late 1940s in resolving the two main outstanding territorial issues facing Ethiopia: the status of the Ogaden and Eritrea. In 1948 Great Britain indicated that it was prepared to withdraw from parts of the Ogaden. Even so, it was 1954 before the entire region was handed back to Ethiopia. The former colonies of British Somaliland and Italian Somaliland jointly gained their independence in 1960, as the new Republic of Somalia. A ruling of the Paris Peace Conference in 1946 decreed that Italy was to relinquish all its former colonies. As a result, a strong independence movement emerged in the British mandated territory of Eritrea, while those who supported union with Ethiopia found themselves in a minority. Nevertheless, the imperial government continued to stridently demand that

Eritrea should be united with Ethiopia, and found a powerful ally in the United States. In 1948, the question of Eritrea's future was entrusted to a UN Commission consisting of delegates from Burma, Guatemala, Norway, Pakistan and South Africa, but it failed to reach a unanimous verdict. Ultimately, then, the matter was put before the United Nations General Assembly, and on 2 December 1950 this body came to a compromise solution, embodied in UN Resolution 390 (V), namely the federation of Eritrea and Ethiopia 'under the sovereignty of the Ethiopian Crown', as the official wording of the document put it.

This federation presented the Ethiopian Empire with a difficult task. There was no question that the Eritrean Highlands were – in economic, cultural and ethnic terms – a part of the old Ethiopian realm. This area had especially close ties with the Ethiopian province of Tigray, with both populations speaking the same language, Tigrinya.[65] However, the years of Italian colonial rule had left their mark on Eritrea. The colonial power had fabricated a totally artificial administrative entity, which it ruled over for decades with an iron fist. Despite this – or perhaps precisely because of it – a feeling of togetherness had grown up among all Eritreans.

For the emperor and the Ethiopian ruling elite, the agreement they were seeking was just one stage in a wider plan to see the lost child of Eritrea reunited with the Ethiopian motherland. And certainly many in Ethiopia understood 'federation' to mean 'union'. Yet there was no denying that Ethiopia and Eritrea during its time under the British mandate had developed in quite separate and distinct ways. In conversation with me, the lawyer and politician *Dejazmatch* Abreha Tessemma, the leader of the anti-unionist party in the Eritrean elections of 1952, summarized the situation:

'After the Second World War, the British dripped "poison" in our ear, and the name of this poison was "democracy". Political parties, trade unions and a free press emerged. My concern was that all these achievements would be steadily dismantled if we chose to join the Ethiopian administration.

Purely political considerations were at stake here; there was no question of us feeling ourselves to be another nation with another religion. After all, it shouldn't be forgotten that the only place where the Ethiopian flag still flew during the Italian occupation was Eritrea. We'd given the Italian authorities to understand that the green and gold and red tricolour was also a symbol of our religious identity, you see. So they allowed us to carry the Ethiopian flag during Church festivals – as long as there was a cross in the centre. And it really was the case that when the federation of Eritrea and Ethiopia came into being, all the democratic achievements were gradually eroded.'[66]

Freedom of the press, freedom of expression and a freely elected parliament: these were things that had also been vouchsafed in an Eritrean constitution drafted by a UN Commission. But the 1931 constitution of absolutist Ethiopia, in force since 1931, did not guarantee such rights. How could these two such differently structured states be brought together under one roof? Eventually, in the view of the Eritrean historian Tesfatsion Medhanie, the emperor only accepted the 'federation' put forward by the UN 'because his dignitaries assured him that he could dissolve it bit by bit and then get rid of it altogether [...] For His Imperial Majesty, the absolute monarch par excellence, the idea of even local autonomy was pure anathema.'[67]

And indeed, the imperial government subsequently set about progressively eroding Eritrea's federal status. All Eritrean political parties were banned, with the exception of those that supported the union with Ethiopia. Democratic rights and fundamental liberties were abolished, and the Eritrean flag was removed from all public buildings. Presently, in place of an 'Eritrean government' there was only an 'Eritrean administration' and instead of a 'head of government' a 'chief executive officer'. The end point of this development was the *coup de grâce* delivered on 15 November 1962:[68] directive number 27 issued by the emperor announced the end of Eritrea's federal status. Eritrea was annexed by Ethiopia and incorporated into the empire as its fourteenth province.

All the same, the 1952 federation arrangement with Eritrea had made a new Ethiopian constitution inevitable. The emperor appointed the Minister of the Pen, *Tsehafe-Tezaz* Wolde-Giorgis, Foreign Minister Akilu and his American advisor John Spencer to the commission that was charged with drawing up proposals for this new legislation. They started work in the summer of 1953 in a building in the palace grounds, where they were under the emperor's constant supervision. Yet the Crown Council, the Church and the country's leading dignitaries also wanted to to be included in the consultations. These negotiations were to last for more than a year. Five versions of the constitution were drawn up and rejected, until the commission finally came up with a proposal that met with everybody's approval.[69] Anyone who had hoped that the 'Revised Constitution' might represent a decisive step away from absolutism towards a constitutional monarchy would have been disappointed. In many respects, it actually corroborated the absolutist position of the emperor.[70] Thus, Article IV of the Constitution stated in no uncertain terms: 'By virtue of His Imperial Blood, as well as by the anointing which he has received, the person of the Emperor is sacred, His dignity is inviolable and His power indisputable.' The emperor's descent from the Solomonic line was confirmed, as was the principle of hereditary monarchy: Article V stipulated that only male offspring of the emperor could lay claim to the succession.

The 'Powers and Prerogatives of the Emperor' set forth in Chapter II of the 1955 Constitution were unrestricted in almost all areas, as before. The emperor had the right to appoint and dismiss the prime minister, the ministers and all the members of parliament, as well as the country's judges; he could also rule by imperial directive if need be without having to involve parliament. Supreme command of the armed forces rested with him. However – and this was a new element – the decision whether to go to war or not now required parliamentary approval. In contrast to the Senate, whose members would continue to be elected by the emperor, delegates to the House of Representatives would henceforth be chosen through universal suffrage. Moreover, legislation passed by the government now needed to be ratified by both chambers. Also for the first time, the budget had to be approved by parliament. Admittedly, if the emperor chose to declare a state of emergency, then parliament would be instantly divested of all these powers, leaving the monarch free to rule by decree.

In addition, the revised constitution contained a new chapter on the 'Rights and Duties of the People'. For the first time in Ethiopia's history, basic human rights such as freedom of religion, freedom of expression and the right to peaceful assembly were guaranteed. Yet at the same time these rights were restricted in as much as they could only be exercised 'in accordance with the law', and 'with respect for the rights and freedoms of others and the requirements of public order and the general welfare.'

There was much wrangling over the text of the Constitution, with *Ras* Kassa, the Premier Prince of the Empire, withholding his assent until the very last moment. In the end, the emperor tasked *Lij* Imru Zelleke, the secretary of the constitutional commission, with the job of presenting the text to *Ras* Kassa for his countersignature. 'Try and impress upon him that he must agree to it,' were the emperor's instructions. According to *Lij* Imru's later account, *Ras* Kassa accepted the draft constitution with a sullen expression and said: 'Come back in two days.' When *Lij* Imru returned, *Ras* Kassa handed back the document with the words: 'So, this is supposed to be modelled on the British constitution, is it?' 'Yes, along those lines,' replied *Lij* Imru. To which *Ras* Kassa responded: 'Fine, I'm fully in agreement with it. I just have one thing to say to you, though: no one will ever observe it.'[71]

In the event, *Ras* Kassa was proved right. The tender green shoots of parliamentarianism that were planted in the Constitution never flourished. In spite of the introduction of elections for the lower house, no steps were ever taken to introduce a parliamentary system in the Western sense. Over the decades leading up to the end of the empire, participation in the elections remained vanishingly small. Independent parties were not permitted, scarcely any distinguished statesmen emerged and the Ethiopian parliament was far from acting as any sort of check and balance on the emperor and his administration. Many Western commentators writing retrospectively on the Ethiopian Empire have sharply criticized Haile Selassie for this backward-looking Constitution and his adherence to absolutism. This may well be justified, but an observation made by the German constitutional lawyer Menno Aden strikes me as being equally pertinent here: Aden quite rightly states that the Western allies of the Empire – Great Britain and the United States above all – voiced absolutely no criticism of the revised constitution at the time. Shouldn't these democratic countries have seen it as their primary role and duty to exert their influence by steering Ethiopia towards a system of constitutional monarchy?[72]

In May 1954, a year before the revised constitution was promulgated, Haile Selassie set off on a grand tour of the United States and Europe. The first and the most important stop on this tour was the USA. In January 1953 Dwight D. Eisenhower had taken up residence in the White House – Haile Selassie held the new US president in high esteem for his generalship and his role as Supreme Allied Commander in the Second World War. A few months after Eisenhower came to office, the long-running negotiations with the USA over a military pact were concluded. Under the terms of the Mutual Defense Assistance Agreement, in return for extensive military aid, Ethiopia granted the USA a 25-year lease on the site of the former Radio Marina in Asmara for use as a military base. In order to expunge all traces of its Italian past, the base was renamed 'Kagnew Station' after the stallion Kagnew, on which Haile Selassie's father had led his troops into battle at the legendary Battle of Adwa in 1896.[73]

The time therefore seemed ripe for a face-to-face meeting between the Ethiopian emperor and the American president. The visit of an African head of state to the United States was not by any means a foregone conclusion, however: the last occasion on which this had happened was a decade before, when Roosevelt had hosted the president of Liberia, Edwin Barclay. The Ethiopian diplomats and the emperor's advisor John Spencer put in months of patient work trying to arrange a mutually-convenient date. At first, Eisenhower's Secretary of State John Foster Dulles was firmly opposed to the whole idea. Yet the energetic support of the new US ambassador-designate to Ethiopia for the planned visit helped bring Dulles around. In October 1953, the secretary of state wrote a memo to the president in which his new-found enthusiasm for the trip is clear: 'The United States has no more genuine friend than Haile Selassie. He has sent troops to Korea and has been most cooperative in our economic and military aid programs [...] We are often accused of placating our potential opponents. Here is an opportunity to reward a constant friend.' Ever the consummate politician, Dulles also spotted a chance to reap political gain from the visit, assuring Eisenhower that it 'would be popular in America and would give the Administration a ready-made and non-controversial opportunity to make a genuine gesture with respect to the Negro population.'[74]

As he embarked on his diplomatic odyssey in 1954, the emperor may well have been reminded of his 'Grand Tour' thirty years before, when, as prince regent, he had spent several months travelling around Europe. Then, *Ras* Tafari had been passed between European capitals like some exotic trophy, as the representative of a backward land of which people knew little and which was looked down upon with the condescending eye of the colonizer. But times had changed. Now he was travelling as an emperor and head of state of a proud nation that had stood up to Fascist aggression and won back its independence – on a continent which, furthermore (with the exception of Libya, Liberia and South Africa) was still largely under colonial rule. For this, the Lion of Judah, who had been restored to His throne, was widely admired and respected throughout the world.

Nevertheless, just as was the case in 1924, there were many dignitaries and officials in the inner circle around the emperor who had serious misgivings about the monarch being absent from his homeland for several months. In the 1960s, the father of one of my fellow pupils at the German School in Addis Ababa, *Kegnazmatch* Ambatchew, told me about a very revealing encounter that his father, *Kegnazmatch* Dehne, had had with my grandfather on this question. *Kegnazmatch* Dehne was one of a number of old imperial dignitaries who had first served under Emperor Menelik. When the details of the 1954 'Grand Tour' were made known, he and many other palace retainers were deeply alarmed. One of them complained: 'This emperor spends too much time abroad, away from his people. Doesn't he know that when a people suddenly realizes that night falls and a new day dawns just the same as always, even when the emperor is absent, one day they might fall to thinking, "So what do we need an emperor for, anyway?"' – 'So what should we do?' said another. And *Kegnazmatch* Dehne answered: 'Let's go to *Ras* Kassa; the emperor will listen to him.' And so the long-serving dignitary went to the residence of my grandfather, told him about their concerns and asked him to speak to the emperor. When he had finished, *Ras* Kassa replied: 'Dehne, I always had you down as a wise man. But now I see you haven't understood the situation in Ethiopia at all.' – 'What do you mean?' –'Well, just because I am the only remaining prince whom the emperor hasn't ostracized to the wilderness, you now expect me to suffer the same fate by telling him this?' This was a rare admission on *Ras* Kassa's part that the emperor paid very little heed to the advice of even his innermost circle.

At Addis Ababa airport on 18 May 1954, the emperor and his entourage stepped aboard a US Army DC-6, which took them to Paris via Khartoum and Tripoli. Among the imperial retinue were the Minister of the Pen, *Tsehafe-Tezaz* Wolde-Giorgis, Foreign Minister Akilu and John Spencer. Because the empress's poor health prevented her from joining her husband on foreign trips, her place was taken by the emperor's youngest son, the 23-year-old Prince Sahle Selassie and by Princess Tenagne-Work. On the later European leg of the tour, Haile Selassie was also accompanied by his favourite son and Prince of Harar, Prince Makonnen, and his wife Princess Sara. During the flight to Paris, after Haile Selassie had already gone up to the flight deck to sit in the co-pilot's seat, the outer port-side engine of the four-engined plane suddenly failed. 'The Emperor's staff froze in quiet terror,' John Spencer reported, 'but Haile Selassie remained up front, amused by their consternation.'[75] In the French port of Le Havre, the Ethiopian delegation boarded the transatlantic liner SS *United States*. 'The Atlantic crossing by ship was uneventful,' Spencer continued, 'except for the initiation of the entourage to the mystery of air-conditioning in the cabins and the magic of steaks which appeared five minutes after the ordering, thanks to the microwave ovens onboard. The last day at sea proved to be unsettling since the stewards declared that they found the $1,100 in gratuities distributed by His Majesty to be inadequate.'[76]

From New York, the emperor was flown to Washington on a presidential plane, where he was greeted at the city's National Airport by Vice President Richard Nixon and a full military honour guard. The emperor glanced around and, turning to his interpreter and chief of protocol *Lij* Endalkatchew – Prime Minister Makonnen's son, who had studied at Oxford – asked him: 'Where is President Eisenhower?' Endalkatchew explained to him that US protocol required that the president receive his foreign guests at a formal welcoming ceremony in the White House, and that it was customarily the duty of the vice president to greet visiting heads of state at the airport. Haile Selassie was further irritated by the fact that Nixon, having escorted the emperor to a waiting black Cadillac open limousine for the ride into the capital, did not get in beside him but instead travelled in a separate car to the White House.[77] There, the President and the First Lady Mamie Eisenhower were already waiting for their imperial guest. In his welcoming speech, Eisenhower paid homage to Haile Selassie as someone 'who has established a reputation as a defender of freedom and a supporter of progress.' The emperor responded: 'This is a moment to which I have looked forward with the keenest anticipation. For years it has been one of my fondest hopes to be able in person to convey to the President and the people of the United States the expression of the profound admiration which I and my people have for your great nation.'[78] That evening, a dinner was held in the White House the emperor's honour, and over the following days Haile Selassie undertook an extensive programme of official functions, visiting the Library of Congress, addressing the delegates of the House of Representatives and going to see the Washington Monument in Mount Vernon.

The talks between the president and the emperor, which were held at the White House and also included the two countries' foreign ministers, resulted in a four-point accord. The United States agreed to advance extra credit for infrastructure projects such as the construction of ports and new highways and the development of air transport, support private investment in Ethiopia, provide assistance for education and supply further military aid in fulfilment of the Mutual Defense Assistance Agreement of 1953.

Unfortunately, the harmonious diplomatic 'mood music' of these talks was seriously compromised when, without consulting his staff, the emperor suddenly asked Eisenhower for further aid in addition to the agreed points. 'I was horrified,' Spencer wrote in his account of the visit. 'Such a move, in my opinion, constituted an abuse of hospitality on a visit designed as a goodwill mission and one that had been arranged over the opposition of the secretary of state.' The end result of this unexpected request, according to Spencer 'was not only a failure of his impulsive initiative, but offense on the part of the officials of the Department of State nearly equal to my own.' Exasperated, the emperor's advisor could only regard this as 'but another instance of His Majesty's superficial approach to foreign affairs without deep appreciation of the substantive and technical issues, or of the obstacles involved.'[79] But above all this incident was evidence of fundamentally divergent conceptions of politics: as an absolute ruler, Haile Selassie was used to taking personal decisions without first clearing them with ministers and officials. And he expected exactly the same of other heads of state whom he met. The fact that in democratic systems, state visits were nothing but atmospheric window-dressing and in the main only served to underscore resolutions that had already been prepared by the ministerial bureaucracy and agreed upon in cabinet meetings, was a totally alien concept to the emperor.

From Washington, Haile Selassie went on to Princeton to visit the famous Ivy League university, and then to New York. In Manhattan, tens of thousands lined the streets to watch the emperor pass by:

'As the 10-car motorcade made its way up Broadway from
Battery Park to City Hall, the ticker tape and other shred-
ded paper was so thick that the emperor could barely be
seen. The tumult brought a rare public smile to the face of
the monarch, who usually maintained an almost sphinx-like
dignity. Beaming from his open car, he stretched wide and
high as he waved and doffed his red-trimmed field marshal's
cap at the sidewalk throngs and the audiences in the skyscrap-
ers' windows above, Spectators snapped photographs of the
King of Kings. Pretty girls blew him kisses. Many usually
blasé Manhattan-ites delayed lunch to see the iconic ruler.'[80]

Even this triumphant ticker-tape parade, though, could not
match the rapturous welcome given to the emperor by a jubilant
crowd of African-Americans when he visited a Baptist Church
on 138th Street in Harlem. The pastor of the church, Rever-
end Dr. Adam Clayton Powell Jr., greeted Haile Selassie 'in the
name of the 700,000 Afro-Americans of New York City, men
and women of every faith, belief, and disbelief'. Powell extolled
the emperor as 'the symbol around which we place all our hopes,
dreams, and prayers that one day the entire continent of Africa
shall be as free as the country of Ethiopia.' A 200-voice choir
then sang the 'Hallelujah Chorus' from Handel's *Messiah*; the
emperor was visibly moved when he heard the refrain 'and he
shall reign forever and ever.'[81]

An equally emotional moment in New York was Haile Selassie's visit to the headquarters of the United Nations on 1 June,
where he was received by Secretary-General Dag Hammarskjöld.
The emperor's welcome speech was a passionate affirmation of
the global system of collective security.

'It is a significant moment for me when, after eighteen years,
I again find myself in a centre where are concentrated the passionate hopes of the thousands of millions of human beings
who so desperately long for the assurance of peace. The years
of that interval, sombre as they were and sacred as they remain
to the memory of millions of innocent victims, hold forth for

In 1954 Queen Elizabeth II hosted the second state visit of her reign,
welcoming Emperor Haile Selassie to Britain. Royal hospitality
on this occasion was markedly warmer than it had been on Haile
Selassie's first visit to the country as regent thirty years before.

us bright hope of the future. The League of Nations failed and
failed basically because of its inability to prevent aggression
against my country. But neither the depth of that failure nor
the intervening catastrophes could dull the perception of the
need and the search for peace through collective security.'[82]

After the United States, the next stages of the emperor's trip
took him on to Canada and Mexico, before he embarked upon
an extended tour of Western Europe.

His first port of call in Europe was Britain, which he reached
after a flight to Malta and a six-day voyage from Valletta to
Portsmouth aboard the cruiser HMS *Gambia*. As the ship passed
through the Straits of Gibraltar, Brigadier G. Lucas, acting governor of Gibraltar, sent a message wishing the emperor 'God

Speed'. The diplomatic courtesy of being taken to Britain on a ship of the Royal Navy stood in marked contrast to the less-than-enthusiastic welcome that country's administration had given him after his exile in 1936. Indeed, the scale of the arrangements undertaken for the official state visit of Emperor Haile Selassie to the United Kingdom in 1954 is a clear testimony to the value and importance that the British government now attached to its relations with Ethiopia.

On their arrival at Portsmouth on 14 October, the emperor, the Duke of Harar and the rest of the royal party were greeted by the Duke of Gloucester. All the warships in port flew the Ethiopian flag and royal salutes were fired; and three flights of Shackleton aircraft from RAF Coastal Command flew over HMS *Gambia*. At Portsmouth Guildhall, the emperor received an address presented by the Lord Mayor and the Corporation of the city before he and his party boarded the special train for London.

The elaborate arrangements were also much in evidence in the British capital. Upon arriving at Victoria Station, the special train drew up at the platform alongside an enclosure formed of red curtains and carpets and decorated with vases of fresh autumn flowers, at the entrance of which were hung the Ethiopian flag and the Union Jack. Waiting within the enclosure to greet the emperor and his party were the Queen, the Duke of Edinburgh, Queen Elizabeth the Queen Mother, Princess Margaret, and other members of the Royal Family along with Prime Minister Sir Winston Churchill, the Foreign Secretary Anthony Eden,[83] other government ministers, and service chiefs.

Drawn up outside in the station forecourt for inspection by the emperor and the Duke of Edinburgh was a guard of honour of the 3rd Battalion, Grenadier Guards. The royal party was then conveyed in a procession of four horse-drawn carriages to Buckingham Palace, where the emperor and the Duke of Harar were to stay for three days (the hospitality extended by the recently enthroned Queen Elizabeth II put to shame that offered by her grandfather George V to *Ras* Tafari thirty years before). In the first of the state carriages sat the emperor, the Queen and the

Duke of Edinburgh; in the second the Duke of Harar and the Duke and Duchess of Gloucester; while the remaining two contained the members of the emperor's suite and of the British suite attached for the state visit. The guards' band played the Ethiopian national anthem as the carriages passed out of the station forecourt.

The route to the palace was adorned with Ethiopian and Union flags. Large crowds also lined the route, loudly cheering the procession as it passed and keen to catch a glimpse of the emperor, seen (and also hailed in the popular press) not just as a valuable ally in the recent war but also as the embodiment of an ancient and romantic kingdom. In the afternoon, the emperor and the Duke of Edinburgh laid wreaths at the tomb of the Unknown Warrior in Westminster Abbey before moving on to Clarence House to visit Queen Elizabeth the Queen Mother.

The next event on the program was a visit to the Guildhall (still to be fully repaired from wartime bomb damage) in the City of London, where the emperor was received by the Lord Mayor and the Corporation, and to which he and the Duke of Gloucester drove in procession. This was a memorable event, and to describe it, it is worth quoting directly from *The Times*:

'When the Recorder, Sir Gerald Dodson, had read aloud the corporation's address of welcome in the library of Guildhall and the Lord Mayor had handed a silver casket containing the illuminated text to the Emperor, who replied briefly, there came a pause, unexpected and protracted. It was broken by the appearance of five men at the far end of the library. They staggered the length of the aisle bearing between them a present from the Emperor that was as much as they could carry. It was a splendid pair of tusks, mounted in the shape of a semi-circle on an ebony base. Silver bands encircled the tusks, which were surmounted by a small globe and cross, and a plate at the baseboard recorded that the gift was to commemorate Haile Selassie's visit. Close behind came the bearers of other gifts – a pair of silver-tipped spears and a round shield, with a boss and other ornaments of gold on a red velvet ground. No one had had previous notice of the imperial presents, except that the corporation had been asked to send a van with a police escort to the Ethiopian Embassy for them. They were accepted with surprise and pleasure in the name of the City by the Lord Mayor.'[84]

Among those present at this event were Sylvia Pankhurst, Lord Amulree, the Archbishop of Canterbury, Mr and Mrs Eden, several cabinet ministers, Mr and Mrs Attlee, and Dominion High Commissioners. Sir Winston and Lady Churchill were not present until the luncheon at the Mansion House that followed the reception. The day concluded with a state banquet in the emperor's honour hosted at Buckingham Palace by the queen and the Duke of Edinburgh.

The report in *The Times* on the day of the emperor's arrival waxed lyrical about Anglo-Ethiopian relations, declaring that 'the visit gives the British people the opportunity to acclaim the transfigured fortunes of a friend whose faith and fortitude they learned to honour when he lived among them, waiting his hour …' and eloquently fused ancient past with present times:

'In the crusading years, Ethiopia was to England and to Europe a land of mystery and hope, the realm of an unknown but mighty ally beyond the besieging hosts of the Paynim, to whom they gave the name of PRESTER JOHN. Trailing these iridescent clouds, with beyond them the even more legendary tradition of SOLOMON and the QUEEN of SHEBA, the EMPEROR would have seemed a figure of romance even if the vicissitudes of his own fortunes had not made him more romantic still. He is in fact a hard-working and very practical ruler in the most modern fashion, in labouring to equip his people with the amenities of twentieth-century civilization with the least possible disturbance to their inherited social order. In his belief that the way of true progress is to graft the new stock upon the ancient roots he has perhaps his closest affinity with the mind of his British hosts.'[85]

At a ceremony at Buckingham Palace the next day, 15 October, the queen made the emperor a 'Stranger (i.e. foreign) Knight of the Order of the Garter', the highest British order of chivalry. Haile Selassie was the first, and to date only, African head of state to be thus honoured. She also conferred on the Duke of Harar the insignia of the Knight Grand Cross of the Royal Victorian Order. In return, the emperor presented to the queen the Chain of the Order of the Seal of Solomon and conferred upon the Duke of Edinburgh and the Duke of Gloucester the Chain of the Most Exalted Order of the Queen of Sheba. The emperor was reported to be 'supremely proud' of his award. As John Spencer later explained, for all Haile Selassie's deep misgivings about British colonial attitudes, and despite his recent wooing of the United States, he remained culturally a great Anglophile:

> 'His Majesty's bitterness against the British also contained elements of strong attraction. He was certainly deeply conscious of the immense debt that Ethiopia had incurred towards the British for her liberation, and in his case at least, there was a genuine ingredient of gratitude. It was that feeling that led him to seek to emulate the British in most matters of style. British town-planners were soon brought in to impart a British solution to the problems of municipal design and management. The Babur Mangued was re-named Churchill Avenue. British interior decorators were brought in to redesign the appointments and furniture in the palace, In the waiting room for visitors, along with Ethiopian publications, were to be found *The Tatler, Punch, Country Life*, and the *Illustrated London News*.'[86]

In the evening, the emperor hosted a candle-lit dinner at the Ethiopian Embassy in Princes Gate. At the emperor's personal instruction, the menu was 'typically English' and the dinner lasted for nearly two hours. There were 58 guests in total. To the emperor's right sat the queen and Sir Winston Churchill, with the Duke of Edinburgh and the Princess Royal to his left. At the opposite end of the table, the Duke of Harar sat with Queen

Elizabeth the Queen Mother on his right and the Princess Royal on his left. There were no toasts or speeches.

During the remainder of his two-week stay in Britain, Haile Selassie's busy itinerary first took him back to Bath (on 17 October), where he revisited Fairfield House,[87] which had been shuttered and unused since he had left it to return to Ethiopia in 1941. On the following day, he received the Freedom of the City of Bath in a ceremony at the Guildhall. Subsequent visits saw him travel to Oxford to receive an honorary degree as a Doctor of Civil Law from the university's chancellor Lord Halifax, and to the Royal Military College at Sandhurst and RAF Duxford (an important Battle of Britain airfield). On his final day in the country, he attended a debate in the House of Commons.

It will be seen that most of this information about the 1954 state visit has been gleaned from *The Times*, which gave the subject the most comprehensive coverage of all in the British press. It is, however, worth concluding with a quotation from the *Daily Mail* of 14 October, given that this newspaper, back in the 1930s, had been notably strident in its support for the dictators:

'The Emperor, who begins his State visit today, last came to Britain in 1938 [*sic*]. What a contrast between the two arrivals! Then he was an exile from his country, which had been overrun by the Italians. Who that saw him in person or picture will ever forget the slight, grave figure with the wide-brimmed hat and the ample cloak? He was the embodiment of pathos and courage. So different from that bullying MUSSOLINI! Merely by standing up, silent, unsmiling and dignified, he did much to kill the Dictator's goose. Now he comes again in the splendour of Imperial Majesty, the welcome guest of the QUEEN and all the British people. For we have seen much and suffered much together.'[88]

From London, Haile Selassie travelled on to Paris, Brussels, Amsterdam, Copenhagen, Stockholm and Bonn. In the Federal Republic of Germany, which was still living in the long shadow cast by National Socialism, the emperor's arrival had special

After Britain, Haile Selassie's European tour of 1954 took
him on to the young Federal Republic of Germany. He is
seen here being greeted in Bonn by Chancellor Konrad
Adenauer (right) and President Theodor Heuss (centre).

significance. As the first foreign head of state to pay it an official
visit, Haile Selassie helped rid the young nation of the pariah
status which the atrocities of the Nazi past had saddled it with.

After two final stops in Berne in Switzerland and the Austrian
capital Vienna – and an absence, all told, of almost six months
– Haile Selassie returned to Ethiopia in mid-November 1954. By
this time, the proud Lion of Judah had turned 62, and his beard
was flecked with grey. Ceremonies marking the 25th anniversary
of the *Negusa Negast*'s ascent to the throne were due to take place
the following year, a celebration that saw Haile Selassie at the
height of his power. As 1955 dawned, there was nothing to suggest
that, just five years later, his throne would be threatened by a coup
attempt that shook the Ethiopian Empire to its very foundations.

CHAPTER SEVEN

Shots across the bows

1955 to 1962

The first fruits of the emperor's attempts at modernisation became apparent in the 1950s, most noticeably in the capital Addis Ababa. Gradually, an urban infrastructure arose – with metalled roads, wide boulevards, shops, factories and ware-houses, hotels and guesthouses, restaurants, bars and night-clubs, plus a handful of cinemas. In addition, this period saw the construction of new administrative blocks, schools and hospitals as well as embassy buildings. The city's growth attracted entrepreneurs and businessmen, advisors, educators and adven-turers from the four corners of the world. And yet in many respects the centre of Addis Ababa continued to resemble the residential seat of some 19th-century German provincial ruler rather than an international capital in the mid-20th century. The heart of the city was occupied by the imperial palaces: the *Genete-Leul* Palace, the emperor's own residence at that time, and the Menelik Palace complex, also known as the 'big *Gebbi*', with its numerous buildings, including the palace ministry. This was also the site of the *Aderash*, the cavernous hall that hosted regular state banquets, and which could accommodate up to 3,000 people.

A first-hand account of the sense of progress pervading many aspects of Ethiopian public life during this period appears in the unpublished memoirs of Donald E. Paradis. Paradis was an American lawyer who worked in the country for eleven years

(1957–68), serving first as an advisor to the Ethiopian minister of foreign affairs and then to the prime minister. His papers offer an insight into the sheer scale of the reforms being undertaken:

'In the legislative and judicial fields, modern Commercial, Civil, Procedural, and Criminal Codes were prepared and enacted, providing the framework for the slow and laborious transition from an ancient and traditional but antiquated and outmoded system to that ideal condition in which men live not under men but under God and the law. Ethiopia's military arm was transformed into a first-rate fighting force which served with distinction in Korea, in the Congo, in Algeria, and in other troubled regions where needed in the service of peace and freedom. [...] The creation of an up-to-date bureaucratic structure, with a pension scheme and merit-based civil service staffed by trained and qualified administrators. The establishment of a flourishing banking system serving the needs of Ethiopia's expanding economy. The enactment of laws permitting the formation of labor unions and the beginnings of the rationalization of ancient systems of land-holdings. These all testify to the labors and foresight of His Imperial Majesty.'[1]

The Menelik Palace was the beating heart of Ethiopia: all business that was of any importance to the country, and quite a bit of inconsequential activity besides, was conducted here. Twice a week, as the nation's chief justice, the emperor presided over the imperial court of law, or *Chilot*, and the imperial cabinet also met here. In 1955, to mark the silver jubilee of the emperor's accession, a new edifice was constructed on a hill in the city: the so-called Jubilee Palace, a European-style building. Yet the emperor only made rare appearances there, since the building had been designed primarily as accommodation for visiting foreign dignitaries. After the 1960 coup d'état, it became his permanent home. In the park surrounding this palace, a small imperial private zoo was created, which became home to several lions, a pair of leopards, two kangaroos, monkeys, gazelles and waterbuck.

Anyone who wanted to get anything done in Ethiopia needed to go to the Menelik Palace and appear before the emperor, or at least apply for an audience and hope for a favourable response. Yet precisely when one didn't have any pressing business to attend to, it was most essential to loiter around the antechamber, to avoid being forgotten about at court. There were two figurative terms for this in Amharic: *fit masmetat* (literally: 'letting your face be slapped'), i.e. doing anything, however drastic, to ensure that the emperor noticed you; and *daj matnat* ('waiting a long time outside the gate'), in other words, showing your face daily in the *Gebbi*. Both terms derive from the daily routine that was played out at the imperial court. Day after day, hundreds of people would assemble there in the hope of being summoned by the *Agafari* for an audience with the emperor. Ministers and senior bureaucrats who had been dismissed from their posts also made the daily pilgrimage to the Menelik Palace. Often it was their only hope of obtaining a new position. Haile Selassie had a good memory and generally noticed if this or that individual was absent from the massed ranks of the dignitaries. And it sometimes happened that he would instruct one of his adjutants to find out why that person hadn't put in an appearance at the palace for the past few days.

One of the first people to arrive at the palace early each morning, even before the emperor, was the prime minister, Aklilu Habte-Wold – regardless of whether he had any government business to discuss that day or not. He would remain there for the entire morning, waiting for the emperor to call him in. And straight after lunch, at the appointed hour he would be back at his post. This led some people to question when he ever found time to hold cabinet meetings. But his presence outside the door of power was key, sending a clear signal to the emperor's courtiers that the prime minister occupied a privileged position. It was also a sensible precaution: as long as the prime minister was *in situ* outside the emperor's chambers, no one could be inside casting aspersions on him to Haile Selassie.

When no state visits were taking place, and no official trips or major celebrations were in prospect, the emperor would invariably arrive at the Menelik Palace just after nine o'clock. As a rule, he would already have done several hours' work by that time. The emperor's daily routine in the capital followed a strict schedule.² He would usually rise sometime between 5.30 and 6 a.m. His morning began with prayers in the palace chapel before he set about the day's business. At 8.30 sharp, breakfast was served, which he mostly ate in the company of his daughter and grandchildren. At 9 o'clock on the dot, a car would arrive to take him on the short ride to the Menelik Palace – escorted by black-uniformed police motorcycle outriders and a car containing his personal bodyguards. At 1 p.m. the emperor would be driven back to the Jubilee Palace to have lunch, generally with a few others in attendance. Very occasionally, he would be joined by some ministers or advisors. A brief siesta would follow before the emperor resumed work at 4 p.m. In the late afternoon, he would break off for his daily excursion into the city. He often visited hospitals, schools and other institutions. Dinner was served in the palace at 8.25 p.m., after which Haile Selassie often retired to the salon with family members to watch a feature film.

An emperor's aura is fed by the monarch remaining aloof and making himself an unapproachable, and often totally invisible, figure to his subjects. At least, this was the principle followed for centuries by the crowned heads of Europe. In this regard, Haile Selassie was not a typical ruler; in fact, he was positively ubiquitous in the capital of his empire. When he wasn't away on a state visit, every afternoon without fail he had himself driven around the streets of Addis Ababa, where he found himself mobbed by ordinary Ethiopians, most of them bowing down low in deference. The emperor paid regular unannounced visits to schools, ministries and public bodies to check that things were running smoothly. At that time, there wasn't a single hospital or school building in the capital that hadn't been dedicated by him personally, and no exhibition or conference not opened by him in person. On one occasion in the mid-1960s, when the crown prince turned up instead of the emperor to cut the ribbon at the opening of a new school, a rumour spread like wildfire around the city that the emperor was about to abdicate. At least once every week, he met with students and other young people whom he had earmarked to achieve great things for the country. And if one of the members of the extended imperial family, or one of the dignitaries or even his cook ever fell ill, he would appear in person at their bedside to ask how they were. Whenever he was told that foreigners had arrived in Ethiopia, he insisted on seeing them – regardless of whether they were diplomats, businessmen or even tourists. Many Europeans who visited Ethiopia at that time still recall their personal audience with the emperor.

Haile Selassie projected an image of himself as a paternalistic ruler, and in this he was aided by his exceptional facility for remembering people, facts and figures. The German scholar and librarian Hans Wilhelm Lockot, who for many years was head of the Ethiopian National Library, later recalled the emperor's phenomenal memory:

'As well as a vast quantity of administrative detail, he stored personal information about thousands of individuals away in his brain: he knew the names, faces, positions, functions, tribal connections and family relationships of officials, military officers or students. All of them he had personally appointed, promoted, transferred or dismissed, or he had supported their education; and reports on all of them had been submitted to him. It was said he never forgot any conversation he had ever had and indeed from his early youth he had been trained to store everything is his memory. He avoided leaving any written records of his actions and never took notes: only his final decisions went into the files. For the population it was a matter of course that the Elect of God should have supernatural qualities, but for officials it was deeply portentous, and it kept them constantly in a state of apprehension. Even when unexpected situations arose, the Emperor would be able quickly and effortlessly to recall accurate details of events which had taken place many years before without consulting files or asking his aides.'[3]

Over time, a pronounced personality cult developed to complement the emperor's personal omnipresence. The government newspaper regularly proclaimed the manifold benefits that flowed from his reign, while the radio played songs praising his deeds. One tune that became popular in the early 1950s had the refrain: *'des jebelesh nafse, des jebelesh nafse, kurat agñiteshalena ba haile-selassie!'* – 'Rejoice, my soul, rejoice! Your pride has been restored by Haile Selassie!' And in 1954, when Haile Selassie set off on his marathon trip to the USA and Europe, a song addressing the emperor by his horse's name, *Abba* Tekel,[4] became a hit in Addis Ababa: *'tekel tollo na, tekel tollo na, yetyopia heseb naf-kohalena'* – 'Tekel, hurry back, Tekel, hurry back, the people of Ethiopia long to see you.' The man responsible for getting such eulogies played on the radio and sung at public events was none other than Makonnen Habte-Wold. In addition to his ministerial posts, he was also president of the 'Patriotic Society', which was dedicated to promoting music and theatre in the country.

Squares, schools, hospitals, the theatre and the sports stadium in Addis Ababa were all named after the emperor. His birthday on 23 July and the day of his coronation on 2 November were declared public holidays. The English-language newspaper *The Ethiopian Herald* always produced a special bumper edition to mark these celebrations: it appeared in large format and was filled with pictures of the emperor and congratulatory advertisements placed by the city's shops, businesses and banks. The emperor kept a very close eye on how he was portrayed in the media. When, as a guest of the US Congress in his capacity as President of the Ethiopian Senate, *Leul-Ras* Asserate Kassa was received by President John F. Kennedy in the White House in the summer of 1963, the *Ethiopian Herald* printed a picture of their meeting on its front page. The next day, the Ethiopian Minister of Information *Dejazmatch* Germatchew Tekle-Hawariat was summoned to the palace. The emperor gave him a thorough dressing-down, telling him: 'The government newspaper isn't there for you to promote the interests of your personal friends!'[5] The following day, the *Ethiopian Herald* reverted to its standard fare of reporting on affairs at court.

On Coronation Day every year, it was customary in the Ethiopian Empire for a so-called *Geber* – a lavish banquet – to be held in the *Aderash* in the palace grounds. Up to 3,000 people from all walks of Ethiopian life – noblemen and dignitaries, soldiers and policemen, but also farmers and even a number of beggars – dined on traditional Ethiopian dishes. On these occasions, the festival hall would decked out with carpets, while blazing torches bathed the room in flickering light. An armada of female cooks, clad in the traditional white *Shamma*, served up *Injera*, flatbreads, with *Wot*, a fiery meat and vegetable sauce. From iron racks suspended above the tables hung cuts of raw meat for the guests to slice pieces off themselves. An army of servants stood by, armed with water jugs, bowls and white hand towels so the diners could wash their hands before and after the meal, since naturally everyone ate using their fingers. The drinks served with the meal were also traditional: *Tella*, Ethiopian barley beer, and *Tedj*, a form of mead. In order to be able to feed as many guests as possible, it was not uncommon for there to be several sittings. Once the first round of diners had left the hall, the servants laid the tables afresh before the next set of guests were let in. Of course, the emperor was in attendance throughout at the head of the hall, pacing his dining over several hours while his banqueting companions changed periodically.

Many foreign observers regarded the various celebrations, festivals and banquets that were held in the Ethiopian Empire as an inappropriate extravagance in the light of the prevailing poverty in the country at large. What they failed to appreciate was that the solemn ceremonial of these events was not enacted in homage to the emperor in person but rather to the age-old institution of the Ethiopian Empire. At least this is how the overwhelming majority of the populace in the capital and in the wider country at that time regarded it, seeing themselves at the same time as an integral part of the patriarchal imperial realm of Ethiopia. And however straitened their personal circumstances may have been, there were hardly any Ethiopians then who questioned these traditions.

Much has been written about life and etiquette at the imperial court in Addis Ababa. Virtually all the accounts written by Europeans about audiences with the emperor make mention of the elaborate welcoming protocol, with all its pitfalls and constant potential for things to go wrong. Especially those visitors who knew nothing of such protocol, or whose countries had long since abandoned it – unlike, say, the English – regarded the court ceremonial as an anachronistic curiosity. The deeper significance of such an arrangement – namely to ensure that an encounter with an emperor always had some mystique about it – escaped many of them. Consequently, many a foreign envoy seemed taken aback by the fact that, on receiving them, the emperor would be sitting on a raised dais a few steps above them. As a boy, I once witnessed the accreditation of the new Soviet ambassador. The diplomatic corps of all the nations with representation in Addis Ababa were assembled in the throne room, together with Ethiopian ministers and dignitaries and governor-generals of various provinces. The emperor stood before his golden throne as the palace minister and his deputy stepped forward with the ambassador. The imperial court officials, who were standing on either side of the envoy in his splendid gold-braided uniform, bowed low before His Majesty. The ambassador, however, who sported an impressive row of medals and decorations on his chest, only deigned to give the emperor the merest hint of a nod. This did not escape the notice of the palace minister and his deputy, and when another bow was called for in response to the emperor's greeting, they took a firm hold of the ambassador's hands and pulled him down with them. The Soviet envoy looked nonplussed, but he had learned his lesson: when taking his leave of the emperor, he bowed down low without any outside assistance, as protocol demanded.

Unquestionably, no publication has made quite such a worldwide splash in its portrayal of Haile Selassie and his court as Polish journalist Ryszard Kapuściński's book *The Emperor: Downfall of an Autocrat*, which appeared in 1978. Its sketches of former imperial dignitaries paint a picture of the Ethiopian court as a pompous, comic-opera kind of spectacle, which had seemingly lost all touch with reality. The opening scene of the book has gained particular notoriety, in which a court functionary identified only as 'F' recounts the following scene:

'It was a small dog, a Japanese breed. His name was Lulu [...] During various ceremonies, he would run away from the Emperor's lap and pee on dignitaries' shoes. The august gentlemen were not allowed to flinch or make the slightest gesture when they felt their feet getting wet. I had to walk among the dignitaries and wipe the urine from their shoes with a satin cloth. This was my job for ten years.'[6]

Anyone who spent time at Haile Selassie's court in those days could confirm that the emperor did indeed have a dog answering to the name of 'Lulu'; yet the idea that he would have allowed his dignitaries to be publicly humiliated in such a manner is preposterous – just as absurd, in fact, as the presumption that there could have been a palace servant whose sole occupation was to go around clearing up the droppings of the emperor's dog.

In the meantime, many of those who know better have given their own assessments, pointing out how little use Kapuściński's book is as a piece of historical reportage. One such commentator, who has lived in Ethiopia for more than forty years, is the Polish gallery owner Barbara Goshu – the wife of the famous Ethiopian painter Worku Goshu, in whose house in Addis Ababa Kapuściński was a frequent guest. In an interview with Kapuściński's biographer Artur Domasławski, she explained: 'Kapuściński was a charming man. Enchanting, warm and friendly. As soon as he arrived in Addis, he always dropped in on us; he liked to chat, to listen and have something to eat with us [...] But, you know what, that *Emperor*: it's like a tale from *A Thousand and One Nights*.'[7] And when quizzed about exactly what was wrong with it, she replied: 'What is untrue? You'd better ask what's true: it'll be easier to say.' According to Kapuściński, his book on the imperial court was made up of interviews which he claims to have conducted with former servants of the emperor in Addis Ababa after Haile Selassie was toppled in 1974. These officials supposedly invited him to their houses to talk under the cover of darkness. This is a highly implausible scenario, though: at that time, the Mengistu regime which took over after the fall of Haile Selassie was intent on hunting down any former servants of the crown. Under constant threat from the Red Terror, they would have been putting their lives on the line by inviting a white journalist into their homes.[8] Eminent historians and scholars of Ethiopian affairs like the American biographer of Haile Selassie Harold Marcus have pointed to numerous passage in Kapuściński's book that clearly do not reflect the actual situation: for instance, his assertion that the emperor spoke no foreign languages and read no books.[9] Even some while later, after the end of the *Derg*'s Red Terror, Ryszard Kapuściński never divulged the names of his anonymous 'sources', not even in the 1990s, when a succession of court officials and former dignitaries came forward to give evidence at the inquest into the circumstances of Haile Selassie's death. Not a single prominent official or servant of the imperial court emerged to confirm the fact that Kapuściński had spoken to him when researching material for his book.

Leaving aside the Polish reporter's work on Haile Selassie, in recent years serious doubts have been raised about Ryszard Kapuściński's journalistic integrity across the board.[10] In his 2010 biography, which deals extensively with the topic of truth and fiction in Ryszard Kapuściński's writings and press reports, Artur Domasławski, foreign correspondent of the Polish newspaper *Gazeta Wyborcza* and a former colleague and friend of his subject, reached the following conclusion: 'Kapuściński pushed the boundaries of journalism into the realm of literature. He fantasized, and made the facts subservient to his narrative objective. [...] He started off in journalism and ended in fiction. Of course, in the process, the credibility of journalism risked being seriously compromised.'[11]

So did the emperor, as some European authors have maintained, live a sybaritic life of indulgence? There is no denying that the imperial family was among the wealthiest in the country. They owned country estates and a string of other properties. The revenue stream from these funded the imperial household, a kind of 'black economy' shadowing the country's official budget and which was subject to no public scrutiny or control. But it is also the case that the emperor used his private income to promote his country's interests abroad and to fund development projects. Many schools in the capital and around the country were financed from this private purse. Unquestionably, Haile Selassie and the royal family were rich in comparison with the rest of the Ethiopian populace. But their wealth did not consist of the major financial assets associated with the European super-rich. There has been much speculation, especially after the emperor's downfall in 1974, about Haile Selassie's foreign investments.[12] The paper trail on this subject is sparse – almost all the records of the Ministry of the Pen went missing during the revolution. However, a telling memorandum from 1959 has survived, written by Haile Selassie's private secretary Teffera-Work Kidane-Wold, to the emperor. In this note, which is signed with the words 'Your slave, Teffera-Work', the private secretary informs the emperor of the balance of his account at the National Provincial Bank in London: Haile Selassie's total assets at that time amounted to £22,000.[13]

Haile Selassie and his family lived a rather modest private life, as those who were around him have attested. For example, the Viennese-born Lore Trenkler, who originally came to Addis Ababa in 1960 as the empress's personal dietary chef and went on to assume responsibility for all the royal family's cooking arrangements in the palace, gave a revealing account of meal times at the court in her memoirs.[14] Breakfast at the palace generally consisted of porridge and cornflakes with milk or cream, followed by eggs of some sort – boiled or scrambled, or an omelette – and to finish a selection of Ethiopian cold meats, butter, marmalade, honey, bread and coffee. On fast days – every Wednesday and Friday, and during the fasting seasons of Easter and Christmas – no breakfast at all was taken. For lunch, there was 'a light starter such as a spinach or cheese soufflé, rice with ragout, a pasta dish, vegetables au gratin, stuffed vegetables, etc.'; and for the main course 'a meat dish with various vegetable and potato accompaniments,' as well as Ethiopian specialities; while dessert comprised either mousse, stewed fruit or cakes 'invariably with a dish of fresh fruit on the side'. For dinner, the same kind of dishes were served as at lunch, except for a more elaborate sweet: 'often substantial hot desserts like steamed puddings, fruit soufflés, pancakes or gâteaux and the like, such as profiteroles, meringues or fruit slices, and so forth.' In the fasting periods, meat was shunned in favour of fish and vegetables. In addition, the Austrian head chef introduced a dish from her homeland that became a firm favourite on fast days in the royal household: apple strudel.

Admittedly, different rules applied when official state guests were visiting Addis Ababa. 'The emperor and his family may have lived frugally in private,' Lore Trenkler recounted, 'but where guests were concerned, nothing was too good.'[15] For such occasions, the emperor vacated his dining room in the Jubilee Palace for the visitors, while his most valued personal staff were placed at his guests' sole disposal. Yet even during state visits, Haile Selassie would scrupulously observe fasting rules; if it so happened that a state banquet coincided with a fast day, the emperor, his ministers and entourage would all be served a separate fasting meal – usually so discreetly that the foreign guests didn't even notice. Only once, according to Lore Trenkler, did visiting dignitaries spot that different meals were being served, during the state visit of the Chinese premier Zhou Enlai to Asmara in January 1964. Having been informed about his host's religious observances, and after a brief consultation with his colleagues, the head of the Chinese delegation announced: 'If the Ethiopians are fasting, then we Chinese will fast too.' Consequently, the state banquet in Asmara went ahead with everyone eating a fasting meal.[16] During the state visit of the German president Heinrich Lübke in October of that same year, his wife was very taken with the porridge that was served for breakfast in the palace at Asmara, and asked the head chef for the recipe. Frau Trenkler went one better, showing the president's wife the special pot she used to prepare the porridge in, in a bain-marie, and at the end of the visit presenting it to her, gift-wrapped in paper and neatly boxed. When the emperor heard about this, he ordered a number of other such porridge pots to be bought and dispatched to Bonn.[17] He couldn't bear the thought of Frau Lübke back home in Germany making porridge for her husband the federal president in an old, used cooking utensil.

But for all the frugality that Haile Selassie displayed in his domestic arrangements, in one respect he was more than happy to indulge himself: the emperor was a car fanatic, and the palace grounds were home to dozens of automobiles with marque names evoking the golden age of motoring. His first official car, which he took delivery of in 1928, was a German Maybach W5 SG Coupé de Ville with a 120-hp engine, a magnificent vehicle with gilded crowns atop the radiator cap and the headlights. The open dicky seat at the back had room for a footman, who could sit behind the emperor and shade him from the sun with a huge parasol. No one knows what became of this car during the Italian occupation. After the war, the emperor acquired a series of other luxury conveyances, mostly as official gifts. We have already mentioned the Cadillac limousine that he was given by Franklin Roosevelt. In the early 1950s, King George VI sent him a dark grey Rolls-Royce Phantom IV. In this context, a notable event occurred in 1966 in Asmara, where King Saud Ibn Abdulaziz, who had been forced to abdicate two years earlier, was due to meet the emperor. To avoid a diplomatic imbroglio, Haile Selassie chose not to receive the king in Addis Ababa but to shift their meeting to Eritrea instead. King Saud came over two weeks beforehand in order to enjoy some rest and recreation on the Red Sea coast. On his arrival, he was met by my father *Ras* Asserate Kassa, who was governor-general of Eritrea at the time. One evening, the Saudi king asked Asserate Kassa to cast an eye over the presents that he had brought for the emperor. These included a monstrous grandfather clock mounted on a vast chest of drawers and two huge and extravagantly decorated vases made of fire-gilded bronze. The king cannot have failed to notice the sceptical look on my father's face. When asked if these gifts would be to the emperor's taste, *Ras* Asserate replied, with all due diplomatic circumspection: 'The emperor already has a great many vases and grandfather clocks.' With a sigh, King Saud enquired: 'But what on earth doesn't he have?' Quick as a flash, the viceroy responded: 'A Mercedes 600 Pullman.'

The king thanked him for the tip and directed his underlings to obtain such a car as quickly as possible. A call was hurriedly put through to the Mercedes-Benz factory at Untertürkheim, and the Swabian car manufacturer duly lived up to its reputation for reliability: 48 hours later, a six-door, burgundy-red Mercedes Pullman was standing outside the palace in Asmara, gleaming in the African sun. And when Haile Selassie arrived in the Eritrean capital a few days later, King Saud picked him up in the Mercedes and announced to him: 'Your Majesty, this is your car!'

I was allowed to witness two state visits to Ethiopia in the 1960s: those of Queen Elizabeth II and Shah Mohammad Reza Pahlavi of Persia. The highest level of protocol applied to visits by royalty, and this was the case for Queen Elizabeth, who came to Ethiopia in January 1965. Accordingly, the emperor went in person to Addis Ababa airport to greet the queen on her arrival, together with a military honour guard drawn from all branches of the armed forces. For this occasion, Haile Selassie wore the official uniform of an Ethiopian field marshal, which had a very British look about it – all except for his headgear, that is: a two-cornered Ethiopian hat adorned with a golden lion's mane. His entire cabinet of ministers and all the country's top generals were present, the former in morning coats and top hats, the latter in full dress uniform. The golden state carriage that had been built to mark the emperor's silver jubilee stood in waiting for the two monarchs, and drawn by a team of powerful white Lippizaners and escorted by a brigade of the imperial life guards in red and green uniforms, the coach made its way into the city centre. The route was lined with cheering crowds. The capital's schoolchildren had been given the day off, and all government agencies and other public bodies were closed. It seemed as though the whole of Addis Ababa had turned out to welcome their distinguished guest. In the evening, a sumptuous banquet was held in the queen's honour at the Menelik Palace, with over a thousand guests attending. This was to be the last such occasion at the Menelik Palace; subsequently, banquets for state visitors were hosted in the more peaceful setting of the Jubilee Palace.

The following day saw the start of the official programme of visits, with the emperor and queen taking a flight down the so-called Historic Route, from the Blue Nile Falls to the rock churches of Lalibela, and then on to see the palaces of Gondar and the giant stelae at the ancient city of Axum. Then their majesties flew to Eritrea, where my father received them with full diplomatic honours at the Yohannes IV airport in Asmara. Limousines with a police motorcycle escort rather than a golden state coach took them into the Eritrean capital. Just days before, the servants at the palace in Asmara had been in a frenzy, with everyone from the butler in his snow-white tailcoat to the chambermaids making sure that every last speck of dust was removed from the furniture, rugs and carpets. For every state visit, nothing was left to chance. A rigid seating plan was in force at the reception in the throne room. The chairs for the Crown Prince and his consort had to be placed at a specified distance from the thrones of their majesties, and set correspondingly lower. The Duke of Edinburgh dutifully performed his allotted role, always walking two steps behind the queen as royal protocol demanded. Prince Philip remained in the background throughout and never committed the gaffe of doing anything that might draw people's attention away from the queen. Only fifty selected guests were invited to the gala dinner in the palace at Asmara that evening; later on, a reception was laid on in the great *Aderash* for over 1,000 people

Three years later, in May 1968, the Shah of Persia and his wife visited Ethiopia. The *Shahanshah* ('King of Kings') Mohammad Reza Pahlavi and the *Shahbanu* Farah-Diba were also escorted from Addis Ababa to Asmara by the emperor. We literally fell over ourselves trying to get close to the enchanting empress as often and for as long as we could. I even managed to exchange a few words with the *Shahbanu* one time, when I took a Polaroid picture of her as she strolled in the palace garden, wearing a light blue silk ensemble with a pleated skirt and an elegant straw hat. A faint smile played across her face, but unfortunately her beautiful eyes were hidden behind a large pair of sunglasses. I do not have the snap, as I presented it to her as soon as I'd taken it, bursting with pride, but the incident has seared itself indelibly on my memory.

Another defining characteristic of Haile Selassie was his devout Christianity. He followed to the letter the strict precepts and dietary proscriptions of the Ethiopian Orthodox Church. Yet he was also well aware of the political power that the Church wielded in Ethiopia – not least through personal experience. After all, it had been *Lij* Iyasu's excommunication in 1916 that catalysed the lords' decision to depose him, thus paving the way for *Ras* Tafari's own accession. As a result, Haile Selassie staked everything on freeing the Ethiopian Orthodox Church from its dependence upon the Coptic patriarch and bringing it under his political influence instead. He entered into negotiations to this end immediately upon his return to the throne following his period in exile. In 1948, an agreement was concluded with the Coptic Pope, in which it was agreed that an Ethiopian should be appointed as primate of the Ethiopian Orthodox Church after the death of the incumbent Coptic head of the Church, *Abuna* Kyrillos. Accordingly, following *Abuna* Kyrillos' death, on 13 January 1951, the Archbishop of Shoa, *Abuna* Basileos, was installed by the Coptic patriarch as the Metropolitan of the Ethiopian Church. In a further round of negotiations, Haile Selassie finally succeeded in resolving the long-running tensions that had existed with the Coptic Pope in Alexandria and in establishing the auto-cephaly of the Ethiopian Orthodox Church. On 28 June 1959 in Cairo, in the presence of the emperor and the foreign minister of the United Arab Emirates, *Abuna* Basileos was consecrated as the first Ethiopian Patriarch by Pope Kyrillos VI of Alexandria.[18] Henceforth, the Ethiopian patriarch would be elected as the head of the Ethiopian Church by members of the country's clergy, confirmed by the emperor and finally enthroned by the patriarch of Alexandria. As protector of the Ethiopian Orthodox Church, the emperor was also proclaimed protector of the five Eastern Orthodox national churches at their conference in Addis Ababa in January 1965. Haile Selassie exploited the influence that this position gave him to ensure that his candidate *Abuna* Theophilos won the election to succeed *Abuna* Basileos in 1971.

The Ethiopian Orthodox Church was enshrined as the state religion in the country's constitution. Even so, Haile Selassie was also at pains to foster a friendly and paternalistic relationship with Ethiopia's Muslim population. His oft-quoted motto in this respect was 'The country is our common concern, but religion is a private matter.' Muslim dignitaries were received by the emperor on Islamic feast days, and there were also a number of Muslim ministers; however, under Haile Selassie no Muslim would ever attain the rank of general. The Ethiopian emperor was also an enthusiastic subscriber to the Christian ecumenical movement. He was the first monarch of the country to travel to Rome to meet the Pope. Paul VI granted him an audience at the Vatican during his 1970 state visit to Italy, though this attracted criticism from the priesthood and other ultra-orthodox members of the Ethiopian Church. Haile Selassie cultivated contacts with the World Council of Churches, and in 1966 opened a conference of the German Evangelical Church in Berlin as their guest of honour. The education he received from Catholic missionary priests like Monsignor Jarosseau may well have had a bearing on the emperor's receptive attitude to ecumenical collaboration over many decades.

The emperor's deep faith also informed his practice of almsgiving. The giving of alms was mandatory in the early Christian Church, and also forms one of the 'Five Pillars' (fundamental obligations) of Islam, and the Ethiopian emperor took this duty extremely seriously. In the course of his customary afternoon excursions, he would have himself driven to the farthest outskirts of the city, where he handed out money from the car in the poorest neighbourhoods. Children, women and old men would arrive in droves, ecstatic at being given banknotes by the emperor. He was also generous towards the people of friendly countries who found themselves in need. When large parts of the east coast of England were devastated by a North Sea storm surge in early 1953, leaving many people homeless, he sent a large shipment of coffee as a mark of the Ethiopian people's solidarity with their liberators. European commentators never failed to register their surprise at these gestures, though some of

them were more disconcerted vis-à-vis the widespread poverty
in the emperor's own country. The German diplomat Hans von
Herwarth, who was head of protocol at the Foreign Ministry in
Bonn, noted of Haile Selassie's 1954 visit to the Federal Republic:
'In Düsseldorf, during his stay at the Breidenbacher Hof Hotel,
he impressed me with a touching gesture of humanity. Glancing
out of the hotel window, he noticed a blind woman newspaper
vendor with a guide dog. He ordered a servant to go out and ask
the woman to come up to his suite, where he promptly bought
her entire stock of newspapers off her and handed her five gold
coins into the bargain.'[19] Even when abroad, the emperor set
great store by projecting himself as a benevolent sovereign.

One notable characteristic of Haile Selassie's paternalistic rule
was the fact that he never allowed ministers and other officials
to remain long in their posts. Before they got themselves into a
position where they could establish a personal power base that
might potentially pose a threat to him, they were transferred to
another post. And the more Haile Selassie mistrusted them, the
further away from the capital they were moved – in case of doubt
they would be appointed to a remote provincial governorship or
– even worse – sent abroad as an ambassador to some far-off
land. This policy became known in Ethiopia as *Shumshir*, the
Amharic term for 'hire and fire'. It is hard now to imagine an age
in which being appointed an ambassador of one's country was
seen as a form of demotion or even shameful ostracism. There
were reputedly occasions when a minister who had suffered such
a fate broke down in tears. At that stage, they had no inkling
that much worse things were later to befall the entire Ethiopian
court and its dignitaries.

One of the few personalities who managed for a long time
to evade the imperial *Shumshir* was the influential Minister of
the Pen, *Tsehafe-Tezaz* Wolde-Giorgis Wolde-Yohannes. He
remained in this post for fifteen years, growing increasingly
powerful in the process. But as his influence grew, so did the deep
mistrust of his internal opponents – both among the old aristocratic class and the *homines novi*. Makonnen Habte-Wold also
eventually became an adversary of the minister. In the winter

Ras-Bitwadad Makonnen Endalkatchew,
prime minister of Ethiopia 1942–57.

of 1953–54, after having formed a successful alliance for over
twenty years, the two men fell out over tax affairs. Presently, the
Minister of the Pen's many enemies, who hitherto had kept their
heads below the parapet, began to gather around Makonnen
Habte-Wold; among their number were Defence Minister *Ras*
Abebe Aragay and Prime Minister *Ras-Bitwadad* Makonnen
Endalkatchew.[20] To try and consolidate his position, *Tsehafe-
Tezaz* Wolde-Giorgis sought to marry into the emperor's family
by asking for the hand of his daughter Princess Tenagne-Work.
But the royal family, first and foremost the Crown Prince, flatly
rejected this and managed to torpedo the planned liaison. This
incident created a permanent rift between the emperor and his
minister.

It is hard to say exactly what prompted the emperor to finally
withdraw his confidence from his most important minister.
During his 'Grand Tour' in 1954, the emperor discovered that

the representatives of foreign governments were approaching *Tsehafe-Tezaz* Wolde-Giorgis, rather than him personally, to discuss Ethiopian affairs. It turned out that their staff had been briefing them that the Minister of the Pen was the 'real power' in Addis Ababa. British newspapers took to calling him the 'strong man of Ethiopia'.[21] But before a direct assault was launched against the Minister of the Pen, his opponents began spreading allegations about his brother, Makonnen Wolde-Yohannes, whom they accused of corruption and embezzlement of public funds. The fact that the powerful Minister of the Pen was unable to prevent legal proceedings from being instigated against his brother was a clear sign that his star was on the wane.[22] Eventually, in April 1955, the Minister of the Pen was charged with high treason for having allegedly plotted an uprising against the emperor. And high treason in the Ethiopian Empire was punishable by execution.

On 25 April 1975, I met *Tsehafe-Tezaz* Wolde-Giorgis in London, where he was living in exile. During our conversation he told me about the circumstances of his fall from power: 'Your grandfather and many of the princes didn't like me. But even so, I owe my life to *Ras* Kassa.' At the time of his minister's trial, to investigate the charges against him, the emperor had appointed a commission chaired by the Crown Prince, who proceeded to appoint as his co-members two of the most prominent opponents of the Minister of the Pen, the prime minister and the defence minister. *Tsehafe-Tezaz* Wolde-Giorgis explained what happened next:

'I refused point-blank to appear before the commission, on the grounds that I was accountable solely to the emperor for my actions. And so *Ras* Kassa was tasked with investigating the facts of the case on the emperor's behalf. After a thorough review of all the evidence, he concluded that the charges against me were groundless. He supposedly told Haile Selassie: "You know that I'm not exactly a friend of this man. But with the best will in the world, I cannot find anything to suggest that he was involved in any conspiracy to topple you from the throne. If you have had enough of him, then simply banish him from your sight for a while." On the day when the emperor was due to announce his final verdict, I was waiting in an annex of the *Genete-Leul* Palace to learn the outcome of my hearing. Finally, *Ras-Bitwadad* Makonnen Endalkatchew and *Ras* Abebe appeared and announced: "It is His Imperial Majesty's most gracious wish and command that you shall be appointed governor of Arussi." They were hoping that I would refuse to give up the powerful role of Minister of the Pen for that of an inconsequential governor of a far-flung province. Had I done so, I would surely have been arrested on the spot for gross insubordination. But I saw through their game and replied: "His Imperial Majesty knows how loyally I have served him all these years and how exhausting this demanding role has been. It is therefore a great honour for me that he has seen fit to send me to Arussi, the land of the great prince Darge, so that I may recuperate there for a while. I should like to kiss His Majesty's feet in gratitude."'

In the end, Wolde-Giorgis was brought before the emperor. The former Minister of the Pen delivered a deeply ingratiating speech, thanking Haile Selassie for his banishment and demotion. *Ras* Kassa, who attended this meeting alongside *Abuna* Basileos, leant over to the archbishop and whispered : 'There! Didn't I tell you – who could have possibly known any better how to please his master?'[23] By accepting his fate of ostracism to the provinces, Wolde-Giorgis saved his neck from the noose. Six years later he returned to Addis Ababa, though he never again played any significant part in Ethiopian politics.

In his study on Haile Selassie's government, Christopher Clapham offers a Machiavellian interpretation of this affair: 'Not least among the emperor's achievements was the way in which he caused the resentment both of the nobility and of frustrated reformers to be directed at Wolde-Giorgis rather than himself, thus remaining detached from policies for which he was essentially responsible.'[24] For one basic fact could no longer be ignored: Haile Selassie's paternalistic form of rule, which largely condemned both the cabinet and the parliament to inactivity, was now being stretched to its limits. The emperor insisted upon taking every conceivable decision; and in cases where he reached no decision, matters were left in limbo. And the more complex things became in the increasingly industrialised world of the 1950s, the greater the number of important decisions that were simply kicked into the long grass.

Clearly, a single person controlling the engine of the state was no longer enough to keep the motor of reform turning over. Despite the fact that many changes were evident in the cities, the lives of most people in the Ethiopian countryside had not improved noticeably since the liberation in 1941. Ethiopia was still fundamentally an agrarian country, with over 90 percent of the population engaged in farming. Nor had the imperial government done anything to bring about reform in land ownership; just under a third of economically viable land remained in the hands of the extended imperial family, while an overwhelming proportion of the rest was divided between the Church and the nobility. Most agricultural land was worked by tenant farmers, who were hamstrung by high tribute payments and taxes. There was little incentive for them to cultivate more land than was absolutely necessary for their own subsistence. Moreover, as a result of the introduction of modern farming methods, a considerable number of agricultural labourers had lost their jobs. Many young people quit the land and migrated to the overcrowded urban centres of Addis Ababa and Asmara, where factories and processing plants were springing up apace, producing mainly clothing, shoes and edible oils. On the other hand the government attempted to boost the export of agricultural goods, especially coffee, so as to enable to import badly-needed industrial machinery and other new technology.[25] Up to the mid-1950s the Ethiopian economy continued to expand steadily, but in the second half of the decade suffered an abrupt slump. The country was now faced with fierce competition in the coffee market from both Latin America and increasingly also from other African countries, while a huge surplus on the world market led to a drastic fall in the price of the commodity. In turn, the closure of

Tsehafe-Tezaz Wolde-Giorgis Wolde-Yohannes,
'Minister of the Pen' 1941–55.

the Suez Canal as a result of the Suez Crisis of 1956 triggered a
collapse in the export of grain, oilseed and coffee beans. How
outmoded most farming practices still were in Ethiopia and the
extent to which agriculture there was weather-dependent was
brought home forcefully by the widespread famine that hit the
provinces of Wollo, Tigray and Harar in 1959. The imperial
government ran into severe difficulties in meeting its financial
obligations. While the emperor continued to press for further
assistance from his most important ally, the United States, at the
same time he embarked on a state visit to the Eastern Bloc, a trip
that proved to be a resounding success. The Soviet Union and its
Eastern European satellite countries promised to bankroll Haile
Selassie to the tune of US $100 million.[26] In turn, this develop-
ment was not without influence on US foreign policy. Washington, which was desperate not to lose its key ally on the Red Sea
to the Warsaw Pact, was quick to offer Ethiopia a new tranche
of credit.

The crisis in the Ethiopian economy in the second half of the 1950s also led to growing discontent among precisely that sector of the populace in which Haile Selassie and his government had formerly placed most faith. In the changed economic climate, those elite students whom the emperor had personally handpicked to complete their higher education abroad were now failing to find appropriate positions on their return. Worse still, they had experienced life in the United States and Europe, and in comparison with the advanced Western democracies, they were now forcibly struck by the economic and political backwardness of their own country. As a result, their clamour for root-and-branch reforms in their homeland grew ever louder.

One of these *homines novi*, who as a protégé of Haile Selassie had enjoyed a glittering career in the Ethiopian Empire, was Workneh Gebeyehu. The emperor had first spotted this talented young man on a trip to Gondar. Though he had had only a few years' schooling, after joining the military academy in Harar he became one of the youngest candidates in the country's history to be commissioned as an officer. During the Korean War in the early 1950s, he was a member of the battalion that Ethiopia contributed to the United Nations deployment there. There followed a meteoric rise at court, under the emperor's personal patronage, from head of security at the interior ministry to head of the secret service and finally acting chief of staff in the private office of the emperor. No one there or in the emperor's inner circle could fail to notice that Colonel Workneh was fast becoming a particular favourite of Haile Selassie and had developed a far closer relationship with him than, say, the Habte-Wold brothers, or indeed the most important members of the emperor's government.

Colonel Workneh filled the void left by the forcibly rusticated Minister of the Pen. It was Workneh's initiative to set up another committee alongside the cabinet, in which important decisions were to be reached: the so-called Private Cabinet of His Imperial Majesty.[27] In 1959, Workneh was promoted to the rank of Lieutenant Colonel; he moved into his own apartment in the palace and he and the emperor were often seen sitting deep in discussion until late in the night. In the course of these tête-à-têtes, a feeling of disappointment at the monarch must have grown in Workneh. No one knows exactly what prompted the Lieutenant Colonel to join a group that was plotting the emperor's overthrow. However, one pointer was given by Haile Selassie's former adjutant Brigadier General Makonnen Deneke, to whom Workneh recounted the details of a conversation he had had with the emperor during his trip to the Soviet Union in 1959. On the long train journey from Leningrad to Moscow, the Lieutenant Colonel and Haile Selassie got involved in a wide-ranging discussion about the political situation in Ethiopia, which ended with Workneh apparently pleading with His Majesty to abdicate in favour of the Crown Prince and so help usher in the sort of constitutional monarchy seen in the United Kingdom or Japan. The emperor's response was uncompromising: 'Workneh, up to now We had thought you had reached the necessary level of maturity for your important role; but now We are dismayed to find that you are in fact still a child. We shall continue to exercise the power that the Almighty has vested in Us to the end. Accordingly, God shall do with Ethiopia what He will. And besides: have you ever heard of anyone voluntarily relinquishing his power?' The emperor's reaction must have confirmed Lieutenant Colonel Workneh in his decision; in any event, he told Brigadier General Makonnen Deneke: 'This person [i.e. the emperor] is very short-sighted. He neither has any vision for Ethiopia, nor does he wish the country well.'[28]

It is possible that Workneh might never have attained his key position at court had not the man who for decades had been the emperor's most trusted comrade-in-arms and closest advisor not died in 1957: *Ras* Kassa. The Premier Prince passed away on 19 November that year, aged 76. He was visiting the old monastery of Mitak Amanuel that day, not far from the city of Debre Berhan in the northeastern part of the province of Shoa. There was no road to this sacred site, which could only be reached on muleback. *Ras* Kassa celebrated Mass there and received Holy Communion, which in the Ethiopian Orthodox Church only happens on very special occasions. The moment he left the monastery and started to climb back onto his mule, he suffered a heart attack and died on the spot. The emperor was away on a state visit to India at the time. *Ras* Kassa was buried with full military honours befitting that of a field marshal – an honour never again given thereafter to any Ethiopian. The emperor had insisted upon this singular honour, and ordered three days of official mourning. The Ethiopian emperor had scarcely ever been seen weeping or lamenting in public. But when he returned from Delhi, his grief at the loss of *Ras* Kassa was etched on his face for all to see. When he came to visit the residence of my family, he heard a woman mourner cry out: *Yemekakeralu, lebetcha, lebetcha kawandinum qorbal, mech kamistu betcha* ('They discussed everything together. The deceased not only took communion with his wife [at his wedding] but with his brother [the emperor] too'). This was a reference to the blood brotherhood the two men shared, which had been sealed by their taking the sacrament of Holy Communion together. And in accordance with traditional funeral ceremonial, my father handed Haile Selassie a photograph of the deceased. In front of everybody, he snatched the picture and, clutching it to his breast, began to weep bitterly.

The same year that *Ras* Kassa died also saw the death of the emperor's second son, Prince Makonnen, who was tragically killed in a car crash. The emperor had already lost two of his daughters and now he had to bury his favourite son as well. *Ras* Asserate recounted to me that the emperor often remarked to him that he himself had actually died when his brother *Ras* Kassa had died and that he was buried when his son, Prince Makonnen, went to his grave. Three years later, in December 1960, he would then be forced to witness those in whom he had invested his greatest hopes for the leadership of the country conspiring against him. Alongside Lieutenant Colonel Workneh, the ringleaders of the palace revolt also included the emperor's favourite general – the commander of the Imperial Guard Mengistu Neway – and his brother Germame Neway, who came from an old aristocratic family in Shoa province.[29]

Yet the brains behind the palace revolt was undoubtedly Germame Neway. He, too, had enjoyed an outstanding education. After graduating from Haile Selassie Secondary School, he was among the first cohort of students to win a scholarship specially endowed by the Crown Prince and be sent to study in the United States in the late 1940s. Initially, he was a student at the University of Wisconsin, where he took his undergraduate degree. He was active in the Union of Ethiopian Students in America and wrote articles for the magazine *Ethiopian Student News*, which was published in New York. Germame had an immense thirst for education and knowledge. He studied the history of the American Revolution, immersed himself in Locke's and Hobbes' theories of the state, and avidly read the works of Marx and Engels as well as the manifestos of the co-founder of the Pan-Africanist movement, George Padmore. Later he transferred to Columbia University, where he wrote a master's dissertation entitled 'The Impact of the Colonial Policy of the Whites in Kenya'. With his head full of ideas, he returned to Ethiopia in 1954, eager to participate in the modernisation of his country. In no time, he obtained a position in the Interior Ministry, where he quickly attracted attention, not only for his radical ideas but also for his unorthodox dress sense. He shunned formal dinner jackets and lounge suits, preferring instead to go around in khaki-drill, sometimes accessorised with a bright red tie.[30]

It didn't take long for the emperor to send him away from the capital, appointing him governor of the Wollamo region in the province of Sidamo. The people there gave him a warm welcome; one of his forebears, *Dejazmatch* Germame, had already been governor of the same region under Emperor Menelik II, and was very popular in this role. Germame Neway set to work with gusto, and soon made a name for himself through his unorthodox approach to discharging his duties. He began distributing fallow farmland to the people. As a result, the rumour began to spread – even reaching the capital – that he was a communist sympathiser and was trying to incite the rural population to revolution. The emperor summoned him to an audience at the palace. In answer to the emperor's question as to why he had taken it upon himself to interfere in the country's tenancy system, Germame coolly replied: 'Because I am the governor, and people have nothing to eat because they have no land.' The emperor was not happy with this response, and so shifted the rebellious governor a little further still from the centre of power, to the Jigga region in Harar province. Haile Selassie was certain that there would be no problem with tenant farmers there, since the only inhabitants of this desert region were Somali nomads. But in Jigga, too, Germame was determined to make a difference. On his arrival he discovered that, although eight hospitals had been built in the region, they had never actually entered operation. They were simply sitting there and falling into disrepair because the Ministry of Public Health had failed to equip them properly. Time and again, Germame went to the capital to raise the question of maladministration in the region he governed, but always came away empty-handed.[31] It is impossible to say when he first conceived the idea of rebelling against the emperor and the whole political system, but sometime during 1960 he succeeded in winning his brother Mengistu over to his plan. They counted on the majority of the 5,000-strong Imperial Guard under Mengistu's command rallying to their cause, so enabling them to stage a successful coup d'état. In addition, their recruitment of secret service chief Lt.-Col. Workneh meant that they now had one of the emperor's closest confidants on their side.

The putsch against the emperor was planned and prepared well in advance. The rebels made their move when Haile Selassie was far away from the capital. He had embarked on an extended trip to Brazil, where he planned to travel with the Brazilian president Juscelino Kubitschek and his wife Donna Sara to see the new capital Brasília, which had only been inaugurated a few months before. In his absence, the emperor had left the business of state in the hands of Workneh and Mengistu Neway – in other words, precisely those men who had been waiting for months for the opportunity to stage their coup. In making their preparations, they had studied in particular Colonel Anwar el Sadat's book *Rebellion on the Nile and the Egyptian Revolution*: seven years before, a bloodless coup had ousted King Farouk of Egypt and driven him into exile, and this scenario now served as the Ethiopian putschists' blueprint for their own plot to topple the Lion of Judah from his throne.

The plan to overthrow the emperor was carefully engineered. On the night of 13–14 December 1960, *Ras* Asserate was roused from his sleep by a telephone call; on the other end of the line was Crown Princess Medfariash-Work. Her husband Crown Prince Asfa-Wossen had gone to dinner the evening before at the empress's villa but had thus far failed to return. When she called the empress to find out what had happened, she was told that at around half-past nine the previous evening, the commander of the Imperial Guard had appeared at the villa and asked to speak to the Crown Prince. *Abba* Gebre Hanna Jimma, the emperor's aged confessor who had known Haile Selassie since childhood, was also summoned, together with Interior Minister *Ras* Andargatchew Masai, Defence Minister *Ras* Abebe and Trade Minister Makonnen Habte-Wold. They had then all left the house together, the empress continued, to go to the headquarters of the Imperial Guard, but since then nothing had been heard of them. *Ras* Asserate Kassa didn't hesitate for an instant, and drove straight away to the Crown Prince's palace, where the Crown Princess had gathered her most trusted friends around her. By this time a clear picture had emerged from the earlier fragmented reports: the Crown Prince, the emperor's confessor, and the ministers were in the custody of the commander of the Imperial Guard and were being held as hostages in the unit's headquarters, just a stone's-throw from the Crown Prince's palace. As if that weren't bad enough, under the pretext that the empress was on her deathbed, many other ministers, generals and dignitaries had also been lured to the Imperial Guard HQ and taken prisoner. In the meantime, the rebels had cut the telephone lines and occupied the state broadcaster, the national bank and the finance ministry building. Officers of the Imperial Guard were in the process of posting armed motorised units on the streets and squares of Addis Ababa and surrounding the capital's high schools and universities.

Even so, the putschists had not managed to seize all the key players and take them hostage. Alongside *Ras* Asserate Kassa, who at that time occupied the post of senate vice-president, the chief of staff of the Ethiopian army, Major General Merid

Mengesha, had also slipped through the net. These two men were determined to confront the rebels; over the course of the next twenty-four hours, they were instrumental in coordinating the response of forces loyal to the emperor, and were ultimately responsible for ensuring that this meticulously-planned attempt to seize power failed. Asserate Kassa made it his top priority to inform the emperor in distant Brasília of the alarming situation back home. Even before daybreak, he succeeded in making it through, in a camouflaged car, to the compound of the British Embassy and having a private discussion with the ambassador Sir Denis Wright. He, in turn, radioed the Foreign Office in London, which relayed *Ras* Asserate's message to Brasília. However, news of the attempted coup in Addis Ababa also reached the emperor from another source. Prince Sahle Selassie, one of the emperor's sons and an avid amateur radio ham, raised the alarm over his wireless set; his call for help was picked up by a fellow enthusiast in Middlesex and passed on to the Ethiopian Embassy in London. When Haile Selassie learned of what was happening in Addis Ababa, his response was immediate. He cancelled his visit to Brazil forthwith and ordered his plane to be got ready for the return flight. He was resolved to fight for his crown.

At midday the following day, Radio Addis Ababa announced that it would be coming back on air. Soon after, listeners heard the voice of the Crown Prince. In measured tones, Prince Asfa-Wossen read out a 'Revolutionary Proclamation,' in which it was declared that a new Ethiopian government had been formed with himself at its head. 'In the last few years,' the Crown Prince announced, 'Ethiopia has been in stagnation. An atmosphere of dissatisfaction and discontent has grown up amongst farmers, merchants and professional people, amongst members of the armed forces and the police and amongst the younger educated Ethiopians – in short amongst the entire Ethiopian population.' This had given rise, he went on, to a 'movement', from which the 'new government' had grown, an administration that had 'dedicated itself to the welfare of the whole Ethiopian people.' His declaration continued: 'The few selfish persons who fight merely for their own interests and for personal power, who are obstacles to progress and who, like a cancer, impede the country's development are now replaced.' And he closed his address with the words: 'Today is the beginning of a new era for Ethiopia in the eyes of the whole world.'[32] The Crown Prince's speech was broadcast repeatedly throughout the day, interspersed with a programme of martial music performed by the military band of the rebel Imperial Guard. And that same evening, Crown Prince Asfa-Wossen was proclaimed as the new regent at the head of a constitutional monarchy, with the emperor's liberally-inclined cousin *Ras* Imru as prime minister and Major General Mulugeta Bulli as supreme commander of the country's armed forces.

Right though the putschists were to claim that there was political stagnation in Ethiopia, they were deluding themselves in thinking they had the support of the Ethiopian people. The general populace was not in sympathy with the rebels; there were no general strikes and no mass protest movement, nor did the uprising attract any following in the provinces. However, Mengistu Neway did try and get the students on his side. On the morning of the following day, a meeting was held with student leaders at the Imperial Guard headquarters. Asserate Kassa and the army chief of staff had, meanwhile, called together the bulk of the army's generals at the headquarters of the First Division in the south of the city. The regular army and the air force did not support the coup; and although a few of the army's generals bided their time, most were determined to crush the rebellion. And, importantly, another central institution of the Ethiopian Empire came out publicly in support of the loyalists, with the head of the Ethiopian Church, Patriarch *Abuna* Basileos, calling for all the excommunication of all those who supported the coup.[33]

On the morning of 15 December, a group of student demonstrators assembled outside the army's headquarters, chanting: 'Arise, fellow Ethiopians! History is calling you! Break the chains of slavery and regain your freedom once more!' On the banners made from torn-up bedsheets that they were holding aloft were slogans such as 'Ethiopia is undergoing peaceful change for us all!' and 'Revolution without bloodshed!'[34] Thus far, no shots had been fired on the streets of Addis Ababa. But the putschists were now left in no doubt that they could not count on the army's backing. Even so, they were in no mood to surrender. In the meantime, they had moved their hostages to the *Genete-Leul* Palace, opposite the Imperial Guards' HQ. There, they were held in the North Wing, in the so-called 'Green Salon', the green-carpeted and wallpapered room in which the empress received her guests after breakfast. Not far from there, in the cellar of the Crown Prince's palace, my brothers and sisters and I had taken refuge along with the Crown Prince's own children. At midday, Radio Addis Ababa broadcast a second proclamation by the Crown Prince: 'We advised that the new People's Government should be given all possible support. We have now learned that Major General Merid Mengesha and Major General Kebede Gebre do not intend to support the new People's Government. We ordered them to come to our palace, but they have refused to comply. As a result of this unlawful behaviour, they are relieved of all their posts and offices with immediate effect.'[35] Shortly afterwards, around 2.30 p.m., an urgent announcement came over the airwaves, ordering all the inhabitants of the capital to remove themselves on the spot from the city's streets and other public places and to go home and stay there. Ten minutes later the first shots were heard. The battle for Addis Ababa had begun.

That night and the following day, loyalist and rebel forces engaged in fierce fighting to secure control of the city's streets. It soon became clear how one-sided this struggle was, with the Imperial Guard unable to withstand the might of the regular army. Eventually, the scattered remnants of the rebel force barricaded themselves into the *Genete-Leul* Palace, where the hostages were still being held captive. The US Ambassador, Arthur L. Richards, had declared himself willing to mediate, and up to the last moment he tried desperately to bring about a peaceful end to the hostage drama. But even now the rebels were unwilling to lay down their arms. When army tanks broke down the palace gates and lined up in front of the building, their guns trained on the portico, the rebels realised they were in a hopeless position. The hatch of one of the tank turrets opened, and out climbed

Tsehafe-Tezaz Aklilu Habte-Wold, prime
minister of Ethiopia 1961–74.

Captain Dereje Haile Mariam, a son-in-law of the emperor.
Jumping down, he called out: 'In the name of the Emperor,
I call on you to surrender!' Mengistu Neway appeared on the
balcony, but before he could say a word to the captain – who
was running towards the palace doors, waving his carbine – his
brother Germame leapt out from behind him, levelled his pistol
at Dereje and shot him dead. This sparked an all-out assault on
the palace by the army. The American ambassador, who was still
inside the building, managed to save himself by jumping out of
a window. In the general mêlée, Mengistu and Germame Neway
burst into the Green Salon with machine-pistols and opened fire,
killing most of the hostages in a hail of bullets. A little later, when
the rebels heard moaning coming from the room, they returned
and finished off anyone who still showed any signs of life, one of
whom was the trade minister Makonnen Habte-Wold.

A handful of the hostages survived the massacre by playing
dead. Later on, they were to describe how events unfolded in the

imperial palace. The emperor's old confessor, it appeared, had only been fatally hit in the second round of shooting. Fifteen of the country's leading politicians lost their lives, among them Major General Mulugeta Bulli and *Leul-Ras* Seyoum Mengesha, the elderly prince of Tigray. Defence minister *Ras* Abebe died of his injuries a few hours after the attack. Only one of the captives in the Green Salon survived the slaughter there: Brigadier General Makonnen Deneke, the emperor's former adjutant, who escaped with a flesh wound. *Dejazmatch* Bezabeh Sileshi, a member of the Senate and *Ras* Andargatchew Masai, the emperor's son-in-law, had been called by the Crown Prince to the empress' suite before the shooting started. Other survivors of the massacre included Crown Prince Asfa-Wossen and *Ras* Imru, the emperor's cousin, because they were being held separately from the other prisoners on the top floor of the palace. When the army stormed the palace, the rebel ringleaders made good their escape through the garage complex. Finally, the Crown Prince sent a servant out clutching a white sheet to signal to the loyalist troops that they were now safe. At the end of three nerve-wracking days, the coup had been crushed, but it had exacted a heavy death toll: over the preceding 24 hours, some 2,000 people had been killed in the battle for control of the capital.

That same evening, Asserate Kassa travelled to Eritrea to inform the emperor that the revolt had been put down. In the interim, Haile Selassie's flight from Brazil had landed in Asmara. The emperor 'looked somewhat tired [but] relaxed and assured.' A large crowd had gathered to welcome him, and 'the emperor was soon surrounded by innumerable screaming people. Had anyone wished to assassinate him, it would have been very easy.'[36] The emperor could hardly wait to get back to Addis Ababa. From the palace in Asmara, he broadcast a message to his people over the radio, in which he exonerated *Ras* Imru and the Crown Prince from any blame for the revolutionary events.

The next day – a Saturday – a long motorcade made its way to the capital's airport to pick up the returning emperor. At its head was the patriarch's car, followed by the empress, the Crown Prince and his wife and the US ambassador; and somewhere in the middle of the line of cars was the limousine where I was sitting alongside the Crown Prince's children. Thousands of people had ringed the airfield to watch the emperor's four-engined DC-6 touch down on the runway. The gangway was set in place, the red carpet rolled out, and everyone waited with bated breath to see the emperor appear. The first person to exit the aircraft was his adjutant, Brigadier General Debebe Haile Mariam, but the moment the emperor in his trademark military uniform came into view, a loud cheering and screaming rose up from the assembled multitude. No sooner had the emperor set foot again on Ethiopian soil than the Crown Prince stepped forward and flung himself on the tarmac at his father's feet in full view of everyone present. I was standing too far away to hear what the emperor said to him, but I was surprised that His Majesty didn't immediately extend his hand to help him up, which would have been the expected reaction. Some commentators have claimed that, when the Crown Prince approached the emperor at the airport, he was carrying a large rock on his back[37] – a traditional gesture of atonement in Ethiopia from ancient times – but I can state categorically that this was not the case. Many years later my father, who had been standing behind the emperor on the steps of the aircraft, told me what Haile Selassie had said to his son when he was prostrate in the dust at his feet – furthermore, he said it loudly enough for everyone in the immediate vicinity to hear: 'We would have been very proud of you if We were coming to attend your funeral. Get up!'

The burning question people were asking at that time was what role the Crown Prince had actually played during the abortive coup. Had he really been threatened at gunpoint to read out the rebels' proclamation, as the official account of the matter maintained? In retrospect, we should consider the fact that the emperor had appointed Crown Prince Asfa-Wossen as governor-general of the province of Wollo – a truly thankless task, given that the people of that region had never forgotten their 'legitimate' ruler *Lij* Iyasu or how he had met his end; and to his dying day, the emperor bore a grudge against this insubordinate province. Now, in the wake of the attempted coup, Haile Selassie's relationship with his eldest son was damaged beyond repair. The fact that the Crown Prince was one of the very few captives to survive the coup, and that he had not been held with the other hostages in the Green Salon at the palace gave the emperor due cause for suspicion. But all discussion of this matter in public was strictly taboo within the emperor's family. At least, my father forbade all speculation about the Crown Prince and reprimanded me sharply whenever I dared to broach the subject.

Twenty years later in London, I finally met the man who is alleged to have forced the Crown Prince to read out the prepared statement: Captain Asrat Deferessu, the one-time spokesman of the Imperial Guard, who was arrested after the coup but released a little while later. Ever since, he had lived in exile in England. I quizzed him about the role of the Crown Prince in the putsch. 'Do you imagine for a moment,' he told me, 'that your father would have lobbied for my release if he hadn't been convinced that no coercion was exerted on the Crown Prince?' By this stage, the Crown Prince had broken his silence on the affair, too. In an interview that he gave in Geneva to the German news magazine *Stern* in 1974 – shortly after Haile Selassie's own arrest by the *Derg* revolutionary junta in Addis Ababa – he freely admitted to his interlocutor: 'I had always been in favour of change in Ethiopia. As you know, I was involved in the attempted coup in 1960, but of my own free will and not, as has sometimes been claimed, under duress. I have always taken the view that only the military might one day bring about real change in Ethiopia.'[38]

This may well have been the case, then. But the key question is not whether the Crown Prince took part in the attempted coup, but whether he might have made a better emperor after Haile Selassie. Many people, above all Ethiopian intellectuals, regarded him as weak and lacking the necessary leadership qualities. On the contrary, I knew him as a kind and thoughtful person and firmly believe that he could have been a worthy successor to his father – so long as the groundwork for a constitutional monarchy had been laid, that is. All those things that would have been flaws in an absolute ruler, such as the lack of experience and the political weakness his opponents accused him of, would have been transformed into positive virtues in a constitutional monarchy. Prince Asfa-Wossen would have fitted well into a role in which the emperor largely performed ceremonial duties and reigned above politics as a symbol of the sovereignty and unity of Ethiopia. And perhaps the Crown Prince himself also sensed that this would have been the only way of saving the 3,000-year-old Ethiopian crown. Haile Selassie, though, had no intention of abdicating – either before the 1960 coup or after it. When, on a later occasion, the emperor was asked why he did not name the Crown Prince as heir to the throne, according to John H. Spencer, he is said to have replied: 'Why should We? He has already been on the throne!'[39]

The day Haile Selassie returned to Addis Ababa, air force jets flew over the capital and wrote his name in the sky with their vapour trails. Around the same time, the first of the fugitive rebel leaders was captured. A military patrol caught Lieutenant Colonel Workneh unawares hiding under a bridge on the road that wound its way up the slopes of Entoto. In the ensuing fire-fight, he shot dead a number of soldiers before the final magazine of his carbine ran out of bullets. He then pulled out his pistol and, turning it on himself, declaimed: 'Tewodoros has taught me something!'[40] The Lieutenant Colonel's body was strung up outside St George's Cathedral for a week. The corpse had been cleaned of blood and dirt and was dressed in a new uniform, with all the badges of rank stripped off it.

Mengistu Neway and his brother, however, had managed to escape to the south of the country, where they were run to ground by a police unit a week after the storming of the palace. To save themselves from being taken prisoner, Germame Neway first shot his brother and then himself: he died on the spot, but Mengistu Neway was only wounded. The bullet had shattered his right cheek and exposed his eyeball, which hung down blindly. After three months in hospital, he was tried for high treason before a properly-constituted court of law, found guilty and publicly hanged with two co-conspirators on Tekle Haimanot Square on 29 March 1961. Mengistu waived his right to lodge an appeal against his death sentence. He had no wish to be thrown upon the mercy of the imperial *Chilot*.

Outwardly, very little appeared to change in Addis Ababa following the abortive coup of December 1960. The emperor announced before the world's press that there would not be 'the slightest deviation from the path We have followed in running Ethiopia'. He went on: 'There will no change in the system of government or in the government's programmes.'[41] The empress, who was a devout Christian, refused ever to set foot in the blood-drenched palace again. And so the royal family moved into the Jubilee Palace. The *Genete-Leul* Palace was handed over to the university, which still uses it to this day, with different parts of it housing an Ethnographic Museum and the Institute for Ethiopian Studies. Revolution had come knocking on the door of Ethiopia but the country's imperial dynasty had faced it down with courage and determination. The army and the Ethiopian Orthodox Church had proved loyal to the emperor, and the rebels had garnered virtually no support from among the populace at large. The emperor's authority was seemingly undisputed. On the day before the storming of the *Genete-Leul* Palace, Mengistu Neway had got into one of Haile Selassie's prized automobiles, which was still flying the imperial standard, and had himself driven around the capital. He was by all accounts astonished to see of groups of people who, thinking that Haile Selassie had returned to power, gathered by the roadside to cheer and wave at the car, shouting: 'Long Live the Emperor!'

And yet the failed coup was to mark a radical caesura in the country's history. Despite appearances, nothing was in actual fact ever the same again: in the words of Harold G. Marcus, 1960 was 'the year the sky began falling in on Haile Selassie'[42] For the first time ever, the authority of the emperor had been seriously challenged. This was also the first time that popular grievances were aired openly. The foundations on which the emperor's throne rested had begun to show cracks. In public, the emperor could airily dismiss his Imperial Guard's act of betrayal: 'Trees that are planted do not always bear the desired fruit.'[43] But inwardly he was deeply affected. For a long time, he could not countenance the thought that his most trusted confidant Lieutenant Colonel Workneh had been one of the principal conspirators and that most of his bodyguard, who after all had been handpicked to protect him, had risen up against him. From now on, the emperor was to view all those around him with far greater suspicion. The national army that Haile Selassie had created had shown itself to be a decisive element in the power structure of the realm. The putschists had not succeeded in wooing the army, despite promising the soldiers and officers more pay. Now that the coup had been crushed the military flexed its muscles and insisted that the emperor increase their wages. Haile Selassie reluctantly acceded to their demands.[44] Finally, fourteen years later, it was the army that drove the Lion of Judah from his palace. It is a bitter irony of history that the leading rebel general in the 1960 coup bore the same given name – Mengistu – as the man who after the toppling and murder of Haile Selassie in 1974 rose to become the bloody dictator of Ethiopia: Mengistu Haile Mariam.

Did Haile Selassie really believe that everything could carry on as before? In view of the fact that several cabinet members had been killed in the Green Salon, at least he found himself forced to appoint a new government. Seven new ministers were installed on 6 February 1961; moreover, those who had particularly distinguished themselves during the coup could count on a promotion. So, General Merid Mengesha was appointed a lieutenant general and also given the post of defence minister. And *Leul-Ras* Asserate Kassa was promoted from vice president to president of the Senate. However, the emperor hesitated in appointing a new prime minister – essentially, he was convinced that he didn't actually need one. For from 1957 onwards, when *Ras-Bitwadad* Makonnen Endalkatchew had been dismissed from his prime ministerial position, there had only been a deputy PM anyway. Ultimately, though, on 17 April 1961, Haile Selassie made his trusted official Aklilu Habte-Wold jointly Prime Minister and Minister of the Pen, thus empowering him to henceforth use the title *Tsehafe-Tezaz*. An imperial commission was also created by Haile Selassie to consider further reforms.[45]

Meanwhile, Haile Selassie addressed the charge of general stagnation in the country that had been levelled by the putschists by passing the buck to his ministers. In a memorable address to the cabinet, he declared:

> 'Our ministers came to Us with their problems and questions. My constant response was: "But you were given the authority to deal with this yourself." How often have Our words not been heeded. People shirked responsibility, avoided taking decisions and instead referred them to Us. As a result, a whole series of programmes have not been implemented, and questions of the utmost importance have gone unanswered. Today, We say to you: this situation cannot be permitted to continue.'[46]

Yet there was nothing to indicate that Haile Selassie really envisaged a situation where ministers would be expected to act on their own initiative. What he had confided to Lieutenant General Workneh before the coup was even truer now: Haile Selassie saw himself as an emperor who had been ordained by God, and hence it was up to the Almighty to decide who should succeed him. Accordingly, anyone in his cabinet who adopted a position that had not been agreed beforehand with His Majesty could reckon upon falling into disfavour, just as before.

So it was that, after the abortive coup in Ethiopia, a growing number of people in the emperor's inner circle reached the conclusion that something fundamental had to change if the country's monarchy was to be saved. They included many of those who had commanded the loyalist forces and defended the Crown against the insurrectionists in the dark days of December 1960. In early 1961, five of these men met on the shores of Lake Langano in the south of the country to discuss possible reforms. Three of them – *Ras* Asserate Kassa, Lieutenant General Abiye Abebe, who was also interior minister and governor-general of Eritrea, and the defence minister Lieutenant General Merid Mengesha – were also members of the royal reform commission. They were joined by the minister for social affairs and later

Their Imperial Majesties with their six children, their son-in-law,
Ras Desta (standing behind the Emperor) and their daughter-in-law,
Leelt Wolete-Israel (on the Emperor's left) in 1932.

governor-general of Harar, Colonel Tamrat Yigezu and the minister of information *Dejazmatch* Germatchew Tekle-Hawariat.
Their discussions resulted in a 'Memorandum to His Majesty',
which appeared decades later in the Amharic-language newspaper *The Reporter* under the headline 'Our loyalty compels us
to recommend some timely reforms to Your Majesty.'[47] In this
memo, they warned that the 'trust and support of the people
might continue to ebb away', and of 'the danger of revolution
increasing'. To prevent this from happening, the signatories
called for a root-and-branch reform, especially in the realms of
bureaucracy, the parliamentary system, the economy and social
welfare, and the organisational structure of the army. In conclusion, they listed seven concrete demands, including a revision of
the constitution, a widening of parliamentary rights of scrutiny,
and a duty of accountability to parliament on the part of the
prime minister. Such views were seldom expressed around the
emperor, and what's more they were being aired in public. The
government newspapers carried no reports on the memorandum,
but copies were soon being circulated throughout the capital and

in the court. The popular British ambassador in Addis Ababa, Sir John Russell, coined the name 'The Stolypinists' for the five authors of the memorandum – an allusion to the former Russian Prime minister Pyotr Arkadyevitsch Stolypin, a monarchist who implemented certain key reforms at the beginning of the 20th century that he hoped would shore up the Tsarist system.[48] But how did the *Negusa Negast* on his throne in Addis Ababa react to the demands of the Ethiopian Stolypinists?

Haile Selassie showed the memorandum to his prime minister, and *Tsehafe-Tezaz* Aklilu Habte-Wold must have encouraged His Majesty in his conviction that he should reject the suggestions. Even though the premier may well have been of the same mind as the signatories of the memo on many matters, he saw it primarily as an attempt by aristocratic forces to relieve him of his office by the back door and seize control of the post of prime minister themselves.[49] The demands of the Stolypinists were forwarded to the reform commission; but presently, along with all other initiatives for a thoroughgoing reform of the Ethiopian state and society, they had run into the sand. One reform, albeit on a very modest scale, was eventually announced in 1966: from then on, the emperor allowed the prime minister to choose his own ministers, though even they were still subject to the emperor's approval. Furthermore, as the Revised Constitution of 1955 provided, even the prime minister himself was still appointed directly by the emperor rather than being elected by parliament.[50] Despite the fact that elections were held for the Chamber of Deputies, parliament continued to exert very little influence upon the country's destiny, and the other great institutions of state that might have been in a position to limit the absolute power of the monarch – the Ministerial Council and the Imperial Crown Council – were fundamentally of no consequence. People soon started to refer to the 'two garages' in which the great and the good of Ethiopia were simply shuffled around by the emperor: the 'lower garage' was the parliament with its two houses, the House of Representatives and the Senate, while the Imperial Crown Council constituted the 'upper garage'.

Haile Selassie then proceeded to deal with the Stolypinists themselves, who had publicly challenged him, in the familiar way. The emperor now had no desire to have such influential people as those who had conspired to make these kinds of plans in his inner circle anymore. After all, a group of people who had been able to put down a coup might just as easily be in a position to instigate a coup of their own. And so the emperor embarked on a new round in the game of *Shumshir* and banished the dissidents in all directions: Lieutenant General Abiye now became the new president of the Senate, the 'lower garage', while *Dejazmatch* Germatchew was dispatched to the remote region of Illubabor. Colonel Tamrat was sent away to be governor-general of Gondar and *Ras* Asserate Kassa was made viceroy of Eritrea. Only Lieutenant General Merid Mengesha kept his post as defence minister. Even so, he did not play any significant role in Ethiopian politics from now on, and died three years after presentation of the memorandum, in 1966.

After the *annus horribilis* of 1960, in which the sky began to fall in on Haile Selassie, there followed a period that harboured further bad news. On 15 February 1962, Empress Menen passed away after many months of being bedridden, and just a few weeks later, on 23 April, the emperor's youngest son Prince Sahle Selassie died at the age of just thirty-one. Three days of mourning followed the death of the empress, during which all government departments, schools and shops remained closed. In accordance with Ethiopian tradition, the empress was buried on the day she died. And in the days that followed, thousands of people set off from all around the country to make a pilgrimage to the capital and pay their last respects to the departed monarch. The kitchen maids at court dyed their aprons black, and the streets of Addis Ababa were filled with people dressed in black mourning clothes.[51] Many of the grieving ladies-in-waiting at court followed the customary practice of cutting their hair off and wrapping their bald heads in black shawls. The men, for their part, did not shave throughout the mourning period of forty days and went around sporting long beards.

The Stolypinists
The reformists of 1961

Leul-Ras Asserate
Kassa, former Viceroy
of Eritrea and the last
President of the Imperial
Crown Council.

Lt.-Gen. Merid
Mengesha, minister
of defence 1960–66.

Lt.-Gen. Abiye Abebe, president of the Senate and last imperial minister of defence.

Lt. Colonel Tamrat Yigezu, the former Governor-General of Gondar and Minister of Human Development.

Dejazmatch Germatchew Tekle-Hawariat, former minister of information and later crown councillor.

Most studies of Haile Selassie only devote a footnote to the empress; and yet the influence that she exerted on her husband over their many decades of marriage should not be underestimated. Empress Menen was not a political person in the way that, say, Menelik II's queen consort Empress Taitu had been, the woman who in 1896 had commanded her own regiment in the field against the Italian invaders. But she was undeniably a constant and indispensable source of support for Haile Selassie. Nor did she ever leave her husband's side, even during difficult times such as when her uncle *Lij* Iyasu was deposed. She always played host to distinguished foreign guests on the many state visits to Ethiopia that took place after the war, though she never accompanied the emperor on his trips abroad. The very thought of leaving her homeland was anathema to her. It stirred up dark memories of the hard times she had endured in exile. She had no desire ever again to experience the fog and cold that had so impaired her health during her stay in England. After the war, she became an important advisor to the emperor – not in affairs of state, but certainly where humanitarian matters were concerned. As a deeply religious person, she abhorred the death penalty. 'God granted us humans life,' she once explained, 'and only He can take it from us.' Many a person who found himself accused of high treason in the empire ultimately owed their lives to her goodness and warm-hearted nature. She endowed many churches, not just in her native country: for instance, after the war, as thanks for the royal family's sojourn in Palestine, she funded the building of a church in Jericho. The empress was also a staunch champion of women's rights. Before the Italian invasion she opened the first school for girls only out of her private purse. She became the first President of the Ethiopian Red Cross, in which capacity she contributed greatly by supplying food and medical goods to the war effort in 1936. From her return from exile in 1941 until her death in 1962, she was head of the Ethiopian Women's Welfare Association and patron of the Empress Menen Handicraft School.

But above all *Itege* Menen was a family person and a guiding spirit to her children and grandchildren. I can still vividly recall

Haile Selassie accompanied by the Dutch Ambassador to
Ethiopia through the Dutch Pavilion at the Red Cross Festival
in 1963. The author, aged 15, walks behind the Emperor.

the time when my mother was absent for a long spell in England,
where she was receiving medical treatment. During this time, the
empress cared for me and my siblings with touching solicitude,
sending us fruits and sweets on a regular basis and inviting us to
the palace once a week to make sure that we were all right. But
she was also very conscious of her status as the grand-daughter of
the King of Wollo and as a princess in her own right. My mother
once told me the following story: When *Ras* Tafari Makonnen

was about to be crowned king in 1930, he toyed with the idea of leaving his wife and ascending the throne with another woman, the beautiful Aster Mengesha, sister of the Prince of Tigray *Ras* Seyoum. It was *Ras* Kassa who brought his cousin to his senses at this time. He took him to task, telling him: 'Princess Menen has always stuck by you, now it's up to you to show some loyalty to your wife!' As the empress was telling my mother this tale, she also came out with an astonishing confession: 'If he had left me,' she confided, 'I'd have left the house there and then and taken up with *Ras* Hailu!' The powerful Prince of Gojjam and fierce opponent of the emperor had made no secret of his fondness for Menen. Whether she ever really had such a move in mind, I cannot say – perhaps she only said it in jest. But in any event it shows that, when the chips were down, she could be a thoroughly feisty person.

With the death of Empress Menen, the palace became a lonely place. *Ras* Kassa was dead, along with Prince Makonnen, the emperor's favourite son, and now Prince Sahle Selassie was gone as well. The emperor's only surviving children were Princess Tenagne-Work and Crown Prince Asfa-Wossen. The Crown Prince's prospects of ever succeeding to the throne had withered on the vine. Ultimately, he would go down in history as the oldest ever Crown Prince of Ethiopia. Over the last thirteen years of Haile Selassie's life, there was no one left – either in his family or in the circle of his dignitaries or advisors – whose critical views the emperor would accept without suspecting an ulterior motive behind the advice he received. Anyone who gave evidence of any kind of strength or especial popularity was deeply suspect to him. And so the Ethiopian ship of state found itself being tossed about on heavy seas without a helmsman or deck officer until it finally sank beneath the waves a decade later.

CHAPTER EIGHT

Shaking hands with history

1963 to 1973

In the 1950s and 1960s, the geopolitical map of Africa changed fundamentally. Throughout the continent, people started to fight to liberate themselves from their erstwhile colonial masters, with a growing number of states achieving independence: Libya was the first to break free (of Italian rule) in 1951, followed five years later by the Sudan, Morocco and Tunisia, and shortly thereafter Ghana and Guinea. In 1960, the 'Year of Africa', no fewer than eighteen colonial territories gained their independence: alongside British Somaliland and Italian Somaliland, these were Cameroon, Togo, Madagascar, the Democratic Republic of Congo, Dahomey (Benin), Niger, Upper Volta (Burkina Faso), the Ivory Coast, Chad, the Central African Republic, the Republic of Congo, Gabon, Senegal, Mali, Nigeria and Mauretania. The following year saw Sierra Leone and Tanganyika (Tanzania) become sovereign states, and in 1962 Algeria, Uganda, Rwanda and Burundi also achieved independence.

In almost all these countries, the indigenous liberation movements had taken Ethiopia as their model, as the only African country that had successfully resisted white European colonization for centuries. Another such grouping was the African National Congress (ANC), which under its leader Nelson Mandela was fighting against the apartheid regime in South Africa. For decades the ANC had sought through peaceful protest to bring down the racist system of oppression directed from Pretoria by the white supremacist National Party. But in March 1960, after security forces shot dead 69 unarmed demonstrators at the Sharpeville township near Johannesburg, the ANC was banned and went underground. From there, it embarked upon a violent struggle against apartheid. Nelson Mandela was also forced to go into hiding, becoming leader of *Umkhonto weSizwe* ('Spear of the Nation', abbreviated to MK), the armed wing of the ANC. In 1962, using the assumed name of David Motsamayi (meaning 'the walker') Mandela left South Africa to travel to other parts of Africa and Europe and raise support for the ANC cause. His travels also took him to Addis Ababa. The first congress of the Pan African Freedom Movement for East, Central and Southern Africa (PAFMECSA), formed under Ethiopian auspices, was being held there that year, and Mandela planned to attend as the ANC's representative. It was the movement's stated aim to foster solidarity among the newly independent states of Africa and to provide support for liberation movements right across the continent.

Mandela gives an account of this, his first trip to Ethiopia, in his celebrated autobiography *Long Walk to Freedom*:

'Ethiopia has always held a special place in my own imagination and the prospect of visiting Ethiopia attracted me more strongly than a trip to France, England and America combined. I felt I would be visiting my own genesis, unearthing the roots of what made me an African. Meeting the Emperor himself would be like shaking hands with history.'[1]

In Khartoum in the Sudan, Mandela got a shock when he stepped aboard the aircraft that was to fly him to the Ethiopian capital:

'I had never seen a black pilot before, and the instant I did I had to quell my panic. How could a black man fly an airplane? But a moment later I caught myself: I had fallen into the apartheid mind-set, thinking Africans were inferior and that flying was a white man's job. I sat back in my seat, and chided myself for such thoughts.'[2]

Nor was this to be the only surprise for Mandela on this trip. Shortly after arriving in Addis Ababa, he was present on the dais to witness the military parade which marked the opening of the PAFMECSA conference. 'Here, for the first time in my life, I was witnessing black soldiers commanded by black generals applauded by black leaders who were all guests of a black Head of State. It was a heady moment. I only hoped it was a vision of what lay in the future for my own country.'[3] At the congress itself, which was opened by Haile Selassie, Mandela was the sole speaker apart from the emperor. He wrote in his memoirs about the impression that Haile Selassie made upon him at that time;

'His Imperial Majesty was dressed in an elaborate brocaded army uniform. I was surprised by how small the emperor appeared, but his dignity and confidence made him seem like the African giant that he was. It was the first time I had witnessed a head of state go through the formalities of his office, and I was fascinated. He stood perfectly straight, and inclined his head only slightly to indicate that he was listening. Dignity was the hallmark of all his actions.'[4]

Yet Mandela's real mission in Addis Ababa went beyond simply appearing at the PAFMECSA conference: it was decided at a meeting between the ANC leader and the emperor that recruits to *Umkhonto* would be trained by a special unit of the Ethiopian police and prepared for their struggle against the forces of the apartheid regime. Moreover, in that same year, one 'David Motsamayi' began his own course of military training in the Ethiopian capital. In the Ethiopian passport that he was issued with, his occupation was given as 'journalist'. The police commissioner of Addis Ababa, Colonel Tadesse Birru, provided lodgings for the leader of the anti-apartheid movement in his own house. Mandela's instructor was a veteran former Ethiopian freedom fighter, Lieutenant Wondemu Befekadu: 'Our programme was strenuous,' Mandela recalled, 'we trained from 8 a.m. until 1 p.m, broke for a shower and lunch, and then again from 2 p.m. to 4 p.m. From 4 p.m. into the evening, I was lectured on military science by Colonel Tadesse, who was also assistant commissioner of police and had been instrumental in foiling a recent coup attempt against the emperor.'⁵ In Addis Ababa, Nelson Mandela learned how to handle a rifle and a handgun, how to fire a mortar and the techniques of bomb-making, but also the 'art and science of soldiering'. The training programme had originally been intended to last six months, but after just eight weeks, when fighting escalated between the ANC and South African security forces, Mandela was recalled to his homeland. As a leaving present, Colonel Tadesse gave him an automatic pistol with two hundred rounds of ammunition. In the event, Mandela did not have much time to put his newly-acquired knowledge into practice. Six months after his return to South Africa, he was arrested, put on trial for sabotage and for plotting an armed rebellion and sentenced to lifelong imprisonment. It would be twenty-seven years before he was eventually released.

The Ethiopian emperor had been resolute in putting himself at the forefront of the pan-African struggle for independence and unity. He fostered close contacts with nationalist political leaders in Kenya, Tanzania, Uganda and Rhodesia (Zimbabwe). In 1958, the Economic Commission of the United Nations in Africa (ECA) was inaugurated, with the aim of furthering the development of the African continent. This body had its permanent seat in Addis Ababa, and a brand-new building was erected as its headquarters in the centre of the capital – Africa Hall, an impressive symbol of growing African self-confidence. In that same year, at the instigation of the prime minister and later president of Ghana, Kwame Nkrumah, all the leaders of the independent nations of Africa – numbering eight at the time – assembled for their first ever conference in Accra.

The leaders were all in accord on the basic objective of liberating and fostering unity among African states but were at odds over what form this should take and how to achieve it. Before long the African countries had split into two groups: on the one hand was the militantly anti-colonial Casablanca Group around Kwame Nkrumah and the president of Guinea, Ahmed Sékou Touré. In addition to Ghana and Guinea, this group also included Egypt, Algeria, Morocco and Mali. On the other hand, there was the more moderate Monrovia group, which included among others Cameroon, the Central African Republic, Chad, the Ivory Coast, Nigeria, Senegal, Sierra Leone and Tunisia. Haile Selassie, who was not given to extreme solutions, either internally or in his foreign policy, felt a greater affinity to the Monrovia Group; even so, this in no way prevented him from establishing friendly relations both with Nkrumah and with the president of the United Arab Republic, Colonel Gamal Abdel Nasser, who had styled himself as the principal reformer both in the Arabian and African regions. The differences between the Casablanca and Monrovia Groups also hallmarked the afore-mentioned PAFMECSA conference of 1962 that Nelson Mandela had travelled to Addis Ababa for. A meeting of the Monrovia group was fixed for the following year in the Ethiopian capital. But now Haile Selassie conceived a plan to open up that meeting to all African nations and bring into being a common organization for African unity.

The emperor took the occasion of Sékou Touré's state visit to Ethiopia in the autumn of 1962 as an opportunity to unveil his ambitious plan to the Guinean president: political, economic and military interests dictated that African states should stand together and speak to the world with one voice.[6] The two leaders prepared a communiqué in which all African states were invited to a conference in Addis Ababa in May 1963. Over the months that followed, the Ethiopian capital made preparations for this great event: the streets were repaired, and existing hotels were renovated and new ones built in order to welcome the official guests arriving from throughout the continent. On 20 May 1963, in the full glare of the world's media, the heads of state and government of no fewer than twenty-eight countries assembled at the Africa Hall in Addis Ababa to discuss a common way forward. The German news magazine Der Spiegel painted a vivid picture of this meeting of African leaders:

'For the entire four days of the conference, from 22 to 25 May, the Ethiopian monarch presided over proceedings from the honorary chairman's seat on the rostrum, in front of the most colourful assemblage of statesman to come together since the founding of the United Nations in 1945. The Mauretanian president Mukhtar Uld Daddah, dressed in a sky-blue silk burnous and white calfskin slippers, sat next to Madagascar's portly head of state Philibert Tsiranana, who had teamed a red, green and yellow checked raffia hat with his sober grey made-to-measure Parisian suit and who whiled away the time during the lengthy speeches of his presidential colleagues by playing around with his 8-mm cine camera. Despite the fact that he had been excommunicated, the President of Congo (Brazzaville), Fulbert Youlou, could be seen there before every session, praying in the white vestments of a Catholic priest, and wearing a chunky, square golden seal-ring, with his forehead resting on the table top, while the chain-smoking, bald-headed King of Burundi, Mwambutsa IV chatted with the Congolese president Joseph Kasavubu over Youlou's bowed head. On the far left side of the horseshoe-shaped conference table sat Kwame Nkrumah of Ghana, dressed in a severe black revolutionary's tunic, reminiscent of Stalin or Mao Zedong. He would regularly break out in loud applause – often being the only person to do so – whenever a speaker mentioned the word 'imperialists' or 'exploiters'. Emperor Haile Selassie, the very epitome of sober neutrality, greeted every address with an identical degree of polite symbolic applause befitting his imperial dignity, tapping silently with the fingertips of his right hand on the palm of his left, even when the Moscow-educated Oginga Odinga from British-occupied Kenya, armed with a gold-topped walking stick and a horsehair fly-whisk, waved both arms agitatedly in the air and bellowed the Black African battle-cry of *Uhuru*! ('Freedom!') at the assembled delegates.'[7]

Even before the heads of state met, the group of foreign ministers had convened to hammer out the charter of the nascent Organisation of African Unity, though their talks soon ran aground. But now that the leaders of Africa had come together

Emperor Haile Selassie and President Gamal Abdel
Nasser chairing the opening session of the OAU
conference in Addis Ababa on 22nd of May 1963.

in his presence, Haile Selassie saw that his hour had come. He
argued passionately for the establishment of an overarching alliance that would span the continent with a permanent administrative structure. Yet precisely what form such an alliance
should take was the subject of fierce debate among the heads of
state, who had extremely divergent views on the matter. Ghana's
President Kwame Nkrumah was largely alone in advocating a
formal union between states and the formation of a common
government – such close ties seemed inopportune to his colleagues, many of whom were primarily concerned to in their
independence. Opinions were also deeply divided on question
of what powers that should be vested in the Secretary-General
of the organisation. One major bone of contention was whether
such an alliance between African nations should also entail the
formation of a single African army.

Yet however different the delegates' political standpoints may
have been, Haile Selassie threw all his weight behind ensuring
that the conference was a success. When Nkrumah saw that

his plan for a United States of Africa was not well received by his fellow leaders, he was determined to leave the conference without more ado. Even the most impassioned pleas could not alter the Ghanaian president's resolve, and the meeting seemed on the verge of imminent failure. At the eleventh hour, however, Haile Selassie took Sékou Touré on one side. Clutching his hand, the emperor looked deep into his eyes and addressed the president of Guinea: *'Mon fils, je vous prie'* ('My son, I beg you'), imploring him to prevail upon his 'brother' Kwame Nkrumah to come back to the conference table. Moved by this intervention, Sékou Touré replied: *'Oui père, je vais essayer.'* ('Yes father, I'll try').[8] And he did indeed succeed in getting Nkrumah to return to the negotiations.

Eventually, the conference agreed upon a charter of the Organisation of African Unity (OAU), an 'Africa of fatherlands'. Instead of a common army, it was resolved that a common defence committee should be established, which would meet regularly to discuss security matters. The borders between countries that had been drawn up by the colonial powers were generally affirmed. A 'Liberation Committee' was also created to land support to the liberation movements in countries that were still under colonial rule. The heads of government of the OAU would come together every year for a summit, while the foreign ministers would meet at six-monthly intervals. A budget was agreed, and finally the official languages that the organisation would use: alongside English and French, Arabic, Amharic and other African languages were admitted as *linguae francae*. In the night of 25–26 May, the charter was formally signed by the assembled heads of state.[9] Even thought the formation of the OAU was in many respects a compromise between the most divergent ideological views and modes of government, this agreement was nevertheless a milestone in the the history of Africa. And the skill in having reconciled the most conflicting opinions was one of the greatest foreign policy triumphs of Haile Selassie. It earned him the soubriquet 'the Father of Africa'.

At this inaugural conference, Haile Selassie was elected as the first president of the organisation; only the question of where the headquarters of the OAU would be located was deferred for the time being. Two years later, the African heads of state and government, meeting in Cairo, opted for Addis Ababa as the permanent seat of their organisation. With the foundation of the OAU, Ethiopia was accorded a key position within African politics. And on several occasions over the ensuing years the position of authority that the emperor enjoyed among the assembled nations of Africa would play a decisive role in resolving conflicts. The first baptism of fire came just six months after the founding of the organisation, when armed conflict erupted between the member states of Algeria and Morocco. In his capacity as President of the OAU, the emperor succeeded through his mediation in bringing about a cessation of hostilities and in referring the ultimate resolution of the conflict to a conference of foreign ministers. Over the course of the following years, virtually all African states united under the umbrella of the OAU, until the organisation finally transformed into the African Union in 2002.

This ongoing process of decolonisation also served to reshuffle the pack of cards in the game of international relations and alliances. In 1955, at the instigation of the Indian prime minister Nehru and the Yugoslavian leader Marshal Tito, representatives from 29 Asian and African nations who belonged to neither of the emerging global power blocs – the Eastern Bloc under the leadership of Moscow and the Western alliance led by Washington – met in the Indonesian city of Bandung. In addition to Nehru and Tito, the high-ranking guests also included the Egyptian leader Nasser and the Chinese prime minister Zhou Enlai. And despite its alliance with the United States, the Ethiopian Empire, represented by Haile Selassie, also took part in the conference. The Bandung Conference gave rise four years later to the Organisation of Non-Aligned States, which Ethiopia also joined. In particular, Haile Selassie was impressed by the policies of the Yugoslavian leader, who had successfully extricated himself from the clutches of the Soviet Union and put himself at the forefront of the non-aligned movement. The two heads of state became close allies from the first state visit by Marshal Tito to Ethiopia in December 1955. Thereafter they met regularly, and right to the end Haile Selassie referred to Tito as 'my friend'.[10] The Marshal advised the Ethiopian emperor against keeping all his eggs in one basket – a piece of advice that the latter was all too ready to heed.[11] Not to rely solely upon one protecting power, for good or ill, to manoeuvre adeptly between various parties and wherever possible to play one off against the other: these had always been the guiding political principles of Haile Selassie. In an interview with *Der Spiegel* on the occasion of the founding of the OAU, in response to being asked what he understood by 'non-alignment', the emperor responded: 'Our own version, Our conception of non-alignment can be formulated in the following way: whenever a country receives aid of any kind from another, without coming under the influence of that country, or when a country is able to boost its economy with outside assistance without being unduly influenced by a foreign power or a foreign power bloc – that's non-alignment.'[12]

As one of the figureheads of the Organization of Non-Aligned States, the Ethiopian emperor made ample use of this conception. In the General Assembly of the United Nations, the Ethiopian delegates no longer, as they had done in previous decades, automatically followed the United States when it came to casting their vote. As early as 1959, Haile Selassie went on his first state visit to Moscow, where he was received by the Soviet premier Nikita Khrushchev. At the end of this visit – to Washington's astonishment – he returned to Addis Ababa with the promise of over $100 million dollars in development aid from the USSR.[13] This was merely the prelude to several other official visits by the emperor to various Eastern Bloc states. He also fostered close ties with China, which like Yugoslavia had made a clean break with Soviet Communism. In 1971, the emperor visited the People's Republic for the first time. In the Hall of the People on the Square of Heavenly Peace, he met Mao Zedong – one of the rare late appearances by the Chinese party leader, who by that stage had largely withdrawn from public life. At the conclusion of this trip, Haile Selassie negotiated an extensive aid package for Ethiopia with the Chinese prime minister Zhou Enlai. At 25 years, the period of the loan was so generously set that it is more accurate to talk in terms of a gift rather than the extension of credit.[14]

Nonetheless, Ethiopia was still fundamentally reliant, as it had been for some time, upon the support of the United States. The USA supplied the country with guns, tanks and aircraft; it was responsible for training the Ethiopian armed forces, provided economic aid and under the Peace Corps programme sent a steady stream of teachers and instructors to the country. Not least, the United Sates was Ethiopia's principal trade partner, with the great majority of its coffee crop being exported to America. Haile Selassie was well aware of this relationship of dependency, and his occasional flirts with Moscow and Beijing were primarily designed to spur Washington on to supplying even more aid.

Although the country's internal situation continued to give cause for concern, Haile Selassie was a statesman who was widely respected throughout the world. The emperor was happy to bask in the glow of international recognition and played his role of the 'father of Africa' for all it was worth. In 1972, he managed to get the Sudanese president Numeiri and the rebel forces of South Sudan around a negotiating table in the Ethiopian capital and to have them sign the Addis Ababa Peace Accord – thus bringing to an end, at least temporarily, five years of civil war in the Sudan. The more news flooded in about faltering development in his own country, the more inexhaustible the emperor's foreign visits became. With the exception of Fiji and New Zealand, there was scarcely a country that Haile Selassie did not visit during his reign. Between 1954 and 1973, the emperor visited the United States alone on no fewer than six separate occasions. No other head of state in the world would make more state visits to Washington in the 20th century.

One of Haile Selassie's most memorable overseas visits was in 1966, to Jamaica. The emperor was used to widespread public acclaim and adulation, but here he was not simply welcomed as a statesman but as a living God. Marcus Garvey's prophesy of a 'Black King' who would be the saviour of Africans had fallen on fertile ground in Jamaica. This foretelling of a bright new dawn brought hope to the descendants of deported African slaves living in the slums of the Jamaican capital Kingston. In *Ras* Tafari, who had ascended the Ethiopian throne on 2 November 1930, they saw the prophesied Saviour and the returning Messiah. In that year, 1930, Jamaica had suffered a severe drought; and just as the reports and pictures of the coronation in Addis Ababa began to be broadcast around the globe, it started raining on the island. The Rastafarians, as Garvey's adherents soon began to call themselves, identified the Ethiopian emperor with the Biblical 'King of Kings from the House of David' whose coming was foretold in the Book of Revelation.[15] Three times, the Rastafarians believed, God had appeared on Earth in human form: the first time in the shape of the Old Testament figure Melchisedek, the 'King of Justice' from Jerusalem; the second time as Jesus Christ, and on the third occasion as Haile Selassie, who – as prophesied in the Revelation – would break the Seven Seals and usher in the Thousand-Year Realm of Peace. Furthermore, could not the return of Haile Selassie to the throne in 1941, after years of banishment and exile, be seen as a triumph of the Last Judgement? The British colonial administration and the Jamaican authorities did their utmost to suppress the movement, but to no avail: Rastafarianism spread among the poor population of Kingston and beyond. Time and again, Rastas went on pilgrimage to Ethiopia to be close to their 'Messiah'. The emperor even established a settlement for them at Shashamane in the south of the country in 1948. And now, barely four years after Jamaica had gained its independence from its British colonial rulers, the Rastafarians awaited the visit of their revered reborn Messiah to their own country with feverish anticipation.

The day of the emperor's arrival, 21 April 1966, was declared a public holiday in Jamaica. Tens of thousands of delirious Rastafarians had gathered at the airport from right across the island. Wherever one looked, one saw dreadlocks and long beards. The huge crowd swayed in time to an insistent drumbeat, palm leaves and green-gold-and-red flags were waved, and the air was thick with the heady aroma of marijuana.[16] On this occasion, too, Heaven sent a sign: it had been raining incessantly for hours, but as the aircraft carrying the emperor came into view on its landing approach, the sun suddenly broke through the clouds. At the moment when Haile Selassie emerged from the plane, the cheering crowd invaded the airfield – and the emperor immediately withdrew back into the aircraft for his own safety. The welcoming ceremony and the playing of the Ethiopian and Jamaican national anthems were cancelled.

The following day, however, a ceremony to greet the Ethiopian emperor was held in the main stadium in Kingston, at which every seat was sold out. Many Rastafarians were among the crowd that assembled here, too. Finally, Haile Selassie met a delegation of Rastafarians in the King's House, the governor-general of Jamaica's residence in the capital. He gave them gold medallions as gifts, but above all he tried to impress upon them that he was not the Messiah: 'We are not God. We are not a prophet. We are a slave of God', he told them. He expressly proclaimed his devotion to the Christian faith, and to underline this he founded two churches – one on Jamaica and the other on Trinidad – and sent an Ethiopian bishop and several priests to work in the Caribbean.

There were also other occasions on which Haile Selassie denied that he was a reborn Messiah. For instance, in a 1967 radio interview with the Canadian broadcaster Bill McNeil, in response to being asked what he thought about the fact that millions of people around the world regarded him as a reincarnation of Jesus Christ, he said:

'I have heard of that idea. I also met certain Rastafarians. I told them clearly that I am a man, that I am mortal, and that I would be replaced by the oncoming generation; and that they should never make a mistake in assuming or pretending that a human being is emanated from a deity.'[17]

Yet the Rastafarians were not to be shaken in their beliefs. One of their most prominent adherents was the Jamaican reggae singer Bob Marley, and his music and that of other musicians spread the beliefs of Rastafarianism around the entire world.

Nowadays, some 32,000 or 1.1 percent of Jamaica's 2.9 million inhabitants profess this faith.[18] I myself occasionally encounter Rastafarians. Whenever they address me as 'God's Nephew', I tell them that Haile Selassie was a man, and moreover a devout Christian and Protector of the Ethiopian Orthodox Church. It makes little impression upon them, I must confess. One Rasta once told me: 'The nose is right next to the eyes, but we cannot see it.' One thing is certain: if there had been any indications that Haile Selassie regarded himself as a deity or the Messiah, he would have been excommunicated by the Ethiopian Patriarch. After all, another emperor – *Lij* Iyasu – had been deposed for a far less serious offence, when rumours began to circulate that he had converted to Islam (see Chapter 2).

There is no doubting that the Rastafarians have their merits, though. I personally greatly value their unshakeable belief in the Pan-African ideal. It deserves to be supported – especially in these current times, when enthusiasm for a unified Africa is by no means as great as it was in the 1960s. As an Ethiopian, I am proud that Rastas wave the flag of Ethiopia throughout the world. For many African nations, the green, gold, and red flag became the symbol for African independence, and they adopted elements of it into their own standards. For Rastafarians, the flag – emblazoned with the Lion of Judah in its centre – became the characteristic banner for their worldwide movement.

If Rastafarians wanted to do Haile Selassie a genuine and lasting service (though I absent myself from taking the initiative on this score), instead of venerating him as a god or as the Messiah, they might lobby the General Synod of the Ethiopian Orthodox Church in Addis Ababa to canonize the former emperor – just as the Russian Orthodox Church has done with the last Russian tsar, Nicholas II, and other members of the Romanov dynasty. There are many examples in Ethiopian history of rulers being venerated as saints, such as the emperors Lalibela and Gebre-Maskal. For no one disputes that all saints were human beings.

As the emperor increasingly took refuge in foreign policy and constantly went off on foreign visits, the business of state in Ethiopia ground to a halt, to all intents and purposes. The pile of unresolved tasks in he country continued to mount, with no one willing or able to tackle them. The decision to dissolve the federation with Eritrea and to incorporate the region into the empire proved fateful. The declaration of Eritrea as the fourteenth province of Ethiopia in 1962 gave birth to the guerrilla movement against Ethiopian rule. Conflict began with isolated attacks on police stations, before the violence steadily escalated over the following years to acts of sabotage, assassinations and aircraft hijackings. To counter the Muslim-oriented Eritrean Liberation Front (ELF), whose aim was to transform Eritrea into an Arab-Islamic state, the Eritrean People's Liberation Front (EPLF) was formed in the mid-1960s, which drew its support overwhelmingly from the Christian-dominated Highland region. Before long, these liberation movements were not only fighting the Ethiopian authorities but principally also one another, and the violence erupted into an open civil war. Ultimately, the emperor capitulated in the face of this violence when he decided to declare a state of emergency in Eritrea.

Repeatedly throughout the 1960s, the prime minister *Tsehafe-Tezaz* Aklilu Habte-Wold had urged the emperor to issue a decree placing Eritrea under military rule. But *Ras* Asserate Kassa, who had occupied the post of Governor-General of Eritrea from 1964 onwards and from his residence in Asmara, believed he had a far better grasp of the situation on the ground there than the central government in Addis Ababa, set his face firmly against such a measure. On taking up his position in Asmara, he had adopted a policy of 'benign neglect', for which he had the emperor's backing. This policy involved avoiding any military over-reaction and isolating the guerrillas in terms of international geopolitics. The German political scientist and Africa expert Volker Matthies gave the following assessment of this approach: 'The imperial regime's strategy of ignoring the Eritrean uprising politically and isolating the rebels was clearly evident in its attempts to play down the violence there as traditional *shifta* (banditry) and criminalise such activity. Although the imperial administration recognized the danger of the insurrection, it never publicly admitted as much.'[19] But there was strong opposition to this policy, both on the part of disgruntled army officers and by prime minister Aklilu Habte-Wold, who called for a tough military crackdown against the liberation movements. Another point of dissension was the viceroy's demand that at least 60 percent of the taxes collected in Eritrea should be used for development projects in the province, a point the central government opposed vehemently.

In a secret memo to the prime minister in June 1970, *Ras* Asserate registered his protest against the government's planned introduction of a state of emergency in Eritrea.[20] He was convinced that even just the persistent rumours that martial law was about to be imposed would lead to a further escalation of the violence. But this time *Ras* Asserate's advice was not heeded by the emperor. Instead, Haile Selassie authorised the military commander in Eritrea, General Teshome Ergetu, to take action without first consulting the Governor-General. *Ras* Asserate responded by decamping to London and putting all affairs of state in the hands of his deputy Tesfa-Yohannes Berhe.[21] As *Ras* Asserate had feared, the situation grew steadily worse. On 21 November, guerrilla fighters from the ELF ambushed General Teshome and assassinated him. Haile Selassie reacted by declaring the long-threatened state of emergency in Eritrea, and appointed the new commander-in-chief there, General Debebe Haile Mariam, as the military governor of the province. A few days later, the Ethiopian army launched a major offensive against rebel forces. The conflict escalated, developing into a bloody civil war that was only brought to a provisional conclusion in 1993 with the independence of Eritrea.

It was not only in Eritrea, however, but also in the southeastern region of Ogaden, inhabited principally by Somalis, that the local populace sought to break away from the central government – and these separatist movements could not be suppressed by military means. The empire was now afflicted by conflicts which continued to smoulder in a number of different areas: between the periphery and the central government; between farmers and large landowners; and between the country's old aristocracy and the new elites. Archaic farming methods were still in force almost everywhere and the ossified tenancy system largely restricted the country's agriculture to a subsistence level. Although a new Ministry for Land Reform had been established within the imperial administration in 1966, the root-and-branch reform of land distribution that many in the country were clamouring for was endlessly postponed.

Within the ruling echelons of the empire, the groups of supporters who gathered around the two most important men in the emperor's inner circle viewed one another with deep suspicion and bent all their efforts towards thwarting each other: on the one hand the aristocrats who behind the scenes had thrown their weight behind *Ras* Asserate, and on the other the 'technocrats' around prime minister Aklilu Habte-Wold, who like most of his fellow ministers was not a member of the aristocratic class. During his years of service to the emperor, the prime minister had achieved a great deal, primarily in the realm of foreign policy, but he also had one major shortcoming: only on very rare occasions did this European-minded head of government leave the capital and travel to the Ethiopian provinces. For example, he only visited Eritrea officially once – on the occasion of the visit of the Chinese premier Zhou Enlai, who for diplomatic reasons could not be received in the capital. *Ras* Asserate, who had got to know all the provinces of his homeland, even presiding over many of them as governor-general, made no secret of the fact that he found the prime minister's knowledge of his own country woefully inadequate. Nevertheless, the mere fact that Aklilu Habte-Wold was not of noble birth ensured him a high level of support among the Ethiopian intellectual elite.

In turn, the prime minister feared that *Ras* Asserate might make a bid for power. Quite a few people imputed designs on the throne to the son of *Ras* Kassa. For instance, a communiqué sent by the British embassy in Addis Ababa to the head of the East Africa division of the Foreign Office in November 1969 makes reference to the widespread rumour that *Ras* Asserate had promised to restore the status of a federation to Eritrea if the ELF liberation movement agreed to renounce the use of violence.[22] The

embassy discounts the rumour as scarcely credible in the following terms. 'It is Asserate's aim to become prime minister, not
an Eritrean Ojukwu [head of the breakaway state of Biafra in
Nigeria at that time].'[23] To me, and to many foreign diplomats,
Ras Asserate always strenuously denied that he had any ambition to seize the crown: right to the end, it was inconceivable to
him that he might ever show disloyalty to his emperor.

The disputes in the palace between *Ras* Asserate and *Tsehafe-
Tezaz* Aklilu were notorious, and not infrequently they would
descend into full-blown shouting matches. The emperor sat
serenely above the two of them and played them off against one
another according to the time-honoured principle of 'Divide and
Rule'. Who knows how productive this rivalry might have been if
only the emperor, after one of the frequent clashes between *Ras*
Asserate and the prime minister, had taken the initiative and told
them: 'I've had enough of your endless quarrels. Get out there and
found political parties and let the Ethiopian people decide on your
future!' But to the bitter end, Haile Selassie never had the slightest
intention of rowing back from absolutist rule and setting in train a
process of democratisation. The Italian journalist Oriana Fallaci
interviewed the emperor in June 1973 – one of the few occasions
on which Haile Selassie faced the foreign press. Fallaci asked him
his opinion of democracy. His answer was revealing:

> 'Democracy. Republic: what do these words signify? What
> have they changed in the world? Have men become better,
> more loyal, kinder? Are the people happier? All goes on as
> before, as always. Illusions. Illusions. Besides, one should
> consider the interests of a nation before subverting it with
> words. Democracy is necessary in some cases and We believe
> some African peoples might adopt it. But in other cases it is
> harmful, a mistake.'[24]

According to the journalist, the emperor finally broke off the
interview with the words: 'Who's this woman? Where does she
come from? What does she want? Enough, go away, *Ça suffit!
Ça suffit!*'

Following his removal as Governor-General of Eritrea, *Ras* Asserate spent over a year without an official position. He withdrew to his country estate at Tibila on the Awash River. He was kept under surveillance there by the security services, and before long news reached Haile Selassie that this place had become a magnet for people who were rumoured to be discontent with the imperial administration. Accordingly, the emperor decided that it would be better to keep *Ras* Asserate close to him. Henceforth, the prince travelled in the emperor's retinue, accompanying him on state visits abroad to such places as Spain and China, among others. In July 1971 Haile Selassie offered *Ras* Asserate a post that he could not refuse: President of the Imperial Crown Council, in terms of protocol the highest office in the Ethiopian Empire after that of the *Negusa Negast*.

The constitution stipulated that the Crown Council should guide the country's destiny, but in practice this body had been in a state of suspended animation for some years – and the emperor was the last person who might show any inclination to wake it from its slumber. The Council comprised forty members, many of whom were men with whom the emperor had grown uneasy over the years or whom he deemed in some way unreliable: his answer was to 'kick them upstairs' by pensioning them off to this hallowed institution.[25] It was unusual for all forty members to assemble, and the post of President had even remained unfilled for the past fifteen years. In fact the last President of the Imperial Crown Council had been *Ras* Kassa; after his death in 1957, the emperor himself had taken on the role of acting president. The President of the Imperial Crown Council did not even have his own suite of offices – another clear indicator of how little importance was now accorded to the post. Under the chairmanship of *Ras* Asserate, for instance, the Council met just once, to decide what present the emperor should be given for his eightieth birthday, in 1972. Then the Crown Council sank back into its usual torpor once more.

The state of terminal inertia within the government saw an increasing number of – predominantly young – Ethiopians lose faith in the leadership of their country during the 1960s. This was especially true of the nation's students. Even in the Palace Revolt of 1960, many of them had been prepared to show their solidarity with the putschists. In the years that followed, the student movement developed into a highly visible centre of opposition to the imperial administration. The emperor found it incomprehensible that resistance should be coming from precisely those people who had him personally to thank for their educational opportunities. After all, he reasoned, had he not done all he could after his return from exile to promote the building of schools and other educational institutions in the country? Using funds from his own pocket, he had founded schools like the Haile Selassie Secondary School in Addis Ababa. This high school enjoyed an outstanding reputation, as did the institution named after the leader of Gideon Force, the General Wingate Secondary School, likewise situated in the capital. The empire's future elite would be trained at establishments like these; the palace kitchens even supplied the school named after the emperor with its school dinners. And in the 1950s, various seats of higher learning were established in Addis Ababa, Gondar and Harar. In 1961, these were combined to form the Haile Selassie University. The government relied first and foremost on American aid to develop education. As part of the Peace Corps Programme founded by President John F. Kennedy, between 1962 and 1971 more than 2,500 American graduates came to the country. Most of them were sent to the high schools and the Haile Selassie University to teach English and other subjects. Around 300,000 Ethiopian school pupils and students passed through their hands over the years.[26] In addition, the imperial government sent Ethiopian students to study at universities abroad, especially in the United States. The figures spoke for themselves: while there were just 71 Ethiopians studying in the USA in 1950, by 1973, this number had risen to over 10,000.[27]

Yet among the student body the demand for political change proved stronger than any bonds of loyalty to the emperor and his administration. In much the same way as students everywhere became radicalised during the 1960s, students in Addis Ababa also grew ever more impatient and radical in their demands

and the way they voiced them.[28] Whereas at the outset of the
decade, agitation had overwhelmingly been for a free press, free
trade unions and land reform, as the 1960s progressed, students
began to advocate a socialist reorganization of society according to the precepts of Marxism-Leninism. Everything that was
labelled as 'Western' soon came to be regarded as 'imperialist'
and 'colonialist'. It is not without a certain irony that many of
those who came out onto the streets to chant anti-American
slogans owed their education to American teachers and instructors, either in the form of the Peace Corps volunteers in Ethiopia
or American lecturers at Berkeley or other US universities. From
the mid-1960s on, these demonstrations became more militant,
leading to violent clashes with the police. The emperor tried to
quell the growing wave of protest with tried-and-tested paternalistic methods, going on television to appeal for calm. The
parents of student leaders who had been taken into custody
were summoned to police stations, and their sons were released
to go home with them provided they gave a written undertaking that they would stand surety for their future good conduct.
Such methods were hardly an effective way of mollifying the
student unrest.

The wave of protest reached a new high point in 1969. The
police had by now started to crack down hard on the demonstrators, using water cannons and baton charges to break up the
protests. The government banned the radical student newspaper *Tagel* ('You Must Struggle'), and Haile Selassie University
was temporarily closed. On 28 December 1969, the leader of
the radical student organization the USUAA (Union of Students
of the University of Addis Ababa) was shot dead by two men
outside the college campus. The background to the murder of
Tilahun Gizaw remains a mystery to this day, but at the time
a rumour spread like wildfire that the imperial security police
were behind the attack.[29] Students from the university took the
victim's body from the hospital and carried it to the grounds of
the university, where thousands of mourners soon gathered on
the campus. The students refused to hand over the body of their
murdered comrade to his family. Finally, troops of the Imperial

Guard were called upon to storm the campus with rifles and fixed bayonets.

The death of Tilahun Gizaw further fomented the anti-government protests. Yet in the end the students were not sufficiently organised or determined to mount a serious challenge to the government. Ethiopian students demonstrated against the Vietnam War and against fashion shows in the capital featuring mini-skirts, chanted 'Land to the Peasants!' and demanded the immediate withdrawal of the American Peace Corps. Ethiopian student organizations in the USA and elsewhere supplied them with plenty of theoretical ammunition, notably the works of Marx, Lenin and Chairman Mao. But the protestors had nothing to offer in the way of practical proposals on how to change the country. It has often been claimed that the Ethiopian student protests of the 1960s paved the way for the 1974 revolution. This is only partially true: the students were a permanent thorn in the side of the government, because they demonstrated to the watching world that everything was not perfect in the realm of the Lion of Judah. But they never garnered any support to speak of among the populace at large. And ultimately they found themselves just as surprised by the events that unfolded in the spring of 1974 as the imperial administration in the Menelik Palace.

As the student unrest grew to fever pitch in Addis Ababa in the late 1960s, I had a memorable discussion with my father. I pointed to the urgent need for reform in Ethiopia in order to head off the threat of a violent revolution, and I accused him of not speaking plainly to the emperor about the crisis. I have never forgotten his answer: 'You young people think that we don't have the guts to speak our minds to the emperor. You have no idea how many of us have demanded root-and-branch reforms so that the institutions can be modernised, or how often we've done so. But his response is always the same: "So, you imagine you're more democratic than the British or the French, do you? We have just received the ambassadors of both countries, and We didn't get the impression that these two diplomats were at all unhappy with Us."'

Haile Selassie with US President John F. Kennedy in the
White House in October 1963, a month before Kennedy's
assassination. Between 1954 and his downfall, the
Emperor made six state visits to the United States.

The emperor always set great store by his image in the wider
world, particularly in the USA and Europe. Might the Western
states have been able to bring about a thoroughgoing change if
they had only made concerted representations to the emperor on
this score? The US administration at least made some attempts
to influence Haile Selassie and steer him towards reforms. For
example, Edward M. Korry, whom Kennedy appointed as
ambassador to Ethiopia in 1963, urged the imperial government
to put in place concrete measures to create a modern market
economy and a government with a democratic mandate. Furthermore, without bothering to mince his words diplomatically,
the envoy flatly turned down Ethiopian demands for an increase
in military aid, telling the Ethiopian defence minister Lieutenant-General Kebede Gebre that the United States was engaged in

an extremely costly war in Vietnam and that, instead of asking for help, Addis Ababa would do better to consider how it might support Washington at a time when the US President had had to go cap in hand and ask his people to pay higher taxes.'[30] Haile Selassie's reaction to this was instant: the imperial government politely but in no uncertain terms requested that the United States change its ambassador to Ethiopia, a request to which Washington acceded.[31]

In 1968, Richard Nixon unexpectedly won the US Presidential race. Nixon was a longstanding acquaintance of the emperor: as Dwight D. Eisenhower's vice-president, he had greeted the official guest from Africa at Washington's National Airport on his first state visit to the United States in 1954. And, initially at least, the relationship between the two leaders was correspondingly cordial. The Ethiopian emperor was the first African leader to be invited to the White House by the new president, in July 1969. During his toast welcoming Haile Selassie, Nixon made great play of his personal friendship with the emperor:

> 'He has wisdom. He has had a long life, and, I know from personal experience, an understanding heart. I share that with you for one moment. I had the great privilege [...] of visiting his country in 1957. My wife and I were received as royal guests at that time and treated royally. I returned again to his country in 1967, holding no office, having no portfolio whatever. I was received again as a royal guest and treated royally. This is a man with an understanding heart. [Laughter]'[32]

Yet for all the warm words of friendship, over the course of the next four years, Washington was to withdraw its support from its hitherto most significant ally in Africa. The USA began step by step to disengage itself with the growing recognition by Washington that the emperor was losing control of his empire. For a long time, operations at the US Kagnew Station base had been one of the principal reasons for American involvement in Ethiopia. This base was a key listening post from which the USA monitored all communications in the Red Sea region. Kagnew

Station was a city within a city (the Eritrean capital Asmara), comprising some 200 buildings spread over a site covering 14 square kilometres. In its heyday it was home to around 4,200 American troops and their dependants, and was equipped with every conceivable amenity – including a cinema, a swimming pool, a supermarket, a golf club, several restaurants and even its own television station. The rent that Washington paid for use of the facility formed the bedrock of American military aid to Ethiopia. Even as late as 1960, President Eisenhower had stressed the importance of 'maintaining an atmosphere in Ethiopia which would assure continued unimpaired use of the key facilities at Kagnew.'[33] Even President Nixon was inclined to adhere to this policy, but increasingly the American administration came to realize that developments in satellite technology had rendered this costly base dispensable. As a result, Haile Selassie was faced with the loss of his most important bargaining chip, which he had used to great effect over many decades to extract ongoing military and economic aid from Washington.

And at the onset of the 1970s, military aid appeared more pressing than ever to Haile Selassie: in Eritrea, he needed to halt the advance of the Muslim Eritrean Liberation Front (ELF), which was being supplied with weapons and ammunition by Arab countries. In turn, in the neighbouring country of Somalia Major General Siad Barre had seized power in a coup in 1969 and proclaimed the Democratic Republic of Somalia. Barre was receiving military aid from the Soviet Union and publicly laid claim to the Ethiopian territory of the Ogaden. In the light of such threats, could Washington really turn down its hard-pressed Ethiopian ally's request for additional military assistance?

Between 1969 and 1973, Haile Selassie visited Washington no fewer than three times, to press home the urgency of his demands in face-to-face talks with President Nixon. His firm conviction that important decisions were best reached through personal contacts between heads of state remained unshaken to the last. Parliamentary procedures, white papers, resolutions by standing committees and plenary sessions of parliament – such matters were totally alien to the emperor. Yet even one-on-one discussions could not achieve the desired aim this time. In 1971, the US government not only rejected any increase in military aid to Ethiopia; it also voted to reduce its annual contributions from $12 million to $10.8 million.[34] In March 1972, Haile Selassie wrote a personal memorandum to President Richard Nixon:

> 'At a time when We were expecting an increase in the US military aid to Ethiopia because of our geographical location and the continued critical condition in our part of the world, it is with dismay and deep concern that We have learned of the envisioned cut in the US military aid program to Our country.'[35]

The emperor ended his letter by expressing the hope that 'Our observations will reach Your Excellency in time for your reconsideration of this important matter.' Even in the preceding year, Nixon had informed the newly-appointed ambassador in Addis Ababa, E. Ross Adair, that 'the emperor must be prevailed upon to see that he bears absolute responsibility for ensuring an orderly and beneficial succession.' After all, Nixon continued, Haile Selassie had done 'too much good work to permit it all to collapse because of a failure to face up to the necessity of providing for his succession.'[36] But Haile Selassie, who celebrated his eightieth birthday in 1972, made no attempt to address the question of what would come after him. Only a direct descendant of the House of David was worthy of wearing the Ethiopian crown – this principle had been enshrined in Haile Selassie's revised Constitution of 1955. Of the emperor's six children, only two had survived: Crown Prince Asfa-Wossen and his eldest daughter, Princess Tenagne-Work. It was an open secret that the Crown Prince no longer had the absolute backing of his father. In addition, in January 1973 Prince Asfa-Wossen had suffered a stroke that left one side of his body paralysed, and there was little to suggest that his condition would improve in the foreseeable future. He was sent to Britain and Switzerland for treatment. The emperor appointed *Ras* Asserate to be the Crown Prince's constant companion, and he accompanied him to Europe. Now that the Crown Prince's affliction was plain for all to see, the question of the succession could not longer be swept under the carpet. The whole country was agog to learn whom the emperor could possibly have chosen to direct the fate of Ethiopia after his death.

Several names were bandied about, chief among them two grandsons of the emperor, one of whom was Princess Tenagne-Work's son, Rear-Admiral and Commander of the Ethiopian Navy Prince Iskender Desta, and the other Prince Wossen-Sagad Makonnen, son of the deceased Prince Makonnen. After his father's untimely death, he had inherited the title of Duke of Harar. But over the course of the years, he too had fallen from favour with the emperor. Yet the emperor did nothing to stem the tide of speculation. One key question became ever more pressing: What would become of Ethiopia when the venerable emperor was no more? And the longer this question remained unresolved, the greater the power vacuum became. And when, in the spring of 1974, the emperor finally brought himself to name a successor, it was too late. The sparks of the revolution that was to bring the empire tumbling down could no longer be stamped out. At the celebration of Easter in Ethiopia that year, Haile Selassie announced that he had chosen the son of the Crown Prince – the 20-year-old Prince Zera-Yakob, who had just begun his course of study in Oxford – to be the 'acting heir apparent'. To many in the country and to foreign observers, this announcement made it sound for all the world as though Haile Selassie still planned to be sitting on the throne of the Lion of Judah at the age of 100.

In May 1973, Haile Selassie made one last attempt to persuade President Nixon in face-to-face negotiations to increase US military assistance to Ethiopia. At the top of the shopping list that the emperor brought with him to Washington were F-4 Phantom fighter-bombers, M-60 main battle tanks and surface-to-air missiles.[37] Initially the decision was deferred, but shortly thereafter, in August 1973, the US government announced a shock decision: all the important facilities at Kagnew Station would cease operations by the end of 1974. It was a slap in the face for the emperor – all the more so since he was not even consulted prior to the decision being made public.[38] This announcement effectively signalled the United States' de facto resolution to drop the empire as an ally. In the end, it came down to a dispassionate consideration of its own interests by Washington: on the one hand, the decades-long alliance with the Lion of Judah and the Ethiopian Empire as its most important ally on the Red Sea, and on the other an economic and strategic *Realpolitik* which recognised that it was useless to continue to supply weapons and other equipment to a tottering regime, with no way of knowing into whose hands these might eventually fall. The prevailing view now in the White House was that Haile Selassie's regime could only survive if it was propped up by American help. There was no room for sentimentality: Washington relocated the headquarters of the US Information Service for East Africa from Addis Ababa to Nairobi and encouraged American firms investing in Africa to focus their efforts on Kenya henceforth, rather than Ethiopia.[39]

At this juncture, did the emperor really believe that he might be able to change the US government's mind once more? In 1959, Haile Selassie had blindsided Washington by making his state visit to the Soviet Union. The worry that it might lose Ethiopia to the Eastern Bloc had persuaded the US government at that time to meet all the demands of its troublesome ally in the Horn of Africa. Now, in the autumn of 1973, the emperor decided to go on another state visit to Moscow. When weighing up the emperor's options, the White House had envisaged just such a move on his part and took a sober view of his chances of success. Secretary of State Henry Kissinger sent round an internal memo on this subject which read: 'My experience is that Haile Selassie does nothing unless it is that he makes the most boring toasts of anybody I have ever heard.'[40] The Soviet Union was financing the rearmament of Siad Barre's 'Socialist Somalia'. Haile Selassie was confident that he would at least be able to persuade Moscow to stop arms shipments to Somalia. But this time the Ethiopian emperor was not received with open arms in Russia. The Kremlin did not want to flatly refuse to grant him a state visit, but tried its utmost to thwart it through diplomatic means all the same. So, Haile Selassie was told that the only available dates were at the end of October, knowing full well that every government agency in Ethiopia would be frantically busy at that time making preparations for the celebrations marking the anniversary of the emperor's coronation on 2 November.[41] The emperor had no choice. He accepted the Russian offer, and had an audience with Party Secretary Leonid Brezhnev, but his pleas fell on deaf ears: the Soviet Union was not prepared to distance itself from Siad Barre.[42] Haile Selassie's strategy of manoeuvring between the superpowers and trying to play them off against one another was at an end. Ultimately, the Ethiopian emperor was left empty-handed.

In the meantime, a pall of paralysis had settled on the palace and the capital. The Lion of Judah had grown old and weak. He was no longer willing or able to tackle the fundamental reforms that the country so urgently required. In the summer of 1972, festivities were held to mark the emperor's eightieth birthday. My father told me that he and my mother went to the palace first thing in the morning to offer their congratulations.[43] Haile Selassie received them in the drawing room that adjoined his bedroom. For his birthday present, *Ras* Asserate gave His Majesty a bespoke leather travel writing case specially designed by Algernon Asprey in London, which the emperor was evidently delighted with. Then my father suddenly fell at the emperor's feet. Alarmed, Haile Selassie asked him: 'What on earth has happened?' The prince replied:

'Your Majesty! In the name of my father, your loyal friend and servant *Ras* Kassa, I beseech you to grant me one great favour. Today is the day when Your Majesty has it in his power to give Ethiopia its greatest gift ever. When you go before the Ethiopian people presently to address them, please say this to your subjects: "My beloved people of Ethiopia. I have served you for almost sixty years. Now the time has come for me to retire and hand the reins of power to a new generation. Here is my son, into whose care I commend you. Serve him as faithfully as you have served me and be as loyal to him as you have been to your Emperor during all these years.'[44] If you do this, I guarantee that you will go down in history as the greatest emperor.'

The emperor was visibly moved and said nothing for a while. Then he told my father to get up and answered him: 'Tell me, did King David abdicate? Or can you think of any other Ethiopian ruler who has done so? We shall reign as long as the Almighty allows Us to. And when the time has come for Us to depart, He will know what is best for Ethiopia.'

My father left the palace that morning downcast. Nor did his mood improve over the following three days of celebration for the emperor's birthday, which passed off with great pomp and circumstance. Once again, magazines around the world were filled with pictures of the jamboree: 'Huge Jamboree for the King of Kings' ran the headline in the German magazine *Bunte*, 'the most magnificent birthday parade ever seen in Africa.'[45] Once more, people flooded into the capital from every province of Ethiopia, filling all the squares and streets, dancing to music and forming spontaneous choirs chanting 'Haile, Haile!' Once again, imperial troops, complete with their military bands, performed a march-past for the emperor, squadrons of Air Force jets roared over the palace, and balloons were released. Once more, the Ethiopian emperor received congratulations from all four corners of the earth and accepted lavish gifts from a string of accredited ambassadors. The German ambassador sent three cases of the finest Rhine wine, while the Swiss envoy presented an ornate timepiece in the Louis Quinze style.[46] Once again, the Patriarch of the Ethiopian Orthodox Church bestowed his blessing upon the defender of the faith and the 'Elect of God'. And once more, torches were handed out in the flag-bedecked streets and a grand firework display let off on the stroke of midnight.

And just a few months later, on 2 November, the anniversary of the emperor's coronation was celebrated and a new session of parliament opened – a parliament that had got used, over the preceding years, to posing some awkward questions but which still made no key decisions. A new ambassador, Willie Morris, had arrived in Addis Ababa from London; the celebrations he witnessed in the Ethiopian capital reminded him irresistably of Evelyn Waugh's mocking description of *Ras* Tafari's accession to the throne in November 1930:

'It was a Waugh touch that when the Emperor seated himself between [the Liberian] President [Tolbert] and Mrs Tolbert at the Opening of Parliament last week, he waited in dignified silence for fifteen minutes while someone went to fetch the gracious speech which everyone had forgotten to bring along. On the occasion of that coronation 42 years ago, the visiting Royal Marine band drank champagne for breakfast, luncheon, tea and dinner all the way from Djibouti. I note that it is still served almost as regularly on all royal occasions. And at the actual Coronation ceremony, Waugh noted that "there was plenty for room for all, except, as it happened, for the Abyssinians themselves". As, sandwiched between the cars of His Excellency from Reykjavik (Long live Icelandic–Ethiopian friendship!) and Her Excellency from Trinidad and Tobago, one looks through the car window at the mixed racial features and variegated dress of the Ethiopians in the street (some of them earning a few extra cents by carrying pictures of President and Mrs Tolbert, or yesterday, even more improbably, of [the Belgian] King Baudouin and Queen Fabiola) then the Ethiopians in the street seem very far removed from the charade in which one is taking part. It must take quite an effort to cross the divide.'[47]

Was it really the case that nothing had changed fundamentally in Ethiopia in the forty-two years between the emperor's coronation and its anniversary in 1972? It was certainly wilfully ignorant of the new envoy to disregard everything that the emperor had achieved for his country over those four decades. But in the interim, things had reached a stage where the emperor was no longer judged by what he had achieved but by what he had failed to do. For Ethiopia was still one of the most economically

The author, as head boy of the German School in Addis
Ababa in 1968, delivers a welcoming address to Haile Selassie
and the German ambassador to Ethiopia, Kurt Müller.

backward countries in the world. The per-capita gross national
product stood at just US$83 in 1973, one of the lowest in the
whole of Africa. Average life expectancy was thirty, and 60
percent of all newborn children died before they reached their
first birthday. In almost all statistical measures of international
development, the Ethiopian Empire found itself in the last five
places.[48]

At the beginning of 1973, isolated reports began to filter
through to Addis Ababa about the worsening food supply situation in the provinces of Tigray and Wollo. Starving refugees had
started streaming from there towards the capital. Throughout
its history, Ethiopia has been afflicted by many famines, but his
time the famine escalated into a hunger crisis on an unimagi-
nable scale. This was the third dry season in a row that had
hit the provinces, with the result that three harvests had now
failed. It had not rained for an entire year, before suddenly, in

August, torrential downpours washed away the last few ears of cereal crop off the fields in many regions. Farmers had resorted to pulling the straw roofs off their *Tukuls* to feed their oxen and mules. They sold their last few possessions to buy food for their families. First their livestock perished, then their children. In May 1973 the Ethiopian Ministry of Planning informed all aid agencies working in Ethiopia that their help was urgently needed. Many international organizations had already set up facilities in the drought-stricken north of the country and were quietly getting on with providing any help they could. But they found it hard gaining access to the most remote areas where there were no roads, the village and settlements that could only be reached on muleback along rocky paths. The country was completely unprepared for a catastrophe of this magnitude, and this may explain the helplessness with which the imperial government reacted to the crisis.[49]

In September 1973, the emperor set off on another state visit to Germany – this would be the last time that he left the African continent. He was welcomed in Stuttgart by the premier of Baden-Württemberg Hans Filbinger, who was keen to show him that the region he governed could provide every bit as much pomp and ceremony as the Federal Government had laid on during the emperor's official visit in 1954. But this time, unlike his trip almost twenty years before, Haile Selassie was not only met by cheering crowds but also by student demonstrations. In the meantime, the first reports of the famine had reached Europe. I was studying in Germany at this time and I can still vividly recall the encounters I had with Haile Selassie during his visit. I have already referred in the Prologue to my first audience with the emperor on 11 September 1973, when he summoned me to Stuttgart and had me translate the protestors' leaflets for him. A few hours after this meeting, the emperor asked me to come and see him again. He was just about to set off for the Institute for Foreign Relations, where he was due to open an exhibition entitled 'The Religious Art of Ethiopia.' Without more ado, he stuffed a $100-dollar bill into my hand and told me to take a cab to the PX-supermarket on the US forces base at Burgholzdorf

north of Stuttgart, where I was to buy a dozen bottles of his preferred 'Vitalis' brand of hair tonic, which was difficult to obtain
in Ethiopia. When I duly brought him the bottles that evening
and handed him back his change, he looked at the money and
exclaimed: 'What? They cost almost thirty dollars!' – 'Yes, Your
Majesty,' I replied, and showed him the receipt. He muttered:
'Unbelievable, how expensive this stuff is.' Finally, he let me
keep the change, telling me: 'There's some pocket money for
when you go back to Frankfurt.' At the time I was astonished
how much attention the emperor paid to the cost of things. But
as has already been mentioned, where his private life was concerned Haile Selassie was anything but a profligate person. He
set great store by frugality, though he could also, when the occasion demanded, be extremely generous. And clearly it wasn't
every day he had a fistful of US dollars; in those days, only a very
limited supply of hard foreign currency was available in Ethiopia, even to the emperor.

The following day, Haile Selassie moved on to Bonn to meet
the Chancellor of Germany, Willy Brandt. Their agenda that
day was to discuss questions of development aid, but the famine
crisis in the northern provinces of Ethiopia was not a topic that
warranted their attention. Just a few weeks later, the hunger
crisis dominated the front pages of the newspapers and was the
lead story on broadcast news reports the world over. It was an
English reporter who put Ethiopia in the global spotlight: for
several months. Jonathan Dimbleby and a film crew had been
travelling through the provinces of Wollo and Tigray, capturing
on film the dreadful scenes of people dying en masse of hunger.
On 18 October 1973, the British broadcaster ITV screened
a documentary on the crisis entitled *The Unknown Famine*.
Before long, the report had been beamed right around the world.
Even for Ethiopians, who had witnessed lots of starving people
in their time, the film presented a shocking picture: countless
children with spindly legs, their bodies mere skin and bone, and
their bellies distended by the malnutrition disease known as
kwashiorkor. The starving people cowered on the ground and
stared out emptily from hollow eye sockets. Boys' and girls' hair

was dessicated, and in many cases had begun to fall out. The flies settled on them in dense clumps, but the children were too weak to shoo them away. The TV report closed with the words; 'These people need food, medicine and blankets – and they need these things now.'[50] This was the first time that television viewers in Europe had witnessed such scenes during prime-time screening – unfortunately it would not be the last.

In Germany, the first news organ to bring the story to public attention was the magazine *Stern*, in November 1973. 'Help!' ran its headline, 'Hundreds of Thousands Will Starve if We Do Nothing', and beside it the picture of a tiny, emaciated Ethiopian boy, gazing directly out at the readers with sad eyes.[51] The magazine's reporter Randolph Braumann was clearly deeply moved by what he had seen: 'As a journalist, one becomes immune to being shocked. But what is happening here defies all comprehension,' he wrote.[52] The fundraising drive that *Stern* set in motion unleashed an unprecedented wave of charitable giving in Germany. In the very week after the report, the first German army transport aircraft lifted off, bound for Dessie, the capital of Wollo. They were carrying helicopters, jeeps and all-terrain Unimog trucks, food supplies, medicines, medical equipment, blankets and tents. They also ferried countless doctors, nurses and aid workers to the famine regions. Nor was the support confined to short-term food aid and healthcare; many infrastructure projects were also set in train: cisterns were installed to help with the water supply, roads were built, while in Mekele, the capital of Tigray, an entire emergency village was built to house orphaned children. When the editor of *Stern*, Henri Nannen, took stock of the aid initiative after a year, he was able to report that over 20 million marks had been raised for Ethiopia.[53] The Federal Government also instigated a special programme to the tune of 10 million marks. The story was the same in many other countries where reports of the famine in Ethiopia were broadcast. Jonathan Dimbleby estimated that the sum of money raised worldwide as a result of his initial report ultimately amounted to some US $150 million.[54] My own initiative was crowned with success after the Philips Foundation topped up the 40,000

Deutschmarks that I had raised in Frankfurt to DM 500,000, thus enabling me to go ahead with the Flying Doctor programme from Kenya. We were able to give medical assistance to famine-stricken victims in the far-flung areas of Wollo for nearly a year. The emperor, who some months before earlier had been sceptical as to the outcome of my enterprise, now embraced it with open arms , and the minister of health was given orders to incorporate the project into the ministry's latest action plan for the Wollo province.

There has been some speculation over whether the government in Addis Ababa deliberately hushed up news of the famine. There is no firm evidence to corroborate such a claim, but we may say with certainty that the regime underestimated the magnitude of the catastrophe for a long time. In November 1973 the emperor travelled in person to Tigray and Wollo to see the situation on the ground for himself, but this was far too late, as many did not hesitate to point out. And without a doubt the terrible effects of the famine – in Wollo alone, between 40,000 and 80,000 Ethiopians died of starvation between 1972 and 1973[55] – could have been mitigated if only the administration had sought help from international aid agencies sooner. But also, the many years of foot-dragging over comprehensive land reform now began to take its toll. In Tigray, which like Wollo was hit by drought, the famine did not have nearly so devastating an effect: the difference was that here many farmers owned their own land, whereas in Wollo most peasants were tenant-farmers.[56] Incomprehension and outrage over the lack of action by the central authorities mounted when it came to light that, at the height of the famine in 1973, the Ethiopian government had exported more than 200,000 tons of grain – the largest export surplus since 1967.

Shouldn't the Ethiopian dignitaries have seen this disaster looming? Were they living in an ivory tower? The Ethiopian author Mammo Wudineh tells of an incident that occurred in the palace at Massawa in Eritrea in the late 1960s. The chief of the Ethiopian police, Brigadier-General Tadesse Birru, was paying his respects to the then Governor-General of Eritrea, *Ras* Asserate; Mammo was accompanying Tadesse at the time

Haile Selassie carries a torch to the *Demera*, a bonfire traditionally
lit at the Ethiopian Orthodox Church festival of *Maskal* in
late September. Behind the Emperor are Crown Prince Asfa-
Wossen and *Ras* Asserate Kassa, while to his left is the Greek
Orhtodox Archbishop of Addis Ababa, *Abuna* Nikolaos.

as a journalist. *Ras* Asserate and General Tadesse fell to dis-
cussing the country's future, in the gloomiest of terms. In 1960,
both men had played a key role in putting down the palace
revolt staged by the Neway brothers. Now the general posed
the question: 'When the earth finally receives our bodies, will
we be worthy of it?' The *Ras*'s response was unequivocal: 'Why
should we be? No, the earth should not receive our mortal
remains! We are divided amongst ourselves and all we can
think of is destroying others' work. This country is descending straight into a chaos that can never be made good.' And he
added: 'Yesterday's events [i.e. the 1960 putsch] will come back
to haunt us tomorrow!'[57]
  These pessimistic sentiments regarding the future of the
empire were not confined to the enlightened aristocracy, but
were shared by the technocrats in Haile Selassie's administration. One such individual was *Ato* Yilma Deressa. A member of

the Crown Council in 1974, *Ato* Yilma was better known for his long cabinet career as finance minister. There is a very interesting story which shows how frustrated many of the closest confidants of Haile Selassie were in the twilight years of the empire.

The following account was related to me by Dr Dima Nago Sarbo, who was present at the meeting, in an interview in June 2015: In March 1974 a group of elders from the province of Wollega went to see *Ato* Yilma Deressa at his home in Addis Ababa to consult with him on who would be the best man to be appointed Governor-General of Wollega, as the present Governor was very unpopular with the people. In response to their queries, *Ato* Yilma advised them to plead for an elder son of *Dejazmatch* Gebre Igziabher (better known as Kumsa Moroda), the hereditary ruler of the region early in the 20th century, *Dejazmatch* Yemane. The reason *Ato* Yilma advised the Elders in this manner said it all: 'In a situation where the government's tenure would be short-lived, at best a couple of months, it is better for you to just demand that the elderly Yemane remain there in a caretaker capacity as the situation in the country is fluid and no one could be certain about the future.'

The elders were bewildered by Yilma's advice as they thought he had lost hope in the fate of the government and asked him why he was so pessimistic. His remarks were prophetic. He said things would never return to the pre-February order; the soldiers had tested the power of the government and their own in the streets by arresting senior officers and cabinet ministers, and were unlikely to return to their barracks. They would eventually dismiss the government and seize power. He added that the future of the country was uncertain and the emperor's government in disarray and unable to control the situation. The elders were shocked to hear such a grim reading of the situation from none other than a senior figure of the Emperor's government. They asked him why, in these bleak circumstances, he remained in the country and did not go abroad. His response was fatalistic. He told them he had been in exile before during the Italian occupation, and his experience was not very pleasant. At least then he was a young man, but now at his advanced age (he was probably in his late sixties at that time) he could not contemplate going into exile again and would remain in the country to face whatever fate awaited him. A few months later *Ato* Yilma was taken into custody and died in prison in 1979 at the age of 72.

Another example of how disheartened Emperor Haile Selassie's ministers became in the last stages of his reign is given by Dr Abebe Ambatchew, who was the first director of the Haile Selassie I Prize Trust.[58] In 1972 Dr Abebe met *Ato* Akale-Work Habte-Wold, then Minister of Justice, in a hotel in Paris on his way to the United States to join the United Nations Development Program in New York. The minister was there on official business and invited Dr Abebe and his family for breakfast. As they said farewell he took the young man aside and, in a fatherly way, gave him the following advice: 'You have to think about your family from now on. Stay in the United Nations, where you want to work, and educate your children. As far as we in Ethiopia are concerned, it is finished.' *Ato* Akale-Work would be one of the 60 officials who were brutally executed without trial two years later on 23 November 1974.

It was not the case that the imperial dignitaries lacked the will to institute reforms. But neither the prime minister nor *Ras* Asserate were prepared to face down the emperor. Loyalty to Haile Selassie eclipsed every other consideration. They had hitched their own fates to that of their emperor, and in the end they were even ready to go to their graves for him. They vacillated between fatalism and torment. And many times, like the one outlined above, they even despised themselves for having this mindset.

CHAPTER NINE

An empty house

1974 to 1975

The imperial regime's death throes in the palace were eventually to culminate in the revolution of 1974 – the year in which not only Haile Selassie, the King of Kings and the Lion of Judah, was deposed but also the 3,000-year history of the Ethiopian Empire finally drew to a close. The events that unfolded in Ethiopia in 1974 have gone down in posterity as the 'Creeping Coup', since the revolution occurred over several months in incremental stages and almost without bloodshed, and because for a long time it lacked any centre. No individual or group proclaimed it, nor did it follow any overarching plan. Only gradually did a single organisation emerge from the various disparate groups, and proceeded to seize the reins of power while the old regime looked on more or less helplessly. Yet even this grouping, which called itself the 'Provisional Military Administration Council (PMAC)' but which would become commonly known as the *Derg* – a Ge'ez term meaning 'council' or 'committee' – did not have a concerted political programme. For a long time it remained a faceless entity to the outside world. No one knew how many members it had or which of the military's foremost officers was actually supporting it.

As with all violent uprisings throughout history, the revolution in Ethiopia cannot be traced to any single decisive cause. Many factors combined to trigger it: the seething resentment among the country's students and the frustration felt by its elites;

the government's inertia and the ongoing famine, which undermine the authority of the ruling class still further; the worsening
economic situation and rising prices; and last but by no means
least an emperor who had grown old yet who had shown himself
resistant to organising his succession. And like all revolutions,
the Ethiopian uprising also required a spark to ignite the pro-
verbial tinder-box.[1] In this instance, it was the failure of a water
pump in the town of Negele Borane near the Kenyan border in
January 1974. The officers of the Fourth Army Division who
were stationed there banned their thirsty troops from drink-
ing from the well used by the commissioned ranks. The soldiers
rebelled and took their officers captive. Over the radio, the mutineers broadcast a demand to Addis Ababa for an increase in
their pay.

In the capital, the drought had caused the cost of basic food-
stuffs to skyrocket, while the international Oil Crisis had the
same effect on the price of petrol and imported goods. The
trade minister announced a 50 percent rise in the cost of fuel.
Taxi drivers were the first to go out onto the streets in protest.
They were soon joined by students, who had just been waiting
for an opportunity to resume their demonstrations. Presently,
their numbers were swelled by the capital's teachers, who were
angry about a proposed education reform and were also calling
for higher wages. The demonstrators attacked the bus company's vehicles with stones, and services in Addis Ababa ground
to a halt. On 25 February, the soldiers and officers of the Second
Infantry Division, based in Eritrea, mutinied. They took control
of the regional capital Asmara and closed the airport. Meanwhile, in Massawa, the commander-in-chief of the Ethiopian
Navy and grandson of the emperor Rear-Admiral Iskender
Desta, was placed under house arrest. It did not take long for
the mutiny to spill over to the capital, as the air force and the
airborne forces division in Addis Ababa refused to attack the
rebels in Eritrea.

The imperial administration tried to counter the insurrection
as best it could: the increase in the price of petrol was rescinded
in some measure, soldiers' pay was raised by 20 percent, and

Lij Endalkatchew Makonnen, Imperial Prime Minister
from the 28th of February to the 22nd of July 1974.

the education reform shelved. The emperor called a joint sitting
of the Imperial Crown Council and the Ministerial Council for
27 February. However, the meeting was interrupted by the news
that the Fourth Division, the most highly trained and largest
unit of the Ethiopian Army, had joined the mutiny. On learning
of this, *Tsehafe-Tezaz* Aklilu Habte-Wold immediately tendered
the cabinet's resignation. This was the first time in the history
of the country that a serving prime minister had resigned; the
assembled dignitaries argued long and hard whether a step such
as this weakened the authority of the emperor. The prime minister's adversaries urged His Majesty to formally dismiss Aklilu
Habte-Wold. His supporters, on the other hand, suspected that
an aristocratic conspiracy lay behind the whole affair.[2] In the
end, the opposing factions settled on a diplomatic ploy: the official communiqué announced that the cabinet had offered its resignation to the emperor and that he had accepted it.

The emperor chose a popular military figure to be Aklilu
Habte-Wold's successor as prime minister: General Abiye Abebe,

who during the Palace Revolt of 1960 had stood loyally by his ruler as governor of Eritrea. In addition, he was a son-in-law of the emperor. But as it turned out, Haile Selassie would no longer have a free hand in deciding who should head his country's government. The army mutineers had despatched a negotiating delegation to the palace, which refused to consent to the emperor's appointment of Abiye. The general had to be content with the post of defence minister, while *Lij* Endalkatchew Makonnen, a politician with much experience in the Ethiopian Empire, was named as the new prime minister. Twenty years previously, he had accompanied the emperor on his grand tour to America as head of protocol and an interpreter. Since then, he had enjoyed a remarkable career. He had spent many years as Ethiopia's envoy to the United Nations and from time to time had even been in the running for the post of UN Secretary-General. Latterly, he had held the post and telecommunications portfolio in the Ethiopian government. Within just a few days, *Lij* Endalkatchew had gathered around him a group of ministers who were some of the country's ablest and most experienced men. No fewer than three of them, the prime minister included, were Oxford graduates.[3]

For a brief while, it seemed as though a democratic spring might be about to dawn in Ethiopia. On 5 March, the English-language newspaper *The Ethiopian Herald* ran a sensational leader by its editor Tegegne Yeteshawork, who also had a post in the ministry of information, where he was responsible for maintaining and monitoring censorship in the country. Under the headline '*Speaking Out*', he made the following announcement:

'It is the job of the press to impart not only information making the public aware of the government's wishes, but also information about what the people want to hear. The press should listen to the heartbeat of the people and not just speak to them, but also in their name. The press should serve as a forum for discussion about leadership of the country, in order to bridge the chasm between the government and the people by acting as the "Nation's Conscience".'[4]

As soon as it came off the press, this edition of the paper sold like hot cakes, and people could be seen reading the editorial on the streets throughout the capital. On the same day, the emperor gave a television address to the nation, in which he announced that he was setting up a commission charged with drafting a new constitution for Ethiopia within six months. 'Our actions shall henceforth be guided by the Will of the People,' Haile Selassie proclaimed.

It began raining leaflets on the streets of Addis Ababa, in which the most diverse groups issued clarion calls for change. The trades unions' governing body called for a general strike, the first in Ethiopian history, and 100,000 manual and office workers promptly downed tools. A demonstration by thousands of women demanded equality. Even a group of Ethiopian Orthodox priests threatened to withdraw their labour, demanding better rates of pay and pension provision 'comparable to other state employees' for themselves and their 200,000 colleagues.[5] However, it did not take long for the tone of these flyers, proclamations and articles to become more abrasive. A torrent of abuse was heaped on ministers and members of the imperial family. As one pamphlet stated, they should be 'taken out of circulation as quickly as possible.' The armed forces had ensured that a commission was called into being which in the event would spend much of its time investigating increasingly strident accusations of endemic corruption within the imperial government and bureaucracy.

The most dangerous moment for a bad government is when it begins to reform, the French political thinker Alexis de Tocqueville once wrote. The new government in Addis Ababa tried in vain to keep the cacophony of demands and proclamations in check. Yet at the very moment when they were confronted with their greatest challenge, the Ethiopian leadership proved itself once more incapable of action. A joint sitting of both houses of parliament, at which the new prime minister was due to give an address, broke up in chaos. The delegates could not agree among themselves whether the prime minister should talk about the urgent need for land reform or address the question of hunger and corruption. The leadership itself was also deeply divided: *Lij* Endalkatchew Makonnen could not count on the support of either parliament or the emperor. He could see his predecessor *Tsehafe-Tezaz* Aklilu still enjoying free access to the palace. And wouldn't the emperor much rather have had a different prime minister anyhow? *Lij* Endalkatchew did what he could: he announced a comprehensive policy of land reform and named the members of the constitutional commission. He also attempted to restore public order by putting in place a night-time curfew and outlawing strikes and demonstrations. But hardly anyone paid any attention to these edicts. The populace had lost patience with their government, and the authority of all the empire's institutions was in the process of unravelling. Nor was this happening just in Addis Ababa, but in other parts of the country as well. In almost all the major cities, the machinery of state bureaucracy had by now ceased functioning. And in Jimma, the capital of Kaffa province, an angry mob drove the governor from office.[6]

Many years later, one of the student leaders from this time told me: 'It wasn't us who brought down the imperial household; it did it all by itself.' How right he was: power now resided on the streets, and ultimately the country's strongest institution stretched out its hand and seized it. At the beginning of April, rumours began to circulate around the capital that the military were preparing to stage a coup. A leaflet, signed by 'Elements of the Armed Forces', proclaimed:

'Your Majesty promised the representatives [of the armed forces] a swift implementation of the following demands: 1) freedom of the press; 2) freedom of assembly and protest; 3) the right to form political parties and to hold democratic elections; 4) to give ownership of the land to the tiller; 5) an improvement in employment law; 6) the release of political prisoners; 7) free education for all; 8) strict control of market prices; 9) to institute legal proceedings against those who – directly or indirectly – have misused public funds; 10) to grant higher pay to soldiers and other workers in the light of current prices; 11) the formation of a committee of civilians and soldiers to monitor the implementation of the demands outlined above.'[7]

This list of demands concluded with a threat: 'Unless these demands are met within a short space of time, we shall regard them as not having been fulfilled and will take the necessary measures to ensure that they are.'[8] Many of the demonstrators now began calling for the arrest of Aklilu Habte-Wold. Soon a military council was specially convened to press for the detention of the former prime minister and the whole of his old cabinet. Twice, an armed forces' delegation met with Haile Selassie to bring this about, and twice the emperor refused to give in to their pressure. Finally, the military resorted to marching Aklilu into the Jubilee Palace. In the presence of the emperor and the serving prime minister *Lij* Endalkatchew, General Abiye announced to the former premier that the armed forces deemed it necessary to arrest him. Before he was led away, Aklilu addressed the emperor: 'If our imprisonment and even our death can save Your Imperial Majesty and Ethiopia, then we are prepared to sacrifice ourselves, but we assure you that it will not stop there. All those present here will soon be joining us.'[9] In that same week, all the former ministers in Aklilu's cabinet also disappeared behind bars and on top of that, hundreds of the empire's leading politicians were incarcerated – without any attempt by the current prime minister or the emperor to intervene. Each arrest was accompanied by the public statement that it was being done in the name of the emperor. The emperor kept silent and raised no protests at this. He did not speak up publicly on behalf of a single one of his ministers, governors or generals. Before long, as if by some invisible hand, the chessboard of Ethiopia had been swept clear of all the key pieces belonging to the imperial party. First it was the pawns and bishops, then the knights and castles – until the board was almost empty and just a single figure was left in play: that of the King of Kings.

Sometime in April 1974, at about 9 p.m., while I was having dinner with my parents, the guards at our gate announced the arrival of Lieutenant General Abebe Gemeda, the commander of the Imperial Bodyguard. My father ordered them to let him in and instructed me to go and meet him at the stairs. I already knew General Abebe from the previous year, when I visited him in the American Army Hospital in Frankfurt, where he was being treated. We embraced each other and I led him to my father's panelled study.

The general was in uniform and looked distraught and haggard. The two men greeted each other warmly and I left them alone. About half an hour later our major-domo, Ketema, came up to my rooms and told me that my father wanted to see me in the hall. When I got there, my father asked me to ring the palace and tell the operator to specifically connect me to *Kegnazmatch* Fantaye Jimma, the Master of the Imperial Bedchamber and then come to the study with the phone.[10] I stood there for a while until my father was finally connected to the Emperor. He rose from his chair, as did the general, and bowed low to the telephone. He then continued: 'Your Imperial Majesty, if it was not so late I would have come to report a most important matter to you now, but I will not bother you tonight. Instead I would be most grateful if you could grant me an audience early tomorrow morning'. He then bowed again and added: 'May the Almighty protect your Majesty.' Saying this, he handed the phone back to me. Presently, General Abebe bade us farewell and we all retired.

The next morning my father left the house very early and did not return until lunchtime. Now it was his turn to look careworn and worried. After lunch we went for a walk in the gardens and he confided in me what was troubling him: General Abebe's visit the previous evening had been to let my father know that he, the general, had just been to see the emperor to tell him that he knew the whereabouts of the rebel officers and to seek the permission of the emperor, who was also Commander-in-Chief of the Imperial Armed Forces, to arrest them before they had the chance to create more havoc in the country. The emperor, though, had refused his request, telling him: 'Everything is under control', and that he would let him know when his assistance was required. General Abebe had pleaded with my father

to intervene in this matter and impress upon the emperor the
necessity to act immediately. He added that he had also asked
the Minister of Defence, General Abiye Abebe, to do likewise.
My father then told me that he and General Abiye had gone to
the Palace together that morning to jointly persuade the emperor
to change his mind and accept General Abebe's offer. However,
the King of Kings was adamant that he was still the master of
the situation, a response that dismayed his two senior advisers.

At the end of our walk my father sighed and told me: 'I am
afraid the end is near. There are certain forces within the palace
who are feeding the poor emperor with fraudulent hope and
telling him that the rebelling soldiers are still loyal to him and
only hostile to the men surrounding him. However, he will soon
realize that he himself is their main target. I suppose we now
have no alternative but to join all the rest aboard the sinking
ship.' I had never heard my father speak so pessimistically about
the state of affairs in Ethiopia before. Forty years later, I still
wonder whether General Abebe's suggested intervention might
indeed have saved the Empire.

A few days after the arrest of *Tsehafe-Tezaz* Aklilu on 1 May
1974, I had another memorable conversation with my father. It
was the day of his fifty-second birthday, and at the end of a small
family celebration, I found myself sitting alone with him in his
study for several hours. It would be our final evening together:
two days later, I flew back to Germany to resume my studies
there. That evening he confided in me his fear that, unless a
miracle were to happen, things looked very black indeed for the
monarchy, and that in his opinion the new administration of *Lij*
Endalkatchew would not be in office long, either. He was well
aware that the real danger for the Crown did not come from
the students and other demonstrators on the streets, but from
the army. He had been concerned for quite some time that the
events of 1960 might recur – though in an even worse way than
back then. In the middle of our conversation, he got up and went
over to his English Regency cabinet and took an envelope out of
the safe that was built into it. Opening the envelope, he pulled
out a crumpled and bloodstained slip of paper. This document,

he told me, had been in his possession since December 1960. It had come from the pocket of General Tsige Debu, the chief of the Ethiopian police force, who had thrown his lot in with the putschists and had subsequently been shot dead by troops loyal to the emperor. He passed me the note. On it was a list of the foremost princes, ministers, and holders of other high offices in the empire. Next to each person's name and address, the name of one of the ringleaders of the revolt had been jotted down. It was a list of who would take possession of whose house after the successful coup.[11] Our family home was also included, and next to it the name of Brigadier-General Mengistu Neway, the leader of the 1960 putschists. As it turned out, a year after the events of 1974, our residence was destined to become the '*Monrepos*' of the eventual victor of the Ethiopian Revolution, the dictator Mengistu Haile-Mariam.

I asked my father if he'd informed the emperor of his fears about a military coup. 'More than once,' was his reply. He wanted to persuade the emperor and his prime minister to impose a state of emergency lasting six months on the country. This would give the administration enough breathing space to draft a new constitution, present it to the people and have it proclaimed by parliament. But the emperor would hear none of it, and tried to placate him by telling him: 'Don't worry, We have everything under control, and the army is loyal to Us.' It was at this point that *Ras* Asserate recounted to me the incident on the emperor's eightieth birthday, when he had begged Haile Selassie to abdicate in favour of the crown prince.

I was loath to leave my father and family behind in Ethiopia in circumstances like this, and proposed cancelling my flight back to Germany there and then, but my father wouldn't hear of it. 'You must finish your degree,' he told me, 'Make sure you complete it, then you can come home. You won't miss anything while you're away.' I now know, of course, that he was just trying to set my mind at ease by saying this. Whenever one of our family was due to go abroad for a long spell, it was customary for us to take our leave of the emperor personally. And so, a few days before, I and my father had set off together for the Jubilee Palace to fulfil our obligation. This was the last ever time I saw the emperor. On greeting my father and me, His Majesty seemed tired and dispirited – but he was still in full control of his faculties. As always, he wasted no time on trivialities: 'So when are you finishing your studies?' he asked me. – 'I don't have much longer to go, Your Majesty,' I replied. Haile Selassie nodded in the direction of my father. 'At your age, your father was already a governor-general, you know.' – 'Indeed, Your Majesty, but those were different times.' For a moment, his eyes flashed animatedly before a look of utter exhaustion passed across his face once more. His parting words to me were: 'Come back as soon as you are able so you can be there for your country. It is important that people from Our House should serve Ethiopia in future, too.' Saying this, he kissed my forehead and dismissed me with his blessing.

Two weeks later, the new cabinet of *Lij* Endalkatchew Makonnen was in the process of being dissolved. A quarter of its members had already either been arrested or fled abroad. The constitutional commission and the Anti-Corruption Committee established by the military had begun their work, and in Addis Ababa one strike followed another. On 12 June 1974 Haile Selassie travelled to the summit of the Organisation of African Unity, which was being held in neighbouring Somalia. Among his entourage were *Ras* Asserate, his son-in-law *Ras* Andargatchew Masai and his grandson Rear Admiral Iskender Desta. Unlike previous such meetings, this summit was not an enjoyable experience for Haile Selassie, the 'Father of Africa'. He became embroiled in fierce clashes with Siad Barre, who in the presence of the assembled heads of state publicly laid claim to those areas of the Ethiopian Ogaden populated by Somalis. The row ended in Haile Selassie leaving the summit early.

The last few days of June saw the emergence of the 'Coordinating Committee of the Armed Forces, Police and Territorial Army,' which became by the name *Derg* and was presently to seize the reins of power.[12] On 1 July, *Ras* Asserate was taken from his house by armed guards. In common with all the other dignitaries of the Ethiopian Empire who were arrested over those weeks and months, the President of the Crown Council offered no resistance.[13] On this occasion, too, the army let it be known that the arrest was being made in the name of the emperor. And Haile Selassie likewise said nothing this time, either. *Ras* Asserate had made preparations for his arrest and left behind a sealed envelope for my brother Mulugeta, with instructions to hand in over to the emperor in the event of his detention. My brother later told me about his audience with the emperor that same day. *Lij* Mulugeta Asserate had himself announced in the palace and Haile Selassie received him in his bedchamber.[14] He struck my brother as being despondent but calm and composed. The emperor greeted him with the words: 'They have deprived me of my right hand today.' Straight away he asked Mulugeta to tell him about the exact circumstances of his father's arrest. At the end he said wearily: 'What can a mother cat do when her kittens have been taken away from her? Scratch, that's all, and that's exactly what we're going to do.' This was nothing other than a simple confession of his helplessness. Then Mulugeta handed His Majesty the envelope. 'You open it,' the emperor told him. Mulugeta did as he was bidden and extracted the contents – all the correspondence that his father had been having in the preceding weeks with the English and American embassies. These letters addressed the question of whether the emperor could be got out of the country and spirited away into exile, and if so how this might be achieved. The United States indicated that it would be prepared to grant Haile Selassie asylum. Moreover, it agreed to guarantee his safety from the moment he left Ethiopian territory. Astonishing as it may appear to outsiders, even as he was being detained and taken away, *Ras* Asserate spared no thought for his own safety, only for that of his emperor.

Events came thick and fast over the next few days. Further waves of arrests swept over the city, with official channels talking of a 'crusade against corruption'.[15] Day after day, dignitaries, civil servants, judges and governors of the empire were dragged from their homes and taken into custody. In July, it was announced that Prime Minister *Lij* Endalkatchew Makonnen had been removed from office; he was arrested soon after. A new prime minister was appointed by the military council and confirmed by the emperor: *Lij* Mikael Imru, a son of the emperor's cousin *Ras* Imru, known for his progressive views that made him popular among the intelligentsia. Yet it only took another few weeks before he too was dismissed. The Crown Council was declared dissolved – in the interim, almost all of its members had been arrested. They were followed by the last few confidants of Haile Selassie: the emperor's adjutant, the former minister of the palace, the Vice-Minister of the Pen and the commander of the Imperial Guard. In mid-August, the Ethiopian capital was treated to an impressive military parade of tanks, army trucks, jeeps, serried ranks of marching policemen and detachments from the army and the air force. The military vehicles were all decked out with flags and pennants bearing the slogan that the *Derg* had devised for itself a few weeks before and which in the meantime was used to sign off every official communiqué: "*Ityopya tikdem!*" – 'Ethiopia First!'

The institutions of the monarchy were de facto set aside, and now it only remained for the *Derg* to do one more thing. The committee set its sights on the monarch himself – in concert with a negative media campaign conducted by state television and radio, which in the meantime were under the control of the military. Up till now, the country's new rulers had refrained from criticising the emperor in public, but now the gloves were off. An avalanche of accusations and abuse began to be heaped upon the emperor. He was no longer referred to as the *Negusa Negast*, but was simply called the *Negus* – the emperor had effectively been demoted to a king. He was accused of having left his country in the lurch in 1936, when Italy invaded the country and he went into exile. Furthermore, it was claimed that he bore sole responsibility for the famine in Wollo. He was also charged with filling his own coffers through the systematic 'exploitation' of Ethiopia and of 'hoarding millions of dollars in numbered Swiss bank accounts'.[16] He was said to be at the head of a class of exploiters who had held Ethiopia in their grasp for decades. At the end of August it was announced that the Jubilee Palace, where the emperor was living with his few remaining followers, had been taken into state ownership and would henceforth be known as the 'National Palace'.[17]

New accusations were levelled at the emperor on a daily basis – right up to 11 September, the Ethiopian New Year. In the New Year's address given by the patriarch *Abuna* Theophilos, the customary homage to the emperor was notable by its absence; after all, Haile Selassie was the *Defensor fidei* of the Ethiopian Orthodox Church. Instead, the patriarch now asked for God's blessing on the 'revolutionary movement', which, with the support of the Ethiopian people, was spearheaded by the armed forces. Unlike the 1960 Palace Revolt, when *Abuna* Basileos had stood firmly on the side of the emperor, now Haile Selassie could not even count on the support of the Church. There was no one left to protect him or to intervene on his behalf – even the Imperial Bodyguard had abandoned him to his fate. Ethiopian state television brought New Year's Day to a close by broadcasting Jonathan Dimbleby's documentary on the famine in Wollo, which until then had not been shown in the country. Now people could finally see it, albeit in a heavily edited version. The images of starving and dying children were intercut with scenes of the royal family's parties and receptions at the palace, including pictures of the celebrations marking the emperor's eightieth birthday.[18]

Haile Selassie watched television that evening, too – the officers of the *Derg* had demanded that he view the film in their presence. A curfew was imposed on the capital that night. A few minutes after it came into force, all international telephone lines from Addis Ababa were cut and the airport closed. At six o'clock on the morning of 12 September a small group of *Derg* officers in combat fatigues entered the former Jubilee Palace, which was now rechristened the 'National Palace' and was the 'property of the Ethiopian People'. The building was like something from a ghost town: by this time only the emperor and a few servants were still living there. The officers had asked three Ethiopian journalists to attend and witness the unprecedented scene that now unfolded within the palace. Haile Selassie was summoned to the library, where he found the officers waiting for him.[19] With his head held high, he listened to the proclamation that one of the officers read out. It was reprinted verbatim in the capital's newspapers three days later:

'Although the people of Ethiopia look in good faith upon the Crown as a symbol of unity, Haile Selassie I has abused the authority, dignity and honour of the throne for his personal ends. As a result poverty and decay have been rife in our country. Now the ruler has reached an age where he is no longer capable of discharging his official duties. Accordingly, His Majesty Haile Selassie I is relieved of his office with immediate effect and replaced by a provisional military government.'[20]

The declaration ended with the battle-cry of the Revolution: "*Ityopya tikdem!*" Haile Selassie had listened to all this without so much as a flicker of emotion. After a short pause, he replied to the officers: 'We have carefully listened to what you have said. If you have been motivated by the nation's interests, it is impossible to place personal interests above those of the nation. We have so far served Our country and people to the best of Our abilities. If you are saying that your turn has now come, you should make sure that you look after Ethiopia.'[21] The emperor was taken from the library by the officers and led out of the palace by a side door. A light-blue Volkswagen Beetle was waiting at the foot of the main steps. When one of the officers opened the front passenger's door, the emperor enquired: 'What, in here?' The officer merely nodded and pushed the passenger seat forward. The emperor climbed in and took a seat in the back. A uniformed captain was sitting behind the wheel. Two jeeps escorted the car as it swept through the palace gates and turned into Menelik Avenue. The emperor was driven to the headquarters of the Fourth Army Division, where most of the imperial dignitaries were already being held. On the same day, parliament was dissolved and the constitution suspended. Tanks appeared on the streets of Addis Ababa: the officers of the *Derg* feared that the capital's inhabitants might rise up in a show of support for the emperor, but in the event no such thing occurred.

In the 1990s I got to know an officer in Addis Ababa, who at the time of the revolution had been one of the first members of the *Derg* but who later fell from grace with the regime. We had a very revealing discussion: 'Do you really think,' he asked me, 'that we drove you from power?' 'Who else?' I replied. I quote his answer in full:

> 'You are deluding yourself. There was no institution we respected more than the imperial household. We were convinced it would take a great deal of time, patience and probably military force too to topple the existing power structure. But in the event we pushed at the very first door and walked into an empty room. So we opened the next door, and again the room was empty. And so we continued until we came to the Crown. We found an empty house that was just waiting to be occupied by someone else.'

Although the command and control centre of power was now firmly in their grasp, the armed forces still fought shy of announcing the abolition of the monarchy. Crown Prince Asfa-Wossen, who was laid up in a sanatorium in Europe, was proclaimed as the 'King-designate'. There was to be no more *Negusa Negast*, 'King of Kings', but the military junta let it be known that if the crown prince were to return to Ethiopia, he would be crowned king. 'The king will be the head of state,' ran the *Derg*'s official statement, 'but will have no direct influence on either the governance of the country or on political affairs.'[22] Yet at the same time no one imagined that the crown prince would actually return to Ethiopia, least of all the country's new masters.

However, after the emperor was deposed, the future shape of the country and the question of who would determine its destiny became the subject of a bitter row within the ranks of the *Derg* itself. The military council, which for so long had operated in the shadows, now acquired a public face: Lieutenant General Aman Andom, a long-serving general who was popular throughout the country and went by the nickname of 'The Desert Lion'. He had won his spurs back in the early 1950s, in the Korean War, when Ethiopia sent a contingent of troops as part of the UN mission to support the United States. In 1964, he commanded the Ethiopian army during the border conflict against Somalia, whose forces

On 12 September 1974, Haile Selassie was led from
his palace and taken into captivity by rebel *Derg*
forces. A year later he was put to death.

had invaded the Ogaden. Aman Andom was now named Chairman of the Provisional Military Administration Council, with
the *Derg* issuing conflicting statements as to whether he should
henceforth be known as the 'president' of the military committee or simply its 'spokesman'. General Aman Andom was widely
regarded as a thoughtful, circumspect person and a man of reconciliation. But he was not one who would be content to play
the role of a prominent figurehead. He might be compared to the
last Russian prime minister Alexander Kerensky, who was overthrown by the Bolsheviks in the October Revolution of 1917,
though the two men met very different fates.

At a press conference, the general announced that a referen-
dum would be held on the country's future. Yet in the meantime, a powerful rival had appeared who had very decided
views about what form the state should take in future: the
36-year-old Colonel Mengistu Haile Mariam, formerly a major
in the imperial army and now the First Acting Head of Government of the PMAC. He envisaged a socialist dictatorship
along Soviet Russian lines. And he shied away from no sub-
terfuge or crime to propel himself to the position of absolute
dictator of Ethiopia. On 17 November Mengistu confronted

General Aman with two demands by the *Derg*. Firstly, he was to approve the despatch of more troops to Eritrea in the name of the PMAC in preparation for a military offensive against the armed rebels of the Eritrean Liberation Front. Secondly, his signature was required on a document that authorized the execution by firing squad of leading members of the imperial regime. General Aman resisted both these demands. For one thing, he was an Eritrean himself and believed in the possibility of a solution to the Eritrea conflict at the negotiating table. And he refused point-blank to collude in the shooting of prisoners who had not been given a fair trial and sentenced by a properly constituted court of law. But over the ensuing days, it would transpire that Mengistu was able to unite the majority of the *Derg* behind him.

The Chairman of the Provisional Military Administration Council was placed under house arrest. But General Aman was disinclined to quit the field without a fight, and proceeded to barricade himself in his residence with an armed group of supporters. The following day, tanks entered the grounds. Over a megaphone, the general was ordered to surrender or face an assault. Shortly afterwards, a shot was heard from the heavily defended building. The soldiers of the Fourth Division immediately returned fire: several machine-gun salvoes were loosed off before a tank rumbled up to the building and blew it to smithereens. The 'Desert Lion' was killed, alongside several of his followers who also belonged to the Military Council. That evening, Radio Ethiopia reported that General Aman had been dismissed as Chairman of the PMAC because he had 'refused to cooperate with the security forces.'[23]

In the meantime, the names of those who were on Mengistu's death list were read out to members of the *Derg* in the Menelik Palace. By a show of hands, they voted on who was to be executed that very night. The original list of prisoners whose killing Aman was meant to approve supposedly ran to just six individuals: the two former prime ministers *Tsehafe-Tezaz* Aklilu Habte-Wold and *Lij* Endalkatchew Makonnen, the President of the Crown Council *Ras* Asserate Kassa, Prince Iskender Desta (the grandson of the emperor and commander-in-chief of the navy), the former defence minister General Abiye Abebe and *Ras* Mesfin Sileshi, the governor of Shoa. But by the end of the round of voting, the list had swelled to no fewer than 60 people. Most of them were languishing in the cellars of the Menelik Palace. The prisoners were brought up from the basement, shackled together in pairs and herded onto a large lorry. They were taken to the Akaki Gaol, the large central prison in Addis Ababa, directly opposite the headquarters of the OAU. There, they were led out into the prison courtyard and made to stand with their backs to the wall, two by two. Then each pair was shot dead, one after the other. In one fell swoop, the country's entire former ruling elite – ministers and dignitaries, generals and civil servants alike – was wiped out. My father was among the victims. A shallow trench grave was dug in the courtyard of the gaol. The bodies were hastily buried, and quicklime was scattered over them. A couple of members of the firing squad refused to obey their orders. They were executed on the spot like the prisoners.[24]

The bloody night of 23 November 1974 would form the prelude to a period of terror such as had never been seen before in Ethiopian history. Before long, a person's life counted for very little there. Mengistu's socialist military dictatorship, which came into being over the next few weeks and months, did not even draw the line at innocent family members, the wives and children. The same day that the emperor was led away from the palace, other members of the royal family were also taken into custody – including the emperor's daughter, Princess Tenagne-Work and her children, along with my mother and six brothers and sisters and many other relatives. Soon, the number of members of the former ruling elite in the *Derg*'s gaols ran into the thousands. They remained in prison for many years in degrading conditions – until the collapse of the Soviet Union in 1991 finally led to the fall of Mengistu's socialist dictatorship.[25]

The wider world reacted with disgust and outrage to the massacre of 23 November 1974, and foreign newspapers began to speculate nervously about what fate awaited Haile Selassie in the hands of the Ethiopian military. He spent the first few weeks after his arrest in the headquarters of the Fourth Army Division, where he was interrogated by his captors. They were primarily interested in the supposed millions that he was reputed to have banked abroad – as revolutionary propaganda at the time never tired of mentioning. The Swiss ambassador, Heinz Langenbacher, was summoned in the hope of gleaning information about the emperor's funds in Swiss numbered accounts. The ambassador regretted that banking confidentiality laws prevented him from divulging any such information.[26] The Governor of the Bank of Ethiopia, Taffara Deguefé, was also questioned. He presented the military council with summaries of the trust accounts that Haile Selassie held on behalf of his grandchildren in London and New York – all in all, very modest sums. The military reacted with even greater surprise when the governor of the national bank informed them that the emperor did not even hold a personal account with any Ethiopian bank. 'This may sound incredible to you, but I know it for a fact,' Taffara told them, 'For many years I tried to induce him to open an account in the Commercial Bank of Ethiopia. He never had a deposit account. Each time a crossed dividend cheque was issued in his name by a company, I had to authorise its payment in cash (the preferred method being new Ethiopian $100 notes)...' What's more, the banker had an entirely plausible explanation for such behaviour: 'He never trusted banks since his exile. The explanation is to be sought in the money he lost in foreign banks during his exile as a result of the *de facto* recognition of the Italian occupation of Ethiopia.'[27]

The members of the *Derg* refused to believe it. They questioned the emperor, Princess Tenagne-Work and other members of the royal family about it incessantly, along with the ministers of the imperial court and Haile Selassie's private secretary. Some of these interrogations were conducted by Colonel Mengistu in person in the presence of the Governor of the State Bank. When the Colonel once again accused the emperor of having hoarded away billions of dollars abroad, Haile Selassie responded indignantly: 'How much money did you say we have in foreign banks? Billions? ... fourteen billion dollars! From where would all this money have come? And for what purpose would we keep it abroad? To live in exile? We have seen and experienced exile...'. 'We all fell silent,' wrote Taffara Deguefé, 'and cast our eyes to the ground at this painful mention of exile.'[28]

In the cold light of day it must have struck the country's new rulers themselves just how absurd their accusations were: in 1974 the entire budget of the Ethiopian state amounted to 800 million Ethiopian dollars (around US $320 million). By comparison, the budget of, say, the German city of Frankfurt in that same year was 2 billion marks.[29] Faced with a GNP the size of Ethiopia's, even the most corrupt man in the world would have found it quite impossible to skim off millions. And if more proof were needed that Haile Selassie had not salted away large amounts of money abroad, the imperial family itself was duly to provide it: one had only to see in what straitened circumstances the Crown Prince and all the other members of the royal family lived in exile. Even so, these accusations reverberated around the world, and Ethiopia's new masters never tired of repeating them, even though they themselves knew full well how groundless they were.[30]

It was much the same story with another oft-repeated claim: the emperor, the military junta maintained, had been responsible for presiding over an unprecedented reign of terror. I am not for one moment here defending the autocratic regime of Haile Selassie, which had very little to do with the democratic practices we hold dear in the West nowadays. But when one compares it to the regime that came after it, its record is by no means bad. Haile Selassie can certainly be characterised as a 'benign despot', but in no shape or form was he a bloodthirsty dictator like his successor, who in the decade of the 'Red Terror' alone (1979–89) had more than half a million 'class enemies' in Ethiopia tortured and put to death.[31] One of the principal demands of the protestors in the spring of 1974 was the 'release of all political prisoners', whom they claimed had been gaoled in their thousands. But when the prison gates were opened, there turned out to be no more than a few dozen all told. And many of them were behind bars for spying for Somalia, while one of their number, the emperor's son-in-law

Haile-Selassie Gugsa, had been imprisoned for collaborating with the Italians during their invasion of Abyssinia in 1935. Even then, most of the spies remained in custody under the new regime. And, as the respected political journal *Ethiops* revealed in 1999, the number of people in exile on political grounds during Haile Selassie's reign totalled just seven.[32] By contrast, under Mengistu's military dictatorship, the prison cells began to fill up with tens of thousands of political detainees, while hundreds of thousands of Ethiopians were driven into exile.

Haile Selassie, the victorious Lion of Judah and King of Kings, would ultimately suffer the very fate that *Tsehafe-Tezaz* Aklilu had prophesied for him when he was arrested and taken away. He would survive his prime minister and the others who died alongside Aklilu in November 1974 by nine months. After his weeks of interrogation at the Fourth Army Division HQ, he was taken back to the Menelik Palace. In his former residence, some makeshift quarters had been made ready for the deposed emperor, comprising two sparsely-furnished rooms and a bathroom. By now, he only had a handful of servants around him, including his butler Eshetu Tekle-Mariam, who remained close at hand day and night. Eshetu had sworn a personal vow never to let his master out of his sight. He spent the nights on a camp bed in the anteroom to the imperial bedchamber. I met this last servant of Haile Selassie in Addis Ababa in 1991 and had a long conversation with him about these final weeks.[33] Eshetu told me that Haile Selassie endured his time in captivity with stoical serenity, seldom speaking a word. A few weeks later Haile Selassie was dead. On 28 August 1975, the military regime announced that Haile Selassie had passed away in the preceding night after failing to recover from a prostate operation.[34] The emperor's longtime personal doctor, Professor Asrat Woldeyes, immediately protested at this version of events. The surgery in question had taken place months before, and to the very end Haile Selassie enjoyed the best of health.

Eshetu painted a moving picture of the emperor's final hours:

'On the night of 27 August 1975, I saw Colonel Mengistu Haile Mariam together with another person I could not recognise being in the palace before, pacing up and down the corridor near the room where the Emperor was. I prepared a dinner for His Imperial Majesty. Without uttering a word, I offered it to him and he dined quietly and proceeded into his bedroom. I was then told by the authorities that I had to transfer to another room, to which I replied that I can leave only after I inform my move to His Majesty. I was given the permission to notify the Emperor, at which point I went in and informed Him of the decision. The Emperor commented somewhat sardonically, "Well, if this place is too small for them, we will build them a larger palace." He then commanded me to do as I was told. The Emperor then staggered toward the window facing the Church of Our Lady. He opened it and said, "Oh, Ethiopia, do you ever harbour ill will toward me?" Tears started to roll down his cheeks.'[35]

Eshetu was then taken to the guards' quarters. He was led into a dark room and the door was locked behind him. The next morning the door was opened again and Eshetu went back to the emperor's rooms to serve him breakfast: 'I knocked, but there was no answer. As I entered the bedroom, the first thing that struck me was a powerful smell of ether. Then I noticed the emperor lying motionless on his bed. His face had turned a dark blue colour. His pillow was not beneath his head, but immediately next to it. Everything pointed to his having been drugged in his sleep and then suffocated.[36]

The stench of ether was so overpowering that the butler lost consciousness for a brief moment. When he came to, he found himself out on the veranda. He was then locked up in a room for several hours with two other manservants before finally being released. Neither the emperor's personal physician nor *Abuna* Theophilos, who both demanded to view the body, were permitted to enter the palace. Nor would the officers allow an autopsy to be conducted. In a final act of humiliation, the deceased was even denied a Christian burial. It subsequently came to light that Colonel Mengistu had the emperor's body hidden beneath the floorboards of a toilet in the palace. His mortal remains were discovered there and exhumed after the fall of the Mengistu regime in 1992. Two years later, in the courtyard of the Akaki Gaol, the mass grave was found where the victims of the November 1974 massacre lay buried.

Five months before the death of Haile Selassie, on 21 March 1975, the Military Council officially proclaimed the abolition of the monarchy. The country's new rulers declared that crown prince and princesses had been stripped of their titles.[37] Prior to this announcement, all the imperial insignia of Haile Selassie had been expunged from all buildings, institutions and public squares in the capital and the provinces, as well as from official documents. Nothing was to remain to remind people of the 3,000-year Ethiopian Empire and the last 'Elect of God' on the Ethiopian throne. For a while, Haile Selassie's face still continued to grace the country's banknotes and postage stamps – until these too were changed. Mengistu and his confederates tried their utmost to erase all traces of Emperor Haile Selassie and his reign from Ethiopian history. But in this, they failed dismally.

What, then, perpetuated the tragedy that ended the long and sometimes triumphant rule of Emperor Haile Selassie? In my view it was the simultaneous collapse of the three institutions that hitherto had been the foundation of the Ethiopian state: namely, the Crown, the aristocracy and the Church.

As far as the Crown was concerned, the emperor's reluctance to take any meaningful measures against the rebelling soldiers during the early stages of the 'revolution in instalments' led to the assumption by the rebels that the head of state was a lame duck, whose tenure of the Throne of David depended solely on their benevolence. There is no doubt in my mind that the emperor could have easily rallied the Ethiopian people and the majority of the Ethiopian army to come to his rescue as far back as April and May of 1974, when the demands of the rebelling soldiers became untenable. Unfortunately, he never made a public statement declaring that sections of the Ethiopian armed forces were coercing him and the country was becoming ungovernable. On the contrary, he continued to accept all the demands of the then still secret union of soldiers and officers of the Imperial Armed Forces. He never uttered a word when scores of his ministers, generals and other high-ranking officials were taken into custody by the military, mostly in his name, so leaving the doors wide open for a military takeover.

Without diminishing the emperor's merit, I am afraid that by refusing to provide the Ethiopian people with a successor at the right moment and by clinging to power until the very end, history may hold him responsible for the demise of the 3,000-year-old reign of the House of David in Ethiopia.

The failure of the aristocracy was equally stark. After the end of the Italian occupation the power of the once mighty aristocrats of the Empire steadily dwindled until, by 1975, only a handful of them were in leading positions in Ethiopia. The remaining small group of enlightened aristocrats (the 'Stolypinists') were now divided among themselves and however hard they might have tried to establish a truly constitutional monarchy in Ethiopia, they could not imagine doing so without the inclusion of their ruling sovereign, whom they served diligently.

Oliver Cromwell, in one of his meetings with Charles I, is supposed to have declared: 'You, Sir, are not England and England is not You!' Unfortunately the enlightened aristocrats who boldly demanded constitutional reforms after the coup d'état of 1960 were unable to make this distinction. For them, Haile Selassie, by whose name they all swore, was the living embodiment of Ethiopia. For them, thanks to their upbringing, Crown and Nation were synonymous.

Had they been united and determined enough to bring the badly-needed change from above, the aristocracy would have been in a far stronger position to force the emperor to declare martial law for one year, perhaps under the leadership of Lieutenant General Abebe Gemeda, to stabilize the situation in the early stages of the revolt until a new constitution, which was then already being prepared, had come into effect. Instead, the cunning emperor continued to profit greatly from their disunity and their petty rivalries and ruled unopposed until his final overthrow by the Coordinating Committee of the Ethiopian Armed Forces (*Derg*). The men who were his collaborators in ruling Ethiopia for over forty years were to find their inhuman end, without once being defended by their august sovereign whom they served with unswerving loyalty. It is an irony of history that a few months later the King of Kings was to share the same fate.

Until 1974 the Ethiopian Orthodox Tewahedo Church was the official religion of the Ethiopian Empire. Church and State were two sides of the same coin for centuries. During the coup d'état of 1960 the Church played a major role in saving the Ethiopian monarchy. It is because *Abuna* Basileos, the first Ethiopian Patriarch, excommunicated the leaders of the revolt and stood on the side of the Defender of the Faith that Haile Selassie could be restored to his throne.

Regrettably this did not happen in 1974. The Church kept quiet throughout the early stages of the revolution until 11 September, the day before the overthrow of the Emperor. That evening Patriarch Tewoflos appeared on Ethiopian television to bless the revolution in progress. It was the first time that the special relationship between Crown and Church was destroyed. Furthermore, the Ethiopian Orthodox Church did not condemn the illegal killings of 23 November 1974 when 60 Ethiopian dignitaries, all of them staunch members of that Church, where massacred without the due process of law. Not only that, it went on to forbid all churches in Ethiopia to hold the traditional requiems for the slaughtered victims. No reaction was forthcoming from the Synod either when the mysterious death of the Defender of the Faith was announced in August 1975. Alas, this inglorious act did not help the Church authorities to save their own necks. Only a few years later the Head of the Ethiopian Orthodox Tewahedo Church, Patriarch Tewoflos, was also murdered in cold blood by the military junta.

The collapse of all these three institutions, which had been the soul of Imperial Ethiopia for millennia, was instrumental in paving the way for the reign of terror, which was to last for over seventeen agonizing years. At the end of it, Ethiopia had lost over half a million souls through the indiscriminate massacres of the Mengistu regime. Another million Ethiopians were to become refugees in all five continents of the world.

Haile Selassie's legacy

On 5 November 2000, twenty-five years after his death, Haile Selassie would finally be accorded a fitting burial. Even the regime that followed the socialist military dictatorship of Colonel Mengistu Haile Mariam – under the leadership of the Ethiopian People's Revolutionary Democratic Front (EPRDF) with Meles Zenawi at its head – had long resisted holding any such public ceremony; yet it could not stop it from going ahead. A large rostrum was erected in front of the steps of the Ba'ita Church in the centre of Addis Ababa. In the presence of the assembled faithful, the Ethiopian Orthodox Church took leave of its *defensor fidei*. The patriarch *Abuna* Paulos offici-ated at the ceremony. The bishops and ecclesiastical dignitaries were seated on the right hand of the patriarch, while to his left were numerous guests of honour, including the aged Princess Tenagne-Work. She was the last surviving direct descendant of the emperor, Crown Prince Asfa-Wossen having died in exile in London three years previously.

I, too, had travelled to the Ethiopian capital that day to attend the funeral service. The crowds on the street kept on growing as the cortège formed up in front of the church. Tens of thousands of people had gathered there. The coffin holding the remains of the emperor was borne on a decorated pallet truck, draped with a huge flag of the Ethiopian imperial household in the national colours of green, gold and red and proudly emblazoned with the Lion of Judah. Finally the funeral procession moved off. Flanking the coffin to the left and right, the priesthood

paraded solemnly in their magnificent vestments under shimmering parasols covered with velvet and brocade and adorned
with silver tinsel. Behind walked deputations of former Imperial Guards in the uniforms of yesteryear, alongside veterans of
the Italo-Ethiopian War. Some of them were wearing traditional
warriors' garb, complete with face masks and lion's-mane head-
dresses, and carrying spears and shields. Others had put on their
old military uniforms, and their breast pockets shone with military decorations and campaign medals. A group of hundreds of
dancing Rastafarians, led by Bob Marley's widow Rita, mingled
with the crowd of mourners. Many of those who lined the route
of the funeral procession held aloft pictures of Haile Selassie and
his empress.

The cortège halted once more in front of St George's Cathedral, where almost seventy years earlier to the day Haile Selassie had been crowned *Negusa Negast*, King of Kings, for the
coffin to lie in state, before the procession set off again to its
final station, the Cathedral of the Holy Trinity. On the steps of
the cathedral, hundreds of *Debteras* – lay masters of church ceremony, dressed in their long robes – began intoning their characteristic chants, swaying in time to the rhythm of their drums and
sistra. In the cathedral, Haile Selassie I was carried to his final
resting place alongside his wife, Empress Menen. It had always
been his express wish to be buried alongside his empress. Now,
finally, twenty-five years after his death, his wish was fulfilled.
Crown Prince Asfa-Wossen, who had passed away in January
1997, was also eventually interred here. The 60 dignitaries who
had been murdered on the Bloody Saturday of 23 November
1974 had already been laid to rest some years before in the cem-
etery of the Cathedral of the Holy Trinity.

In the end, a person can only perform to the limits of his or
her abilities. No one would deny that Haile Selassie served his
country in good faith, or that he achieved great historical triumphs in the process. He stood up against Italian Fascism and
assured the multi-ethnic state of Ethiopia its unity and independence. He was a brilliant exponent of foreign policy and played
a significant role in the decolonisation of Africa. Yet ultimately

Haile Selassie was unequal to the challenges that accompanied the headlong technological and economic development of the world in the second half of the 20th century. The Ethiopian historian Bahru Zewde has rightly claimed that: 'Haile Selassie's greatest fault was that he reigned for far too long – and that he did not realize it.'[1]

Haile Selassie was not a weak monarch, quite the contrary in fact: never before in the country's history had an Ethiopian emperor wielded so much power. Yet despite this – or perhaps precisely because of it – he was also fated to be the last of his line. He would and could not understand that a modern state in the mid-20th century could no longer be governed along paternalistic and autocratic lines like some absolutist empire of the 18th century. All his policies were geared toward centralism, and to share power was unthinkable for him. He harboured a deep mistrust of all those around him and proved incapable of delegating decisions.

Count Edouard von Taaffe, who served as Austrian prime minister under the Habsburg emperor Franz Joseph, once memorably said: 'The art of ruling the Danube Monarchy involves keeping all its constituent parts in an equal state of mild dissatisfaction.' And it is true that all of Haile Selassie's actions were aimed at treating all the various different ethnic groups within the country equally. The emperor made no distinction between skin colour, ethnic background, status or religious affiliation. Only one quality mattered to him: his subjects' unconditional loyalty to him.

The 'divide and rule' policy that Haile Selassie pursued enabled fundamental shortcomings and the fatal state of stagnation in the country to be whitewashed over for decades on end. In the final years of his reign, it seemed that Haile Selassie's primary aim was no longer to promote the development of his country but instead to shore up his own power at all costs. His closest confederates simply accepted this, some of them with a mixture of agony and despair. They placed personal loyalty to the emperor above everything else, even their own safety. And possibly also above their responsibility to their own native land.

Even critical voices among his entourage could not envisage their nation's future without the King of Kings. Right up to the eleventh hour, Haile Selassie neglected to pass the sceptre of office on to the next generation. He regarded himself and his destiny as being in God's hands – and likewise the fate of the country over which he held sway.

The revolution of 1974 which overthrew imperial rule opened the floodgates to an era of terror and lawlessness. Not content with that, Mengistu's bloody regime also subjugated the thousands of years of Ethiopian history to its new ideological worldview by condemning the Ethiopian Empire lock, stock and barrel.

If one removes the ideological blinkers and considers the history of Ethiopia over the last hundred years, it is fair to say that the country never before underwent the kind of upheavals and twists of fate that it experienced in the 20th century. This is especially true of the period following the Italian invasion of 1935. The period after the reign of Emperor Menelik was characterised by internecine feuding. The regency of *Lij* Iyasu ended with the coronation of Empress Zauditu, and after her death the crown passed to Haile Selassie. He is to be credited with leading Ethiopia into the modern world – first as regent, then as the King of Kings. In this, he saw himself as the heir to Emperor Menelik. Haile Selassie established schools and universities on the Western model. He introduced a constitution and made Ethiopia a member of the League of Nations. The constitution of 1930 marked the beginning of a constitutional form of government and the end of feudalism. And despite lasting for only five years, the period under Italian occupation further accelerated the process of modernisation, which changed Ethiopia from the ground up. To consolidate their colonial rule, the Italians developed the country's infrastructure, creating a network of roads. This had a direct effect on Ethiopia's economic and social structure, in that it facilitated the exchange of goods and the movement of people from the outlying provinces. Moreover, the central bureaucracy that Italy installed also helped sweep away the country's feudal structures.

The era that followed the country's liberation was one of consolidation. The popularity of the emperor and the fighting prowess of the Patriots enabled Ethiopia's unity to be maintained. Yet the challenges facing it after the war were enormous: virtually no funds were available aside from a modest grant from the British government; there was a dearth of well-educated people in the administration, and very little modern equipment of any kind in the country. The British commandeered everything that the Italian occupiers had left behind, right down to the office furniture and fittings. Throughout the 1940s and 1950s, Great Britain put obstacles in the way of Ethiopia's development at every twist and turn. Nevertheless, Haile Selassie still managed to put a functioning civil service in place. The path of modernisation that he had embarked upon was sustained: regulations and laws were codified, a state bank and a national currency were created, and presently a national airline too, along with a host of other institutions with modernization at the heart of their agenda. Eritrea was reunified with Ethiopia, a move that also saw the empire achieve its long sought-after aim of gaining access to the sea.[2]

However, political developments failed to keep pace with the country's economic and social achievements – or indeed with the demands that arose from Ethiopia's increasing role on the global stage. Addis Ababa became the seat of the Organisation of African Unity (OAU; nowadays the African Union), and many international firms and organisations established branches in the Ethiopian capital. But within the country itself, all power remained firmly in the hands of the emperor, who ruled Ethiopia according to paternalistic principles. Haile Selassie basked in the renown he enjoyed around the world, but all the while he ignored the fact that things were far from ideal within his own country. The attempted coup led by General Mengistu Neway in 1960, in which many of the country's leading politicians were killed, was a warning shot that went unheeded. Before long, discontent was growing among all of Ethiopia's social classes about the state of the country. And so matters took their inevitable course. The famine that hit Wollo province was the catalyst for the revolution of 1974, spearheaded by the armed forces and demonstrating students. It is to the credit of the imperial regime and its principal officials that they did not order a savage crackdown on the insurrection, but instead submitted passively to the course of events. Admittedly, this did not prevent them from paying for this lack of action with their lives.

Thus began Ethiopia's arduous journey to the present day. What began as a student revolt informed by thoroughly high-minded principles descended into the tragedy of the Red Terror, in the course of which hundreds of thousands of Ethiopians were tortured, raped, mutilated and murdered for supposedly being 'class enemies'. Millions of people lost the roof over their heads, along with all their worldly possessions and their fundamental human rights. As with so many such uprisings, the Ethiopian Revolution obeyed the tragic principle that 'the revolution devours its own children'. When it was over, Ethiopia found itself in the grip of a military regime which, freed from all moral constraints, ruled with brutal violence and lawlessness. After seventeen years of military rule, which saw Ethiopia cut adrift from all its historic and traditional values, torn asunder from its cultural roots and with all its institutions destroyed, the country was on its knees. From this point, Ethiopia could sink no further.

Mengistu Haile Mariam's brutal junta was followed in 1991 by a government of the Tigray People's Liberation Front (TPLF) under the leadership of Meles Zenawi. It was thanks to the TPLF – which suffered significant casualties in the process – that Mengistu's military dictatorship was overthrown and its unprecedented reign of terror brought to an end. Shortly afterwards, Ethiopia was divided into regions organised along ethnic lines. Yet the ethnocentric policies pursued from the outset by the TPLF is not the right path for a heterogeneous country such as Ethiopia, with it eighty-plus ethnic groupings and over one hundred languages. In many regards, the 'ethnic federation' the current government is so fond of referring to resembles the apartheid regime in white supremacist South Africa. When the South African prime minister D. F. Malan instituted the system of apartheid in 1948, he was asked what the term meant; he replied: '*Apartheid* means nothing more than an ethnic federation.' Ethiopia's current 'ethnic federation' is far removed from the kind of federal state we see in India, the United States or the Federal Republic of Germany. A policy that makes ethnicity the guiding principle of its system of governance inevitably sets free powerful centrifugal forces. The example of Haile Selassie should remind us that the unity and sovereignty of Ethiopia must be preserved at all costs. Unity in diversity and diversity in unity – this should be the motto of any federation worthy of the name. There is no questioning the fact that the EPRDF regime has had some degree of economic success; yet where people's fundamental democratic rights are concerned, there is a blatant disregard of them by those in power, as repeatedly attested by Amnesty International and Human Rights Watch. We should learn from the mistakes of the imperial era and provide a secure future for the now 90 million Ethiopians in peaceful coexistence with one another and within the framework of a properly constituted state under the rule of law.

When history comes to pass judgement on Haile Selassie and his sixty-year reign over Ethiopia both as regent and as emperor and weighs up his strengths and weaknesses, his many services to the country will carry more weight than the great mistakes he undoubtedly made. The old adage holds good for him, too – namely that the greatness of a leader only becomes clear in the light of the regime and the rulers than come after him or her. I feel sure that future generations of Ethiopians will judge him far more kindly than my generation has done.

Asfa-Wossen Asserate

Notes

Prologue
1. This story was told to me by the Ethiopian author Mammo Wudineh in November 2000.
2. Quoted in *Time* magazine, 6 January 1936.
3. I have in my possession a significant part of my father's correspondence and diaries, which I hope to publish in the foreseeable future.

Chapter 1: A childhood in Harar
1. Christian Ethiopians have two names: a 'wordly' name by which they are referred to on a daily basis, and a baptismal name used by the Church solely for liturgical purposes, e.g. when an individual takes holy orders, dies or becomes king or emperor.
2. On Harar and its history, cf. *Encyclopedia Aethiopica* (EAE). Edited by Siegbert Uhlig, vol. 2, pp.1012–1021.
3. Cf. Leonard Mosley: *Haile Selassie. The Conquering Lion.* London 1964, p.25f.
4. Charles Nicholl: *Somebody Else. Arthur Rimbaud in Africa 1880–1891.* London 1997, p.226.
5. Letter from Armand Savouré to Frédéric Rimbaud, 1897, quoted in Nicholl, *Somebody Else*, p.251.
6. Lord Edward Gleichen: *With the Mission to Menelik 1897.* London 1898, p.45f.
7. Ibid., p. 42/45.
8. Cf. Eloi Ficquet, Taurin Cahagne, in: EAE 1, p.664f.
9. Gleichen, *Mission*, p.50.

10. Haile Selassie I: *My Life and Ethiopia's Progress 1892–1937*. Translated and annotated by Edward Ullendorff. Oxford 1976, p.15.
11. Ibid.
12. Cf. Antonios Alberto, André de Jarosseau, in EAE 3, p.270.
13. Quoted in Harold G. Marcus: *Haile Selassie I. The Formative Years 1892–1936*. Berkeley, Los Angeles, London 1987, p.3f.
14. Ibid., p.16.
15. Haile Selassie, *My Life* I, p.15.
16. Some sources suggest that Menelik II may have named *Ras* Makonnen as the heir apparent as early as 1896, immediately after the Battle of Adwa. Cf. EAE 3, p.687.
17. Haile Selassie, *My Life* I, p.20.
18. Ibid., p.21.
19. Felix Rosen: *Eine deutsche Gesandschaft in Abessinien* [A German legation in Abyssinia]. Leipzig 1907, p.84.
20. Ibid.
21. Haile Selassie, *My Life* I, p.42.
22. Speculation such as that in Leonard Mosley's work (*Haile Selassie*, p.41) that *Ras* Makonnen was poisoned seem scarcely credible, as does the recurring rumour that he did not actually die in 1906 but withdrew from public life to live out the rest of his days in a monastery.
23. Rosen, *Eine deutsche Gesandschaft*, p.286.
24. Monsignor Jarosseau's diary entry of 23 March 1906, quoted in Marcus, *The Formative Years*, p.7.
25. Letter from Basile to Monsignor Jarosseau, quoted in Marcus, *The Formative Years*, p.7.
26. Gleichen, *Mission*, p.153.
27. For the biography of *Lij* Iyasu, cf. Bahru Zewde, *Lij* Iyasu, in EAE 3, pp.253–256.
28. Haile Selassie, *My Life* I, p.29.
29. Many factors point to him having suffered from syphilis (cf. Marcus, *The Formative Years*, p.7).
30. For the biography of the Empress Taitu, cf. the article by Hanna Rubinkowska, in EAE 3, p.878f.

31. Gleichen, *Mission*, p.154.

32. Cf. Haile Selassie, *My Life* I, p.35.

Chapter 2: Two cousins vie for power

1. Monsignor Jarosseau's diary, March 1910, quoted in Marcus, *The Formative Years*, p.7.

2. Cf. Haile Selassie, *My Life* I, pp.37–41.

3. Ibid., p.42. Prior to this marriage, Tafari Makonnen had already conceived an illegimtiate daughter, Romana-Work, who was later to die in Italian custody in Turin. She was married to *Dejazmatch* Merid Beyene, a soldier and Patriot, who was killed in 1936 while fighting the Italians. His widow was taken prisoner and transported to Italy, where she died soon after.

4. Marse Hazan Wolde Qirqos: *YeZaman Tarik Tezetaye BaNegesta Negestat Zawditu Zamana Mangist*. Addis Ababa, undated, p.111.

5. Conversation with *Fitaurari* Nebeye-Leul, *Ras* Kassa's private secretary, Spring 1993.

6. Tekle Hawariat Tekle Mariam: *Autobiography – Yahiwote Tarik*. Addis Ababa 2006, p.249.

7. Ibid.

8. Ibid., p.304.

9. Gebre-Igziabiher Elyas: *Prowess, Piety and Politics. The Chronicle of Abeto Iyasu and Empress Zewditu of Ethiopia*. Quoted in Marcus, *The Formative Years*, p.15.

10. Tekle Hawariat Tekle Mariam: *Autobiography*, p.324.

11. Archive of the British Foreign Office, National Archives, Kew, London FO 371/2227.

12. Haile Selassie, *My Life* I, p.42f.

13. Marcus, *The Formative Years*, p.19. This in turn shows the special closeness between the Church and State in Ethiopia. It was impossible for any Ethiopian ruler to reign without the support of the Ethiopian Orthodox Church.

14. Conversation with *Fitaurari* Nebeye-Leul, *Ras* Kassa's private secretary, Spring 1993.

15. For the biography of *Ras* Kassa, cf. Asfa-Wossen Asserate, Kassa Hailu, in EAE 3, p.350f.

16. Interview conducted by the author with *Dejazmatch* Zawde Gebre-Selassie, 2–5 May 2002 in Munich.

17. Ibid.

18. Ibid.

19. Quoted in Marcus, *The Formative Years*, p.22.

20. Haile Selassie, *My Life* I, p.55.

21. Marcus, *The Formative Years*, p.23.

22. Wilfred Thesiger: *The Life of My Choice*. London 1987, p.55.

23. Haile Selassie, *My Life* I, p.62.

24. Telephone interview in October 2010 with *Dejazmatch* Berhane-Maskal Desta, the grandson of *Ras* Kassa, who as a boy personally witnessed the events in Fiche.

25. Conversation with *Fitaurari* Nebeye-Leul, *Ras* Kassa's private secretary, Spring 1993.

26. Gobeze Tafeta: *Abba Tena Iyasu*. Addis Ababa 1996, p.149f.

27. Marse Hasan Wolde Qirqos: *YeZaman Tarik Tezetaye BaNegesta Negestat Zawditu Zamana Mangist*. Addis Ababa (n.d.), p.166.

28. See for example Paul B. Henze: *Layers of Time. A History of Ethiopia*. London 2000, p.193ff. Hitherto, *Lij* Iyasu's contribution has been little researched, and to date no definitive biography of him has been written.

Chapter 3: The Ethiopian Machiavelli

1. Bahru Zewde: *A History of Modern Ethiopia 1855–1974*. London, Athens, Addis Ababa 1991, p.128

2. Quoted in Marcus, *The Formative Years*, p.26.

3. Bahru Zewde, *A History of Modern Ethiopia*, p.130

4. Marcus, *The Formative Years*, p.28.

5. Giuseppe di Felizziano Graf Colli to the minister, 23 March 1917, IFM, Archivo Politico 66/1135.

6. De Coppet to the Ethiopian ambassador, 21 June 1918, FAM, *Guerre, Affaires politiques générales*, Ethiopie IX, 1918, Vol. 1625.

7. For the biography of Adolf Jakob Meyer, see EAE 3, p.889f.

8. Quoted in Marcus, *The Formative Years*, p.40f.

9. Ibid., p.41.

10. Haile Selassie, *My Life* I, p.125.

11. Quoted in Mosley, *Haile Selassie*, p.125.

12. Haile Selassie, *My Life* I, p.59.

13. On this subject, cf. the entries on the institution of slavery and its history in Ethiopia by Richard Pankhurst, Jonathan Miran, Dirk Bustorf and Wolbert Smidt, in EAE 3, pp.673–681.

14. See Tecola W. Hagos 'King Sahle Selassie, Emperor Menilik II and the Betrayal of Ethiopia', in EthioNL: A site for Ethiopians, November 20, 2004 [http://www.ethio.nl/ethio_country/king_sahleselassie.html]:
According to the *Fetha Negast*, the true nature of a human being is in a state of liberty or freedom. 'The state of liberty is in accord with the law of reason, for all men share liberty on the basis of natural law. But war and the strength of horses bring some to the service of the victors ... To free a slave is one of the deeds of perfection which must be done, for it is an excellent form of alms; it is the granting to a man of the right to become master of himself, according to the original law of his natural liberty.' [*Fetha Negast*, Chapter XXXI].

15. See also Dirk Bustorf, Domestic and Court Slavery, EAE 3, p.678f.

16. Charles F. Rey: *In the Country of the Blue Nile*. New York 1969 (first published 1927), p.219.

17. Haile Selassie, *My Life* I, p.81.

18. Marse-Hazan Wolde-Kirkos: *Yazaman tarik tezetaye – kayahutena kasamahut 1896–1922*. Addis Ababa 2006, p.262.

19. Quoted in the above.

20. Telegrams to Baldwin and Mussolini on 18 September 1923, FO 371/8410; IFM Affari Politici, pacco 1924.
21. Haile Selassie, *My Life* I, p.77.
22. German Embassy in Abyssinia, Addis Ababa, 2 March 1924, to the German Foreign Office, Berlin, AA R77854.
23. *The Times*, 17 May 1924.
24. Ibid.
25. Report by Friedrich Kuhn, Hamburg, to the German Foreign Office, 13 June 1924.
26. German Embassy in Abyssinia, Addis Ababa, 2 March 1924, to the German Foreign Office, Berlin, AA R77854.
27. Haile Selassie, *My Life* I, p.98.
28. Marcus, *The Formative Years*, p.64f.
29. Lord Stamfordham, 10 April 1924, FO 371/9988.
30. Letter from Rowland A.C. Sperling to Prime Minister Ramsay MacDonald, 28 December 1923, FO 371/8408.
31. Note on the principal personalities of the Abyssinian Mission. Memorandum by Mr. C. Russell, 2 July 1924, FO 371/9991.
32. Ibid.
33. Richard Greenfield: *Ethiopia. A New Political History.* London 1965, p.158.
34. *Illustrated London News*, 12 July 1924.
35. *Manchester Guardian*, 8 July 1924.
36. *The New York Times*, 5 May 1924.
37. The original of this caricature hangs in the Sitwell family home of Renishaw Hall near Sheffield. My friend Sir Reresby Sitwell (1927–2009) kindly gave me a copy in the 1980s. It is reproduced here by kind permission of Lady Alexandra Sitwell.
38. Vita Sackville-West: *The Edwardians.* London 1970, p.339.
39. For the complete story of the 'Dreadnought Hoax' cf. Adrian Stephen: *The 'Dreadnought' Hoax.* London 1983 (first edn. 1936).
40. Haile Selassie, *My Life* I, p.112.

41. Quoted in M.G. Smith, Roy Augier, Rex Nettleford: *The Rastafari Movement in Kingston*. Jamaica, Kingston 1960, p.5.

42. Quoted in Haile Selassie, *My Life* I, p.123.

43. Cf. ibid., pp.65–76.

44. On the history of the newspaper *Berahanena Salem*, cf. EAE 1, p.536f.

45. Christine Sandford: *The Lion of Judah Hath Prevailed. Being the Biography of His Imperial Majesty Haile Selassie I*. Westport, CT 1972, p.46f.

46. Cf. Marcus, *The Formative Years*, p.103f.

47. Ibid., p.83.

48. Cf. the text of the treaty in Haile Selassie, *My Life* I, p.147ff.

49. Cf. Sandford, *The Lion of Judah*, p.51.

50. Ibid, p.52f.

51. Haile Selassie, *My Life* I, p.154f.

52. On the wording of the ultimatum directed at the Empress, see Mahtama-Selassie Wolde-Maskal: *Zekra Nagar*. Addis Ababa 1969, pp.719–722.

53. Conversation with *Dejazmatch* Haile Mariam Gessesse, Asmara, July 1968.

54. Sandford, *The Lion of Judah*, p.53.

55. Conversation with *Fitaurari* Nebeye-Leul, *Ras* Kassa's private secretary, Spring 1993.

56. The title *Leul* is equivalent to that of 'Your Highness', and was formerly only ever used as a form of address. The person generally regarded as the originator of the term as a title is the former foreign minister Heruy Wolde-Selassie; it was first applied to *Ras* Tafari and his wife Princess Menen, who were respectively designated *Leul-Ras* and *Leelt Woizero*.

57. Marcus, *The Formative Years*, p.95.

58. Proclamation announcing the appointment of King Tafari as the King of Kings, 3 April 1930, in Mahtama-Selassie Wolde-Maskal, *Zekra Nagar*, p.725.

Chapter 4: The Elect of God

1. Haile Selassie, *My Life* I, p.173.
2. Ibid., p.174.
3. Major Cheesman, diary, quoted in Mosley, *Haile Selassie*, p.169.
4. *Berliner Lokal-Anzeiger*, September 1930.
5. Haile Selassie, *My Life* I, p.174f.
6. Baron von Waldthausen, despatch to the German foreign office, 22 October 1930, AA R77856.
7. Report by the German embassy in Addis Ababa to the German foreign office, 17 November 1930, AA R 77856.
8. Evelyn Waugh: *Remote People*. London 1931.
9. Thesiger, *The Life of My Choice*, p.92.
10. For a detailed description of the coronation ceremony, cf. Mahtama-Selassie Wolde-Maskal, *Zekra Nagar*, pp.729–747.
11. Baron von Waldthausen, despatch to the German foreign office, 22 October 1930, AA R77856.
12. Zawde Retta: *Yakadamawi Haile-Selassie Mengest*. Delhi 2012, pp.18–45.
13. Ibid.
14. Ibid.
15. Ibid.
16. Baron von Waldthausen, despatch to the German foreign office, 22 October 1930, AA R77856.
17. Waugh, *Remote People*, pp.56–58.
18. Ibid., p.59.
19. Ibid., p.63.
20. Baron von Waldthausen, despatch to the German foreign office, 22 October 1930, AA R77856.
21. Ibid.
22. *The New York Times*, 3 November 1930.
23. *The Times*, 22 December 1930.
24. Ibid.
25. German foreign office to the Imperial Ethiopian Consulate-General, Berlin 29 November 1930, AA R77856.

26. German embassy in Addis Ababa to the German foreign office, 10 March 1931, AA R 77856.

27. In the Revised Ethiopian Constitution of 1955, the following articles treat the question of the Solomonic dynasty's claim to the Ethiopian throne: 'The Imperial dynasty shall remain perpetually attached to the line of Haile Selassie I, descendant of King Sahle Selassie, whose line descends without interruption from the dynasty of Menelik I, son of the Queen of Ethiopia, the Queen of Sheba, and King Solomon of Jerusalem' (Article 2); and further, 'By virtue of His Imperial Blood, as well as by the anointing which He has received, the person of the Emperor is sacred, His dignity is inviolable and His powers indisputable' (Article 4).

28. *Lij* Imru Zelleke, secretary of the constitutional commission of 1955, in a telephone conversation with the author, May 2013. *Lij* Imru Zelleke was later appointed as Ethiopian ambassador to the Federal Republic of Germany.

29. Haile Selassie, *My Life* I, p.178.

30. Paulos Tzadua, EAE 2, p.534f.

31. Cf. the entry by Paolo Marrassini, EAE 3, pp.364–368.

32. Conversation with *Fitaurari* Nebeye-Leul, *Ras* Kassa's private secretary, Spring 1993.

33. *Dejazmatch* Zawde Gebre-Selassie in personal conversation with the author, Munich 2002.

34. The full text of the constitution can be found in Mahtama-Selassie Wolde-Maskal, *Zekra Nagar*, pp.767–792.

35. Ibid., p.769.

36. Zawde Retta, *Yakadamawi Haile-Selassie Mengest*, pp.18–45.

37. Ibid., p.39.

38. Bahru Zewde, *A History of Modern Ethiopia*, p.141.

39. Menno Aden: *Überlegungen zur Verfassungsgeschichte Äthiopiens, Memorandum*. Essen, August 2013.

40. Marcus, *The Formative Years*, p.120.

41. For the history of the Hall family of business entrepreneurs and its influence on Ethiopia, see the entries on David and Moritz Hall in EAE 2, p.979f.

42. Treaty Regulating the Importation into Ethiopia of Arms, Ammunition, and Implements of War between Ethiopia, France, Great Britain and Italy, 21 August 1930, in: HMG *British and Foreign State Papers, 1931*. London 1936, pp. 332–351.

Chapter 5: The darkest hour

1. Quoted in Angelo Del Boca: *Yperit-Regen. Der Giftgaskrieg.* [Yperite Rain. Chemical Warfare] In: Asfa-Wossen Asserate, Aram Mattioli (eds.): *Der erste faschistische Vernichtungskrieg. Die italienische Aggression gegen Äthiopien 1935–1941* [The first fascist war of annihilation. Italian aggression against Ethiopia 1935–1941]. Cologne 2006.

2. Bahru Zewde, *A History of Modern Ethiopia*, p.152.

3. Scholars now broadly concur that Mussolini took the decision to invade Ethiopia in 1932. Cf. Angelo Del Boca, *Yperit-Regen. Der Giftgaskrieg*, p.4. Manfred Funke, however, assumes that the decision was made as early as 1928. Manfred Funke: *Sanktionen und Kanonen. Hitler, Mussolini und der internationale Abessinienkonflikt* [Sanctions and cannons. Hitler, Mussolini and the international conflict in Abyssinia]. Düsseldorf 1970, p.9.

4. Funke, *Sanktionen und Kanonen*, p.11ff.

5. Note by Capt. E. H. M. Clifford to the British Colonial Office, Ado, 25 November 1934. FO 371/19100

6. Cf. Anthony Mockler: *Haile Selassie's War*. Oxford 1984 (2nd. edn. 2003), p.37ff.

7. Funke, *Sanktionen und Kanonen*, p.37.

8. Ibid.

9. Ibid., p.43f.

10. Interview by Haile Selassie with S. Groussard, *Le Figaro*, 25/26 March 1959.

11. Konstantin von Neurath, Memoir dedicated to the Imperial Chancellor, 31 October 1934. Quoted in Funke, *Sanktionen und Kanonen*, p.31.

12. Communication by Tekle Hawariat to the Secretary-General of the League of Nations Joseph Avenol, 12 August 1935. FO 371/19125.

13. Covenant of the League of Nations (see Yale Law School, The Avalon Project: Documents in Law, History and Diplomacy: http://avalon.law.yale.edu/20th_century/leagcov.asp).

14. For the details of the Hoare–Laval Plan and its consequences, cf. Henderson B. Braddick: The Hoare–Laval Plan. A Study in International Politics. In: *Review of Politics* 24 (1962), pp.342–364; James C. Robertson: The Hoare–Laval Plan. In: *Journal of Contemporary History* 10 (1975), pp.433–464.

15. Duff Cooper: *Old Men Forget. The Autobiography of Duff Cooper*. London 1953, p.192f. Furthermore, the British secretary of state for war immortalised the Abyssinian conflict in a scurrilous rhyme of his own devising: 'The Duce gives the order / To march against the foe, / And off to Abyssinia / The organ-grinders go, / But now they're quite incapable / Of any sort of grind / And they're back to Mussolini / With their organs left behind …'. Quoted in: John Charmley: *Duff Cooper, The Authorized Biography*. London 1986, p.88.

16. Haile Selassie, *My Life* I, p.255.

17. George Steer: *Caesar in Abyssinia*. London 1936, p.161.

18. Ibid., p.162.

19. Ibid., p.162f.

20. Ibid., p.164.

21. Del Boca, *Yperit-Regen. Der Giftgaskrieg*, p.51.

22. Of the many studies of the Italo-Abyssinian conflict, the following are worthy of mention: A. J. Barker: *The Rape of Ethiopia 1936*. New York 1971. Ibid.: *The Civilizing Mission. A History of the Italo-Ethiopian War of*

1935–1936. New York 1968. Angelo del Boca: *The Ethiopian War 1935–1941.* Chicago 1969. Mockler: *Haile Selassie's War.*

23. Haile Selassie, *My Life* I, p.251.

24. Zewde Retta, *Yakadamawi Haile-Selassie Mengest*, p.227.

25. Stuart Emeny: Under Fire with the Emperor. In: Ladislas Farago (ed.): *Abyssinian Stop Press. With Contributions by Patrick Balfour, Edmund Demaitre, Mortimer Durand, Stuart Emeny, Ladislas Farago and Major-General J. F. C. Fuller.* London 1936, p.187.

26. Steer, *Caesar in Abyssinia*, p.202.

27. Ibid., p.201f.

28. Ibid., p.202.

29. Interview by Angelo del Boca of *Ras* Imru Haile Selassie, Addis Ababa, 13 April 1965, quoted in Del Boca, *Yperit-Regen. Der Giftgaskrieg*, p.53.

30. Ibid., p.51.

31. Marcel Junod: *Kämpfer beiderseits der Front* [Fighters on both sides of the front]. Zurich, Vienna 1947, p.64.

32. John H. Spencer: *Ethiopia at Bay. A Personal Account of the Haile Selassie Years.* Algonac, MI 1984, p.24.

33. Steer, *Caesar in Abyssinia*, p.265.

34. Quoted in Marcus, *The Formative Years*, p.177.

35. Haile Selassie, *My Life* I, p.281.

36. Barker, *The Rape of Ethiopia*, p.97 and p.105.

37. Bahru Zewde, *A History of Modern Ethiopia*, p.157.

38. Conversation with *Fitaurari* Nebeye-Leul, *Ras* Kassa's private secretary, Spring 1993. Nebeye-Leul accompanied the emperor and *Ras* Kassa during this period.

39. Ibid.

40. Hour of Need. *Time* magazine, 20 April 1936.

41. Mockler, *Haile Selassie's War*, p.133.

42. Greenfield, *Ethiopia*, p.222.

43. Steer, *Caesar in Abyssinia*, p.367.

44. Ibid., p.368.

45. Haile's Selassie's second daughter, Princess Zenebe-Work, had died in March 1933.

46. Spencer, *Ethiopia at Bay*, p.64.

47. Ibid., p.69.
48. Extracts from Reports of Proceedings of H.M. Ships *Enterprise* and *Diana*, Concerning the Evacuation of the Emperor of Abyssinia from Djibuti. Despatch by Murray to the Foreign Office, London, 30 June 1936, FO 371/20197.
49. Ibid.
50. Aram Mattioli: *Ein vergessenes Schlüsselereignis der Weltkriegsepoche* [A forgotten key episode in the era of world wars], in: Asserate, Mattioli, *Vernichtungskrieg*, pp.9–25, here p.21.
51. Cf. Gabriele Schneider: *Das Apartheidsystem im Italienisch-Ostafrika* [The apartheid system in Italian East Africa], in: Asserate, Mattioli, *Vernichtungskrieg*, pp.127–152.
52. Ladislas Sava (Saska): 'The Great Massacre of February 19th–21st, 1937', quoted in Sylvia Pankhurst: *Ethiopia – A Cultural History*. London 1955, p.543f.
53. Cf. Angelo del Boca: Graziani Massacre, in: EAE 2, p.878. Among those executed during the Graziani Massacre were two sons of *Ras* Kassa, my uncles Aberra Kassa and Asfa-Wossen Kassa.
54. Quoted in Mosley, *Haile Selassie*, p.238.
55. From the unpublished memoirs of Vice Admiral B.B. Schofield. I am indebted to his daughter, the writer Victoria Schofield, for providing me with this information.
56. Richard Pankhurst (ed.): *Sylvia Pankhurst, Counsel for Ethiopia. A Biographical Essay on Ethiopian, Anti-Fascist and Anti-Colonial History 1934–1960*. Hollywood 2003, p.47f.
57. FO 371/20197, notes and minutes June-July 1936.
58. Lion Incognito, *Time* magazine, 8 June 1936.
59. Spencer, *Ethiopia at Bay*, p.72.
60. Capitulation, *Time* magazine, 29 June 1936.
61. Answering Ethiopia, *Time* magazine, 13 July 1936.
62. Ibid.
63. Spencer, *Ethiopia at Bay*, p.73f.

64. Haile Selassie, Speech to the General Assembly of the League of Nations, 30 June 1936 (http://www.mtholyoke. edu/acad/intrel/selassie.htm).
65. Answering Ethiopia, *Time* magazine, 13 July 1936.
66. Anthony Eden, Earl of Avon: *Facing the Dictators. The Eden Memoirs*. London 1962, p.388.
67. Quoted in Mosley, *Haile Selassie*, p.242.
68. Lutz Haber: The Emperor Haile Selassie I in Bath 1936–1940, in *The Anglo-Ethiopian Society, Occasional Papers*. London 1992 (http://angloethiopian.org/publications/articles.phptype =O&reference=publications/occasionalpapers/papers/haileselassiebath.php). The author of this paper was another exile from tyranny. The son of the renowned German-Jewish chemist and Nobel prize winner Fritz Haber, Lutz Haber fled Nazi Germany and came to Britain in 1934, where he remained for the rest of his life.
69. Haile Selassie I: *My Life and Ethiopia's Progress*, Volume 2. Edited by Harold Marcus with Ezekiel Gebissa and Tibebe Eshete. East Lansing, MI 1994, p.36.
70. Cf. FO 371/20196 (7 May 1936) and FO 371/20198 (12 August 1936).
71. Haile Selassie, *My Life* II, p.36.
72. Cf. Katalog Brunn Rasmussen Kunstauktioner: Fine Art + Antiques International Auction 841, 4–13 June 2013, Copenhagen, Catalogue No. 841/244, p.192f.
73. Mosley, *Haile Selassie*, p.244.
74. V. F. W. Cavendish-Bentinck, First Secretary Foreign Office, 25 March 1938, FO 371/22010.
75. Lord Halifax, Memorandum, 2 March 1938, FO 371/22010.
76. Anglo-Italian Treatment, 16 April 1938. For the exact wording of the agreement, see: http://worldlii.org/int/other/LNTSer/1939/42.html.
77. Letter of Haile Selassie to Farrer & Co., 7 June 1938 FO 1093/82. Death duties that became payable on the death of the anonymous donor shortly after the donation was made effectively reduced this sum to £7,000.

78. Archive of the British Foreign Office, National Archives, Kew, London FO 371/24637.

Chapter 6: The Lion of Judah returns

1. David Shirreff: *Bare Feet and Bandoliers. Wingate, Sandford, the Patriots and the Part they Played in the Liberation of Ethiopia.* London, New York 1995, p.33
2. Quoted in Thesiger, *The Life of My Choice*, p.316.
3. Haile Selassie, *My Life* II, p.127.
4. A thorough treatment of Orde Wingate and Gideon Force's mission to liberate Ethiopia can be found in: Shirreff, *Bare Feet and Bandoliers*, pp.65–225; Thesiger, *The Life of My Choice*, pp.309–354; Mockler, *Haile Selassie's War*, pp.255–389.
5. Thesiger, *The Life of My Choice*, p.350f.
6. Quoted in Mosley, *Haile Selassie*, p.258.
7. Thesiger, *The Life of My Choice*, p.318ff.
8. Quoted in Mockler, *Haile Selassie's War*, p.292.
9. Ibid., p.312.
10. Mockler, *Haile Selassie's War*, p.284f.
11. Mosley, *Haile Selassie*, p.259.
12. Quoted in Mockler, *Haile Selassie's War*, p.316.
13. Shirreff, *Bare Feet and Bandoliers*, p.65f.
14. Quoted in Mockler, *Haile Selassie's War*, p.316.
15. Captain Michael Tutton, diary entry, quoted in Shirreff, *Bare Feet and Bandoliers*, p.73.
16. Ibid.
17. Quoted in Sandford, *The Lion of Judah*, p.94.
18. Quoted in Thesiger, *The Life of My Choice*, p.330.
19. Mosley, *Haile Selassie*, p.265.
20. Brigadier Nott, diary entry, quoted in Shirreff, *Bare Feet and Bandoliers*, p.181.
21. Douglas Newbold, Civil Secretary of the Sudan, in reference to Wingate. Quoted in Mockler, *Haile Selassie's War*, p.372.
22. Mockler, *Haile Selassie's War*, p.372f.
23. Ibid., p.378.

24. Haile Selassie, *My Life* II, p.161.
25. Ibid., p.160.
26. Haile Selassie's speech of 5 May 1941 is reproduced in full in English in the second volume of his autobiography, pp.161–165.
27. For the details of this campaign, readers should consult Shirreff, *Bare Feet and Bandoliers*, pp.197–212.
28. Thesiger, *The Life of My Choice*, p.351.
29. Ibid.
30. Telephone conversation (16 June 2013) between the author and *Dejazmatch* Berhane-Maskal Desta, who was present at the parade.
31. Spencer, *Ethiopia at Bay*, p.93f.
32. Quoted in ibid., p.95.
33. Ibid.
34. Memorandum of 9 December 1940. National Archives, Kew, London FO 371/24645/306.
35. Our second meeting was in December 1974 at St Margaret's Westminster Church, where he attended the memorial service for the 60 dignitaries who were murdered on 23 November 1974.
36. The following report appeared in the Court Circular of *The Times*, 12 May 1971: 'The Anglo-Ethiopian Society held its annual dinner on Friday, May 7, at the Café Royale, London. The Society's chairman, Sir Duncan Cumming, presided. Among those present were the Joint President, the Earl of Avon, and the Ethiopian Ambassador, Lieutenant-General Iyassu Mengasha. Toasts were proposed by Lij Asfa-Wossan [sic] and Sir Thomas Bromley.'
37. Haile Selassie, *My Life* II, p.172.
38. Some years ago, the Africa correspondent of the *Financial Times,* Michela Wrong, made this notorious comment (stripped of its racial slur) the title of her much-praised book on Eritrea: *I Didn't Do it for You: How the World Betrayed a Small African Nation.* New York, 2005.
39. Quoted in Sandford, *The Lion of Judah*, p.109.

40. At the end of 1942, with the signing of the first Anglo-
Ethiopian Agreement, the disagreeable and undiplomatic
Brigadier Lush was posted to Madagascar. However, for
Haile Selassie, Lush remained for many years thereafter
the person whom he felt epitomised British policy towards
Ethiopia. In 1966, to mark the 25th anniversary of the
country's liberation from Italian tyranny, the emperor
invited all the surviving British officers who had taken part
in the campaign to a parade in Addis Ababa. But it was
only at my father *Ras* Asserate's urging that Haile Selassie
agreed to issue an invitation to Maurice Lush. Lush was
at least gracious enough to use the occasion to express his
regret at his former attitudes and behaviour. Cf. Shirreff,
Bare Feet and Bandoliers, p.284.

41. Quoted in Spencer, *Ethiopia at Bay*, p.97.

42. The full text of the agreement is reprinted in: Francis
James Rennell of Rodd: *British Military Administration of
Occupied Territories in Africa During the years of 1941–
1947*. London 1947, pp.539–558.

43. On the Woyane Rebellion, cf. Gebru Tareke: *Ethiopia,
Power and Protest. Peasant Revolts in the Twentieth
Century*. Lawrenceville, NJ 1996.

44. Cf. Bahru Zewde, *A History of Modern Ethiopia*,
pp.179–189.

45. US State Department. Memorandum of 18 June 1941,
National Archives, SD 884.001 Selassie 1372.

46. Spencer, *Ethiopia at Bay*, p.104.

47. Letter by Roosevelt to Haile Selassie, 4 August 1942, quoted
in Harold G. Marcus: *Ethiopia, Great Britain, and the
United States, 1941–1974*. Berkeley and elsewhere 1983,
p.14.

48. Spencer, *Ethiopia at Bay*, p.105f.

49. Roosevelt to Haile Selassie, 11 July 1943, SD 884.24/112.

50. Wallace Murray, Memorandum for the Secretary of State,
20 July 1943, SD 334.014/7–2043.

51. Marcus, *Ethiopia, Great Britain, and the United States*,
p.21.

52. Spencer, *Ethiopia at Bay*, p.149.

53. Ibid.

54. Ibid., p.160.

55. Ibid., p.161.

56. On the following, cf. Bahru Zewde, *A History of Modern Ethiopia*. pp.184–189.

57. On this subject, cf. Christopher Clapham: *Haile Selassie's Government*. London, Harlow 1969, p.19f.

58. For the biography of Wolde-Giorgis and his career at the court of Haile Selassie, cf. Makonnen Tegegn: Walda-Giyorgis Walda-Yohannes and the Haile Selassie Government, in *Northeast African Studies*, 4, 2 (1997), pp.91–138.

59. Seyoum Haregot: *The Bureaucratic Empire Serving Emperor Haile Selassie*. Trenton, NJ 2013, p.21. For the biography of Aklilu cf. especially: Aberra Jembere, Aklilu Habte-Wold in EAE 1, p.170ff., as well as Aklilu's autobiography: *Aklilu Remembers. Historical Reflections from a Prison Cell* (dual-language text in Amharic and English). Uppsala 1994.

60. Bahru Zewde, Makonnen Habte-Wold in EAE 3, p.684f.

61. Telephone conversation between the author and *Dejazmatch* Berhane-Maskal Desta, February 2013.

62. Aberra Jembere, Belay Zeleke, in EAE 1, p.456.

63. Greenfield, *Haile Selassie*, p.244f.

64. Telephone conversation between the author and *Dejazmatch* Berhane-Maskal Desta, 8 August 2012.

65. On the history of Eritrea and Ethiopian_Eritrean relations, see: Elisabeth Furrer-Kreski et al.: *Handbuch Eritrea. Geschichte und Gegenwart eines Konflikts* [Eritrea Handbook: The Past and Present of a Conflict]. Wettingen, undated; Tesfatsion Medhanie: *Eritrea. Dynamics of a National Question*. Amsterdam 1986.

66. Conversation with *Dejazmatch* Abreha Tessemma, Asmara, June 1967.

67. Tesfatsion Medhanie: *Kaiser Haile Selassie und die äthiopisch-eritreische 'Föderation'* [Emperor Haile Selassie

and the Ethiopian-Eritrean 'Federation'], unpublished manuscript. Bremen, September 2013.

68. Ibid.

69. Clapham, *Haile Selassie's Government*, p.37.

70. Cf. ibid., pp.37–44. The complete text of the constitution is reproduced in Perham, *The Government of Ethiopia*, Appendix B.

71. *Lij* Imru Zelleke, secretary of the constitutional commission of 1955, in a telephone conversation with the author, May 2013.

72. Menno Aden, *Überlegungen zur Verfassungsgeschichte Äthiopiens* [Deliberations on the Constitutional History of Ethiopia], unpublished manuscript, p.4

73. The Amharic word *Kagnew* may be translated as 'vigilance' or 'imposing order on chaos'.

74. Spencer, *Ethiopia at Bay*, p.268.

75. Ibid., p.268f.

76. Ibid., p.269.

77. Theodore M. Vestal: *The Lion of Judah in the New World. Emperor Haile Selassie of Ethiopia and the Shaping of Americans' Attitudes toward Africa*. Santa Barbara, Denver, Oxford 2011, p.49. Vestal's book contains an exhaustive account of Haile Selassie's state visit to the United Sates in 1954 (pp.48–94).

78. Ibid., p.53f.

79. Spencer, *Ethiopia at Bay*, p.269f.

80. Vestal, *The Lion of Judah in the New World*, p.2.

81. Ibid., p.60.

82. *Ras* Nathaniel: *50th Anniversary of His Imperial Majesty Haile Selassie I: First Visit to the United States (1954–2004)*. Bloomington, Victoria, BC 2004, p.46.

83. Twenty-one years later to the day, on 14 October 1975, Anthony Eden, Earl of Avon, contributed a tribute to Haile Selassie for a Memorial Evensong held for the deceased emperor in St George's Chapel, Windsor Castle. In this eulogy, delivered by his son, Eden called Haile Selassie 'a man of undiminished stature to the end of his days'.

84. *The Times*, 16 October 1954: 'Emperor in the City'.
85. *The Times*, 14 October 1954: leader 'A Friend from Africa'.
86. Spencer, *Ethiopia at Bay*, p.121.
87. In 1958, four years after his state visit to Britain, Haile Selassie donated Fairfield House to the City of Bath, in recognition of the hospitality the town had extended to him during his years in exile. It became an old people's residential home, a role it fulfilled until 1993. Since then Fairfield House has been used as a community centre; it is a site of great significance particularly to Rastafarians.
88. *Daily Mail*, 14 October 1954.

Chapter 7: Shots across the bows
1. From the unpublished papers of Donald E. Paradis, reproduced by kind permission of Mrs. Martha Paradis.
2. Cf. Lore Trenkler: *Arbeiten und Leben am Hof Haile Selassies I, Erinnerungen 1960–1975* [Work and Life at the Court of Haile Selassie I. Recollections 1960–1975], edited by Rudolf Agstner. Wiesbaden 2011, pp.103–108.
3. Hans Wilhelm Lockot: *The Mission. The Life, Reign and Character of Haile Selassie I*. London 1989, p.53f.
4. For a long time in Ethiopia it was the custom for people to be given a 'horse's name' alongside their baptismal name. The horse's name was said to reflect the character of the person who bore it. As a rule, the name would be that of the noblest mount of the person in question, preceded by the word *Abba* (Father). Haile Selassie's horse name was *Abba Tekel* – 'Father of *Tekel*', in other words, 'the father of him who brings everything together', while Ras Kassa's horse name was *Abba Keskes*, 'father of him who initiates everything.'
5. Conversation between the author and *Dejazmatch* Germatchew Tekle-Hawariat, Bonn, 22 November 1985.
6. Ryszard Kapuściński: *The Emperor: Downfall of an Autocrat*. London 2006 (first edition 1978), p.5.

7. Artur Domasławski: *Ryszard Kapuściński. A Life.* Translated by Antonia Lloyd-Jones. London, New York 2012, p.303.

8. Ibid., p.303f.

9. Harold G. Marcus: Prejudice and Ignorance in Reviewing Books about Africa: The Strange Case of Ryszard Kapuściński's 'The Emperor', *History in Africa* 17 (1990), pp.373–378.

10. In 2005, the Kenyan writer Binyavanga Wainana launched an acerbic attack on Kapuściński, lambasting him in the following terms: 'He is a fraud. A liar. And a profound and dangerous racist.' See also: Thomas Urban: *Mein Freund Che. Lauter Zweifel am großen Reporter Ryszard Kapuściński* [My friend Che. Serious doubts cast on the great reporter Ryszard Kapuściński]. *Süddeutsche Zeitung*, 1 March 2010, p.11.

11. Nationaler Infantilismus. Interview mit Artur Domasławski, *Der Spiegel* 10 (2010). p.109.

12. See Chapter 9 of this book for further treatment of this subject.

13. Memorandum of Haile Selassie's private secretary Teffera-Work Kidane-Wold on the emperor's share portfolio, Addis Ababa 1959 (in the possession of the author, kindly placed at my disposal by Mesfin Gebreyes).

14. Trenkler, *Arbeiten und Leben am Hof Haile Selassies*, p.105f.

15. Ibid., p.107.

16. Ibid., p.110f.

17. Ibid., p.113f.

18. Ernst Hammerschmidt: *Äthiopien. Christliches Reich zwischen Gestern und Morgen* [Ethiopia. A Christian Empire between Yesterday and Tomorrow]. Wiesbaden 1967, p.117.

19. Hans von Herwarth: *Von Adenauer zu Brandt. Erinnerungen.* [From Adenauer to Brandt. Recollections.] Berlin, Frankfurt am Main 1990, p.119.

20. Clapham, *Haile Selassie's Government*, p.115f.

21. Seyoum Haregot, *The Bureaucratic Empire*, p.16.
22. Ibid., p.17.
23. As attested by *Dejazmatch* Berhane-Maskal Desta, who accompanied *Ras* Kassa to the palace that day (Telephone conversation, February 2013).
24. Clapham, *Haile Selassie's Government*, p.22.
25. Cf. Seyoum Haregot, *The Bureaucratic Empire*, p.235f.
26. Harold G. Marcus: *A History of Ethiopia*. Berkeley, Los Angeles, London 1994, p.162.
27. On the role played by the Private Cabinet, cf. Clapham, *Haile Selassie's Government*, pp.120–123.
28. Quoted in Berhanu Assres: *Men yenagar yanabara – yatahsasu gereger ena mazazu*. Addis Ababa 2013, p.143 ff.
29. A full account of the attempted Palace Coup of 1960, including its origins and main protagonists, can be found in Greenfield, *Ethiopia*, pp.315–452; for an in-depth analysis of the putsch, see Christopher Clapham: The Ethiopian Coup d'État of December 1960, in *The Journal of Modern African Studies*, 6 (1968), pp.495–507. I have given an account of how I experienced these events as a twelve-year-old boy in my book *Ein Prinz aus dem Hause David and warum er in Deutschland blieb. Die Erinnerungen.* [A Prince from the House of David, and why he remained in Germany. Memoirs.] Frankfurt am Main 2007, pp. 116–155.
30. Greenfield, *Ethiopia*, pp.352.
31. Ibid., p.373.
32. Revolutionary Proclamation, 14 December 1960, quoted in: Greenfield, *Ethiopia*, p.399.
33. Greenfield, *Ethiopia*, p.410f.
34. Randi Rønning Balsvik: *Haile Selassie's Students. The Intellectual and Social Background to Revolution, 1952–1977.* East Lansing, MI 1985, p.95f.
35. Quoted in ibid., p.416f.
36. Report by the American ambassador to Ethiopia to the US State Department, Addis Ababa, 16 December 1960, SD 775.00/ 12–1660.
37. For example Lockot, *The Mission*, p.83.

38. *Der König, der nur nicken darf* [The King who is only allowed to nod in agreement] *Stern*, 3 October 1974, p.172ff.

39. Spencer, *Ethiopia at Bay*, p.317.

40. Quoted in Greenfield, *Ethiopia*, p.434.

41. Selassie Pledges Unchained Rule, *New York Times*, 21 December 1960.

42. Harold G. Marcus: '1960, the Year the Sky Began Falling on Haile Selassie', in *Northeast African Studies* 6, 3 (1999), pp.11–26.

43. Quoted in Greenfield, *Ethiopia*, pp.433.

44. Bahru Zewde, *A History of Modern Ethiopia*, p.214.

45. In addition to the prime minister *Tsehafe-Tezaz* Aklilu, the other members of this reform commission were the interior minister Lieutenant-General Abiye Abebe, the Senate president *Leul-Ras* Asserate Kassa, the defence minister Lieutenant-General Merid Mengesha and the finance minister Yilma Deressa.

46. Seyoum Haregot, *The Bureaucratic Empire*, p.32.

47. *The Reporter*, 29 Megabit 1995 (Ethiopian calendar = 7 April 2003 AD).

48. I am grateful to Lord Amery of Lustleigh (1917–1996), a lifelong friend of my father, for identifying Sir John Russell as the originator of the term 'Stolypinists' for the Ethiopian reformers.

49. Telephone conversation between the author and *Dejazmatch* Berhane-Maskal Desta, 16 June 2013.

50. Cf. Clapham, *Haile Selassie's Government*, p.43.

51. Trenkler, *Arbeiten und Leben am Hof Haile Selassies*, p.49.

Chapter 8: Shaking hands with history

1. Nelson Mandela: *Long Walk to Freedom. Autobiography.* London 1995, p.349

2. Ibid., p.348.

3. Ibid., p.350.

4. Ibid., pp.350–351.

5. Ibid., p.362.

6. Seyoum Haregot, *The Bureaucratic Empire*, p.150.

7. *Wer soll Afrika führen?* [Who should lead Africa?] Interview with Emperor Haile Selassie I of Ethiopia, *Der Spiegel*, 24 (1963), p.63ff.

8. Berekat Habte Selassie: *The Crown and the Pen. The Memoirs of a Lawyer Turned Rebel*. Trenton, NJ 2007, p.186f.

9. The full text of the Charter of the OAU can be found on the African Union's website: http://www.au.int/en/sites/default/files/OAU_Charter_1963_0.pdf

10. Trenkler, *Arbeiten und Leben am Hof Haile Selassies*, p.108.

11. Seyoum Haregot, *The Bureaucratic Empire*, p.134.

12. *Wer soll Afrika führen?* [Who should lead Africa?] Interview with Emperor Haile Selassie I of Ethiopia, *Der Spiegel*, 24 (1963), p.65.

13. Jeffrey A. Lefebvre: *Arms for the Horn. US Security Policy in Ethiopia and Somalia, 1953–1991*. Pittsburgh, PA 1992, p.101.

14. Seyoum Haregot, *The Bureaucratic Empire*, p.201.

15. Asfa-Wossen Asserate: *Rastafaris: Der Tag, als der Regen kam. Hintergründe und Missverständnisse der Rastafari-Bewegung.* [Rastafarians: The Day When the Rain Came. Background to and Misconceptions of the Rastafarian Movement] In: *Die Presse* (Vienna), 13 March 2010. For the history of Rastafarianism, see; Horace Campbell: *Rasta and Resistance. From Marcus Garvey to Walter Rodney.* Daressalam 1985.

16. Rebecca Tortello: All Hail. The State Visit of Emperor Haile Selassie. In: *The Gleaner*, 21–24 April 1966.

17. Bill McNeil: Radio Interview with Haile Selassie I, Canada 1967 (http://jah-rastafari.com/selassie-sounds/him_canada_1967.mp3)

18. Source: the CIA World Factbook (Jamaica): https://www.cia.gov/library/publications/the-world-factbook/geos/print/country/countrypdf_jm.pdf

19. Volker Matthies: *Der Eritrea-Konflikt. Ein 'vergessener Krieg' am Horn von Afrika* [The Eritrea conflict: a 'forgotten war' in the Horn of Africa] Hamburg 1981, p.56.

20. *Ras* Asserate Kassa: Communication No.1/62/24 v.22 Sene 1962 Ethiopian calendar (= 29 July 1970 AD) to Tsehafe-Tezaz Aklilu Habte-Wold (in the author's possession).

21. Henze, *Layers of Time*, p.278.

22. Richard B. Dorman to Eric G. Le Tocq (Head of the East African Dept., Foreign and Commonwealth Office), 21 November 1969. National Archives, Kew, London FCO 31/301.

23. On 30 May 1967, Lieutenant-Colonel Chukwuemeka Odumegwu Ojukwu, military governor of Eastern Nigeria, proclaimed it a sovereign state, with the name Republic of Biafra, with himself as head of state.

24. Oriana Fallaci: Journey into the Private Universe of Haile Selassie. In: *Chicago Tribune*, 24 June 1973.

25. Cf. Christopher Clapham: The Functions and Development of Parliament in Ethiopia. In: James C. N. Paul, Christopher Clapham: *Constitutional Development. A Sourcebook*. Addis Ababa 1967, p.828; Clapham, Haile Selassie's Government, p.123ff.

26. Theodore M. Vestal: Peace Corps, in: EAE 4, p.126f.

27. Bahru Zewde, *A History of Modern Ethiopia*, p.130, p.221f.

28. On the student movement in Ethiopia, cf. Randi Rønning Balsvik: *Haile Selassie's Students*. East Lansing, MI 1985.

29. Ibid., p.269.

30. Edward M. Korry, Memorandum on a discussion with Lieutenant-General Kebede Gebre, defence minister, and Lieutenent-General Iyasu Mengesha, chief of staff of the Ethiopian Army, Addis Ababa, 18 January 1967, quoted in Marcus, *Ethiopia, Great Britain and the United States*, p.188.

31. Seyoum Haregot, The Bureaucratic Empire, p.194.

32. Richard Nixon: Toast of the President to Emperor Haile Selassie I of Ethiopia, 8 July 1969, quoted in: Vestal, *The Lion of Judah in the New World*, p.170.

33. Quoted in Lefebvre, *Arms for the Horn*, p.103.

34. Vestal, *The Lion of Judah in the New World*, p.176.

35. Haile Selassie, memo to Richard Nixon, 15 March 1972, quoted in: ibid., p.179.

36. Memorandum by Marshall Wright, 21 June 1971, quoted in ibid., p.178.

37. Ibid., p.181.

38. Ibid., p.183.

39. Seyoum Haregot, *The Bureaucratic Empire*, p.194.

40. Washington Special Actions Group Meeting, 24 April 1974, quoted in Vestal, *The Lion of Judah in the New World*, p.184.

41. Seyoum Haregot, *The Bureaucratic Empire*, p.195.

42. Just a few years later, the shifting pattern of alliances had changed. In 1976 the new ruler of Ethiopia Colonel Mengistu flew to Moscow to sign a treaty with the Russian premier Leonid Brezhnev securing Soviet military aid for his country. In July 1977 the Somali president Siad Barre exploited the weakness of the Ethiopian central government to launch an invasion of Ethiopia – with an army which over the preceding years had been liberally supplied with arms by the Soviet Union. Now Moscow turned its back on 'Somali socialism' and threw in its lot with 'Ethiopian socialism'. The USSR sent arms and ammunition, while Cuba supplied 18,000 troops, who fought alongside Mengistu's forces against Somalia. In its turn, the United States forged closer ties with 'Somali socialism' and supplied Siad Barre with weapons.

43. Discussion between *Ras* Asserate and the author, Addis Ababa, 1 May 1974.

44. Robert Kaplan, a renowned scholar of Ethiopian history, once observed: 'Pushing Haile Selassie for reform would have been like tinkering with the divine order.' In Robert

Kaplan: *Surrender or Starve. Travels in Ethiopia, Sudan, Somalia, and Eritrea*. New York 2003, p.16.

45. *Super-Fest beim König der Könige* [Huge Jamboree for the King of Kings], *Bunte*, 10 August 1972, pp.36–43.

46. Ibid., p.40f.

47. Willie Morris, memo to Sir Alec Douglas-Home MP, Addis Ababa, 9 November 1972, in Matthew Parris, Andrew Bryson (eds.): *The Spanish Ambassador's Suitcase. Stories from the Diplomatic Bag*. London 2012, p.57f.

48. Under pressure from Libya, in October 1973 Ethiopia severed its diplomatic ties with Israel, which had previously given the imperial government strategic and military support and advice. This decision, which led to a further distancing from the USA, may also have contributed to the demise of the empire. Cf. Haggai Erlich: *Israel and Ethiopia during the Haile-Selassie Time. A brief summary of Haile-Selassie policy*. Tel Aviv 2013 (unpublished manuscript).

49. On the topic of famine in Ethiopia, see: Africa Watch: *Evil Days. 30 Years of War and Famine in Ethiopia. An Africa Watch Report*. New York, Washington, London 1991.

50. Jonathan Dimbleby: Ethiopia proves that there can be a life after death. *The Observer*, 28 July 2002.

51. *Stern*, 22 November 1973, p.1.

52. *Stern*, 29 November 1973, p.18.

53. *Stern*, 12 December 1974, p.12.

54. Dimbleby: Ethiopia proves that there can be a life after death. *The Observer*, 28 July 2002.

55. Africa Watch, *Evil Days*, p.58.

56. Ibid., p.59.

57. Mammo Wudeneh: *Yadaraskubat – Gela tarik ena tesetawoch*. Addis Ababa 2004, p.218ff.

58. Abebe Ambatchew: *A Glimpse of Greatness – Emperor Haile Selassie I: The Person*, p. 109.

Chapter 9: An empty house

1. On the 'Creeping Coup' of 1974 and the chronology of events, cf. Andargatchew Tiruneh: *The Ethiopian*

Revolution 1974–1987. Transformation from an Aristocratic to a Totalitarian Autocracy. Cambridge 1993, pp.37–81; Bahru Zewde, *A History of Modern Ethiopia*, 2nd edn., pp.228–240.

2. See for example Seyoum Haregot, *The Bureaucratic Empire*, p.257.

3. Bahru Zewde, *A History of Modern Ethiopia*, 2nd edn., p.231. Seyoum Haregot's accusation that the cabinet was dominated by aristocrats is incorrect; the majority of its members belonged to the group of 'technocrats'.

4. Tegagne Yeshatawork: Speaking Out. *Ethiopian Herald*, 5 March 1974.

5. Stephan Brüne: *Äthiopien – Unterentwicklung und radikale Militärherrschaft. Zur Ambivalenz einer scheinheiligen Revolution* [Ethiopia – Underdevelopment and radical military rule. On the ambivalence of a hypocritical revolution] (Hamburg Beiträge zur Afrika-Kunde 26). Hamburg 1986, p.77f.

6. Ibid., p.79.

7. Leaflet 'To the Ethiopian People', signed by 'Elements of the Armed Forces', 4 March 194, quoted in ibid., p.295ff.

8. Ibid., p.296.

9. Seyoum Haregot, *The Bureaucratic Empire*, p.275.

10. It is interesting to note that by this stage my father already harboured deep suspicions about the loyalty of some employees at the Jubilee Palace.

11. A few weeks later, my father also showed this letter to my cousin *Lij* Negga Mesfin, who had visited him to demand he take action against the rebellious army units. Cf. Fantahum Engeda: *Bakadamawi Haile-Selassie astedadar goltaw yawatu politika chegeroch ena tegloch bakerb balamualachew yahewat Tarik manashanat sigamagamu.* Addis Ababa 2004, p.329.

12. Brüne: *Äthiopien – Unterentwicklung und radikale Militärherrschaft*, p.295ff.

13. On the circumstances of Ras Asserate's arrest, cf. Asfa-Wossen Asserate, *Ein Prinz aus dem Hause David*, p.264ff.

14. Conversation between the author and *Lij* Mulugeta Asserate, London, December 1999. In his book *Yanegusu ganama* (Addis Ababa, undated, p.60) Seyoum Tassew, a valet of the emperor, confirms that Mulugeta Asserate had an audience with Haile Selassie that day.

15. Selassie Accepts Ethiopia Cabinet, *New York Times*, 4 August 1974.

16. Selassie is Accused of Hoarding Millions, *New York Times*, 8 September 1974.

17. Ethiopians Say Palace of Emperor is People's, *New York Times*, 26 August 1974.

18. Marcus, *A History of Ethiopia*, p.188.

19. Haile Selassie Goes from Noble Palace to Barren Mud Hut, *New York Times*, 15 September 1974. The writer of this article wrongly claimed that Haile Selassie was wearing his customary military dress uniform when arrested. In fact he was dressed in a dark suit with his black kabba over it.

20. *Derg* (Provisional Military Coordinating Committee) Proclamation No.1, Addis Ababa, 12 September 1974.

21. Guenet Ayele Anbessie: *Yeletena Colonel Mengistu Haile-Mariam Tizzitawotch* [Recollections of Lt.Colonel Mengistu Haile-Mariam]. Addis Ababa 2002, pp.28 and 168. Quoted in: Theodore M. Vestal: The lost opportunity for Ethiopia: The failure to move toward democratic governance. In: *International Journal of African Development*,Volume I, Issue 1(Fall 2013).

22. *Derg* (Provisional Military Coordinating Committee) Proclamation No.1, Addis Ababa, 12 September 1974.

23. Ethiopia Executes 60 Former Officials, Including 2 Premiers and Military Chief, *New York Times*, 24 November 1974.

24. Marina and David Ottaway: *Ethiopia. Empire in Revolution.* New York 1978, p.59ff.

25. My mother and siblings were also arrested and incarcerated. On their imprisonment and the fight to get them released, see Asfa-Wossen Asserate, *Ein Prinz aus dem Hause David*, p.281ff.

26. Taffara Deguefé: *Minutes of an Ethiopian Century*. Addis Ababa 2006, p.421.

27. Ibid., p.420.

28. Ibid., p.428.

29. Source: former city treasurer Gerhard of Frankfurt am Main, November 2013.

30. In 1995, Edward Ullendorff, the translator of the first volume of Haile Selassie's autobiography, recounted one 'urban myth' concerning the emperor's foreign wealth: 'At one stage there was a persistent rumour that pilots of Ethiopian Airlines had been charged by Haile Selassie to deliver parcels filled with gold to the manager of a Swiss hotel at which the Emperor had occasionally stayed. On investigation it turned out that the rumour was substantially accurate and that parcels had indeed been sent to that gentleman, but they did not contain gold – only bags of Ethiopian coffee, for which the manager had developed a penchant. Thus a gesture of royal thoughtfulness was interpreted as an act of imperial plunder.' In: Ullendorff: *From Haile Selassie to H. J. Polotsky*. Wiesbaden 1995.

31. Report by Human Rights Watch 1999 (http://www.hrw.org/legacy/english/docs/1999/11/29/ethiop5495.htm)

32. They were as follows: Captain Kebede Tessema in the Sudan; *Ato* Debebe Ayele, *Ato* Woldemaryam Wolde-Gabriel, *Ato* Getachew Gardadew and Colonel Tesfa Desta in Germany, *Ato* Teferra Sharaw in Sweden and *Ato* Petros Desta in Yemen. Cf. Ethiops, Hedar 1992 Ethiopian calendar = November 1999 AD.

33. Our conversation took place in Addis Ababa in August 1991.

34. Alden Whitman: Haile Selassie of Ethiopia dies at 83. *New York Times*, 28 August 1975.

35. Ibid.

36. In 1991, Paulos Miklias also interviewed Eshetu about the final hours in the life of the emperor, and his responses on that occasion correspond almost exactly with the information given here. Cf. Paulos Miklias: *Haile Selassie*.

Western Education and Political Revolution in Ethiopia.
Youngstown, NY 2006, p.248f. Three years later, Eshetu
testified against the dictator Mengistu at the public tribunal
held in December 1994 in Addis Ababa, and had his witness
statement recorded. However, his accusations were not
followed up by the new Ethiopian government of Meles
Zenawi.

37. Ethiopia's Military Government Abolishes Monarchy and
    Titles, *New York Times*, 22 March 1975.

Epilogue: Haile Selassie's legacy

1. Bahru Zewde: Hayla-Sellase: From Progressive to
   Reactionary. In *Northeast African Studies* 2, 2 (1995),
   pp.99–114, here p.111.
2. See also: Imru Zelleke: *Perspectives of Ethiopia's Future*
   (memorandum sent to the author on 25 September 2014).

Ethiopian Imperial Titles, in descending order of rank

Male titles

Negusa Negast: 'King of Kings', Emperor

Negus: King

Germawi, Janhoy: Majesty

Merid Azmatch: Formerly the title of the rulers of Shoa. Later the honorific title of Crown Prince Asfa-Wossen.

Re'esa Mesafent or *Yamesafent Takadami*: Premier Prince of the Empire

Leul: Highness, a more recent title for princes of the blood

Lij: (literally 'child') equivalent to Spanish *Infante;* traditional title for princes from the House of David

Leul-Ras: Imperial Duke

Ras-Bitwadad: formerly the highest title in the land below that of king, before it was replaced in 1916 by *Ras* Tafari Makonnen with the title of *Leul-Ras*. After the Second World War, this title was only awarded once more, to the first Ethiopian prime minister *Ras-Bitwadad* Makonnen Endalkatchew

Ras: (literally 'head', formerly head of a vast army) Duke

Mesfen (plural *Mesafent*): Highest peer of the empire, member of the high-ranking nobility

Afe Negus: lit.'Mouth of the King', highest judge's title, equates to the title of Lord Chief Justice in England

Dejazmatch: lit. 'Commander of the Gate' (i.e. commander of a central body of a traditional Ethiopian army), equates to the title of 'Count' and formerly to rank of General in the army

Tsehafe-Tezaz: lit. 'Writer of Proclamations', traditional title of the Minister of the Pen, equates to Lord Privy Seal

Begirond: lit. 'Keeper of the Purse', title of ministers of finance

Yamister Tsehafi: lit. 'Writer of Secrets', title of a trusted member of the imperial household

Liqamakwas: Dignitary at court whose duty it was to wait in constant attendance upon the emperor and also act as his double

Fitaurari: lit. 'Commander of the Vanguard', equivalent to the Western title of 'Baron'; this title comes higher in the hierarchy if combined with the post of Minister of War

Nagadras: lit. 'Chief of the Merchants', chief inspector of customs and trade; the title was later applied to the Minister of Trade

Kegnazmatch: lit. 'Commander of the Right Wing', title of the lower-ranking nobility, and formerly equivalent to the rank of colonel

Grazmatch: lit. 'Commander of the Left Wing', title of the lower-ranking nobility, beneath *Kegnazmatch,* and formerly equivalent to the rank of major

Blattengetta: lit, 'Page-master', title given to scholars serving the emperor

Blatta: Ethiopian title given to learned men in governmental service, beneath *Blattengetta*

Makonnen (plural *Mekwanint*): Dignitary and an officer in the army

Ligaba: Lord Steward

Agafari: Master of Ceremonies

Azaj: Master of the Royal Household

Ato: Formerly a title for noblemen in Shoa province; now equivalent to 'Sir,' 'Mr'

Female titles

Negesta Negestat: 'Queen of Queens', Empress

Negest: Queen

Itege: Empress, Queen

Germawit: Majesty

Leelt: Princess, Highness

Mesfenit: Duchess

Emebet-Hoy: Lady

Woizerit-Hoy: Dowager Lady (widowed)

Woizero: formerly lady, now simply 'Mrs'

Glossary

Abbaba: lit. 'little father'; an intimate form of address to a father, uncle or grandfather

Abuna: bishop; the Ethiopian Orthodox Tewahedo Church has been autocephalous since 1959

Aderash: ceremonial room in the royal palace for grand banquets

Deber, Debre: Amharic for 'mountain'; it also denotes a monastery complex (e.g, *Debre* Libanos to the north of Addis Ababa), or a house (e.g. *Debre* Tebor, the family villa of Asserate Kassa in the Entoto Hills

Debtera: 'masters of ceremonies' and performers of the traditional 'Dance of David' in the Ethiopian Orthodox Church and practitioners in traditional medicine.

Derg: *Ge'ez* term for 'committee', used to denote the Ethiopian Military Council, the revolutionary regime that formed the government of Ethiopia from 1974 to 1991

Entoto: range of hills above Addis Ababa, home to the villas of the imperial family

Etshege: senior abbot among all Ethiopian monks; traditionally the title of the Abbots of the monastery of Debre Libanos and St Stephen's monastery in Haiq

Fetha Negast: lit. 'Law Book of the Kings', traditional Ethiopian statute book, translated from the Arabic in the 16th century

Gebbi: Palace, court; usually associated with Menelik II's grand palace in the capital

Geber: a traditional banquet held at the imperial court

Ge'ez: the language of ancient Ethiopia, whose roots go back to the the first century AD. *Ge'ez* is also the language of ecclesiastical liturgy

Genete-Leul: lit. 'Paradise of Princes', name of one of the emperor's palaces in Addis Ababa, now the seat of Addis Ababa University

Injera: a flatbread prepared from *Teff*, national staple dish of Ethiopia

Kabba: traditional Ethiopian cloak

Kebra Negast: lit. 'the Glory of the Kings', principal work of ancient Ethiopian literature; written in the 14th century, it recounts the origins of the Solomonic dynasty

Lanka: gold-brocade robe of a prince or king, worn on ceremonial occasions

Masqal: Feast of the Exaltation of the Holy Cross (27 September), a principal feast day of the Ethiopian Orthodox Tewahedo Church

Shamma: traditional toga-like gown made of white cotton

Shumshir: imperial decree issued for the appointment or dismissal of office holders

Tedj: Ethiopian traditional form of wine, fermented from honey, water and the leaves of the *gesho* tree, a species of buckthorn native to Ethiopia

Teff: a grain native to the Northern Ethiopian Highlands and Eritrean Highlands, used for baking *Injera*

Tukul: traditional Ethiopian round hut, roofed with straw

Wot: a spicy stew of meat or vegetables

Genealogical Table of the House of David

(excerpt)

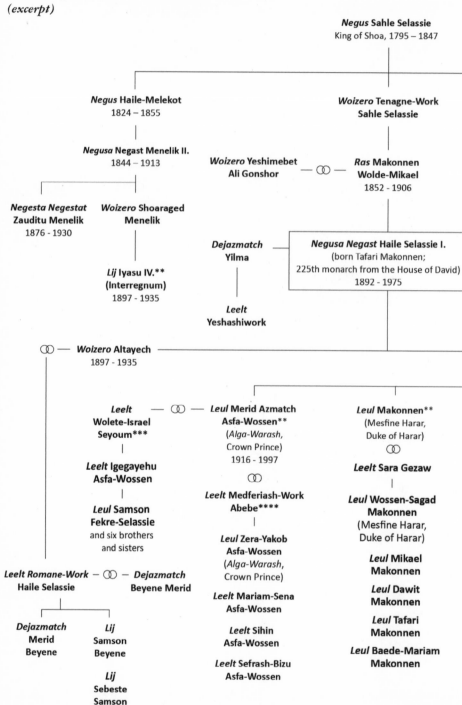

Negus Sahle Selassie
King of Shoa, 1795 – 1847

Negus Haile-Melekot
1824 – 1855

Woizero Tenagne-Work
Sahle Selassie

Negusa Negast Menelik II.
1844 – 1913

Woizero Yeshimebet
Ali Gonshor
— ◯◯ —
Ras Makonnen
Wolde-Mikael
1852 - 1906

Negesta Negestat
Zauditu Menelik
1876 - 1930

Woizero Shoaraged
Menelik

Dejazmatch
Yilma

Negusa Negast Haile Selassie I.
(born Tafari Makonnen;
225th monarch from the House of David)
1892 - 1975

Lij Iyasu IV.**
(Interregnum)
1897 - 1935

Leelt
Yeshashiwork

◯◯ — **Woizero** Altayech
1897 - 1935

Leelt
Wolete-Israel
Seyoum***
— ◯◯ —
Leul Merid Azmatch
Asfa-Wossen**
(*Alga-Warash*,
Crown Prince)
1916 - 1997

Leul Makonnen**
(Mesfine Harar,
Duke of Harar)
◯◯

Leelt Igegayehu
Asfa-Wossen

Leelt Sara Gezaw

◯◯

Leul Samson
Fekre-Selassie
and six brothers
and sisters

Leelt Medferiash-Work
Abebe****

Leul Wossen-Sagad
Makonnen
(Mesfine Harar,
Duke of Harar)

Leul Zera-Yakob
Asfa-Wossen
(*Alga-Warash*,
Crown Prince)

Leul Mikael
Makonnen

Leelt Romane-Work — ◯◯ — **Dejazmatch**
Haile Selassie   Beyene Merid

Leelt Mariam-Sena
Asfa-Wossen

Leul Dawit
Makonnen

Dejazmatch
Merid
Beyene

Lij
Samson
Beyene

Leelt Sihin
Asfa-Wossen

Leul Tafari
Makonnen

Leelt Sefrash-Bizu
Asfa-Wossen

Leul Baede-Mariam
Makonnen

Lij
Sebeste
Samson

Ras Darge Sahle Selassie
(*Re'esa Mesafent*, Premier Prince of the Empire)
1830 – 1900

Woizero Tesseme Darge ——— ⊕ ——— **Dejazmatch** Hailu
Wolde-Kiros*

Leul-Ras Kassa Hailu* ——— ⊕ ——— **Leelt** Tsige Beshah****
(*Yamasafent Takadami*, Premier Prince of the Empire)   d.1945
1881 - 1957

Leul-Ras Asserate Kassa* ——— ⊕ ——— **Leelt** Zuriash-Work
1922 - 1974   Gebre-Igziabher**
and six brothers and sisters   b.1930

The Author**
b.1948
and six brothers and sisters

——— ⊕ ——— **Itege** Menen Asfaw**
1889 - 1962

Leelt — ⊕ — **Ras**	**Leelt**	**Leelt**	**Leul**
Tenagne-Work** Andargatchew	Tsahai-Work**	Zenebe-Work**	Sahle Selassie**
Masai			

⊕   ⊕   ⊕   ⊕

Ras Desta   Lt.-Gen. Abiye   **Dejazmatch**   **Leelt** Mahsente
Damtew****   Abebe****   Haile Selassie   Habte-Mariam*****
                                                      Gugsa***

Leelt   **Leul** Ermias
Aida Desta   Sahle Selassie

Leelt
Hirut Desta

Leelt
Sable Desta

Leelt
Sofia Desta

Admiral
Iskender Desta

Leul
Amha Desta

*	Descendant of the Imperial House of Gondar and the Royal House of Lalibela
**	Descendant of the Royal House of Wollo and of the Holy Prophet Muhammad
***	Descendant of the Royal House of Tigray
****	Descendant of the Noble House of Adisge
*****	Descendant of the Royal House of Wollega

Bibliography

Books

Encyclopaedia Aethiopica. Ed. Siegbert Uhlig. 4 vols [A to X],
  Wiesbaden 2003–2010 (abbr: EAE).
Abebe Ambatchew: *A Glimpse of Greatness – Emperor Haile
  Selassie I: The Person*. Bloomington, IN, p. 109.
Abiye Abebe: *Awqan enetaram*. Asmara 1962 AD.
Africa Watch: *Evil Days. 30 Years of War and Famine
  in Ethiopia. An African Watch Report*. New York,
  Washington, London 1991.
Aklilu Habte-Wold: *Aklilu remembers. Historical Reflections
  from a Prison Cell* (dual language Amharic/English).
  Uppsala 1994.
Andargachew Tiruneh: *The Ethiopian Revolution 1974–1987.
  Transformation from an Aristocratic to a Totalitarian
  Autocracy*. Cambridge 1993.
Asfa-Wossen Asserate: *Ein Prinz aus dem Hause David
  und warum er in Deutschland blieb. Die Erinnerungen*.
  Frankfurt am Main 2007.
Asfa-Wossen Asserate, Aram Mattioli (eds.): *Der erste
  faschistische Vernichtungskrieg. Die italienische Aggression
  gegen Äthiopien. 1935 –1941*. Cologne 2006.
Bahru Zewde: *A History of Modern Ethiopia 1855–1974*.
  London, Athens, Addis Ababa 1991.
Ibid.: *A History of Modern Ethiopia 1855–1991*. 2nd edn.
  Oxford, Athens, Addis Ababa 2001.
Ibid.: *Pioneers Of Change In Ethiopia. The Reformist
  Intellectuals of Early Twentieth Century*. Eastern African
  Studies, Oxford and elsewhere 2002.
Balsvik, Randi Rønning: *Haile Selassie's Students. The
  Intellectual and Social Background to Revolution, 1952–
  1977*. East Lansing, MI 1985.

Barker, A. J.: *The Rape of Ethiopia 1936*. New York 1971.

Ibid.: *The Civilizing Mission. A History of the Italo-Ethiopian War of 1935–1936*. New York 1968.

Bereket Habte Selassie: *The Crown and the Pen. The Memoirs of a Lawyer Turned Rebel*. Trenton, NJ 2007.

Berhanu Assres: *Man yenagar yanabara – yatahsasu gereger ena mazazu*. Addis Ababa 2013 AD.

Berihun Kebede: *Yatse Haile-Selassie tarik*. Addis Ababa 2000 AD.

Blashford-Snell, John: *Something Behind The Ranges. The Autobiography*. London 1994.

Brüne, Stephan: Äthiopien – *Unterentwicklung und radikale Militärherrschaft. Zur Ambivalenz einer scheinheiligen Revolution* (Hamburger Beiträge zur Afrika-Kunde 26). Hamburg 1986.

Burton, Richard: *First Footsteps in East Africa, or An Exploration of Harar*. London 1856.

Campbell, Horace: *Rasta and Resistance. From Marcus Garvey to Walter Rodney*. Daressalam 1985.

Carnochan, Walter B.: *Golden Legends. Images of Abyssinia, Samuel Johnson to Bob Marley*. Stanford 2008.

Charmley, John: *Duff Cooper. The Authorized Biography*. London 1986.

Clapham, Christopher: *Haile Selassie's Government*. London, Harlow 1969.

Ibid.: *Transformation and Continuity in Revolutionary Ethiopia*. Cambridge 1988.

Cooper, Duff: *Old Men Forget. The Autobiography of Duff Cooper*. London 1953.

Darkwah, R. H. Kofi: *Shewa, Menilek and the Ethiopian Empire 1813–1889*. London and elsewhere. 1975.

Deedes, Bill: *At War with Waugh. The Real Story of 'Scoop'*. London 2003.

Del Boca, Angelo: *The Ethiopian War 1935–1941*. Chicago 1969.

Domosławski, Artur: *Ryszard Kapuściński. A Life*. Translated by Antonia Lloyd-Jones. London, New York 2012

Eden, Anthony, Earl of Avon: *Facing the Dictators. The Eden Memoirs.* London 1962.

Fantahum Engeda: *Bakadamawi Haile-Selassie astedadar goltaw ya- watu politika chegeroch ena tegloch bakerb balamualachew yahe- wat Tarik manashanat sigamagamu.* Addis Ababa 2004 AD.

Farago, Ladislas (ed.): *Abyssinian Stop Press.* With Contributions by Patrick Balfour, Edmund Demaitre, Mortimer Durand, Stuart Emeny, Ladislas Farago and Major-General J. F. C. Fuller. London 1936.

Funke, Manfred: *Sanktionen und Kanonen. Hitler, Mussolini und der internationale Abessinienkonflikt.* Düsseldorf 1970.

Furrer-Kreski, Elisabeth, et al.: *Handbuch Eritrea. Geschichte und Gegenwart eines Konfliktes.* Wettingen (undated).

Gebre-Igziabiher Elyas: *Prowess, Piety and Politics. The Chronicle of Abeto Iyasu and Empress Zewditu of Ethiopia.* Edited and translated by Reidulf K. Molvaer. Cologne 1994.

Gebru Tareke: *Ethiopia. Power and Protest. Peasant Revolts in the Twentieth Century.* Cambridge 1991.

Getatchew Bekele: *The Emperor's Clothes. A Personal Viewpoint on Politics and Administration in the Imperial Ethiopian Government 1941–1974.* East Lansing, MI 1993.

Gleichen, Lord Edward: *With the Mission to Menelik 1897.* London 1898. (http://www.archive.org/stream/ withmissiontomeoogleigoog/ withmissiontomeoogleigoog_ djvu.txt)

Gobeze Tafeta: *Abba Tena Iyasu.* Addis Ababa 1996 AD.

Greenfield, Richard: *Ethiopia. A New Political History.* London 1965.

Guenet Ayele Anbessie: *Yeletena Colonel Mengistu Haile-Mariam Tizzitawotch* [Recollections of Lt.Colonel Mengistu Haile-Mariam]. Addis Ababa 2002.

Haberland, Eike: *Untersuchungen zum äthiopischen Königtum.* Wiesbaden 1965.

Ibid: *Demystifying Political Thought, Power, and Economic Development.* Washington, DC,1999.

Haile Selassie I.: *Hiwate ena yaitiyopiya ermega*. 2 vols., Addis Ababa 1973.

Ibid.: *My Life and Ethiopia's Progress 1892–1937*. Translated and annotated by Edward Ullendorff. Oxford 1976.

Ibid.: *My Life and Ethiopia's Progress*. Vol. 2. Edited by Harold Marcus with Ezekiel Gebissa and Tibebe Eshete. East Lansing, MI 1994.

Hammerschmidt, Ernst: *Äthiopien. Christliches Reich zwischen Gestern und Morgen*. Wiesbaden 1967.

Henze, Paul B.: *Layers of Time. A History of Ethiopia*. London 2000.

Herwarth, Hans von: *Von Adenauer zu Brandt. Erinnerungen*. Berlin, Frankfurt a. M. 1990.

Höhnel, Ludwig Ritter von: *Mein Leben zur See, auf Forschungs-reisen und bei Hofe. Erinnerungen eines österreichischen Seeoffiziers*. Berlin 1926.

Junod, Marcel: *Kämpfer beiderseits der Front*. Zurich, Vienna 1947.

Kaplan, Robert: *Surrender or Starve. Travels in Ethiopia, Sudan, Somalia, and Eritrea*. New York 2003.

Kapuściński, Ryszard: *The Emperor. Downfall of an Autocrat*. London 2006 (first edition 1978).

Lefebvre, Jeffrey A.: *Arms for the Horn. US Security Policy in Ethiopia and Somalia, 1953–1991*. Pittsburgh, PA 1992.

Lockot, Hans Wilhelm: *The Mission. The Life, Reign and Character of Haile Selassie I*. London 1989.

Mahtama-Selassie Wolde-Maskal: *Zekra Nagar*. Addis Ababa 1969 AD.

Mammo Wudeneh: *Yadaraskubat – Gela tarik ena tesetawoch*. Addis Ababa 2004 AD.

Mandela, Nelson: *Long Walk to Freedom. Autobiography*. London 1995.

Marcus, Harold G.: *The Life and Times of Menelik II. Ethiopia 1844–1913*. Oxford 1975.

Ibid.: *Ethiopia, Great Britain and the United States, 1941–1974*. Berkeley, Los Angeles, London 1983.

Ibid.: *Haile Selassie I. The Formative Years. 1892–1936.* Berkeley, Los Angeles, London 1987.

Ibid.: *A History of Ethiopia.* Berkeley, Los Angeles, London 1994.

Marse-Hazen Wolde-Kirkos: *Yazaman tarik tezetaye – kayahutena kasamahut 1896–1922.* Addis Ababa 2006 AD.

Matthies, Volker: *Der Eritrea-Konflikt. Ein 'vergessener Krieg' am Horn von Afrika* (Arbeiten aus dem Institut für Afrikakunde). Hamburg 1981.

Messay Kebede: *Ideology and Conflicts. Autopsy of the Ethiopian Revolution.* Lanham, MD and elsewhere 2011.

Milkias, Paulos: *Haile Selassie, Western Education and Political Revolution in Ethiopia.* Youngstown, NY. 2006.

Mockler, Anthony: *Haile Selassie's War.* Oxford 2nd edn. 2003 (first published Oxford 1984).

Mosley, Leonard: *Haile Selassie. The Conquering Lion.* London 1964.

Nathaniel, Ras: *50th Anniversary of His Imperial Majesty Haile Selassie I: First Visit to the United States (1954–2004).* Victoria, BC 2004.

Nicholl, Charles: *Somebody Else. Arthur Rimbaud in Africa 1880–1891.* London 1997.

Ottaway, Marina, and David Ottaway: *Ethiopia. Empire in Revolution.* New York 1978.

Pankhurst, Richard: *Sylvia Pankhurst, Counsel for Ethiopia. A Biographical Essay on Ethiopian, Anti-Fascist and Anti-Colonialist History 1934–1960.* Hollywood, CA. 2003.

Parris, Matthew, and Andrew Bryson (eds.): *The Spanish Ambassador's Suitcase. Stories from the Diplomatic Bag.* London 2012.

Paul, James C. N., and Christopher Clapham: *Ethiopian Constitutional Development. A Sourcebook.* 2 vols. Addis Ababa 1972.

Perham, Margery: *The Government of Ethiopia.* London 1948 (2nd edn. 1968).

Potyka, Christian: *Haile Selassie: Der Negus Negesti in Frieden und Krieg.* Bad Honnef 1974.

Raunig, Walter (ed.): *Das christliche Äthiopien. Geschichte – Architektur – Kunst*. Regensburg 2005.

Rey, Charles F.: *In the Country of the Blue Nile*. New York 1969 (first published 1927).

Ibid.: *Unconquered Abyssinia as it is Today*. London 1923.

Rosen, Felix: *Eine deutsche Gesandtschaft in Abessinien*. Leipzig 1907.

Sackville-West, Vita: *The Edwardians*. London 1970 (first published 1930).

Sandford, Christine: *The Lion of Judah Hath Prevailed. Being the Biography of His Imperial Majesty Haile Selassie I*. Westport, CT 1972.

Seyoum Haregot: *The Bureaucratic Empire. Serving Emperor Haile Selassie*. Trenton, NJ. 2013.

Seyoum Tassew: *Yanegusu ganama*. Addis Ababa (undated).

Shirreff, David: *Bare Feet and Bandoliers. Wingate, Sandford, the Patriots and the Part they Played in the Liberation of Ethiopia*. London, New York 1995.

Sohier, Estelle: *Portraits Controversés d'un Prince Éthiopien. Iyasu 1897–1935*. Paris 2011.

Spencer, John H.: *Ethiopia at Bay: A Personal Account of the Haile Selassie Years*. Algonac, MI 1984.

Steer, George: *Caesar in Abyssinia*. London 1936.

Ibid.: *Sealed and Delivered. A Book on the Abyssinian Campaign*. London 1942.

Taddesse Tamrat: *Church and State in Ethiopia*. Oxford 1972.

Taffara Deguefé: *Minutes of an Ethiopian Century*. Addis Ababa 2006 AD.

Tecola, Hagos W.: *Democratization: A Personal View*. Cambridge, MA 1995.

Tekle Hawasiat Tekle Mariam: *Autobiography – Yahiwot Tarik*. Addis Ababa 2006 AD.

Tesfatsion Medhanie: *Eritrea. Dynamics of a National Question*. Amsterdam 1986.

Ibid.: *Towards Confederation in the Horn of Africa. Focus on Ethiopia and Eritrea*. Frankfurt am Main, London 2007.

Thesiger, Wilfred: *The Life of My Choice*. London 1987.

Trenkler, Lore: *Arbeiten und Leben am Hof Haile Selassies I. Erinnerungen 1960–1975.* Edited by Rudolf Agstner. Wiesbaden 2011.

Ullendorff, Edward: *The Ethiopians. An Introduction to Country and People.* London 1960.

Vestal, Theodore M.: *The Lion of Judah in the New World. Emperor Haile Selassie of Ethiopia and the Shaping of Americans' Attitudes toward Africa.* Santa Barbara, Denver, Oxford 2011.

Volker-Saad, Kerstin, and Anna Greve (eds.): *Äthiopien und Deutschland. Sehnsucht nach der Ferne.* Munich, Berlin 2006.

Waugh, Evelyn: *Waugh in Abyssinia.* In: *Ibid.: Waugh Abroad. Collected Travel Writing.* New York, Toronto 2003.

Ibid.: *Remote People.* London 1931.

Wrong, Michela: *I Didn't Do It For You. How the World Betrayed a Small African Nation.* New York 2005.

Zewde Retta: *Yakadamawi Haile-Selassie Mengest.* Delhi 2012.

Zischka, Anton: Abessinien. *Das letzte ungelöste Problem Afrikas.* Bern, Leipzig, Vienna (undated).

Essays and articles

Agstner, Rudolf: Der Besuch Kaiser Haile Selassies von Äthiopien in Wien vor 50 Jahren. In: *Wiener Geschichtsblätter* 59, 3 (2004), pp. 231–237.

Asfa-Wossen Asserate: Das Äthiopische Kaiserreich bis 1974 – Revolution – Volksrepublik bis 1991. in: Horst Haselsteiner, Heinrich Schuschnigg (eds.): *Die Kaiserreiche. Roms Erben.* Vienna 2004, pp. 144–163.

Ibid.: Rastafaris: Der Tag, als der Regen kam. Hintergründe und Missverständnisse der Rastafari-Bewegung. In: *Die Presse* (Vienna), 13 March 2010.

Bahru Zewde: Economic Origins of the Absolute State in Ethiopia. In: *Journal of Ethiopian Studies* 17 (1984), pp. 1–29.

Ibid.: Hayla-Sellase. From Progressive to Reactionary. In: *Northeast African Studies* 2, 2 (1995), pp. 99–114.

Braddick, Henderson B.: The Hoare-Laval Plan. A Study in International Politics. In: *Review of Politics* 24 (1962), pp. 342–364.

Clapham, Christopher: The Ethiopian Coup d'Etat of December 1960. In: *The Journal of Modern African Studies* 6 (1968), pp. 495–507.

Courlander, Harold: The Emperor Wore Clothes. Visiting Haile Selassie in 1943. In: *The American Scholar* 58 (1989), pp. 271–281.

Fallaci, Oriana: Journey into the Private Universe of Haile Selassie. In: *Chicago Tribune*, 24 June 1973.

Haber, Lutz: The Emperor Haile Selassie I. in Bath 1936–1940, in: *The Anglo-Ethiopian Society, Occasional Papers*, London 1992 (http://www.anglo-ethiopian.org/publications/articles.php?type= O&reference=publications/occasionalpapers/papers/haileselassie- bath.php).

Hardy, Deborah: Haile Selassie Remembered in Shropshire, in: *The Anglo-Ethiopian Society News File Summer 2013*, London 2013, pp. 17–19.

Hedemann, Philipp: Wenn Bob Marley das wüsste. Rastafaris in Afrika. In: *Cicero* 11 (2012), pp. 84–89.

Makonnen Tegegn: Walda-Giyorgis Walda-Yohannes and the Haile Selassie Government. In: *Northeast African Studies* 4, 2 (1997), pp. 91–138.

Marcus, Harold G.: Haile Selassie and Italians, 1941–1943. In: *Northeast African Studies* 10, 3 (2003), pp. 19–25.

Ibid.: 1960, the Year the Sky Began Falling on Haile Selassie. In: *Northeast African Studies* 6, 3 (1999), pp. 11–26.

Ibid.: Prejudice and Ignorance in Reviewing Books about Africa: The Strange Case of Ryszard Kapuścińskis 'The Emperor'. In: *History in Africa* 17 (1990), pp. 373–378.

Molvaer, Reidulf K.: About the Abortive Coup Attempt in Addis Ababa from 5 Tahsas to 8 Tahsas 1953 (14–17 December 1960). A Synopsis of Dubb-Ida by Balambaras

Mahteme-Sillasé Welde-Mesquel. In: *Northeast African Studies* 3, 2 (1996), pp. 97–125.

Pankhurst, Richard: Emperor Haile Sellassie's Arrival in Britain. An Alternative Autobiographical Draft by Percy Arnold. In: *Northeast African Studies* 9, 2 (2002), pp. 1–46.

Robertson, James C.: The Hoare-Laval Plan. In: *Journal of Contemporary History* 10 (1975), pp. 433–464.

Sbacchi, Alberto: Secret Talks for the Submission of Haile Selassie and Prince Asfaw Wassen 1936–1939. In: *The International Journal of African-Historical Studies*, 7 (1974), pp. 668–680.

Spencer, John H.: Haile Selassie. Triumph and Tragedy. In: *Orbis* 18 (1975), pp. 1129–1152.

Tortello, Rebecca: All Hail. The State Visit of Emperor Haile Selassie. In: *The Gleaner* 21–24, April 1966.

Ullendorff, Edward: Haile Selassie at Bath. In: *Journal of Semitic Studies* 24 (1979), pp. 251–264.

Vestal, Theodore M.: The lost opportunity for Ethiopia: The failure to move toward democratic governance. In: *International Journal of African Development*, Volume I, Issue 1 (Fall 2013).

Newspapers and magazines

The Ethiopian Herald, Addis Ababa.
Ethiops, Addis Ababa.
Frankfurter Allgemeine Zeitung, Frankfurt am Main
The New York Times, New York.
Die Presse, Vienna.
Der Spiegel, Hamburg.
Stern, Hamburg.
The Reporter, Addis Ababa.
The Times, London.

Unpublished manuscripts and documents

Asfa-Wossen Asserate: Family Memories on the Captivity of *Lij* Iyasu. A Personal Account.

Asserate Kassa: Letters, documents and diaries (in the author's possession).

Bahru Zewde: The Dynamics of Political Succession in Ethiopian History. Paper presented at the 18th International Conference of Ethiopian Studies, Dire Dawa, 29.10.–02.11.2012.

Bairu Tafla: Progress and Retrogress in Ethiopian History. An Appraisal of 18th and 19th Century Cultural Development. Paper presented at 8th Orbis Aethiopicus Conference: Continuity and Innovation in Ethiopian Culture, Gonville & Caius College, Cambridge 12.–14.09.2003.

Erlich, Haggai: Israel and Ethiopia during Haila-Selassie Time. A brief summary of Haila-Selassie policy. Tel Aviv 2013.

Marse Hazan Wolde Qirqos: YeZaman Tarik Tezzettaye BaNegesta Negastat Zawditu Zamana Mangist. Addis Ababa (undated).

Menno Aden: Überlegungen zur Verfassungsgeschichte Äthiopiens, Memorandum. Essen, 3 August 2013.

Teffera-Work Kidane-Wold: Memorandum über das Auslandsvermögen des Kaisers in England, Addis Ababa 1959 (handwritten manuscript).

Tesfatsion Medhanie: Kaiser Haile Selassie und die äthiopisch-eritreische 'Föderation' (unpublished manuscript), Bremen, September 2013.

Documents from archives

Archive des Auswärtigen Amtes, Berlin (AA).

The Public Record Office, London, Foreign Office (FO).

Archive of the State Department, National Archives, Washington, DC (SD).

Archives of the French Foreign Ministry (FFM), Paris. Guerre, Affaires politiques générales, Ethiopie, vol. 1617–1625.

Historical Archives of the Italian Foreign Ministry (IFM), Rome: Archivio Politico 1914–1918, Archivio degli Affari Politici 1919–1930.

Picture credits

My heartfelt thanks to the families of Lt Gen. Abiye Abebe, Lt Gen. Merid Mengesha, *Dejazmatch* Germatchew Tekle-Hawariat and Lt. Col. Tamrat Yigezu for granting permission to use images on pages 242 and 243. Also to Lady Alexandra Heywood for her kind permission to reproduce the sketch by Rex Whistler on page 64 and to Zewde Retta for the photograph on page 70. Special thanks to Dr Günter Klatt, who provided the picture of *Negus* Tafari which appears on the spine.

Acknowledgements

I had it in mind to write this book since the time of the Ethiopian Revolution in 1974, but it is my readership in the German-speaking world whom I have to thank for giving me the final impetus to put pen to paper. At various readings of my works, I was urged time and again to write something about the 'life and times of the King of Kings'.

For the original German edition of 'King of Kings', I am extremely grateful to Rainer Wieland, my reader of many years' standing, for encouraging me to embark on the project and for giving me the benefit of his professional input every step of the way during the book's creation.

I would also like to thank my agent Joachim Jessen from the Thomas Schlück Agency in Garbsen, as well as Christian Seeger and his colleagues at Propyläen Verlag in Berlin, publishers of the German edition.

My thanks must go to Professors Menno Aden, Tesfatsion Medhanie and Haggai Erlich for observations in their own special fields of expertise that were of great benefit to me in researching and writing this book. I am also much indebted to *Ato* Mesfin Gebreyes for sending me the list of the assets held by the Emperor in Great Britain in 1959.

A number of high office-holders in the former Ethiopian Imperial government provided me with some enlightening insights into many different aspects of the day-to-day business of Haile Selassie's regime: *Tsehafe-Tezaz* Wolde-Giorgis Wolde-Yohannes (deceased), *Dejazmatch* Germatchew Tekle-Hawariat (deceased), *Dejazmatch* Zawde Gebre-Selassie (deceased), *Dejazmatch* Berhane-Maskal Desta (deceased), Ambassador Imru Zelleke, *Ato* Tekalign Gedamu and *Ato* Taffara Deguefé (deceased). I am greatly obliged to all of them for taking the time to talk to me and for revealing the inner workings of the very complicated system of the imperial administration. Dr Dima Nago Sarbo's advice and numerous discussions on the relevance of deep-rooted reforms in Ethiopian politics is highly appreciated.

Mrs Jennifer Dummer's and Mr Stephen Bell's help in tracking down numerous official documents from both the German and British national archives was invaluable.

A host of relatives, colleagues and friends of Ethiopia were kind enough to supply me with many eyewitness accounts and images of life in the country during the Emperor's reign. My heartfelt thanks are due to all of them, along with my humble apologies that it was sadly impossible to publish all of this fascinating material.

For the current edition, I should like to express my thanks, first and foremost, to Dr Barbara Schwepcke and Harry Hall at Haus Publishing in London for raising the possibility of, and then bringing to fruition, an English translation of the book. Aided by the editorial skills of Emma Henderson, they have done a magnificent job in seeing this project through to completion. My English translator, Dr Peter Lewis, has produced a very sensitive rendition of my German text, and I am much indebted to him for his extremely collegial approach to working with me on this undertaking.

Thomas Pakenham, a distinguished writer on Ethiopian history and author, *inter alia*, of *The Mountains of Rasselas* and *The Scramble for Africa*, has been a long-standing family friend and I am deeply honoured that he agreed to write the foreword to the English edition.

Professor Tecola H. Hagos has been a friend since my student days; I am greatly obliged to him for his kindness in proofreading and endorsing my book.

Finally, Anthony Mockler, the author of *Haile Selassie's War*, is a firm friend of Ethiopia and my family, and I thank him warmly for his generous endorsement of this biography of the King of Kings.

Asfa-Wossen Asserate, Frankfurt-am-Main, July 2015

Index

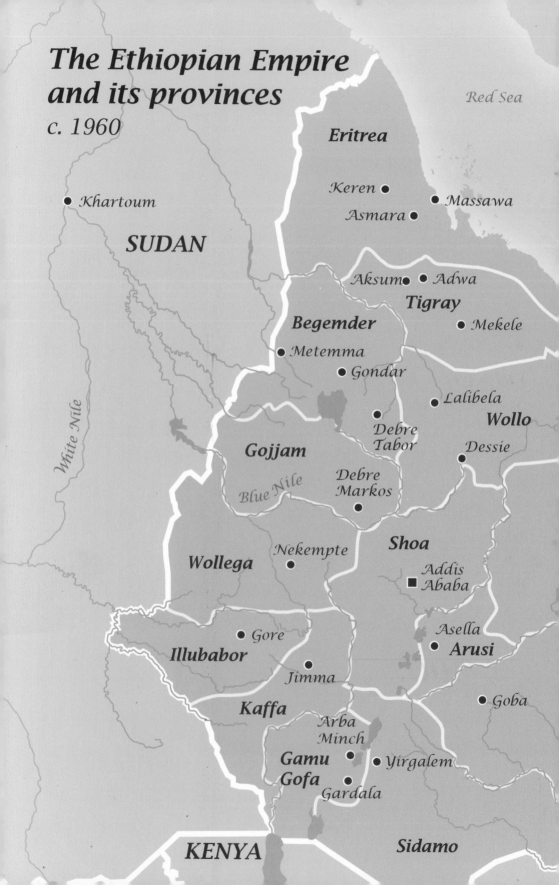

The Ethiopian Empire and its provinces
c. 1960

Red Sea

Eritrea

Khartoum

SUDAN

Keren

Massawa

Asmara

Aksum

Adwa

Tigray

Begemder

Mekele

Metemma

Gondar

Lalibela

Wollo

Debre Tabor

Dessie

Gojjam

Blue Nile

Debre Markos

White Nile

Shoa

Nekempte

Addis Ababa

Wollega

Asella

Gore

Arusi

Illubabor

Jimma

Goba

Kaffa

Arba Minch

Gamu Gofa

Yirgalem

Gardala

KENYA

Sidamo